DECISIONS

MAKING PERSONAL ECONOMIC CHOICES

Second Edition

TEACHER'S EDITION

DECISIONS

MAKING PERSONAL ECONOMIC CHOICES

Second Edition

TEACHER'S EDITION

Annotation Author

Judith Staley Brenneke, Ed.D.

Developed by

Changing Times Education Service
A Division of EMC Publishing
St. Paul, Minnesota

and

Visual Education Corporation
Princeton, New Jersey

ISBN 0-8219-0850-2

Published by EMC Publishing
300 York Avenue
St. Paul, Minnesota 55101

Printed in the United States of America
0 9 8 7 6 5 4 3 2 1

Contents

Introduction

Economic literacy is becoming an increasingly important goal of our nation's secondary schools. Educators—along with business leaders, public officials, and parents—are calling for emphasis on the skills students need to become intelligent decision makers and responsible economic citizens. The rapidly changing marketplace—producing new products in electronics and new alternatives in banking and telecommunications—requires consumers to evaluate their alternatives carefully in order to get the most out of their resources. The transformation in industry creates the need to consider the changing face of the job market. The major economic issues facing our nation—productivity and unemployment, energy and the environment, inflation and the role of the government—demand that citizens analyze and choose among complex solutions to complex problems.

Economic literacy has two dimensions: a personal one and a social one. The aim is to teach individuals to make intelligent decisions about how to use personal and national resources. Economics is the ideal discipline for achieving that aim because economics is a tool for making informed decisions. The concepts of economics are used to identify and evaluate alternatives in an effort to solve problems by using the least resources. The same concepts can be used by all sorts of decision makers: business owners, public officials, and individuals acting as workers, citizens, or consumers. By mastering those concepts, students will be able to make more informed decisions. By understanding how their decisions relate to the economy as a whole, students will be able to make more responsible decisions.

Decisions provides a valuable resource for teachers who wish to promote economic literacy. The text explains basic economic concepts, discusses the relationship between the individual and the American economy, and explores the individual's roles as worker, citizen, and consumer. It does so while emphasizing throughout the benefits of making informed decisions.

ORGANIZATION

Decisions is divided into five parts that move from the general to the specific. Part One uses decision making as a means of introducing basic economic concepts and showing how individuals can apply them. Part Two relates these concepts to our economic system to provide a frame of reference for what follows. Parts Three, Four, and Five introduce students to the core of information and skills they will need to manage their resources as workers, consumers, and citizens. Throughout the book, personal decisions are connected to the economy as a whole. The chapters in Parts Two through Five each end with a section called "You Interact with the Economy," which details how individual decisions affect the economy and vice versa.

Part One

The first part establishes the decision-making framework and introduces the basic economic concepts that recur throughout the book: resource management, scarcity, opportunity costs, and trade-offs. Chapter 1 describes a systematic decision-making method students can use to get the most out of their resources. It also explains how the individual's decisions occur in various economic roles. Chapter 2 focuses on how the conflict between unlimited wants and scarce resources forces consumers and producers to make choices. It also sketches the basics of the circular flow of goods and services and outlines the workings of supply and demand.

Part Two

The second part describes the economic setting in which individual decisions are made. Chapter 3 begins by exploring various ways groups make economic decisions and details the dynamics of our own modified market system by analyzing the circular flow and supply and demand. Chapter 4 focuses on business and the individuals that work within a business. It reveals the relation of profit to risk and explains the role of the entrepreneur. Chapter 5 describes the role of the federal government in the economy: how it acts as provider of services, regulator, and spender, and how it raises the revenue necessary to perform these functions. The chapter ends by exploring the influence that the individual can exert on group decisions.

Students will benefit by studying these three chapters before learning in detail about personal economic decisions. First, these chapters provide the context students need to see that their decisions do not occur in a vacuum. Second, these chapters introduce important concepts that will enrich students' understanding of later material. The principles of supply and demand detailed in Chapter 3, for instance, are referred to in later chapters as factors to consider when making certain decisions. Profit as a reward for risk, introduced in the business chapter, reappears in the discussion of saving and investing.

Part Three

The third part turns the students' attention to their roles as workers. Chapter 6 helps students identify a career they want and then develop a strategy for getting a job within that career. Chapter 7 focuses on the challenge of working with other people by detailing the rights and responsibilities of workers and managers. Chapter 8 explains the rewards of working—income and fringe benefits—and the financial responsibilities of citizenship—taxes.

These chapters give concrete advice on how students can develop skills needed for their chosen careers and how to construct a résumé to exhibit those skills. They present essential information on how to work successfully with others and be productive members of the work force.

Part Four

The fourth part is actually a consumer guide in itself. Chapter 9 begins by emphasizing the ideas that spending money to consume goods or services is but one of many alternative uses of resources and that individuals get the most out of their resources by using them in various combinations. The chapter also outlines a basic consumer method that the subsequent chapters explain in detail. Chapter 10 focuses on how to get and evaluate information, outlining the sources of information and explaining how to separate influence from information in advertising. Chapter 11 addresses the three central questions a consumer must answer: what to buy, where to buy, and when to buy. It explains how to compare competing goods and services and the businesses that sell them and discusses how consumers can shop for the best price. Chapter 12 turns to the question of how to pay for a purchase by comparing cash and cash substitutes to credit and saving. By discussing these alternatives together, the text helps students compare the advantages and disadvantages of each method. The final chapter of this section, Chapter 13, outlines the rights and responsibilities of consumers by exploring the legal relations of sellers and buyers, describing how consumers can solve the problems that sometimes arise, and linking individual action to consumer protection.

Part Five

The chapters in Part Five each focus on buying certain kinds of goods or services. Each chapter is organized to follow the consumer shopping method outlined in Part Four. Chapters 14 and 15 focus on the basic needs consumers must meet: food, clothing, housing, and transportation. The next three chapters form a unit on shopping for financial services. Chapter 16 establishes the relationship between credit, saving, and other financial services and introduces the basic institutions that provide these services. The next two chapters then focus on how to shop for credit and for savings and investments. Chapter 19 explores the basics of the four most common types of insurance: life, auto, health, and property. It also explains how careful actions can reduce risk and limit the need for insurance.

The final chapter of the text ties together the book's main themes and points to students' responsibility to take control of their lives. The goal of the text is to help students learn to make their own decisions. Students learn to use tools that are appropriate to solve immediate problems and that will be appropriate 20 years from now, when they are choosing among jobs, systems, products, and services that are not even dreamed of yet.

COURSE ALTERNATIVES

Decisions was designed for either one- or two-semester courses and was developed to be comprehensive enough that it could be used alone or with some supplementary activities. Still, some teachers may wish to use the text to teach certain topics deemed most important. Various alternatives exist:

- A teacher who wishes to emphasize basic consumer skills but is less interested in detailed information on various goods and services could teach Part Four and eliminate Part Five. The chapters in Part Four, by outlining a basic consumer method, are actually a consumer guide in themselves.
- A teacher who wishes to stress the individual's worker role could concentrate on the chapters in Part Three, supplementing them with Part Two's overview of the economy and perhaps with Chapter 9, which gives general guidelines on how to use effectively the income that the worker earns.
- A teacher who does not wish to emphasize economics can eliminate Part Two. By expanding slightly on the coverage of economic relations in Chapter 2, he or she can provide an overview of the economy's workings on a more basic level.

With these and the many other variations possible, we strongly recommend beginning the course with the first and second chapters before assigning any others. The material presented in those chapters is so basic and the concepts explained in them used so often throughout the book, that students' understanding of later material will be greatly enhanced by first taking time with Part One. A teacher who wishes to can reverse the order of these chapters and focus first on the central economic problem, then teach the first chapter as a way of finding solutions.

Following this introduction is a scope and sequence chart showing where key economic concepts are used throughout the book.

OTHER COMPONENTS OF THE PACKAGE

Decisions has many valuable supplements and teaching aids that can increase its adaptability in the classroom.

First, of course, is this *Teacher's Edition,* which contains the following teaching aids for each chapter of the text: an overview of the chapter's key points; a list of suggestions for introducing students to the chapter's ideas and enhancing their understanding of the material; a set of discussion questions; answers to the text's vocabulary matching exercises; answers to the text's review questions; and notes on teaching the text's projects. After this chapter-by-chapter guide, the *Teacher's Edition* contains a list of resources.

The second component is the *Student Workbook,* a helpful adjunct to the textbook. Each workbook chapter includes a two-page review of the material covered in the textbook chapter, content applications, case problems, and analyses of related current issues. A unique, end-of-part project provides a finely focused exercise applying the concepts learned in each of the five parts of the textbook. A Teacher's Edition of the workbook is available.

A third component is the microcomputer software package. This software concentrates on the decision-making principles and their application to everyday problems.

A fourth component is a *Teacher's Resource Binder.* It includes classroom teaching suggestions, reproducible activity masters, and reproducible tests for every chapter.

Scope and Sequence Chart *

TOPIC	PART ONE	PART TWO	PART THREE	PART FOUR	PART FIVE
Wants	**2** (17-26)	**3** (46-48)	**8** (135)	**9** (141-142,144-152) **10** (161-163)	**20** (327-330)
Scarcity	**2** (17-26)	**5** (78-81)	**6** (101-103)		**14** (239-241) **15** (256-258) **20** (327-330)
Roles Worker	**1** (3-5) **2** (22-26)	**3** (39-45) **4** (55-58) **5** (72-78)	**6** (89-103) **7** (107-119) **8** (123-135)		**20** (327-330)
Citizen	**1** (3-5) **2** (26-29)	**3** (46-48) **5** (78-83)	**8** (128-135)	**13** (220-223)	**20** (327-330)
Consumer	**1** (3-5) **2** (22-26)	**3** (39-48)		**9** (152-154) **10** (158-171) **11** (176-188) **12** (192-206) **13** (210-223)	**14** (231-241) **15** (245-258) **16** (262-273) **17** (277-279) **20** (327-330)
Actors Producer	**2** (22-26)	**3** (35-48) **4** (52-64)	**6** (91-103) **7** (107-119) **8** (123-135)	**9** (152-154) **10** (163-171) **11** (176-188) **12** (193-197) **13** (220-223)	**14** (231-241) **18** (294-305) **19** (321-322) **20** (333-337)
Government	**2** (26-29)	**3** (35-48) **5** (69-83)	**6** (91-103) **7** (107-116) **8** (123-135)	**9** (152-154) **10** (163-171) **13** (210-223)	**14** (231-239) **16** (269-273) **17** (282-287) **18** (294-305) **19** (321-322) **20** (333-337)
Decision method	**1** (5-12)		**6** (89-90)	**9** (141-142)	**20** (327-330)
Trade-offs	**1** (5-12) **2** (17-22)	**3** (46-48) **4** (58-63) **5** (70-81)		**9** (144-152) **10** (171) **11** (176-178) **12** (192-193) **13** (220-223)	**15** (245-256) **16** (269-270) **17** (277-280) **18** (296-302) **19** (312-321) **20** (327-330)
Opportunity cost	**2** (17-22)	**5** (70-81)		**9** (144-152) **11** (176-178) **12** (192-193) **13** (220-223)	**15** (245-256) **16** (269-270) **17** (277-280) **18** (301-302) **19** (312-321) **20** (327-330)
Risk	**1** (5-12)	**4** (52-58)	**8** (123-128)	**13** (214-217)	**15** (245-251) **18** (293-305) **19** (309-312, 322-323) **20** (327-330)
Values	**1** (5-12) **2** (17-22)	**3** (35-39) **5** (69-70)		**9** (142-152) **11** (176-183)	**20** (330-333)
Goals	**1** (5-12) **2** (17-22)	**3** (35-39) **5** (70-78)	**6** (91-101) **8** (123-128)	**9** (142-152) **11** (176-183)	**14** (231-239) **15** (245-256) **16** (269-270) **18** (293-294) **19** (310-321) **20** (330-333)
Managing resources	**1** (3-13) **2** (17-26)	**4** (55-58)	**6** (91-96) **8** (135)	**9** (141-154) **10** (158-161) **13** (220-223)	**14** (239-241) **15** (256-258) **17** (279-282) **19** (309-312, 322-323) **20** (327-333)
Economic principles	**2** (26-29)	**3** (35-39) **5** (69-70)			**20** (333-337)
Supply and demand	**2** (22-26)	**3** (39-45)	**6** (101-103) **7** (112-118)	**10** (166-171) **11** (184-188) **13** (220-223)	**15** (256-258) **16** (270-273) **20** (333-337)

*The numbers in bold refer to the chapters, and the numbers in parentheses refer to the pages within chapters. For example, information on scarcity can be found in Chapter 2, pages 17-26, etc.

TOPIC	PART ONE	PART TWO	PART THREE	PART FOUR	PART FIVE
Rights and responsibilities	**1** (12-13)	**3** (46-48) **5** (81-83)	**7** (109-112) **8** (129-132)	**10** (166-171) **12** (203-206) **13** (210-223)	**15** (245-251, 256-258) **17** (280-289) **19** (322-323) **20** (333-337)
Family	**1** (12-13)		**6** (89-90)	**9** (144-152)	**14** (231-236) **15** (245-251) **17** (282-287) **18** (294-295) **19** (310-312, 322-323)
Planning			**8** (135)	**9** (141-154) **10** (158-161) **12** (197-203) **13** (217-220)	**14** (231-239) **15** (245-258) **16** (264-267) **17** (277-282) **18** (293) **19** (309-312)
Getting information	**1** (5-12)		**6** (91-103) **8** (123-128)	**9** (141-142) **10** (158-171)	**14** (231-239) **15** (245-256) **16** (267-269) **17** (282-287) **18** (296-301) **19** (312-321)
Comparison shopping				**9** (141-142) **10** (158-161) **11** (176-188)	**14** (231-239) **15** (245-256) **16** (262-263, 260 270) **17** (287) **18** (301-302) **19** (312-323)
Determining how to pay				**9** (141-142) **10** (158-161) **12** (192-206)	**14** (231-236) **15** (245-256)
Wages/income	**2** (22-26)	**3** (39-45) **5** (76-78)	**7** (112-116) **8** (123-135)	**9** (142-152) **12** (192-206)	**17** (277-279)
Taxes		**5** (78-81)	**8** (128-135)		**18** (296-302)
Credit				**12** (192-197)	**15** (245-256) **16** (262-270) **17** (277-287)
Saving				**9** (144-152) **12** (192-197)	**16** (262-270) **18** (293-302)
Prices	**2** (22-26)	**3** (39-45) **5** (78-81)		**9** (152-154) **10** (163-166, 171) **11** (184-187)	**14** (231-236) **15** (256-258) **16** (270-273) **17** (277-279, 287-289)
Competition	**2** (26-29)	**3** (35-48) **5** (72-76)	**6** (101-103)	**11** (176-188) **12** (203-206)	**14** (231-239) **16** (262-270) **17** (277-279, 282-287) **18** (296-301)
Identifying alternatives	**1** (5-12) **2** (17-26)	**5** (69-70, 72-76, 78-81)	**6** (89-90, 101-103) **7** (118-119)	**9** (142-144) **10** (158-171) **11** (176-183) **12** (192-206)	**14** (231-241) **15** (245-258) **16** (262-269) **17** (282-287) **18** (293, 296-301)
Others (coworkers, consumers)	**1** (12-13)		**6** (91-101) **7** (107-109, 112-116)	**10** (161-166) **11** (187-188) **13** (220-223)	**15** (256-258) **17** (279-280) **18** (294-295) **19** (321-323)

Chapter-by-Chapter Teaching Plans

Contained below are the following aids to teachers for each chapter of *Decisions:*

- An overview of the chapter's key points
- A list of suggestions for introducing students to the chapter's ideas and enhancing their understanding of the material
- A set of discussion questions
- Answers to the text's vocabulary matching exercises
- Answers to the text's review questions
- Notes on teaching the text's projects

CHAPTER 1 Making Decisions

CHAPTER OVERVIEW

The text and vignette in Chapter 1 will help the student:

1. Identify personal, family, and public resources that can be used to achieve goals.
2. Identify the three economic roles of worker, citizen, and consumer involved in economic decisions.
3. Describe how simple choices can be made by following experience, habit, another's example, or impulse.
4. Explain how to use the systematic decision-making method to make more important or complex decisions.
5. Describe the benefits of the systematic decision-making method.
6. Explain how all decisions affect others in some way and how others' decisions affect him or her.

NOTES ON TEACHING THE CHAPTER

1. This chapter begins with an open-ended vignette that should provoke much discussion. Use it to introduce students to the complex decisions people face, which can most easily be resolved by using the method outlined in the chapter. The variety of views students offer should help them see how goals and values affect decisions. (See also the first project in this chapter.)
2. Brainstorm to generate ideas on how to use resources other than money to satisfy wants.
3. Ask students to identify what role or roles are being illustrated in the following examples:
   a. Linda decides to volunteer to join her local first aid squad to gain experience for a future career in medicine. (citizen, worker)
   b. Roger works overtime on his summer job to buy a new stereo. (worker, consumer)
   c. Marie agrees to help Armen with the anniversary party for his parents in exchange for skiing lessons this winter. (consumer)

   Develop similar examples.
4. Have students complete several open-ended statements. Some examples follow, but the teacher may wish to add more.
   a. I have the hardest time making decisions about . . .
   b. The biggest decision facing me is . . .
   c. After I make a big decision, I feel . . .
5. Invite a businessperson to class who works in middle- or upper-level management for a local company. Have him or her give examples of how decision-making techniques—especially cost-benefit analysis—are used when making management decisions. This may help students to see how the process can be applied.

DISCUSSION QUESTIONS

1. Do you think that the only important resource is money?
2. When confronted with a problem, is it always a good idea to make a decision right away?
3. Is it really necessary to follow each step of the systematic decision-making process?
4. Do you agree with the statement in the text that all decisions involve risk?
5. Some people believe that the economy is so complex, it's impossible to say that the actions of one individual affect others. Do you agree or disagree? Can you think of examples in which the economic actions of one person do affect others?

ANSWERS TO KEY TERMS

a. worker role b. goals c. principle of least cost d. benefits
e. systematic decision-making method f. personal resources g. risk h. trade-off
i. citizen role j. alternative k. consumer role l. costs m. economics n. values
o. public resources

ANSWERS TO REVIEW QUESTIONS

1. Managing resources helps get the most out of them. Resources include time, money, skills, and energy.
2. Two other resources are family and public resources. Examples will vary.
3. The three economic roles are worker, citizen, and consumer. Examples will vary.
4. Simple decisions are made by using experience, by habit, by following an example, or on impulse.
5. Systematic decision making consists of defining your problem, identifying and ranking your goals, determining your alternatives, analyzing the consequences of each alternative, selecting the best alternative for achieving your goals, putting your decision into action, and evaluating your decision.
6. Defining a problem in a general way helps create more possible alternatives. To satisfy hunger, someone could buy a meal in a restaurant, buy and warm prepared food, cook a meal from scratch, or persuade someone else to prepare the meal.
7. Analyzing the consequences of alternatives enables someone to see if an alternative fulfills his or her goals.
8. Cost doesn't mean only dollars. It means anything that must be given up in order to get an alternative.
9. Alternatives are chosen by following the principle of least cost, or selecting the alternative that offers the most benefits for the fewest costs.
10. Decisions involve risk because the future is uncertain. Risk is reduced by gathering information before deciding, by evaluating decisions, and by evaluating how well decisions are made.
11. Systematic decision making helps people use resources wisely, set their own goals, discover more alternatives, make the decision more easily, and avoid future problems.
12. Examples will vary.

NOTES ON PROJECTS

1. The discussion of Liz's decision should be lively. By brainstorming in class, students may be able to identify more alternatives—be sure that the costs and benefits of each are explored fully. *Variation:* the teacher may wish to alter some of the circumstances of the vignette to see if students' views change. What if Mrs. Carstairs weren't Steve's mother, for instance? What if Liz didn't like Steve?
2. Guide the students to select a service that is provided publicly (though the class could discuss why some services—food preparation, for instance—aren't). They'll generally find that public services have less cost to the individual user, though they may entail some restrictions on use (as with public transportation, which may run less frequently on weekends or not at all during the night). Students should also explore beyond the user cost to the less obvious cost of services in taxes.
3. This project leads students to see that they already make some decisions in a systematic way. By evaluating the results of their decisions, they'll see whether they should use the method more often or more completely. When the class com-

pares notes, teachers may want to tally how many unsatisfying decisions fell into each category. Presumably there will be more in the "unsystematic" column, which can be the starting point for an analysis of why: the inability to take all costs and benefits into account and the failure to identify alternatives are probably the most common reasons.

4. By standardizing the circumstances for all students, this project reduces individual differences to a question of goals and values, rather than resources. Students could discuss their choices, which would produce a thorough understanding of the costs and benefits of each alternative. The teacher may choose to let students introduce other alternatives by using other resources, as long as those options are reasonably within the grasp of the students using the resources they, their families, or their community possess.

CHAPTER 2 Why You Make Choices

CHAPTER OVERVIEW

The text and vignette in Chapter 2 will help the student:

1. Explain that, because resources are limited, not all wants can be satisfied.
2. Identify the opportunity cost—the thing that must be given up to get something wanted more—in his or her choices.
3. Explain how goods and services are exchanged between those who feel they can both derive benefits.
4. Describe how producers use human, natural, and capital resources to produce goods and services for society.
5. Describe the five principles on which our economy is based: free choice, self-interest, free competition, the right to property, and limited government.

NOTES ON TEACHING THE CHAPTER

1. Before introducing this unit, a brief lesson in clarifying values may help students to apply the principles they learn to a personal situation. The following exercises developed by Howard Kirschenbaum, Sidney B. Simon, and Leland W. Howe are a start. The teacher may also wish to use some original exercises or other references.
   a. Have students list 20 things they like to do. Then have them code each response as to (1) whether or not it costs them money, (2) whether they prefer to do it alone or with others, (3) when they last engaged in that activity.
   b. Have students fill in the blanks to the following questions:
      (1) If I had a million dollars, I would . . .
      (2) What I want most out of life is . . .
      (3) The one thing I would change about myself if I could is . . .
      (4) I get very angry when . . .
2. Using the vignette as an example, ask the students to recall a personal experience where they had to make a choice similar to George's. In retrospect, do they feel they made the right choice? Why or why not? What resources did they use and how?
3. Illustrate the concept of scarcity by using various examples throughout history (e.g., decreased supply of rubber and rubber products in the 1940s, the gas crisis of the 1970s).
4. Explore the variety of exchanges made possible by money (where barter wouldn't be effective) by identifying the manufacturing source of familiar goods, from cars to soaps to meats and cereals to radios and CDs. Hearing the distances that goods must travel, students will clearly see how money makes exchanges easier.
5. The balancing-out of self-interest that theory predicts is a difficult concept. Remind students that a key is that all actors must be pursuing similar goals—thus, competition results. Also important is a certain agreement on acceptable ways to pursue those goals.

DISCUSSION QUESTIONS

1. How do the following influences affect us in our three economic roles?
   a. social changes
   b. technology
   c. family status
2. Introduce the term "conspicuous consumption" (an individual's way of expressing status or prestige through purchases). Ask each student to think of someone they know who made a purchase that illustrates this concept (they shouldn't name names).
3. Do you agree with the text's statement that secondary wants are as important as primary wants?
4. Some people say that the economy would be more fair and people would benefit if the government made more choices about how to use society's resources. Do you agree or disagree?

ANSWERS TO KEY TERMS

a. capital resources b. producers c. goods d. barter e. natural resources f. wants g. scarcity h. consumers i. human resources j. substitution k. opportunity cost l. interdependence m. medium of exchange n. voluntary exchanges o. services p. price q. wage

ANSWERS TO REVIEW QUESTIONS

1. Wants motivate people to do something to satisfy them. Wants are satisfied by using personal resources—time, energy, skills, and money.
2. People decide what resources to use by applying the principle of substitution, which means satisfying a want in the way that uses the least resources.
3. Scarcity exists when the desire for a resource exceeds the ability to satisfy it. Planning prevents scarcity from becoming worse by helping people use their resources carefully.
4. Scarcity forces people to choose which want to satisfy because there are not enough resources to satisfy all wants.
5. Choices are made after considering goals, values, the benefits of each alternative, and the cost of lost opportunities.
6. Opportunity cost is the value of the next most attractive want that cannot be satisfied when an alternative is chosen. It helps people choose by making the results of choices clear.
7. Interdependence increases the ability to satisfy wants because society is able to produce more goods and services than individuals could produce alone, and because society is able to produce more complex goods.
8. Producers hire workers to help produce goods and services. They exchange these goods and services with consumers for money. Producers and consumers make exchanges because both believe they will benefit from the exchange—the consumer will satisfy a want, and the producer will make a profit.
9. Money is useful because it can be carried and stored easily, it is not perishable, and it can be divided easily into smaller amounts without losing its value.
10. Prices are determined by the availability and desirability of goods and services. Wages are determined by the availability and desirability of workers with specific skills.
11. Producers use human, natural, and capital resources to produce goods and services. Examples will vary.
12. The U.S. economy is based on the principles of free choice, self-interest, private property, free competition, and limited government. It doesn't always work just as theory describes it. Competition isn't always free and the government's role is not limited.

NOTES ON PROJECTS

1. The length of the list students write should lead them to appreciate how many choices they make daily. Asking if the want was satisfied makes them evaluate their actions—a key part of decision making. The last question leads them to consider how their wants can multiply. *Variations:* the teacher may ask students what things they weren't able to do because of what they chose to do, driving home opportunity cost; the

teacher may wish to assign this as homework before students read the chapter.

2. By introducing substitution, this project helps students start exercising their creativity—being a resource manager sometimes entails formulating creative solutions to problems. After students hand in these sheets, the teacher may read to the class some particularly imaginative or colorful substitutions for money, or draw on examples from personal experience. *Variation:* each student could write a short essay on how he or she used substitution.
3. The teacher should help students identify all the essential ingredients in a good or service (for example, if they select a haircut as the service, they need to think about the equipment and materials used, as well as the labor itself). Students should also discuss such tasks as transporting goods from the manufacturer to their location. *Variations:* each student could make an oral presentation on the jobs located, or all students could collect their charts into a large "Job File."
4. Give students some pointers on good interviewing techniques—preparing questions in advance, having follow-up questions ready, rephrasing a question that hasn't been answered, and pursuing an unanticipated but potentially interesting issue. Some role playing in class may be a helpful warmup exercise. Students must be cautioned not to ask too sensitive questions. *Variation:* bring a local businessperson into class to discuss a decision for all students.

CHAPTER 3 The Marketplace in the United States

CHAPTER OVERVIEW

The text and vignette in Chapter 3 will help the student:

1. Explain that economic systems determine how a society makes economic choices.
2. Describe the four basic types of economic systems.
3. List and explain the seven basic goals of our U.S. market system.
4. Describe how individuals, businesses, and government interact in our economic system.
5. Explain how supply and demand determine price.
6. Evaluate how imports and exports affect an economy.

NOTES ON TEACHING THE CHAPTER

1. The vignette that opens this chapter, like that for Chapter 1, is open-ended, which allows students to assimilate the material in the chapter and come to their own conclusion. The issue is an important national question and one students will have heard much about—all will have an opinion. It may be interesting to take an informal poll of students after they read the vignette but before reading the chapter and then again after reading the chapter—have students' attitudes changed? Why or why not?
2. The teacher may wish to have one or more students research current figures for the following:
   a. gross national product
   b. consumer price index
   c. minimum wage
   d. rate of inflation/deflation

   These data may be defined and discussed in terms of the economic trends that they illustrate.
3. Encourage students to begin reading the financial section of a major newspaper. What future economic trends are forecast and by whom? How might these trends affect our life-style and personal economic choices in years to come?
4. Try to obtain an old mail-order catalog. Have students scan it to see what, if any, items were marketable then but would not be today. Which items seem to have fluctuated a great deal in price, and which seem to have remained fairly constant? Have students speculate on why this might be.
5. In reviewing the list of economic goals, explain to students that economists use *equity* not to measure fairness (a question of values, which economists avoid), but simply as a tool for analysis. That is, they try to determine which groups a given action will benefit and from which groups it will exact a cost.
6. Students may have difficulty understanding that a good's price is only one point in a range of

possibilities. It should help to point to examples of foodstuffs—especially meat and produce—where variations often occur in a short period of time.

DISCUSSION QUESTIONS

1. Are there any situations where you feel a monopoly or oligopoly should be permitted to exist, in order to provide a higher quality product or service? In what areas and why?
2. How would a society's goals differ under each of the three pure types of economic systems?
3. How much effect do you feel your *local* government has upon the economy? Should it have more or less control?
4. Do you believe that consumers really have the power to determine prices? If not, why not? If so, how do they exercise that power?

ANSWERS TO KEY TERMS

a. mixed system b. exports c. equilibrium price d. public monopoly
e. traditional system f. supply g. demand h. economic system i. oligopoly
j. market system k. imports l. market demand m. market n. substitutes
o. modified market system p. command system q. complements r. monopoly
s. monopolistic competition t. prevailing wage

ANSWERS TO REVIEW QUESTIONS

1. An economic system enables a society to determine what is produced, how much is produced, and for whom it is produced.
2. The four types of systems are traditional, command, market, and mixed. There are no examples of a pure type. All systems contain some mix of elements.
3. The seven basic goals our economic system pursues are freedom to choose, equity, security, full employment, efficiency, price stability, and growth. Different individuals within our system disagree about the relative importance of these goals. Examples will vary.
4. The economic system in the United States is a market system that is modified by command and traditional elements. It differs from a pure market system in that markets are not always competitive and the government plays a much larger role than theory suggests.
5. A monopoly is a market for a particular product that is controlled by one firm; an oligopoly is controlled by a few large firms. Oligopolies control the automobile, oil, tobacco, and military aircraft industries, among others. There are few pure monopolies today, though the government allows some public monopolies to exist.
6. Individuals sell their labor, land, and capital to producers, and (as consumers) they buy finished products from those producers. Producers make goods and services. Governments regulate the interaction of the other two and provide public services.
7. The two important features of demand are willingness and ability to purchase a good or service.
8. Paula Abdul and Janet Jackson are so popular, and demand for their albums so high, that producers can sell virtually all they can produce at a higher price (say $8.98) — there is usually no need to lower the price to reduce excess inventory.
9. The equilibrium price is the price at which supply and demand are equal. A product priced higher than equilibrium will sell slowly and leave the producer with unsold inventory. A seller who sells a product below equilibrium will sell out quickly but may not earn a profit.
10. Prices go up if people's incomes rise, producer costs rise, or the demand for complements goes up. Prices go down if supply increases but demand doesn't, competition increases, substitutes are introduced, or producer costs decrease.
11. The circular flow is the exchange of money for goods and services that takes place between individuals and producers. Individuals sell their factors of production—labor, land, and capital—to producers. Producers use the factors to make finished products (goods and services), which they sell to individuals (acting as consumers). Imports take money out of the circular flow, but exports add money to it. If imports and exports are about equal, the circular flow is not changed much. But if either imports or exports are greater than the other, money leaks out of or pours into the economy.

NOTES ON PROJECTS

1. This group project may reveal interesting differences in the way people respond—identifying interviewee's approximate age and sex will help students see if answers follow a pattern. The teacher should caution students on how to ask the questions: first politely ask if it is possible to take a few minutes of the respondent's time; explain the concepts clearly, but don't lead a response; and thank the interviewees for their cooperation. (Handing respondents a card that lists and explains the concepts may make it easier for them to rank the goals.)
2. Material can be found in encyclopedias or magazine articles and even in works of social history or novels—in those cases students will have to draw conclusions. The teacher can make the material come alive for students by asking them to compare the choices they have to make with the choices they would face in this other society. In evaluating systems, students must be cautioned to make their own goals clear. The final report could be written or oral.
3. Research into the era of trust busting can be quite entertaining, as well as instructive. Standard Oil is probably the most well-known of the trusts, but students will find many others. The third option invites students to look into a recent major breakup—that of AT&T. The changes in the prices of phone equipment and services should show students the effects of competition on price and of size on economic efficiency.
4. Students should be able to gather the information from business or mass-market periodicals. Students should gather information for at least five years—it may be best to have the data fall at two-year intervals. Without knowing how many computers were produced, students cannot do full supply and demand curves, but by charting actual purchases they'll see the effect of demand increasing as prices decrease. Further research will show causes: technological changes reduced price, lower price opened the product to more buyers, and increased awareness of the need for computer skills also increased demand. Students can use this exercise to investigate other aspects of price as well. They could look at substitutes and see whether increased sales for home computers mean lower sales for home video games. They can also check on complements—has the price of software packages changed?
5. This debate can get quite heated unless the teacher guides it carefully. The additional question—if imports are restricted, how to do it effectively—may help students focus on less emotional topics.

CHAPTER 4 What Business Is All About

CHAPTER OVERVIEW

The text and vignette in Chapter 4 will help the student:

1. Explain how businesses combine human, natural, and capital resources to produce goods and services for profit.
2. Describe the four roles of entrepreneur, owner, manager, and worker that a person can play within a business.
3. Describe the functions of producers, distributors, and service firms.
4. Evaluate the costs and benefits of organizing a business as a sole proprietorship, partnership, corporation, cooperative, or franchise.
5. Assess the significance of small businesses within our economy.

NOTES ON TEACHING THE CHAPTER

1. Invite several local businesspeople to class to discuss how they established their business, the risks involved, and how free competition and government regulation affect their profit. The teacher may wish to include representatives from a sole proprietorship, partnership, and corporation, or from a producer, distributor, and service firm.

2. Ask students to use the systematic approach to decision making from Chapter 1 to make a choice for Randy. The teacher may also ask students to assume Otis's role—was he wise to offer his resources in forming a partnership? What should he be certain of before he enters into a formal agreement with Randy?
3. Ask some students to write to the local Chamber of Commerce, Small Business Administration, and regional office of the Federal Trade Commission to request literature available to those interested in establishing a small business. Have them share this information with the rest of the class.
4. Have several students interview several local franchisees to determine the extent of the franchisor's involvement with the start-up of the business and how they continue to oversee the day-to-day operation.
5. Ask students to brainstorm the types of businesses that are often successful as "work at home" careers. What might be the pros and cons of such businesses?

DISCUSSION QUESTIONS

1. What risks would be involved in starting a business that specializes in the sales and service of home computers? Do you feel such a business would be successful in your community? Why or why not?
2. Who is most important to the success of a business—the entrepreneur, the owner, the manager, or the worker?
3. Since World War II, the percentage of businesses that are service firms has risen steadily. Some say this is a problem because service firms create fewer jobs than manufacturers. Others say that the trend simply shows a change in the economy's focus. What do you think?
4. Some critics say that corporations do not act responsibly because stockholders cannot control them. Do you agree or disagree?

ANSWERS TO KEY TERMS

a. partnership b. managers c. service d. cooperative e. loss f. personal liability
g. stockholders h. entrepreneur i. distributor j. workers k. charter l. business
m. owners n. stock o. franchises p. profit q. dividend r. producer s. corporation
t. sole proprietorship u. limited partnership v. Small Business Administration (SBA)

ANSWERS TO REVIEW QUESTIONS

1. Profit is the amount by which a business's income is greater than its expenses. It is the reward the business owner receives for taking the risk of going into business in the first place.
2. Every entrepreneur has the *willingness* to take a risk (there is no guarantee that he or she will succeed in the new business), the *ability* to combine resources to produce goods or services and raise the money needed, and an *idea* that people will want to buy the good or service.
3. The four roles are entrepreneur, owner, manager, and worker. Some, and sometimes even all, of these roles do overlap, especially in new, small businesses.
4. Managers *plan* to meet the business's goals; they *organize,* marshalling available resources to meet those goals; they *direct,* leading and motivating workers in their efforts toward those goals; and they *control,* checking to see that goals are being met and met efficiently.
5. *Producers* produce goods; *distributors* help producers and consumers exchange goods; and *services* provide services to other businesses or to consumers. Examples will vary.
6. *Advantages:* easy to form; not much money needed; taxed at individual rate; owner is free to act as he or she pleases; owner gets all profits. *Disadvantages:* hard to raise money; success limited by owner's abilities; dies when owner dies; owner has unlimited personal liability for debts and obligations.
7. *Advantages:* easy to form; access to more capital than sole proprietorships; earnings taxed at individual rate; two heads are better than

one. *Disadvantages:* amount of money to be raised still limited; success limited by partners' abilities; success endangered if partners disagree; owners have unlimited liability.

8. *Advantages:* can raise far more capital; can outlive individual owners; owners' liability for losses and damages is limited to amount of their investment. *Disadvantages:* owners have little direct control; earnings taxed at a high rate; many legal restrictions and reporting requirements.
9. Franchises are legal arrangements in which one business pays a fee to another business for the right to use that business's name or sell its products. *Advantage:* a franchise allows an individual with limited money the chance to own a business and to receive training and advice. *Disadvantage:* the franchisee doesn't have complete control.
10. SBA helps business owners by guaranteeing or granting loans, by providing information, and by providing business executives who can give advice.

NOTES ON PROJECTS

1. The teacher may find this project most appropriate for group work—brainstorming may make it easier for students to identify an entrepreneurial idea. Once they have their ideas, students should do some research to identify the resources they'll need. By learning what's required to make comparable goods or services, they can better estimate their own needs.
2. The teacher should guide students to encyclopedias and history books for long-lived major corporations like the automakers, oil companies, or chemical firms. More recent arrivals—franchises or computer firms, for instance—may be described in periodical articles. Local newspapers may outline the development of a local success story. Students should notice that control of the business changes over time, especially as it grows larger. *Variation:* students could form into groups and investigate different firms in the same industry.
3. Students should, after a brief interview, be able to find answers to all the listed questions, which will make clear that the concepts discussed in this chapter are relevant to every business, large or small. The first question will tell them about entrepreneurship; the second about risk and profit; the third about the role of the individual in business; the fourth about the functions of the business; and the fifth about ways of organizing a business.
4. An alternative would be to invite an official of a local SBA office to talk to the class. The SBA person could describe the common problems that small business owners meet and how SBA helps them.
5. The debate should be lively, though the teacher can help by reminding students to focus on profits and not confuse them with markup. Students may want to keep in mind that lower profits could mean fewer goods and services or less efficiency in production.
6. Arrange for a librarian to direct students to resources where they can find company addresses and telephone numbers. If they plan to write a letter to the company requesting an annual report, emphasize the need to use correct grammar and spelling. Their letters should be typewritten or word processed on a computer. You may want to plan a class period to discuss the information contained in an annual report before scheduling the group presentations.
7. To prepare for this project, conduct a literature search of current articles on family-owned businesses. Have students prepare their own questions in advance of the presentation. Afterward, ask a student to write the guest presenter(s) a thank-you note on behalf of the class.

CHAPTER 5 The Government and the Economy

CHAPTER OVERVIEW

The text and vignette in Chapter 5 will help the student:

1. Evaluate the role all levels of government play in our economy.
2. Distinguish between public and merit services provided by the government.
3. Describe government regulation of competition, of the workplace, of public resources, for public safety, and of the amount of money in the economy.
4. Explain how government spends and collects revenue.
5. Describe the effect citizens can have on government policies, programs, and spending.

NOTES ON TEACHING THE CHAPTER

1. Ask the students to take a stand on the issue presented in the vignette—do they favor a user fee or continued support for the pool from property taxes? Do they think that Kim's view is selfish? What else might she consider? Is she simply acting out of self-interest, as theory says she will?
2. Divide the class into two groups to debate the issue of government regulation. One group may argue that government regulation is necessary to keep citizens and their property safe. The other may reason that government involvement is excessive and creates too many regulations for too few benefits.
3. Suggest that some members of the class interview someone who lived through a time of many government economic controls such as the Depression or World War II. Ask them how those controls limited their freedom to choose. Do they find that they now appreciate some things more because of limitations during that time?
4. Have students research and report on some of the recent reforms in the social security system. Discuss why such reform was necessary and encourage students to consider the fairness of these reforms. If social security payroll deductions were made optional, how many students would still choose to participate in the program?
5. Assign some students to investigate voter turnout in a recent election. Encourage them to register to vote and do so, if they are eligible. What are some reasons people may give for *not* voting? How might they be encouraged to exercise this basic right?
6. Emphasize the difference between public services, which tend to be such essentials as a legal system and defense, and merit services, which vary from locality to locality.

DISCUSSION QUESTIONS

1. What things can government do to lessen the problems of recession in a troubled economy?
2. What are some of the advantages of a sales tax to produce revenue for the government? What are some advantages of an income tax?
3. There are many differences in the services a local government provides from community to community. For example, some governments provide a full-time paid fire department; others rely strictly on volunteers. Some provide free trash collection; others ask citizens to assume the responsibility. Do you feel there should be more consistency in the services local governments provide?
4. Some people argue that the corporate income tax should be abolished—first, because it represents double taxation (first as corporate income and again as individual income), and second, because consumers pay the tax anyway, in the form of higher prices. Do you agree or disagree?

ANSWERS TO KEY TERMS

a. fines b. real estate tax c. ability-to-pay standard d. merit services
e. social security tax f. sales tax g. regressive tax h. wealth i. excise tax
j. income transfers k. user fees l. progressive tax m. tariff n. taxes
o. public services p. income tax q. Federal Reserve System r. benefits-received standard
s. license fees t. trust

ANSWERS TO REVIEW QUESTIONS

1. According to theory, the only functions of government in a market economy are to preserve law and order, to enforce contracts, and to ensure free and fair competition. The role of government has changed in the United States because people want to meet goals other than freedom and efficiency.
2. In the United States there are about 80,000 local governments, fifty state governments, and one federal government.
3. Public services are services that must be provided and that only government can provide to ensure that everyone can enjoy their benefits. Merit services are services government chooses to provide because it decides people should have them. Examples will vary.

4. Governments regulate business activity to ensure competition; to oversee industries that use public resources, or otherwise affect the public interest; to preserve fairness and safety in the workplace; to ensure the safety of the public at large; and to control the economy.
5. OSHA has been streamlining regulations (since 1977); the CAB has stopped setting passenger air fares and routes (since 1978); and government control of banking practices has been lessened (other examples may be given). The reason, in each case, is to increase competition, except in the case of OSHA, where it is to reduce costs to businesses.
6. Governments spend money to employ workers, to buy goods and services, and to give aid to individuals and businesses.
7. Such payments are called *income transfers* because they transfer income from those who earn it (who are taxed) to those government feels need or ought to have it (who receive payments).
8. Taxes are based on *income* (personal and corporate income and the social security tax), on *sales of goods and services* (sales and excise tax and tariffs), and on *wealth* (property tax and inheritance tax).
9. The four standards for evaluating taxes are fairness (using the benefits-received and ability-to-pay standards), directness, collectibility, and effect on the economy.
10. To influence government decisions, individuals can vote; join political parties or groups; sign petitions; campaign for candidates for office; speak at public hearings; and call or write their representatives.

NOTES ON PROJECTS

1. Leading the debaters to the second question—how to pay for it—should help them see that government decisions—like personal ones—require trade-offs. Debaters opposing the service could be required to say what they would do with the money saved—provide a different service or cut taxes?
2. In general, the reason should be one of the five or so discussed in the chapter. Be sure students choose a *regulation* of business, not just a *law*. Finding the local (or regional) administrator should not be hard—government directories in the reference room of the local library provide names and addresses.
3. Dissatisfaction with a tax could be over its existence or over its rate—ask students to separate the two questions. *Variation:* a class consensus on reforming a given tax could be turned into a letter to a government official, as in the next project.
4. The district office of your state or federal representative should be able to provide information on pending legislation. By checking the periodicals' indexes and writing to or calling interest groups, students should be able to get plenty of information on both sides of the issue. The important thing, of course, is that they write informed letters. Guiding them to do so may take the form of asking students to assume the role of the representative—what kind of letter (tone, persuasive style, and presentation) would convince them? *Variations:* if the vote on the issue is close, the losing side could also write a letter that serves as a "minority report"; the class could also ask the official to come to class to explain his or her position on the issue.
5. Ask students to find out where they can register to vote and when. There could even be a class demonstration of the mechanics of voting. *Variation:* students could, as a class, construct a voter registration handbook to keep in the school library.

CHAPTER 6 Planning for the Job You Want

CHAPTER OVERVIEW

The text and vignette in Chapter 6 will help the student:

1. Identify the importance of job satisfaction.
2. Explain how one's life-style and future goals direct a career choice.

3. Find information on potential careers.
4. Identify how to get the job he or she wants.
5. Write a résumé and prepare for an interview to help in obtaining a job.
6. Identify future economic trends when choosing a career.

NOTES ON TEACHING THE CHAPTER

1. It may be helpful to invite the school's career or guidance counselor to administer an occupational preference test or interest inventory to the class. Results of such tests can often be scored by the students themselves, or perhaps the counselor can arrange for speedy results. Students may use the results from such tests to do further research on a particular career or as background for projects 2 and 3 in the text.
2. To help students better understand how employment agencies work, recruit several class members to canvass and interview managers of several nearby agencies, including the local government employment service. Have them develop questions to ask (submitting them to you first for approval). Some possibilities: does the agency specialize in filling certain kinds of positions? what is the average fee charged for locating most jobs? who pays the fee? and what percentage of jobs are filled in a given time period?
3. Require students to write a letter to an appropriate professional organization, trade association, or labor union asking for more information on the career they have chosen to research. Figure 6.3 can be used as a sample for format.
4. When reviewing résumés and cover letters, stress the importance of good grammar, spelling, and punctuation.
5. Distribute a list of commonly asked interview questions such as those listed below.
   a. Why do you want to work for us?
   b. Tell me about yourself . . .
   c. What do you consider to be your major strengths and weaknesses?
   d. Where do you plan to be 5–10 years from now in terms of your career?
   e. How well do you work under pressure?
   f. Would you be willing to relocate?
   g. Describe how you handled a major problem or responsibility successfully.

   Have students familiarize themselves with how to respond to such questions during their interview. Encourage them to give thoughtful, concise answers, and to use the opportunity to develop their strong points fully. Discourage common, often meaningless responses such as, "I like people" and "I'm a hard worker," suggesting instead *how* one could prove these qualities in a potential job. Remind them that they too can and should ask questions of the interviewer before deciding whether the position is right for them.

DISCUSSION QUESTIONS

1. Pose the following question to the class: "If you didn't *have* to work (for economic reasons) *would* you? Why or why not?" This is apt to initiate a lively discussion on the value of work, economic conditions, and the like. The teacher might wish to use examples of lottery winners who suddenly find themselves millionaires. Do most of them quit their jobs after winning?
2. Ask each student in the class to fill in the following open-ended sentence with an appropriate ending: "A good job should. . . ." When all students have contributed, discuss which responses have a broad application to most work situations, and which are clearly indicative of certain types of jobs. Are there some that all students agree on? If so, why?
3. Ask the class to compare some of the pros and cons of each source of job training noted:
   a. vocational/technical school
   b. apprenticeship
   c. two- or four-year college
   d. military service
   e. on-the-job

   Encourage discussion on how they compare financially, the time involved, and opportunity cost. As a discussion leader, it is important to be as objective as possible so as not to influence student responses.
4. Ask the class to respond to this provocative statement: "It doesn't matter what you do to get a job—it's who you know that counts."

ANSWERS TO KEY TERMS

a. job b. interview c. job satisfaction d. résumé e. references f. career
g. occupational ladder h. job application i. life-style j. apprenticeship
k. private employment agency

ANSWERS TO REVIEW QUESTIONS

1. By influencing income, leisure time, family, friends, education, and interests, career influences life-style. Because interests, education, family, and friends influence career choice, life-style also affects career.
2. Evaluating a career is very important—first because career helps determine life-style, second because job satisfaction influences happiness. People are likely to have more than one career. Being ready for that possibility prepares them to change when they're not satisfied.
3. People get more information about careers by doing research in the library, writing to a trade or professional group, interviewing people in the career, or doing part-time work.
4. To evaluate careers, look at their income and benefits, the education and training they require, any personal or physical characteristics they call for, their economic future, the working conditions they offer, the type of work required, the degree of control workers have over that work, and the amount of responsibility involved.
5. To learn about oneself, conduct a self-analysis, make lists, talk to family, friends, teachers, or counselors, or take a test. The purpose is to identify interests, abilities, and resources to find a career that matches them.
6. A job seeker plans a strategy to persuade an employer to hire him or her for a job.
7. Information about job openings comes from contacts, private or government employment agencies, applying directly, reading want ads, and keeping informed from news reports. Government jobs are filled through military recruiters and civil service applications. Some people also create job openings by offering skills as a way of solving a problem a business has.
8. An effective résumé includes the applicant's name, address, and job objectives. It lists work experience and education that relate to the job objective. It may or may not include references. It is neatly typed and is usually one page long.
9. An interviewee should appear on time for the interview and should be dressed appropriately. He or she should be polite. Practicing the interview beforehand can prepare the interviewee for answering difficult questions. Briefly rereading the résumé before going in can help, too. The interviewee should do some research on the employer beforehand, if possible, and prepare questions to ask.
10. People learn about the prospects of various careers by reading books and magazines and studying reports of economic and technological trends. Doing so helps protect them from being locked into a declining career.

NOTES ON PROJECTS

1. Trying to group jobs into occupational ladders will help students see the connections between jobs. By looking into the economic future of various jobs and the salaries they command, students will form habits that will benefit them later. *Variation:* present the material in a written report.
2. To find people to talk to, students can consult the yellow pages, local Chambers of Commerce, unions or professional associations, or can draw on their own acquaintances. The teacher should review questions beforehand, to see that students aren't missing possible leads. Questions can cover the nature of the work, the extent and cost of training, the number of potential employers, and all other factors. Students should also be cautioned about politeness when calling to arrange the interview, as well as during the interview. The thank-you note can serve as an introduction to formal business letters. The teacher can use the sample cover letter in the book as a model for form, but should advise stu-

dents on proper style and diction. *Variation:* make an oral report to the class on what was learned.

3. The question of training is difficult. Because for some jobs, students will not yet have the training or education they'll need, they must assume that training in order to do this project. The teacher can suggest that students use such résumés as goals for their future—they can plan how to get the experience in a certain amount of time that will produce that résumé. Completed résumés should, of course, be typed neatly.
4. This project can be used in place of the third. Both get students to organize the details of a résumé around the job objective, but by using a fictional character, students may practice résumé writing with more ease. Later they can transfer the skill to their own job objectives and experience. *Variation:* expand the project by asking students to write a cover letter for Raymond in response to a want ad for a specific job.
5. This role playing should be good practice for students on interviewing. The teacher will need to guide the employer students in creating realistic jobs, in terms of work required and wages paid. Applicant students can, of course, use the résumé they wrote in project 3. (In fact, the students could play the parts of Raymond and a prospective employer from project 4.) *Variations:* ask students to change positions, giving them a chance to play both roles; pick two students to do this project in front of the class, opening up the last questions (hire or don't hire, take the job or not) to a class vote.

CHAPTER 7 Entering the Work Force

CHAPTER OVERVIEW

The text and vignette in Chapter 7 will help the student:

1. Explain the need to work cooperatively with others in order to help an organization achieve its goals.
2. List the rights and responsibilities of workers and management.
3. Describe the nature of a labor union and its relationship with management.
4. Identify changes in work status.
5. Explain the relationship of worker productivity to economic growth.

NOTES ON TEACHING THE CHAPTER

1. This chapter has one of the book's open-ended vignettes on a controversial topic. Use the dilemma faced by Sheila and her coworkers to make the chapter's point that working cooperatively promotes an organization's survival and enhances workers' security. Point out that workers are understandably concerned about job security. The role-playing project should allow students to explore this issue.
2. To reinforce the point about working cooperatively, point to the students' own experience with group projects—did group work succeed because members worked together or fail because they didn't?
3. One volume of the *Martindale-Hubbell Directory,* the *State Law Digest,* contains all state employment laws limiting women and minors from working in various fields. If a copy is available, the teacher will find some fascinating provisions that could be used in class as examples of child and female labor laws.
4. Ask a local businessperson to come to class to detail the qualities management looks for in workers. Relate this point to the previous chapter by asking this businessperson to explain how students can demonstrate these qualities in résumés and interviews.
5. Have students research the history of the Professional Air Traffic Controllers Organization (PATCO) and its 1981 strike. What major factors do they believe contributed to the trouble encountered by this 11,000+ member union? Have them find evidence of other strikes that resulted in improved working conditions for other influential unions. This can result in a discussion on the pros and cons of strikes as a negotiating tool for unions.

6. Ask students to interview several people asking how they feel labor unions affect wages, working conditions, supply and demand of labor, and the balance of imports and exports.
7. Invite a representative from the local state unemployment service to explain the terms under which one may collect unemployment benefits, for how long, and how to file a claim.
8. Ask students to pick an organization, local or national in which they are interested. It could be a business, a charity or educational group, or part of the government. Find out what the organization's goals are by doing research or by talking to members or leaders. Find out what jobs are in the organization to get that work done. How does each worker's performance help the organization achieve its goals? Describe the work of this organization.
9. Have students ask one of their parents, or another family member or friend, about the last time he or she left a job. How did he or she decide and prepare to leave? What effects did he or she expect the change would have on his or her life? What effects did it actually have? Have students write the findings from their interview in a "case history of a worker's status change."

DISCUSSION QUESTIONS

1. Ask students to brainstorm possible reasons for the decline in union membership in recent years. What are the advantages and disadvantages of union membership?
2. Discuss the implications of lowering the federal minimum wage for workers under eighteen. Will it actually raise the number of job opportunities for teenagers or is it an attempt to get less costly labor?
3. Ask students to assume that they have recently been promoted to a management position that requires them to manage other workers who are friends, in a supervisory capacity. How could they ward off some of the resentment or jealousy felt by their former coworkers and still see that management's goals are met?
4. Debate the issue of new technology and its effect on the work force. Does technology actually replace a worker or does it ultimately *create* more jobs in manufacturing, service, and the like?
5. Critics of labor unions charge that union contracts drive up prices, harming workers who don't belong to unions. Hold a class debate on this issue.

ANSWERS TO KEY TERMS

a. layoff b. mediator c. union shop d. work permit e. managers f. retirement
g. boycott h. organization i. open shop j. transfer k. productivity l. closed shop
m. firing n. antidiscrimination laws o. raise p. labor unions q. resign r. strike
s. arbitrator t. grievance procedures u. cost-of-living adjustment v. promotion
w. collective bargaining x. agency shop y. injunction

ANSWERS TO REVIEW QUESTIONS

1. Cooperation involves *communication* with managers and with other workers, *performance* to the best of a worker's ability, and a friendly and considerate *personality*. Examples should reflect the issues discussed in the text.
2. A work permit is a document that allows a worker who is under a state's minimum working age to hold a job. Depending on the state and the job, workers under sixteen or under eighteen must get such permits.
3. Workers have the right to a minimum wage (except food service workers), to time-and-a-half wages for overtime work (except some workers), and to equal pay for equal work. Workers also have a right to be paid the promised wage and to be paid on time.
4. Managers have a right to expect that workers will do quality work, be reliable, be productive, be efficient, act safely, show initiative, be adaptable, cooperate with managers and with other workers, be honest, and have a good attitude. Answers about the importance of a quality should reflect understanding of the worker's responsibility to help the organization meet its goals.

5. A union is a group of workers who join together to bargain more effectively with management.
6. Collective bargaining is the negotiation of a labor contract by representatives of a union and of management. The contract spells out pay and other benefits, working conditions (including safety procedures and perhaps worker output), worker security, and grievance procedures.
7. Before deciding to go on strike, union workers should consider whether their gains from striking will equal the wages they will lose while on strike; whether the settlement they seek will endanger the health of the business, and thus their jobs; and whether their action will have an adverse effect on other workers in other businesses.
8. Before asking for a raise, a worker should analyze his or her performance objectively to see if a raise is deserved. To ask for a raise, carefully explain what has been contributed to the organization—and what will be done in the future.
9. A promotion is a movement within a company to a position with new responsibilities. A transfer is a move to a different work place.
10. A layoff, whether temporary or permanent, is related to economic conditions or the performance of the organization. Firing is the result of poor performance by an individual worker.
11. When productivity goes up, workers have greater job security; businesses become more competitive and their profits go up; society benefits from a healthy economy, more jobs, and more goods and services.

NOTES ON PROJECTS

1. This project introduces students to one of the major issues of our time and helps them realize that all public policy decisions affect the economy. They should be able to locate much information in recent periodicals, for the topic is a current one. Government sources may also provide useful information. Guide students to base their summary evaluations on reasonable analysis—what would they give up in current goods and services for the sake of more research? You may ask students to focus on a particular industry or type of good. And it may be best to steer them away from nondurable consumer goods (cosmetics, toiletries)—although food would be a useful topic to pursue.
2. The role-playing exercise will give students a chance to put themselves in the center of a major national question. Some reading in magazines of opinion and in books—to give their arguments more basis—could be helpful before beginning.

CHAPTER 8 Earning a Paycheck

CHAPTER OVERVIEW

The text and vignette in Chapter 8 will help the student:

1. Describe how workers are paid for their labor.
2. Explain what fringe benefits are and how they affect one's payment for labor.
3. Distinguish between gross pay, net pay, and common payroll deductions.
4. Define income taxes and explain what must be done to file a return.
5. Explain income security provided by the government to workers and their dependents.
6. Describe the effect one's disposable income has on the economy at large.

NOTES ON TEACHING THE CHAPTER

1. Invite a local businessperson to speak to the class about fringe benefits. The individual could be a personnel officer or a member of the local Chamber of Commerce. Ask this person to discuss common fringe benefits in the area and their average cost to employers per employee. If a major corporation in the area offers a cafeteria plan of benefits, ask a personnel officer to explain how the plan works.
2. Have students discuss the average wage earned by teenagers in their area for part-time jobs. (Some may be unwilling to share with the class exactly how much they earn in their job. The teacher should stress that this is acceptable.) Compare wages for private services such as babysitting to the figures for part-time jobs in businesses, which will probably be closer to the minimum wage.
3. Since many students have part-time jobs and will need to file a tax return, obtain enough copies of the current year's IRS booklets and forms for each student to complete. Form 1040EZ is simple enough to understand and will be appropriate for most students. If the time of year is right, encourage some students to bring in their own W-2 forms, or duplicate some mock W-2 forms for students to use. Reproduce one form on an overhead transparency and slowly review the step-by-step instructions to help students understand how each entry is arrived at.
4. Ask an accountant to come to class to discuss the kind of expenses that can be taken as deductions.
5. Have students investigate the system of worker's compensation in force in the state. Must all employers contribute to this fund? What about those who are self-employed? Give a hypothetical example such as a painter who has been injured while working in someone's home—to what extent would the homeowner be liable? What questions should a homeowner ask before contracting with someone to do work on his or her property?
6. Have students interview the human resources manager or personnel director of a large local employer. Ask him or her about a fringe benefit the company provides for all its employees: health insurance, life insurance, day care, or whatever. Find out how much it costs the company per worker. Then have students do some shopping around, and find out how much it would cost a worker to buy the same benefit acting as an individual consumer. Is there a difference? What is the difference? What does this tell them about fringe benefits? If they were working for a company that did *not* provide this benefit, would they buy it on their own?

DISCUSSION QUESTIONS

1. Initiate a class discussion on social security. If social security deductions and benefits were made optional, how many students would choose to belong to the system? How many would not? What would they do instead to provide for themselves during retirement?
2. Ask students to assume that they are involved in contract negotiations at their workplace. Management's representative has offered them the choice between a 10 percent salary increase or an 8 percent increase with the addition of a dental insurance plan. Which would they choose? What personal considerations would influence their decision? As a negotiator representing others, what would they want to know about other workers before accepting or rejecting the offer?
3. Some legislators propose changing the federal income tax system to a so-called flat tax. In some flat tax proposals, all wage earners pay the same percentage of income. In other proposals, the tax rate will still be graduated, but within a smaller range (4 percent to 20 percent, for example). Many proposals exempt all wages below a certain amount. Many also couple the change in the tax rate with the abolition of all deductions. Do you favor a flat tax? Why or why not? If you do favor this kind of tax, what form should it take?

ANSWERS TO KEY TERMS

a. W-2 form b. bonus c. payroll deductions d. tax deductions e. earned income
f. salary g. unemployment compensation h. pension plan i. gross pay j. W-4 form

k. wage   l. tips   m. social security   n. net pay   o. fringe benefits
p. worker's compensation   q. piecework rate   r. profit-sharing plan   s. commission
t. income tax return   u. exemption   v. social insurance

ANSWERS TO REVIEW QUESTIONS

1. A wage is a rate of pay per hour of work. Workers are not paid for hours they do not work, but they are paid time-and-a-half for any overtime hours (more than forty a week). A salary is a rate of pay that covers a longer period—a week, a month, or a year. The one rate covers all the work done in that period. Workers may not be paid extra for extra hours.
2. Commissions are paid to sales workers. They serve as an incentive to encourage salespeople to work harder and sell more.
3. Common fringe benefits include vacation days, sick days, holidays, and personal days; health and life insurance; tuition reimbursement; day care; pension plans; and profit-sharing plans. Benefits help companies compete for good workers, boost workers' morale, ensure workers' economic security, and improve productivity.
4. Net pay is what is left after payroll deductions are deducted from gross pay.
5. Some common payroll deductions are federal income tax, social security tax, state and local income taxes, charitable contributions, union dues, and insurance premiums.
6. Any person who earns more than a certain amount of income must file a federal income tax return. In 1990 that limit was $5,100 for single persons and $9,200 for married persons filing a joint return.
7. Taxpayers file by filling out a tax form and sending it to the IRS by April 15. They can send the return in later if they have asked for and received an extension.
8. Taxpayers receive a refund if more tax was withheld than they owe. They must pay the difference if they owe more than was withheld.
9. All workers except some state and city government employees pay taxes to the social security system. From those taxes payments are made to retired and disabled workers, their spouses and dependents, and to the spouses and dependents of dead workers.
10. Employers contribute to state-run unemployment compensation funds. These funds are then used to pay benefits to workers who are fired without cause or laid off as long as they are willing to do comparable work.
11. Disposable income is what is left of income after all income taxes are paid. People use it to satisfy their wants.

NOTES ON PROJECTS

1. The teacher can guide students to talk to food-service workers (though not in fast-food restaurants) about tips and to sales workers about commissions. The class debate on these forms of payment should be lively. The teacher can ask students to consider the benefits, such as not being tied to the output of low-productivity workers, and the costs, such as reduced income in bad economic times when consumer spending is low.
2. The debate may start by focusing on why the tax deduction is allowed—to help reduce the abuses of campaign financing. Did it succeed? Related issues would include spending limits and whether public funding of campaigns limits choices to candidates with large personal fortunes. Students should be able to find much material in magazines that cover public issues.
3. Students should be able to locate much material on this important and current topic. The class could also bring in the district's representative or a member of a local SSA office to explain the history of the program and changes in coverage, benefits, and taxes.

CHAPTER 9 Planning to Use Your Resources

CHAPTER OVERVIEW

The text and vignette in Chapter 9 will help the student:

1. Explain and use the seven-step basic consumer method.
2. Describe how personal resources are used to satisfy wants.
3. Identify the alternatives to buying goods and services.
4. Assess the value of planning and of managing resources.
5. Describe the processes for managing time, skills, energy, and money.
6. Identify the effects of inflation and deflation on buying power.

NOTES ON TEACHING THE CHAPTER

1. Have the students use the seven-step basic consumer method to make a consumer decision. Have the first few who complete all seven steps share their experiences with the class. Ask them to evaluate the value of the process as a consumer tool.
2. As a demonstration of the effectiveness of bartering, have a group of students volunteer to form a bartering unit. They should each have a skill or item valued by the other members of the group. At the completion of a designated time (e.g., two weeks), ask the unit to describe their transactions to the class; have the class determine whether fair value was received in each case.
3. Have students complete the following open-ended statements:
   a. I never seem to have enough time to . . .
   b. I wish I could afford . . .
   c. I wish I knew how to . . .
   Ask students how, through effective management of personal resources, their statements could change.
4. Invite a member of the school board to explain how the school budget is determined. As a follow-up, have students look for similarities and differences of school budgets and personal budgets.

DISCUSSION QUESTIONS

1. Can you think of any item or service for which an alternative to buying would not be acceptable?
2. Of the personal resources we have—money, time, skill, and energy—which is most important? Why?
3. Why do you suppose the text suggests that you set long-term goals before short-term ones?
4. Do you agree that a good reason to save money is that it is a good habit to acquire?
5. How have you, and your families, been affected by inflation? What measures have you and your families taken to fight inflation?

ANSWERS TO KEY TERMS

a. long-term goals b. renting c. skills d. budget e. variable expenses
f. deflation g. basic consumer method h. short-term goals i. product care and maintenance
j. personal energy k. fixed expenses l. savings m. inflation n. buying power

ANSWERS TO REVIEW QUESTIONS

1. The seven steps consumers follow are planning, getting information, comparison shopping, determining how to pay, reviewing the decision to buy, buying, and evaluating the purchases. The planning step follows the same method as systematic decision making: listing your wants, identifying your goals and resources, and selecting which wants to satisfy and which resources to use.
2. Alternatives to buying include substitution, doing it yourself, barter, product care and maintenance, renting, and doing without. Instead of buying a desk, a person could make one by improvising, build one, or trade something he or she no longer needs for a desk.
3. Planning helps in using resources effectively, including living within a budget and using time to gain more resources. Planning makes it pos-

sible to rank wants so that the most important ones can be satisfied first. Planning prevents buying on impulse. Planning what kind of gift to buy and how much to spend can save time and help avoid impulse buying. Students' examples should reveal understanding of these benefits.

4. Managing time results in using it efficiently to gain money, skills, and energy.
5. People develop skills by going to school, learning from others, reading, or using a home computer. All skills can increase with practice. Skills are used to satisfy wants or to increase other resources.
6. Energy can be increased by getting proper rest, eating well, and exercising regularly. Substances like drugs, nicotine, and caffeine decrease energy and should be avoided.
7. Making a budget involves noting past expenses, setting goals, estimating income, expenses, and savings, and balancing the budget. After making a budget, the most important thing is to use it.
8. A fixed expense is a cost that does not change over time, like a loan or insurance. A variable expense is a changeable cost that may be easier to control, such as clothing and entertainment.
9. People save to buy expensive purchases, to provide for retirement and emergencies, and to build a reserve fund.
10. Inflation is a general increase in prices that results in a decrease in the buying power of consumers. Consumers can fight inflation by switching to less expensive items or brands, buying at sales, and avoiding impulse buying.

NOTES ON PROJECTS

1. The teacher should guide students into ranking their goals to make wiser decisions. Students may also need help in seeing the implications of some of their goals. Follow-up is crucial: students must compare their actual time expenditure to their budgeted time to see whether they made mistakes in either.
2. This project should start the students thinking about income enhancement in a meaningful way. Use class discussion to introduce the project by having students discuss their skills. The teacher might share how he or she uses a skill to supplement other resources. Encourage students to find other class members with related or complementary skills; have them devise ways they could combine their skills to make money. Hearing about other people's skills might spark self-discovery in students who have not yet examined their own skills.
3. The project should help students see how critical goal-setting is to wise money management. Although the budget exercise is too short to uncover major spending patterns, it will give the students a chance to think about many aspects of resource management, like savings, alternatives to buying, and impulse buying. The teacher will probably need to emphasize the importance of accurate record-keeping. It may be helpful to have each student indicate his or her method of noting expenditures prior to starting the project. *Variation:* the teacher may want to follow this project with a similar budget covering a longer time.
4. This exercise should get students thinking about why prices change. By looking at more than one item, they may be able to draw conclusions about the dynamics of the economy as a whole. Discussion should lead students to consider the prices of other goods. *Competing products* are goods that vie for the same consumer dollars. For instance, if the cost of video rental goes up relative to the cost of movies, more entertainment dollars will be spent on movies. *Complementary products* are goods for which demand rises and falls together. If computer prices go down, prices of software may increase — more consumers may have more money to spend on it. By trying to consider what causes these changes, students will prepare for Chapter 12, which discusses timing purchases to take advantage of supply and demand.
5. Arrange class time for students to share their journal entries. The challenge for you is to try this experiment yourself and share your thoughts with the class.
6. Compile inflation-fighting suggestions into a handout for each student, or prepare a bulletin board on your students' top 10 inflation-fighting suggestions.
7. Review membership information with students. If possible, arrange a field trip to a buying cooperative.

CHAPTER 10 Getting and Using Information

CHAPTER OVERVIEW

The text and vignette in Chapter 10 will help the student:

1. Evaluate sources of information as well as the information itself.
2. Distinguish between information and influence.
3. Locate information to help in making decisions.
4. Identify the appeals that advertisers use.
5. Analyze which technique an advertiser is using.
6. Explain the controls and regulations set to ensure the fairness of advertising.

NOTES ON TEACHING THE CHAPTER

1. In order to recognize how much influences affect the buying decisions we make, ask the students to identify what personal or external influence is being illustrated in the following examples.
   a. John has just gotten a job at the local service station every day after school and on Saturdays. His first thought when he heard that he had been hired was, "Now I can buy my own car!"
   b. Alice and Sue have been friends all through high school. Now that they have graduated, Alice is going away to college, while Sue has taken a position as a secretary at a realtor's office. On a recent shopping trip, Alice eagerly spent all her money on new clothes. She couldn't understand why Sue preferred to wait until she had worked awhile before buying many new clothes.
   c. Each year, a different member of the Wilson family hosts the entire family for Christmas dinner. This year it's Dan's turn. Although he has recently had to take a cut in pay, he is determined to provide a lavish meal.
2. To provide students with the experience of dealing with an especially aggressive salesperson, have students role play various resistance techniques.
3. Invite a representative from a Better Business Bureau to class to explain their consumer services. A member of a local trade or business association can perform the same function. Ask him or her to emphasize the regulatory role the organization plays.
4. The power of advertising can best be recognized when we realize the number of products we know by their commercial slogan, jingle, or song. Have students come up with as many examples as they can.
5. Ask students to watch one hour of children's television on Saturday morning and analyze the advertisements; have them pay particular attention to the amount of useful information given and the various appeals used. As they share their observations in class, a pattern of very little information and a large number of similar appeals and techniques should emerge.

DISCUSSION QUESTIONS

1. Is it right or wrong to allow personal or external influences to affect our buying decisions? Why?
2. It has been said that the strongest influence on a teenager's buying decisions is peer pressure. Do you agree or disagree?
3. If you were about to buy a particular make of car and your father said that members of the family had always bought another make and were consistently satisfied, would you change your mind?
4. Are organizations that test and rate products absolutely objective? Explain your answer.
5. Which advertising technique is most informational and objective?
6. Are you for or against advertising? Explain.

ANSWERS TO KEY TERMS

a. rational appeal b. testimonial c. influences d. emotional appeal e. peer pressure
f. advertising g. sales pressure h. information i. warranties

j. trade and professional associations k. Better Business Bureaus
l. Federal Trade Commission m. bait-and-switch advertising

ANSWERS TO REVIEW QUESTIONS

1. Family and friends, business sources, organizations that test and rate products, and governments all provide information. Evaluate information by checking the source for reliability and objectivity and by checking the information itself for completeness and relevance.
2. Information is facts about goods and services that can be used to evaluate alternatives. Influences are forces within and outside a person that affect how he or she thinks and behaves. Examples will vary.
3. Business sources of consumer information include product labels, warranties, information booklets, trade and professional groups, and the BBBs.
4. Products are tested and rated by Consumers' Research, Consumers Union, and Consumer Guide. Although their test results are valuable, they test only national brands and they may be looking for different qualities in their tests than a consumer wants.
5. The agencies named will vary but should be found in Table 10.1.
6. Advertising is both an influence and an information source. Advertisements can be used by learning to screen them carefully to get the information they provide and ignore their attempts to influence.
7. Answers should include any three of the following: rational, emotional, positive or negative, humor, sex, or fear. (Descriptions are in the text.)
8. Answers should include any three of the following: testimonial, endorsement, problem solving, demonstration, scientific test, product comparison, life-style, and bandwagon. (Descriptions are in the text.)
9. The media controls itself through standards set by the Direct Marketing Association, Outdoor Advertising Association of America, and the American Association of Advertising Agencies. Industry controls itself through the National Advertisers Division and the National Advertising Review Board, both part of the BBBs.
10. Arguments for advertising include any of the following: it doesn't force anyone to buy, gives valuable information, promotes competition, lowers prices, and pays for entertainment. Arguments against advertising include any of the following: it creates unnecessary wants, wastes money, limits competition, raises prices, and invades our lives.

NOTES ON PROJECTS

1. By making the chart and comparing their results, students should see the importance of peer pressure in their choices. Ask the students if they think their parents would be subject to different influences from the ones that affected them.
2. The teacher should guide students to make the product they select something the testing organization will rate: an appliance, brand-name food, or hobby article. The teacher should also caution students not to consult material printed by the three organizations before picking the brand they prefer. The class might compare their decisions and the views of CU, CR, and CG. Different results may point out how much taste varies and what an important consideration it is.
3. Different groups of students should test different types of products. The teacher will want to guide students to select relatively inexpensive products that can be tested easily. Limiting the number of criteria to be judged will simplify the project.
4. Students should notice differences between print, radio, and TV ads and their impacts. Have them discuss which medium is most influential. Have students tell how they evaluated the fairness and honesty of the ads. Stimulate debate on how to make judgments about ads and their effects. *Variation:* if equipment is available, the teacher may tape the ads, making comparison in class easier; having different students react to the same ad will demonstrate that ads affect people differently.
5. This project is very adaptable to group work. The teacher may help students identify a mar-

ket for their products—which consumers would want to buy it and what features would they be looking for? *Variation:* ask students to perform their two commercials in class. The students who watch the performance can then identify the ad's appeal and technique. They can also decide which is more effective and why. The class could even award an honorary "Obie," the ad industry's prize, to the best commercial.

CHAPTER 11 Comparison Shopping

CHAPTER OVERVIEW

The text and vignette in Chapter 11 will help the student:

1. Compare competing goods using ten standards.
2. Compare competing services using six standards.
3. Distinguish the differences among various kinds of sellers of goods.
4. Analyze what factors affect prices.
5. Time purchases correctly to get the best value for the money spent.
6. Describe the impact of consumer choices on businesses.

NOTES ON TEACHING THE CHAPTER

1. Ask each student to select a product he or she would like to purchase and list, in order of importance, the ten standards to be checked. Are there any other factors considered important?
2. Students probably don't realize how many services they purchase. Ask them to name as many as they can.
3. The text states that catalog selling saves consumers money. To enable students to test this for themselves, divide the class into groups. Ask each group to select an item and price it in a department store. Then have them price a comparable item in a catalog (remember to have them add shipping charges and any taxes that are applicable). Have each group share its findings. Do they agree or disagree with the information in the text?
4. Invite someone to class to give a demonstration product party, comparable to one he or she would do in a home. Try to find a product with appeal to both sexes (some type of home product). After the party, students should discuss why they liked, or didn't like, this method of selling.
5. Using Table 11.4, ask students to try to determine why certain products are typically on sale during particular months. Often the reason can be traced to supply and demand.

DISCUSSION QUESTIONS

1. From the vignette in this and the preceding chapters, it appears Ian's family gave him the

responsibility of finding the best home computer for them. Would your families give you the responsibility for a major family purchase? Why? Would you accept the responsibility for such a choice?
2. Comparison shopping takes time; how can the time spent be minimized?
3. Suppose you had spent a lot of time and energy comparison shopping for a product, bought what you believed was the best one, and then the product was recalled, as many products have been, because of faulty production. How do you think you would feel?
4. Of the five factors that influence price changes—demand, supplier's cost, competition, technology, and government regulation—which do you think causes the greatest price fluctuation? Why?
5. Do you think the phrase "suggested list price" is misleading to consumers? Explain your answer.

ANSWERS TO KEY TERMS

a. department stores b. supermarkets c. specialty stores d. discount department stores
e. factory outlet f. catalog selling g. discount supermarkets h. comparison shopping
i. direct selling j. vending machines k. convenience stores l. loss leaders
m. promotional sale n. suggested list price o. warranties p. flea market
q. clearance sale r. generic or unbranded products s. rebate t. brand u. auction
v. mail-order clubs

ANSWERS TO REVIEW QUESTIONS

1. Comparison shopping helps consumers decide what, where, and when to buy, and how to pay for the purchase.
2. Sometimes it's impossible to comparison shop. Some goods and services are available from only one seller. Some purchases aren't important or costly enough to warrant comparison shopping. Consumers should comparison shop more often than they do, especially for expensive or complex goods or services.
3. In comparing goods consumers look at price, intended use, accessories, performance, product life, care, safety, consumer protection, service availability, and the maker's reputation. While price is important, it is not the only feature to consider. The question is what the buyer gets—or gives up—for the money spent.
4. Consumers compare services by looking at what they want done, how well it will be done, how long it will last, what consumer protection there is, and how reputable the provider of the service is. Price is also important but not the only thing to consider.
5. Consumers locate alternative sellers of goods and services by using their own experience, asking family and friends, checking ads and the yellow pages, and requesting information from local trade, professional, or business groups or a government agency.
6. To compare competing sellers of goods and services, consumers look for competitive prices, selection, quality, convenience, the chance to use different methods of payment, courteous and helpful salespeople, and reputation.
7. Any four of the following can be named: department stores, discount department stores, supermarkets, discount supermarkets, convenience stores, specialty stores, and factory outlets. Answers to the second part of the question should contain the major characteristics listed in the text.
8. Any three of the following can be named: catalog selling, mail-order clubs, direct selling, vending machines, flea markets, garage or yard sales, auctions, and shopping by computer. Answers to the second part of the question should contain the characteristics listed in the text.
9. The five factors that change prices are demand, supplier's costs, competition, technological changes, and government regulation. Consumers can watch these conditions and buy when they cause lower prices.
10. Promotional sales stimulate demand; clearance sales unload unwanted supply. A sale is not useful if stores have lured customers with misleading price advertising, or if the sale leads consumers to buy items not really marked down.
11. National brands are well known but have high advertising and packaging costs; store brands are usually equal in quality but cheaper because of lower costs; generic products cost the least.
12. Consumer decisions affect businesses by deciding the fate of their products and services. If

too few consumers buy a product, it fails and producers will not make money. Businesses care what consumers think because they need consumer purchases to survive.

NOTES ON PROJECTS

1. Encourage class members to cover a wide variety of products and services so that the reports will be more meaningful (and less repetitive). A good way to start off is by having students write a brief description of what they're looking for in a product or exactly what service they want performed. *Variation:* the end product could also be a written report.
2. Nonstore sellers will be available for all goods—remind students that consumers do buy from each other. Students need to develop a single list of questions they can ask each seller to get the information they'll need to compare each one.
3. Encourage students to watch out for misleading advertising. Encourage them to tell the class about any new sale gimmicks they encounter in their research. As they share their experiences, they may develop a list of stores that regularly seem to mislead consumers with their advertising.
4. This could be done as a group project in order to spread the expense. Group work will also make the comparisons interesting—different students may prefer the taste of different brands. Students should be able to discuss when it might be preferable, desirable, or necessary to select one brand instead of another.
5. Ask: Have you ever dialed a teen "talkline?" What was your phone bill for that call?

CHAPTER 12 Saving, Spending, or Borrowing Money

CHAPTER OVERVIEW

The text and vignette in Chapter 12 will help the student:

1. Evaluate the three methods of paying for a purchase—cash or cash substitutes, credit, or savings.
2. Explain how interest is calculated.
3. Describe the three methods used by lenders to calculate the balance of an open-end credit account.
4. Explain how to use the five cash substitutes.
5. Describe how to operate a checking account.
6. Identify the range of services available through electronic funds transfer.

NOTES ON TEACHING THE CHAPTER

1. To give students experience in comparing the cost of buying on credit to saving, use the following exercise. Divide the class into pairs of students, asking each pair to choose an item they want to purchase. One student of each pair should assume that he or she has $25 saved for the item and will save an additional $10 each week. That student should calculate how long it will take him or her to save enough to buy the good. The other student should assume that he or she has $25 to make a down payment and will finance the rest of the purchase through a bank card or the store's charge plan. He or she should find the finance charge (and the APR) to discover how much more it will cost to buy the good on credit. The pair should then decide which method they prefer and explain their choice to the class. The class as a whole may discuss the different choices made—do preferences vary according to the kind of good being purchased?
2. To illustrate the advantages and disadvantages of the various cash substitutes, pose the following situation for students. Suppose you just won

$10,000 in a sweepstakes. How would you prefer to receive the money—cash, personal check, cashier's check, certified check, money order, or traveler's check? Also ask students how they would feel about a personal check made out to someone else but endorsed over to themselves.

3. People are often careless about the way they write checks. Invite a local bank officer to speak about the importance of accurate check writing. Ask him or her to describe some of the more unusual checks the bank has received and to tell about any difficulties that arose as a result. He or she might also discuss the rights and responsibilities of consumers and financial institutions in regard to checks and statements.
4. Students will never learn to reconcile a checking account unless they actually do it. Give them practice with this exercise. The following checks were written in a month: #231, $14.95; #232, $11.12; #233, $27.19; #234, $17.15; #235, $13.39; #236, $50.00; #237, $21.50; #238, $13.42; #239, $25.00; #240, $18.79. A deposit of $100.00 was made after check #235 was written. The opening checkbook balance was $150.13; the closing balance was $37.62. The statement returned all checks except #238 and #240; the deposit had been credited to the account. Check #230 for $35.00, which had been written in the previous month, was also returned. There was a $2.50 service charge. The opening statement balance was $185.13; its closing balance was $67.33. After deducting the service charge, the checking account balance should be $35.12, which agrees with the statement balance minus the two outstanding checks.

DISCUSSION QUESTIONS

1. Some people believe that a purchase should not be made unless one has the money on hand to pay for it. Do you agree or disagree?
2. Would you want to operate a checking account to handle your income and monthly bills? Why or why not?
3. Can you think of any disadvantages to electronic funds transfer? Would you use these methods of getting cash or paying bills? Why or why not?

ANSWERS TO KEY TERMS

a. personal check b. interest c. principal d. compound interest e. finance charge
f. certified check g. adjusted balance method h. traveler's checks
i. average daily balance method j. endorsement k. cashier's check l. check register
m. annual percentage rate n. interest-bearing checking account o. previous balance method
p. money order q. regular checking accounts r. stop-payment order
s. automatic teller machine t. overdraft u. bank statement v. reconcile an account
w. debit card x. effective annual yield y. closed-end credit z. open-end credit

ANSWERS TO REVIEW QUESTIONS

1. Consumers buy with cash or cash substitutes, credit, or savings.
2. When evaluating buying methods, consumers consider the immediacy of their need for the purchase, the price of the purchase, the frequency with which the purchase is made, and the availability, convenience, cost, and opportunity cost of the method.
3. Calculate interest by multiplying the principal times the rate of interest times the time. Compounding means that a financial institution adds interest to the principal as it is earned so it also earns interest. Daily compounding is most advantageous for the consumer.
4. Calculate the effective annual yield by dividing the dollar amount of interest earned in one year by the principal. Calculating it helps in comparing different interest rates.
5. Finance charges include interest on loans plus any other charges such as service charges or insurance.
6. Compare the terms offered by different lenders by comparing the annual percentage rate—the yearly cost of a loan—which lenders are required to state.
7. The three ways of figuring the balance in open-end credit are the previous balance method, the average daily balance method, and the adjusted balance method.

8. Any of the following are substitutes for cash: personal checks, cashier's checks, certified checks, traveler's checks, and money orders.
9. A depositor puts money in a financial institution, which gives the depositor blank checks. The depositor (or drawer) gives a check to a payee, who presents it to the financial institution (the drawee) for payment. With a stop-payment order, the drawer asks the institution to refuse to pay a particular check.
10. Check registers are the record books of deposits and withdrawals. Statements are the financial institution's records, which also include service charges and interest payments. Reconcile an account to make sure that personal records match the institution's.
11. Consumers using electronic funds transfers can limit their liability for the use of lost or stolen cards to $50 if they notify the financial institution within two days of discovering the loss. Otherwise, liability is $500. They can also limit their liability if they notify the financial institution within 60 days of any errors on statements.

NOTES ON PROJECTS

1. By having the whole class work on the same items, the teacher can point out how individual differences influence choices.
2. Remind students to be sure to ask how much interest would be earned in a year—only with those dollar figures can they calculate the rate. To explain a higher annual effective rate, students should look at the stated interest rates, the frequency of compounding, and the time that money starts earning interest.
3. This project will help students read bills and understand them. It should make them aware of how significant interest costs can be. It will provide them examples of written credit terms and give them experience in looking for the annual percentage rate figure. *Variations:* the teacher may want to give students figures for hypothetical charges and payments made and ask them to calculate the interest costs at those rates; if local department stores are not available, students can do the same project using mail-order catalogs.
4. This project will acquaint students with the ever-increasing range of services. Before deciding which institution is best, students will need to determine what their criteria are—what services they want. As students share their choices with each other, encourage them to explain the disadvantages they discovered as well.

CHAPTER 13 Consumer Rights and Responsibilities

CHAPTER OVERVIEW

The text and vignette in Chapter 13 will help the student:

1. Describe the four requirements of a contract.
2. Identify which contracts must be written and what a written contract contains.
3. Describe the various kinds of warranties and the protection that each offers.
4. Develop effective solutions to consumer problems.
5. Locate sources of assistance for solving consumer problems.
6. Explain what consumer responsibilities accompany consumer rights.

NOTES ON TEACHING THE CHAPTER

1. From the vignette, it is clear that Maria has a problem but doesn't know how to resolve it. Ask students to role play various solutions, such as returning to the store to talk to a salesperson or to the manager, calling the manufacturer, and visiting a local Better Business Bureau. Which course do students think will get the best results?
2. Most people neglect to read a warranty until there is a problem with a product—then they often find that the problem is not covered. Ask each student to select a product and write a warranty for it, including all coverage and protection that they think is essential. Then have them locate a real warranty for a comparable item. Is there protection that they wanted that the warranty doesn't offer? Is there protection they hadn't thought of that the warranty provides?
3. Take examples of consumer problems from a

consumer-aid service in a newspaper or magazine or on a radio or TV show. Ask the students how they would solve the problems. Then compare their solution with the advice originally offered—do the students prefer their own solution or the original?

4. Many people hesitate to use the legal system, such as small claims court, to help resolve consumer difficulties because they feel unable to represent themselves. To give the students preparation for such an appearance, split the class into groups of three students. Ask each group to develop a hypothetical consumer grievance, then select one group member to be the consumer, one to be the other party, and the third to be the judge. Have each group present its case to the class, with the judge settling the dispute. Does the class agree with the judge's decision? Why or why not?
5. Invite a local store manager to class to discuss the costs of shoplifting. Ask him or her to talk about how much merchandise is lost this way, how much prices must be increased to cover this loss, and how much it costs to institute safeguards against shoplifting. Also ask the manager to describe the store's policy for dealing with shoplifters.

DISCUSSION QUESTIONS

1. There is a familiar expression about consumers—*caveat emptor,* which means "let the buyer beware." How do you feel about this statement?
2. Do you think that the parents of a non-emancipated minor should be held responsible for the contracts entered into by that minor? Why or why not?
3. The Magnuson-Moss Warranty Act requires written warranties for goods selling for more than $15. Do you agree with that dollar limit, or do you think it should be lowered or raised?
4. When products are found to be unsafe or faulty, the manufacturer recalls them and fixes the problem. Do you think that is a sufficient handling of the problem or should the manufacturer be asked to replace the product or give a full refund if requested. If that were the policy, would there be any effect on products' prices?
5. If you saw someone shoplifting or committing a worker crime, what would you do? Why?

ANSWERS TO KEY TERMS

a. warranty of fitness b. small claims court c. offer d. warranties or guarantees
e. puffery f. acceptance g. warranty of merchantability h. shoplifting
i. competent j. legal aid society k. consideration
l. breach of contract m. worker crime n. contract o. full warranty
p. consumer action panel q. minor r. limited warranty s. responsibility
t. recall u. sue

ANSWERS TO REVIEW QUESTIONS

1. Minors can void contracts. The minor must return what was received in consideration. The minor must void the whole contract, not just part of it. Lying about age removes the right to void a contract. Contracts for food, clothing, shelter, and medical care may not be voided by an emancipated minor. Parents of a non-emancipated minor may be held responsible for such contracts.
2. Contracts for the sale or purchase of real estate, contracts for the sale of goods priced at more than $500, contracts that will not be completed within one year, and contracts to undertake the debt of another must be in writing. Examples will vary.
3. When a contract is breached, the consumer can cancel it, sue to have the contract fulfilled, or sue for damages.
4. Goods sold "as is" include any express warranties the seller may make, but they do not include the warranty of merchantability or fitness.
5. Written warranties must state whether they are full or limited and must specify the limitations. They must state how long the warranty lasts,

what the owner has to do to qualify, what the seller will do to correct any problems that may arise, and whether parts and labor are covered. Retailers must make written warranties available for consumers to read.

6. Consumers should first check for warranty coverage and follow instructions. For other problems, consumers should return to the place of purchase, explain the problem, and propose a solution. If it cannot be resolved there, consumers should write, call, or see the head of the manufacturing or selling company. If that doesn't work, they can contact the Better Business Bureau, Chamber of Commerce, trade or professional associations, industry consumer action panels, a local media consumer complaint representative, government consumer offices, or government officials. If these steps fail, the consumer can sue.
7. Small claims court is an informally run court where, for a small fee, consumers can represent themselves to settle quickly problems involving small amounts of money.
8. Some consumers shoplift or switch price tags to pay a lower price. Some workers steal supplies or goods; some lie about their work or time records. These practices all drive up prices for consumers.
9. Consumers must act responsibly to protect their rights and to protect each other. By using their rights, consumers solve problems that they encounter and may prevent others from having the same problems.

NOTES ON PROJECTS

1. This project will help students learn to think about warranties when they are shopping. It will also force them to ask to see warranties, which many consumers neglect to do. Finally, it will get them used to reading warranties—seeing the kinds of items covered, interpreting terms, and determining whether they are full or limited warranties.
2. Students' letters should present all the information concisely and clearly. The sample in the text can serve as a model format, although the students should express the problem in their own words. The teacher should remind students to include their proposed solution. *Variation:* as a follow-up assignment, tell students that their request was not met because the company denied fault — what will they do now?
3. This project should familiarize students with an option that many consumers neglect. In those states not having a small claims court, consumers still have recourse to the court system. If students are stumped on where to begin, direct them to the state attorney general's office or to local consumer action groups.
4. This is a good group project. Each small group can focus on a type of business group or government agency that assists consumers. Remind students to include consumer-aid services in the media. The final product can be a valuable addition to the school resource center. The school parent association may even want to contribute toward printing it in a professional manner and selling it in the community as a fund raiser.
5. To prepare for this project, conduct a literature search of current articles on how stores prevent shoplifting. Have students prepare their own questions in advance of the presentation. Afterward, ask a student to write the guest presenter(s) a thank-you note on behalf of the class.
6. Use product recall articles as the basis for a bulletin board display. If students plan to write a letter to a trade organization requesting additional information, emphasize the need to use correct grammar and spelling. Their letters should be typewritten or word processed on a computer. Ask a librarian to show students how to use the *Directory of National Trade and Professional Associations of the United States.*

CHAPTER 14 Shopping for Food and Clothing

CHAPTER OVERVIEW

The text and vignette in Chapter 14 will help the student:

1. Analyze the central importance of the four basic needs: food, clothing, housing, and transportation.
2. Describe how to plan food purchases by considering nutritional needs and food preferences.
3. Identify what constitutes a balanced menu and plan one.

4. Evaluate foods by using labels, grade marks, and freshness dates, and compare them using unit pricing.
5. Determine what clothes are needed to complete a wardrobe.
6. Evaluate clothes before buying them.
7. Explain how each of the four stages of the food distribution system uses the principle of substitution.

NOTES ON TEACHING THE CHAPTER

1. Since most students will not have housing expenses, a pie diagram similar to Figure 14.1 drawn for their own situation would not include a wedge for housing. Still, they can compare how their income is spent. Ask them to total their income for a fairly long period—at least a month—and add up what they spent their money on by category (food, clothing, entertainment, and so on). They should then calculate the percentage spent on each type. (Of course, if students are keeping budgets as a result of reading Chapter 9, they will be able to do these calculations quickly.)
2. Invite the school system's nutritionist or dietitian to class to speak about how to maintain a well-balanced diet.
3. To get students accustomed to analyzing menus, ask them to compare the lunches offered in the school cafeteria to Table 14.2. If, after a week, they find that the menus are too heavy in one food group or too light in another, encourage them to form a committee to discuss the matter with the dietitian.
4. Time, or lack of it, is often the critical personal resource that determines how consumers will purchase a particular food. Split the class into groups of three, asking each group to identify a food to investigate. One student in the group will purchase the food ready-made from a store or restaurant (e.g., a bottle or carton of orange juice). The next will purchase it in a processed form that still requires some preparation (e.g., a can of orange juice concentrate). The third will buy the raw ingredients and make the food from scratch (e.g., oranges for squeezing). Ask the students to compare the cost in money and time of each method. How do they feel the various alternatives compare in taste? Which would they prefer to use in the future, and why?
5. Gather some magazines at least three years old that contain pictures of men and women wearing clothing for different occasions. Allow the students some time to browse through them, then discuss what clothing fads existed compared to the present. Ask them, too, to identify what clothes are still fashionable now. During the discussion, it will become clear that some items do not change in style frequently and are good to include in a wardrobe.

DISCUSSION QUESTIONS

1. Tremendous weight loss claims are made for certain one-food diets—the dieter eats only one food, or very few foods, for a period of a few weeks. Is anything wrong with these diets?
2. When young people first leave home to live on their own, they often live with a roommate. The way food is packaged, however, it is more economical to buy in large quantities. How would you take advantage of this?
3. What was the most recent article of clothing you purchased? Did you consider any of the factors of fit and construction listed in the text? If you were to do so now, would you still buy the item?

ANSWERS TO KEY TERMS

a. nutrients b. protein c. carbohydrates d. fats e. vitamins f. minerals
g. water h. balanced diet i. grades j. open dating k. unit price l. fibers
m. construction n. U.S. Recommended Daily Allowance

ANSWERS TO REVIEW QUESTIONS

1. The four basic consumer needs are food, clothing, housing, and transportation. The five-step basic consumer method can be followed to satisfy them.
2. Menus should provide the following nutrients: protein, carbohydrates, fats, vitamins, min-

erals, and water. The amounts are shown in the U.S. Recommended Daily Allowances.

3. Choosing food from the five basic food groups every day helps ensure a balanced diet, but it is important to have the correct number of servings from each group, to select different foods from within the groups, and to use caution with foods in the fifth group.
4. Grades help consumers select the correct grade of meat or poultry according to how they plan to prepare it.
5. The pull date is the last date on which the product should be sold. The expiration date is the last date on which the product should be used. Open dating helps consumers buy and use foods when they are at their best and freshest.
6. Since unit pricing shows the price of an item as it relates to a certain unit of measure, it enables consumers to compare different size packages. Examples will vary.
7. Determine wardrobe needs by considering intended use, flexibility, style, and color.
8. Natural fibers include cotton, wool, and linen. Manufactured fibers include nylon, polyester, and rayon.
9. Analyze clothing for fit and construction. Tests for fit include comfort, tightness or looseness, roominess of movement, and attractiveness. For construction, inspect finishing, stitching, fasteners, hems, linings, and fabric construction.
10. The four stages in the food marketing system are production, processing, distribution, and consumption. The participants use substitution when a resource becomes too expensive.
11. Consumers can grow their own food, process food themselves, buy and cook fresh or processed foods, or eat in a restaurant.

NOTES ON PROJECTS

1. Students should begin by developing a menu plan with foods they especially like first. Then have them compare this with the five basic food groups. Discuss how they can bring their ideal diets into balance while still retaining their preferences and staying within their budgets. Try to accommodate as much diversity in ethnic cooking as possible. Remind them to include their snacks in their weekend plans.
2. The students' wardrobe lists for Walter should reflect an understanding of his clothing needs for school, for sports, and for his new job. He'll need more dress items and seasonal clothing. Discuss the alternatives of mixing and matching, buying at different types of stores, and ways to use his old clothing. The teacher should also discuss whether Walter needs three distinct wardrobes (school, work, play). Input from students should reflect their understanding of flexible, multi-use clothing.
3. Assigning different articles of clothing to different pairs or groups of students will prevent duplication of information. Students should be encouraged to investigate a variety of sellers of goods (see Chapter 11).
4. Material in encyclopedias, books, and periodicals should be abundant. The teacher should encourage students to read current periodicals for information on recent techniques like hydroponics, computer-run farms and agribusiness. Assign each topic to a group of students. The teacher can thus ensure that the class has an overview of the whole food system.

CHAPTER 15 Shopping for Housing and Transportation

CHAPTER OVERVIEW

The text and vignette in Chapter 15 will help the student:

1. Determine housing needs and compare the advantages and disadvantages of renting and buying.
2. Locate and analyze information on housing.
3. Inspect housing.
4. Explain the legalities of renting or buying housing.
5. List and evaluate the many alternative forms of transportation.
6. Compare new cars and shop for used cars.
7. Describe the importance of saving energy and various energy-saving steps that can be taken.

NOTES ON TEACHING THE CHAPTER

1. Unless students are considering leaving home as soon as they finish high school, shopping for housing may seem irrelevant. Try to make the topic as meaningful as possible by inviting two or three recent graduates who are now living on their own. Ask them to describe the pleasures and problems they have encountered in establishing their housing arrangements.
2. It may be difficult for students to see that individual needs and wants really influence housing choices. Ask each one to describe the apartment he or she would look for if about to leave home and live alone. Now pair students off and have each pair compare their different needs and wants. Based on their combined requirements, have each pair describe the apartment needed to satisfy both parties. Ask several pairs to share with the class what compromises were made and what wants were kept as housing requirements.
3. Ask any class member who has purchased an unsatisfactory car to share his or her experience with the class. Many states have enacted laws protecting consumers against the purchase of lemons. Invite a state legislator to class to speak about similar legislation in your state or about laws that exist in other states and how your state compares.
4. Invite a car salesperson to speak to the class about how to negotiate effectively for price.
5. Most students are undoubtedly familiar with gas, electricity, and oil as sources of energy. Ask students who may have some knowledge and interest to explain to the class about alternate sources, such as wind, sun, and water. Ask the class to discuss the advantages and disadvantages of each for the local area.

DISCUSSION QUESTIONS

1. The average person moves about five times during his or her life. In view of this, do you think people should rent or buy housing?
2. If you were moving to an unfamiliar place, how would you find a place to live? If you were renting, would you use a real estate agent, even if that meant paying extra?
3. Many people feel that it is essential to have a car, even though it is costly to own one. Do you agree or disagree?
4. How do you feel about tax dollars being spent to help one part of the traveling population—to fix the superhighways, upgrade or maintain trains, or buy buses?
5. To encourage people to save energy, should the federal government give tax incentives to people who take steps to cut down the amount of energy used in their homes? Since these people will already be rewarded by having lower energy bills, should the government reward them again with a tax credit?

ANSWERS TO KEY TERMS

a. public mass transit systems b. equity c. mortgage d. point e. condominium
f. cooperative g. title search h. closing i. lease j. options k. landlord l. tenant
m. sticker price n. subletting o. down payment

ANSWERS TO REVIEW QUESTIONS

1. In planning to obtain housing, first determine the number and kinds of rooms needed, the type of housing desired, and the location desired.
2. The three expenses of housing are immediate expenses, monthly expenses, and upkeep. Examples will vary.
3. Rental advantages: smaller initial cash outlay and less responsibility for upkeep. Buying advantages: equity and freedom to redecorate or remodel.
4. Consumers get information on housing from family, friends, coworkers, schoolmates, signs, bulletin boards, classified ads, and realtors.
5. In inspecting housing, check for cleanliness and condition; size, number, and layout of rooms; energy consumption; plumbing, electric outlets, and appliances; storage space; outside features; and security provisions.
6. Landlords and tenants sign leases to protect themselves. The lease states the names of the landlord and tenant, describes the property and its contents, describes the length of the lease and conditions for changing it, specifies the amounts to be paid in security deposit and rent and when they're due, describes any promises either party makes, and specifies any restrictions.

7. To choose between public and private transportation, consider each method's cost, convenience and reliability, time available, flexibility, and safety.
8. Compare new car models' mileage, safety record, handling and braking, warranty and maintenance record, operating costs, comfort and room, and options. To get this information, read government and consumer publications and test drive the car.
9. To shop for a used car, determine what model is wanted and what extras it should have, examine the car carefully, test drive the car, and ask a mechanic to check it.
10. Consumers can get information on dealer cost (for a new car) and average retail price (for a used car) so they can negotiate a better price. They can also comparison shop.
11. Transportation and housing are consumer areas that influence the nation's energy. Conserve energy by using the car for multipurpose trips or by using public transit. In the home, conserve energy by leaving unused rooms unheated and buying appliances that are energy efficient.

NOTES ON PROJECTS

1. The teacher should remind students to start this project by first answering the three sets of questions to determine their housing wants. *Variation:* the teacher may want to set a budget that all students follow to standardize the assignment—tailor that budget to local costs.
2. Students should prepare for the landlord's visit by gathering their questions. They might ask for examples of repairs the landlord pays for and those that tenants are charged for, whether the state or city has any rental laws and how the lease reflects them, and what rights landlords have to evict tenants and tenants have to protect themselves. *Variation:* the teacher may want to invite someone who is knowledgeable about tenant rights—such as the leader of a tenant organization—to come to class, either on the same day or another, to respond to the same questions.
3. Use the concept of opportunity cost to get students thinking about other methods of transportation that may cost less and what they might want to do with any money they can save by not owning a car.
4. Students should find that the new car buying price is near or less than the sticker price, although it will be more than dealer cost. Used car prices will vary more from the *NADA* average, depending on the car's condition.
5. Ideas for improvement could include additional insulation, heavy curtains, reduced use of appliances, and so on. Local utility companies may be able to assist the class by providing a speaker or literature on home energy savers that will include ideas the students may be unaware of.
6. Ask an interested student to research local or national companies that offer incentives to their employees who carpool. What incentives do the companies offer? The student might also investigate state-run programs. In Minnesota, the Metropolitan Transit Commission operates a program called Minnesota Rideshare. Minnesota Rideshare matches potential drivers/riders with others who live and work in the same general area. Have the student discuss the findings of the research in class. Also, assign small groups of students to form their own "carpool." Each group will be responsible for setting up schedules and drivers and determining the costs involved (gas, insurance, etc.)
7. Ask a creative student to arrange a bulletin board of the display advertisements. Lead a class discussion of the merits of renting housing versus buying housing.

CHAPTER 16 Shopping for Financial Services

CHAPTER OVERVIEW

The text and vignette in Chapter 16 will help the student:

1. Explain how financial institutions compete for consumers' money.
2. Plan and comparison shop for financial services.
3. Describe the types of financial services available.
4. Distinguish between the four basic types of financial institutions.
5. Evaluate financial institutions.
6. Describe the role of the Federal Reserve System in regulating the money supply.

NOTES ON TEACHING THE CHAPTER

1. Have a group of students collect advertising pamphlets from local banks. Prepare a bulletin board collage to illustrate competition between banks.
2. Invite local bank representatives for a panel discussion to explain and compare services offered to the community. Have the class summarize in writing the highlights of the panel discussion. Students could use the summary to decide which bank would best meet Connie's needs.
3. Prepare short case studies for class discussion. For example, John is in need of a $7,000 low-interest loan for college. What type of financial institution would best fit his needs?
4. If the school system has a credit union, ask an officer to explain its operation to the class.
5. To emphasize the rights and responsibilities of consumers who use EFT, have students contact the Federal Reserve Board for a copy of the Electronic Funds Transfer Act. Discuss the literature with the class.
6. Obtain a video from the nearest Federal Reserve Bank that explains the operation of the Fed. (The address of the nearest Federal Reserve Bank can be obtained from the *Rand McNally Bank Directory* or the Federal Information Center at 1-800-366-2990.)

DISCUSSION QUESTIONS

1. Would uniform banking fees be more beneficial to the consumer than competitive rates?
2. Are computer-aided methods of banking causing the consumer to lose financial privacy?
3. Are financial institutions attempting to be all things to all people? Do overlapping services cost consumers money?
4. A number of S&Ls went bankrupt and closed in the 1980s. Was this a side effect of deregulation? Will deregulation mean less competition?
5. Should the power of the Federal Reserve Board be limited?

ANSWERS TO KEY TERMS

a. foreign exchange b. safe deposit box c. commercial bank d. savings and loan association
e. mutual savings bank f. credit union g. float h. deposit insurance
i. Federal Reserve System j. reserve k. trust l. open market operations
m. discount rate n. invest

ANSWERS TO REVIEW QUESTIONS

1. Financial institutions compete in benefits—the interest rates and services they offer to depositors—and in costs—the fees charged to customers for the services.
2. The four types of financial services are obtaining cash and paying bills, credit, saving, and investing. Examples will vary.
3. Answers should include any three of the following: location, business hours, automatic teller machines, automatic deposit, automatic transfers between accounts, and bank by phone.
4. Insured financial institutions display a sign stating this fact in their windows and in their interiors. Deposit insurance makes money safe up to certain limits even if the financial institution fails.
5. Wise consumers consider and plan for their financial needs as a total package because financial services often overlap.
6. The four main type of institutions are commercial banks, savings and loan associations (S&Ls), mutual savings banks, and credit unions.
7. (a) Credit—department stores, oil companies, finance companies, automakers. (b) Savings and investment—stockbrokers, realtors and dealers, and mutual funds. (c) Cash substitutes—money market funds, local retail stores, check cashing stores, post office, sellers of traveler's checks.

8. The Fed helps local institutions cope with the flood of checks written while at the same time keeping charges low for the service.
9. To control the money supply, the Fed can change the reserve requirement, buy and sell government bonds, change the discount rate, or control some types of credit. It takes these steps to be able to increase or decrease demand when the economy needs to grow or the inflation rate must be lowered.

NOTES ON PROJECTS

1. The teacher may wish to create a hypothetical financial situation, so that all students would be analyzing the same conditions to identify what services are needed. *Variation:* ask smaller groups of students each to focus on a different service, with each member of the group checking a different institution.
2. This research project will involve the students not only in the history of deposit insurance but also the evolution of the country's banking system. It should illustrate more clearly the changes in institutions and services that were mentioned in the chapter.
3. Students should be able to find many articles in current periodicals that mention actions the Fed has taken. *Variation:* debate the Fed's independence—should the Fed be more responsive to a president's wishes or is its independence more valuable?
4. To prepare for this project, conduct a literature search of current articles on banking services for the 1990s. Have students prepare their own questions in advance of the presentation. Afterward, ask a student to write the guest presenter(s) a thank-you note on behalf of the class.
5. Assign this project to a student who may be interested in a career in banking. Have the student share the information from the American Bankers Association with the class.
6. Ask a creative student to arrange a bulletin board of print advertisements from banks. Discuss the appeals used in the ads and the targeted customer in each ad. Ask: How do banks target their customers?

CHAPTER 17 Shopping for Credit

CHAPTER OVERVIEW

The text and vignette in Chapter 17 will help the student:

1. Explain why people use credit.
2. Plan for the use of credit.
3. Explain how a credit rating relates to the ability to borrow.
4. Identify the types and sources of credit available to consumers.
5. List borrower and lender rights.
6. Compare the cost of different credit plans.
7. Explain how consumer credit affects the economy.

NOTES ON TEACHING THE CHAPTER

1. Assign students to interview senior citizens, middle-aged adults, and young adults to find out their past and current opinion of credit. Are there age differences in attitudes about credit?
2. Obtain an auto installment loan contract from a local bank, duplicate it for each class member, and analyze the important parts of the contract. Identify Truth-in-Lending requirements.
3. Contact the Federal Reserve Bank and obtain a free copy of the *Consumer Credit Terminology Handbook* for each student to keep. The book will reinforce credit vocabulary and can be used after high school.
4. Prepare a transparency in chart form comparing types of open-end credit. Compare card cost, interest rates, advantages, and disadvantages. Have students do the research for the chart information.
5. Prepare a transparency illustrating logical steps to take when one falls into the trap of overborrowing. Follow the discussion with a visit from a representative of a local credit counseling agency. Contact CCCS-Consumer Credit Counseling Services, sponsored by National Foundation for Consumer Credit.

DISCUSSION QUESTIONS

1. From your study of Chapters 16 and 17, discuss the role the Federal Reserve plays in a local bank's decision to loan or not to loan money for a new auto.
2. Does the misuse of credit contribute to the financial problems of a family? Can those financial problems have any other effects on a family?
3. Have TV advertisements encouraged people—particularly young people—to overbuy and misuse credit by creating the image that material goods make happiness?
4. How does the cost of credit affect taxes? Should we restructure tax laws relating to credit?
5. Are we becoming a cashless society? Do you think that a cashless society would be beneficial or harmful?

ANSWERS TO KEY TERMS

a. credit rating b. debt consolidation loan c. repossession d. bankruptcy
e. credit bureau f. closed-end credit g. collateral h. open-end credit i. credit limit
j. character k. open charge account l. revolving charge account
m. overdraft protection n. capacity o. single-payment loan p. passbook loan
q. finance company r. cosigner s. industrial bank t. collection agency u. capital

ANSWERS TO REVIEW QUESTIONS

1. People use credit to have the use of an item while they pay for it, to make purchases more conveniently, to meet emergency expenses, to buy an expensive item, and to build a credit record.
2. The opportunity cost of not using credit is doing without an item until enough cash can be saved to purchase it. (Any example of putting off the use or enjoyment of a product or service is acceptable.)
3. Answers should include any four of the following: use credit only when necessary, compare credit cost with cash cost, shop for credit, reduce the cost of credit, read all credit contracts carefully, don't feel pressured, don't take on more debts than you can handle.
4. Overusing credit may result in needing debt counseling, taking out a consolidation loan, repossession of items not paid for, or bankruptcy.
5. Character—how the borrower will behave; capacity—the borrower's ability to pay; capital—the property a borrower owns.
6. Favorable qualities for getting credit include a good credit history, stability in residence or employment, and operating checking and savings accounts. Other answers may be acceptable. Difficulties in getting credit include no identification, floating address, unstable employment history, age, bad credit history, and no credit history.
7. Closed-end (installment) and open-end (noninstallment). Examples will vary.
8. Sources of credit include commercial banks, S&Ls, mutual savings banks, credit unions, finance companies, industrial banks, retailers, life insurance companies, and families. Students who mention pawnbrokers and loan sharks should also say that these sources are undesirable.
9. The Consumer Credit Protection Act makes lending requirements easier to interpret. The Fair Credit Reporting Act lets borrowers see their credit files. The Equal Credit Opportunity Act deals with discrimination in lending. The Fair Credit Billing Act details billing procedures for open-end credit. The Fair Debt Collection Practices Act covers debt collection by collection agencies.
10. Benefits of consumer credit—any two of the following: gives consumers a better standard

of living, helps businesses expand, gives banks the income they need to pay interest on savings, offers a way for consumers to beat inflation. Disadvantages of consumer credit: may worsen inflation by increasing demand and pushing up prices, pushes up the price of individual items as retailers try to cover credit costs.

NOTES ON PROJECTS

1. The point of this project is to familiarize the students with forms and the questions asked on credit applications. Discuss with the students the best way to answer questions so that applicants show themselves to best advantage. Use the exercise to help them see what they can do now to make it easier to obtain credit in the future.
2. Before the visit, the class should decide what questions they want to ask. The teacher may suggest that students pick a panel of students to do the actual interviewing. *Variation:* students could prepare credit histories for a few imaginary consumers desiring to borrow different amounts; the credit officer can then comment on the probability that each consumer would be granted credit.
3. In this project the students will be able to see themselves in a situation where they are actually thinking about and applying for credit. The reports can lead to a discussion of similarities and differences among findings and choices.
4. Knowledge of debt collection practices—both legal and illegal—will help students when they enter the credit market. Discuss how the law has protected borrowers.
5. This project will emphasize that the government's credit decisions also affect the economy. An abundance of background material should be available from recent periodicals. Make sure that all pros and cons of the government debt issue are brought out in the student debate.
6. To prepare for this project, conduct a literature search of current articles on consumer credit problems. Have students prepare their own questions in advance of the presentation. Afterward, ask a student to write the guest presenter(s) a thank you note on behalf of the class.

CHAPTER 18 Shopping for Personal Investments

CHAPTER OVERVIEW

The text and vignette in Chapter 18 will help the student:

1. Distinguish between saving and investing.
2. Describe the goals of saving and investing.
3. Locate sources of information and advice useful in planning saving and investing goals.
4. Describe different methods of saving and investing.
5. Read and interpret stock and bond listings.
6. Identify eight factors to use in comparing investments.
7. Explain how personal and business investments affect the country's economy.

NOTES ON TEACHING THE CHAPTER

1. Have students read an article from the business section of a magazine—*Money, Changing Times,* or others. Discuss and interpret it with students.
2. Visit a stock exchange or brokerage house if possible. If such a trip is impossible, invite a broker to speak to the class.
3. Obtain copies of *The Language of Investing Glossary* and *You and the Investment World* from the New York Stock Exchange to use as additional reading material. Both booklets are free.
4. Have students choose a company in the local area for study. Chart the company stock for a school term. Draw conclusions on how the company affects the economy in the area.
5. To emphasize the decision-making process, use case studies from the "Beginning Investor" chapter of *Saving and Investing,* a consumer education kit from Changing Times Education Service.
6. Investigate municipal bonds offered in the area. Find out how funds were obtained to build your school, a firehouse, and other projects.
7. Encourage students to examine local real estate. Clip real estate ads reflecting current property values.

8. Have students listen for the Dow-Jones Average on TV newscasts. Discuss why this figure is given nationwide attention.

DISCUSSION QUESTIONS

1. Are stocks too risky? Could there be another stock market crash?
2. What is meant by the statement "It takes money to make money?"
3. Some people claim that IRA, Keogh and 401(K) plans are unfair tax breaks for the rich because all consumers cannot afford them. Do you agree or disagree?
4. Some investors believe that the number of land fraud operations in the United States make real estate a poor investment. Do you agree or disagree?
5. Leaving money in a passbook savings account means losing money during inflation. Do you agree or disagree?
6. Some people say that U.S. savings bonds are poor investments. What do you think?

ANSWERS TO KEY TERMS

a. saving b. investing c. wealth d. brokerage e. passbook account f. time deposit
g. face value h. stock exchange i. over-the-counter trading j. default
k. bond l. mutual fund m. investment club n. real estate o. collectibles
p. maturity date q. trustee r. dividend s. annuity

ANSWERS TO REVIEW QUESTIONS

1. People save for emergencies, for a large purchase, for retirement, and to get into the habit of saving. People invest to increase wealth.
2. Get information or advice from daily newspapers' business pages, business sections of general news magazines, special business magazines, trade publications and investor newsletters, the library, knowledgeable friends, financial institutions, brokerage houses, special dealers and traders, and community colleges and adult education courses.
3. *Advantages:* safety, easy access for deposit or withdrawal, small or no minimum required to open the account. *Disadvantage:* rather low interest rate.
4. *Advantages:* higher return than passbook, guaranteed rate, safety, and relatively low capital requirement. *Disadvantages:* fixed interest rate (bad when rates are rising), penalties for early withdrawal, and a higher minimum initial investment than a passbook account.
5. *Advantages:* security, low minimum investment, easy redemption, easy replacement, and higher income than for passbook accounts. *Disadvantages:* lower rate of return compared to other types of investments and penalties for early withdrawal.
6. *Advantages:* tax-reducing and tax-exempt provisions and the opportunity to manage one's own investments. *Disadvantages:* money is taxed when withdrawn and penalties charged for early withdrawal.
7. Stocks are bought and sold on a stock exchange, in over-the-counter trading, or between individual investors themselves.
8. Investors hope to gain from stocks by receiving dividends and being able to sell the stock for more money than they paid for it (growth). *Disadvantages:* prices vary and dividends aren't guaranteed.
9. *Advantages:* guaranteed interest and tax-free income from municipals. *Disadvantages:* possibility that other rates will rise and possibility of default.
10. (a) *Advantages:* opportunity to participate in higher-income investments and management by professionals. *Disadvantages:* risk and lack of individual control over investments. (b) *Advantages:* members can control investments and small investors can take part in large investments. *Disadvantage:* performance is limited to the members' skills.
11. (a) *Advantages:* investment is likely to increase in value, the purchase of a home provides shelter as well as investment, and renting can provide income. *Disadvantages:* high

capital requirement and low liquidity. (b) *Advantage:* investor can pursue a personal interest. *Disadvantages:* high risk and the need for knowledge.

12. The factors for evaluating investments are liquidity, growth, income, security, capital, knowledge, time, and taxability.
13. Personal investment aims to increase individual wealth. Business investment increases the capital resources of a business. Business investment has the greater impact on the economy, because it increases or decreases the production of goods and services—and the creation of jobs.

NOTES ON PROJECTS

1. This project will put the theory of the eight factors into practice for the students. Refer them to the basic decision-making method, which is what they'll be using to compare and decide among the alternatives. The second part of the project should point up the fact that more capital involves more risk, more chance for high return, and more alternatives.
2. Splitting the class into groups should provide a large variety of results. This is a long-range project, as the students will chart the progress of their hypothetical investments over a period of time of a month or more. Actual charts and interim status reports would enhance the project. Setting a deadline for selling off the investments will get the students to think about the importance of planning their investing with future goals in mind.
3. One of the key factors in judging whether the economy will be healthy or not is the amount of planned business investment. Stress that perceived consumer demand plays a great role in how much investment businesses decide to make. *Variation:* make this an overview of the economy by assigning different industries to specific students (or groups). Each student can then report to the class, giving everyone a broad idea of where the economy is headed. The teacher may wish to use these reports as a springboard for discussing personal investment—use the information students gather on industries' and companies' futures as guidelines for evaluating stocks.
4. To prepare for this project, conduct a literature search of current articles on investments. Have students prepare their own questions in advance of the presentation. Afterward, ask a student to write the guest presenter(s) a thank-you note on behalf of the class.

CHAPTER 19 Shopping for Insurance

CHAPTER OVERVIEW

The text and vignette in Chapter 19 will help the student:

1. Describe the basic principle of risk-sharing.
2. List ways to reduce risk.
3. Determine insurance needs.
4. Describe the details of the various types of insurance.
5. Compare insurance sources.
6. Explain how driving habits affect the total economy.

NOTES ON TEACHING THE CHAPTER

1. Have students find out the number of accidents occurring within a 5-mile radius of school. Determine the major cause of the accidents. If the cause is poor road construction or conditions, have students write a letter of complaint to local officials explaining the problem and advocating a solution.
2. To reinforce insurance terminology, create a crossword puzzle or scramblegram the students can use.

3. Invite a local police official to speak to the class about the number of accidents occurring in the area involving people under the age of 25. Have the speaker stress the major causes of these accidents.
4. Students are often covered by school insurance. Investigate the plan. Ask the school official in charge to explain the plan to the class.
5. Consumers often receive mail-order insurance offers. Have students write to the insurance commissioner in the state to find out what regulations are imposed on this practice.

DISCUSSION QUESTIONS

1. For problem-solving and discussion questions, use case studies and related reading from *Insurance*—Parts 1, 2, 3, and 4, a learning resource from Changing Times Education Service.
2. Do you agree with the concept of no-fault insurance?
3. In many states, women pay lower auto insurance rates than men in the same age group. Is this sex discrimination?
4. What affect does inflation have on life insurance payments to the beneficiary? Do benefits go up with the cost of living?
5. Do you feel the laws on drunken driving in your state are tough enough? Are they too tough? If you think they need changing, how would you change them?
6. Some people propose that the federal government provide health insurance for all citizens. Do you believe such a program is needed?

ANSWERS TO KEY TERMS

a. pure risk b. premium c. insurance policy d. liability e. beneficiary
f. cash surrender value (CSV) g. term insurance h. whole-life insurance
i. limited-payment life j. endowment k. universal life insurance l. no-fault insurance
m. bodily injury protection n. property damage protection o. medical payments coverage
p. collision coverage q. deductible r. uninsured motorist protection
s. comprehensive coverage t. wage loss and substitute services coverage u. health insurance
v. replacement cost w. health maintenance organization (HMO) x. homeowner's insurance
y. coinsurance z. actual cash value

ANSWERS TO REVIEW QUESTIONS

1. People buy insurance to protect themselves from the money losses that may occur.
2. Premiums depend on the following (any three): the law of averages; the number of people sharing the risk; the cost history of past claims; the characteristics of the individual; the value of what's insured; the presence and size of a deductible; and state law.
3. *Life*—taking care of ourselves, maintaining health, driving carefully, freeing the home of hazards, and avoiding dangers. *Motor vehicles*—driving defensively; obeying traffic laws; maintaining the vehicle in good condition; not mixing drinking and driving; using seat belts. *Health*—getting proper nutrition and exercise; practicing preventive medicine; and avoiding harmful drugs. *Home and property*—taking precautions against fires; making needed repairs; removing hazards; and improving the security of the home.
4. The deductible is the amount of loss the insured agrees to bear before the insurer begins to pay claims.
5. The forms of life insurance are term, whole life, limited payment, universal life, and endowment. Term is the least expensive. All others include savings.
6. All states require drivers to obtain a minimum amount of insurance or to post a bond. No-fault laws allow the driver who suffers an injury to collect up to a specified amount from his or her insurer, regardless of fault.
7. Auto insurance includes uninsured motorist protection, bodily injury and property damage liability, comprehensive, collision, medical payments, and wage loss and substitute services coverage.
8. Health insurance includes the following (any three): hospital expenses, surgical expenses, regular medical expenses, major medical expenses, emergency services, maternity care,

disability, psychological care, alcohol or drug abuse treatment, nursing care, and dental expenses.

9. Coinsurance means that the insurer does not pay all of the charges but some lesser amount. The insured pays the rest. Health insurance plans may include yearly and lifetime limits for the individual or family.
10. Homeowner's insurance covers property damage and personal liability. The insured must be sure to increase the amount of insurance as the property value increases.
11. Consumers get insurance through their own purchase, through employers, and through the government.
12. To evaluate insurance plans, consumers must get all unclear terms explained and get all conditions clarified.
13. Drivers can reduce the risk of costly accidents by observing speed limits, not mixing drinking and driving, using seat belts and child restraints, and wearing helmets while riding motorcycles. Doing so saves the driver—and society—dollars and lives.

NOTES ON PROJECTS

1. The second part of the project is the key—what can students do to reduce premiums? While one answer may be discouraging (it takes time to grow older), students should identify other methods that are within their reach—driver education, more careful driving, taking deductibles, and avoiding the purchase of high-risk cars.
2. Encourage students to talk to HMO members to see how *they* feel about the quality of the care. Especially valuable would be members who had experience with other forms of health care. To evaluate HMOs, students must identify their health care goals. What is most important—cost, personal service, or preventive medicine? They must establish criteria before they can evaluate whether an HMO or private insurance is better. For comparison, they can get information from a parent's health insurance policy or from the state Blue Cross and Blue Shield program.
3. Students will need help in estimating the value of their family's property. *Variation:* to make it easier—and to make the project less sensitive—the teacher could outline a hypothetical home and possessions at certain estimated values. Then all students could work from common information. To help in estimating value, the teacher could invite an insurance agent to come to class and give some rough guidelines based on the type of item (furniture, jewelry, and so forth) and its characteristics (age or manufacture).

CHAPTER 20 It's Up to You

CHAPTER OVERVIEW

The text in Chapter 20 will help the student:

1. Explain why decisions are needed to solve problems.
2. Identify the three roles in which decisions are made.
3. Use the systematic decision-making method to make important decisions in all roles.
4. Describe the ways to reduce risk.
5. Identify values, resources, and goals in making decisions.
6. Describe the five principles that are the basis of our economy.
7. Identify the three types of economic actors—individuals, businesses, and governments.
8. Explain the importance of keeping informed about changes in oneself and in society.

NOTES ON TEACHING THE CHAPTER

1. Ask students to interview people who were teenagers twenty-five and fifty years ago to learn the nature of the decisions they were making and the risks involved. Ask students to compare these choices to those that they face.
2. Invite an economist or community planner to class to discuss some predictions of what the local community will be like in ten years. Have the students discuss what implications these predictions have for them and for their role in the economy at that time.
3. Ask interested students to research a country whose economic system is different from ours. Ask them to share with the class how the economy affects the decisions made by the people living in that country.
4. Ask students to identify all the ways they can imagine to get information or education on the following topics: career choice, buying a car, home or car repair, investing, cooking. (The teacher can add any number of similar topics.) This brainstorming exercise should help them see that there are many places they can turn to to get help and data when they are making decisions in the future.

DISCUSSION QUESTIONS

1. What important decision have you made recently and what risks were involved? How did you try to reduce those risks?
2. If you could have more of one personal resource, which would you prefer to have more of? What other resource do you think you'd have to give up to be able to increase the first resource?
3. Do you think your most important economic decisions are made in your role as a worker, citizen, or consumer? Why?
4. What goal do you have now that may be unimportant in five years? What goal do you have now that will probably still be important in five years?

ANSWERS TO REVIEW QUESTIONS

1. The three basic ideas of this text are that people need to make decisions, and are better off making informed decisions; that to make informed decisions, people need to understand themselves; and that to make informed decisions, people need to understand the economy.
2. Wants motivate us to satisfy them, which requires using resources. The ability to satisfy wants is limited by the quantity of resources possessed.
3. In making decisions, define the problem, identify goals, identify alternatives, analyze the consequence of each alternative, select the best alternative in light of the goals, put the decision into action, and evaluate the decision.
4. To analyze alternatives, people trade off their costs (what must be given up to get them) for their benefits (what satisfaction they provide). To select alternatives, people must consider opportunity cost—the next most attractive alternatives that they cannot have.
5. Decisions are risky because of limited knowledge and the uncertain future. Risk is reduced by learning as much as possible before deciding and by evaluating decisions and how they are made.
6. In deciding which want to satisfy, people take into account their values—what they believe is important—and resources—what they'll use to satisfy the want.
7. Plans help people achieve goals by providing a method for reaching them. In planning, be reasonable, take time to plan, make one's own plan, follow the plan, and evaluate the plan.
8. The principles underlying the economy are free choice, self-interest, competition, private property, and limited government involvement. In practice the economy works differently—competition isn't always free and the government often plays a larger role than some think it should.
9. *Workers* provide labor for businesses in return for a wage. With that wage they buy goods and services from *producers* which makes them *consumers*. Everyone depends on the work that others perform (as well as their own). Decisions of how to spend, how to work, and how to vote influence other people.
10. Supply and demand set price. Understanding supply and demand helps people to make more intelligent decisions—such as knowing whether to enter a particular career or when is the best time to make a particular purchase.
11. Individuals should know their rights so they can guard them, exercise them to protect themselves and others, and keep informed to see if their rights change or are threatened.
12. No. People need to continue learning about changes in the economy and in themselves.

NOTES ON PROJECTS

1. This project asks students to make the decision that is uppermost in their minds. By tackling this important choice, they should get good practice using the method. The last part of the project—asking those, such as graduating seniors, who've already decided, to evaluate their decision—will provide valuable practice as well.
2. Students must recognize that they will need to keep learning new skills—it may help them realize this important fact to see that even new products demand new skills from their owners. The teacher can guide students to resources they can use—product designers and engineers and specialized library materials—to find the predictions they need. *Variation:* the teacher may prefer to change this activity into a group brainstorming session in which the class as a whole predicts the world twenty-five years from now, and individual students can then focus on one aspect.

List of Resources

Federal Government

U.S. Office of Consumer Affairs, 1009 Premier Bldg., Washington, DC 20001

Consumer Product Safety Commission, Washington, DC 20207

Department of Agriculture, Meat & Poultry hotline, 1-800-535-4555

Environmental Protection Agency, 401 M St., SW, Washington, DC 20460

Federal Deposit Insurance Corporation (FDIC), 550 17th St., NW, Washington, DC 20429

Federal Trade Commission, 6th Street and Pennsylvania Avenue, NW, Washington, DC 20580

Department of Housing and Urban Development, Fair Housing and Equal Opportunity, 451 7th St., SW, Washington, DC 20410

Internal Revenue Service, 1111 Constitution Ave., NW, Washington, DC 20224

Superintendent of Documents, Government Printing Office, Washington, DC 20402

Food and Drug Administration, 5600 Fishers Lane, Rockville, MD 20857

Consumer Information Center, General Services Administration, 18th and F Streets, NW, RM-G102, Washington, DC 20405; for catalog of publications, write Consumer Information Catalog, Pueblo, CO 81002

Federal Reserve Board, Constitution Avenue, Washington, DC 20051

Department of Energy, Office of Energy Conservation and Renewable Energy, Box 8900, Silver Spring, MD 20907

Professional, Trade, and Labor Associations and Organizations

Council of Better Business Bureaus, 4200 Wilson Blvd., Suite 800, Arlington, VA 22203

Association of Home Appliance Manufacturers, 20 N. Wacker Dr., Chicago, IL 60606

Gas Appliance Manufacturers Association, 1901 N. Moore St., Arlington, VA 22209

National Automobile Dealers Association, 8400 Westpark Dr., McLean, VA 22102

National Homebuilders Association, 15th and M Streets, NW, Washington, DC 20005

AFL-CIO Education Department, 815 16th St., NW, Washington, DC 20006

Society of Consumer Affairs Professionals, 4900 Leesburg Pike, Alexandria, VA 22302

American Council on Consumer Interests, 240 Stanley Hall, University of Missouri, Columbia, MO 65211

Joint Council on Economic Education, 432 Park Ave., S., New York, NY 10016

American Bankers Association, 1120 Connecticut Ave., NW, Washington, DC 20036

American Council of Life Insurance, 1001 Pennsylvania Ave., NW, Washington, DC 20004

Health Insurance Association of America, 1025 Connecticut, NW, Washington, DC 20036

Magazines and Newsletters

Changing Times, Editors Park, MD 20782 (subscriptions)

Kiplinger Washington Letter, 1729 H St., NW, Washington, DC 20006

Money Magazine, Time Customer Service, PO Box 60001, Tampa, FL 33660-0001 (subscriptions)

ACCI Newsletter, 240 Stanley Hall, University of Missouri, Columbia, MO 65211

Status Report, Insurance for Highway Safety, 1005 N. Glebe Road, Arlington, VA 22201 (newsletter)

Consumers Report, PO Box 53029, Boulder, CO 80322 (subscriptions)

MMI, Consumer Education Newsletter from Money Management Institute, 2700 Sanders Road, Prospect Heights, IL 60070

Career-related Software

Career Design 1.4, Career Design Software, Box 95624, Atlanta, GA 30347; 1-800-346-8007, in Atlanta (404) 321-6100; IBM compatibles only

Career Navigator, Drake Beam Morin Inc., 100 Park Ave., New York, NY 10017; 1-800-345-JOBS; IBM compatibles only

Instant Resume System, Lightning Word Corp., 5825 Vargas Ct., San Jose, CA 95120; 1-800-462-2571; IBM compatibles

Three more computer-assistance programs for career guidance widely available on college campuses include the Self-Directed Search software, Discover, and SIGI (System of Interactive Guidance and Information). The Self-Directed Search software, which helps users determine appropriate occupations for beginning research, is based on the well-regarded research of Dr. John Holland. Discover and SIGI provides users with a printout of appropriate career options to fit the pattern of answers the user gives when questioned.

Miscellaneous

National Foundation for Consumer Credit, 8701 Georgia Avenue, Silver Spring, MD 20910

Teacher's Notes

Teacher's Notes

DECISIONS

MAKING PERSONAL ECONOMIC CHOICES

SECOND EDITION

Consultants

Richard Campbell
Director, Cooperative Education/ Youth Employment
Nebraska Department of Education

Les R. Dlabay
Department of Economics and Business
Lake Forest College

Margaret Ann Ferguson
Specialist, Business Education
Los Angeles Unified School District

Mamie Hardy
Director, Professional Services
Changing Times Education Service

Dennis Lupher
Associate Professor of Economics
Ohio University—Lancaster

Gene R. Moore
Social Studies Teacher
Winterhaven Senior High School
Polk County, Florida, Public Schools

Deborah Siegelaub
Home Economics Teacher
Hillcrest High School
New York City Public Schools

Gerald E. Talbot
Personal Finance Teacher
Nyssa Senior High School
Nyssa, Oregon, Public Schools

Pat Tennison
Coordinator of Career Education
School District of Kansas City, Missouri

Barbara Ann Ware
Specialist, Occupational Education
Dallas Independent School District

DECISIONS

MAKING PERSONAL ECONOMIC CHOICES

SECOND EDITION

Consulting Authors

Judith Staley Brenneke
Cleveland Center for Economic Education

Mary Lou Hamill
New Jersey Network

Developed by

Changing Times Education Service
A Division of EMC Publishing
St. Paul, Minnesota

and

Visual Education Corporation
Princeton, New Jersey

Program Editor	Rosemary J. Barry
Project Editor	Dale Anderson
Writer/Researchers	Timothy J. Kenslea, Harry Wagner, Linda Wiesner
Editors	Wendy Warren Keebler, Nancy B. McLane
Production Manager	Gary F. Pugh
Text Designers	Art Ritter, Liz Waite
Text Illustrators	Jim Edwards, Patricia Pereira
Picture Researchers	Ellen Horan, Mark Schaeffer
Special thanks to	Cindy Feldner, Adrienne Klein, Richard Lidz, Robert Waterhouse

ISBN 0-8219-0849-9

Published by EMC Publishing
300 York Avenue
St. Paul, Minnesota 55101

Printed in the United States of America
0 9 8 7 6 5 4 3 2 1

Preface

Take a look at the following money IQ test, and answer 'yes' or 'no':

- Do you earn a portion of your own money?
- Have you ever set and achieved a specific savings goal for something you wanted such as a camera, bicycle, or vacation?
- Do you keep your debts paid up?
- If you have a checking account, do you know how to keep your checkbook balanced?
- Are you current on your financial obligations?
- Are you responsible when it comes to money?

How well did you do? Of course, a perfect score of all 'yes' answers shows you keep an eye on your wallet. 'No' answers signal trouble spots.

A very interesting pattern developed between teens and money during the 1980s. According to the Rand Youth Poll in New York, teen spending grew from $39.1 billion to $55.9 billion annually. That's in spite of a 15.5 percent population drop among teens to 23.2 million. There's a whole lot of buying going on!

Even car ownership by teens rose: during the 1980s 36 percent of those eligible to drive owned cars.

All this economic activity involves decision making, so by opening this book you have made a great start! *Decisions* has been written out of two beliefs. First, you will be better able to pursue your interests as citizens, workers, and consumers if you understand basic economic principles. Second, these economic principles are best understood when they are related to the practical decisions of everyday life. These are decisions that you will be actively involved in soon.

Here is how *Decisions* is organized: Part One of the book opens with two chapters on individual choice making. Part Two presents a brief overview of how our economy works. Parts Three, Four, and Five return to the individual and explore our decisions as workers, consumers, and citizens.

Decisions uses personal involvement, clear writing, and structured learning throughout:

- Each of 20 chapters opens with a vignette dramatizing an economic dilemma facing young teens.
- Featured sections called "You Interact with the Economy" appear in most chapters and show how personal economic decisions affect the economy and vice versa.

- Basic economic principles are reinforced throughout the text by showing how they apply to decisions that people make in all economic roles.
- Various features help you to master the vocabulary of economics. Boldface type highlights terms where they first appear, with clear definitions provided in italics. Matching exercises help you recognize and remember terms and their definitions. A glossary combines all of the major key terms in a handy reference section.
- Lists highlight important information. End-of-chapter summaries review, item by item, the chapter's key points.
- End-of-chapter materials reinforce and expand your understanding of the chapter's main ideas.
- Full-color illustrations sustain interest and emphasize content.

Economics is a tool for making informed decisions — a way of analyzing and choosing among the many and varied alternatives available to you. *Decisions* is designed to help you use this tool effectively to make intelligent, responsible decisions.

Contents

PART FIVE Your Shopping Decisions

Photo Credits

Page 1 (Part One opener): Craig Aurness/Woodfin Camp; page 2 (Chapter 1 opener): Jim Anderson/Woodfin Camp; page 4: Tony Freeman/PhotoEdit; page 6 (top left): Glenn R. Steiner/FPG; page 6 (top right): Sybil Shackman/Monkmeyer; page 6 (bottom): W. Marc Bernsau/The Image Works; page 9: Tony Freeman/PhotoEdit; page 11: Richard Hackett/International Stock; page 13: Bob Daemmrich/The Image Works.

Page 16 (Chapter 2 opener): Exxon; page 18: Richard Hackett; page 19: Dan McCoy/Rainbow; page 22: Tom Dunham; page 25: Dennis Stock/Magnum; page 27: Palmer & Brilliant; page 29: Beringer/Dratch/The Image Works.

Page 33 (Part Two opener): Palmer & Brilliant; page 34 (Chapter 3 opener): Kent Oppenheimer/Alpha; page 40: Tom Dunham; page 48: Dan McCoy/Rainbow.

Page 51 (Chapter 4 opener): Tom Dunham; page 56: Jim Raycroft/Ocean Escapes, Inc.; page 57: Dan McCoy/Rainbow; page 59 (bottom left): Michael Newman/PhotoEdit; page 59 (bottom right): Tom Dunham.

Page 68 (Chapter 5 opener): Palmer & Brilliant; page 71: Harvey Barad/Monkmeyer; page 72: Peter Arnold; page 74: Robert Pathe/Alpha; page 80: John Freeman; page 82: Zachary Singer/Greenpeace USA.

Page 87 (Part Three opener): Paul Fusco/Magnum; page 88 (Chapter 6 opener): Paul Fusco/Magnum; page 92 (top): Erich Hartmann/Magnum; page 92 (bottom): John Coletti/Stock Boston; page 95: Tom Dunham; page 100: Tom Dunham.

Page 106 (Chapter 7 opener): Tony Freeman/PhotoEdit; page 108: Tom Dunham; page 109: Tony Freeman/PhotoEdit; page 110: Charles Harbutt/Archive; page 112: FPG; page 115: PhotoEdit.

Page 122 (Chapter 8 opener): Bob Peterson/FPG; page 124: Century 21 Real Estate Corporation; page 125: National Restaurant Association; page 126: William Campbell/Sygma; page 127: Robert Bruschini/Studio B; page 132: Tony Freeman/PhotoEdit.

Page 139 (Part Four opener): Tony Freeman/PhotoEdit; page 140 (Chapter 9 opener): Michael Heron/Woodfin Camp; page 143: Abigail Heyman/Archive; page 145: Tom Dunham; page 147: Ned Skubic; page 151: Tom Dunham.

Page 157 (Chapter 10 opener): Steve Bourgeois; page 159: Tom Dunham; page 160: John Freeman; page 162: Lisa Law/The Image Works; page 167: Tom Dunham.

Page 174 (Chapter 11 opener): Richard Hutchings/InfoEdit; page 178: Hank Morgan/Rainbow; page 180: Steve Bourgeois: page 181: John Freeman; page 183: AT&T Archives; page 187: Bob Daemmrich/The Image Works.

Page 191 (Chapter 12 opener): Palmer & Brilliant; page 193: Tom Dunham; page 198: Bob Daemmrich/The Image Works; page 204: Steve Bourgeois; page 205: Tom Dunham.

Page 209 (Chapter 13 opener): Tom Dunham; page 215: Tom Dunham; page 216: Tony Freeman/PhotoEdit; page 217: Toby Mosko; page 221: James L. Shaffer/PhotoEdit; page 222: Richard Hackett/International Stock.

Page 227 (Part Five opener): Richard Hutchings/InfoEdit; page 228 (Chapter 14 opener): Todd J. Weinstein; page 236: Tom Dunham; page 238: Steve Bourgeois; page 240: Jeff Jacobson/Archive; page 241: Super Valu Stores, Inc.

Page 244 (Chapter 15 opener): Burt Glinn/Magnum; page 247: Chris Brown/Stock Boston; page 249: Tom Dunham; page 252: Michael O'Brien/Archive; page 257: William Moriarty/Rainbow.

Page 261 (Chapter 16 opener): Tony Freeman/PhotoEdit; page 265: Tom Dunham; page 266 (top left): Tom Dunham; page 266 (bottom left): Tom Dunham; page 268: Tom Dunham.

Page 276 (Chapter 17 opener): Palmer & Brilliant; page 279: Tom Dunham; page 284: Steve Bourgeois; page 286: Peter Russell Clemens/International Stock; page 288: Tom Dunham.

Page 292 (Chapter 18 opener): Alan Oddie/PhotoEdit; page 294: Clyde H. Smith/Peter Arnold; page 295: Tom Dunham; page 297: U.S. Treasury; page 340: Ford Motor Company.

Page 308 (Chapter 19 opener): Innerfield/International Stock; page 311: Propix/Monkmeyer; page 316: Carey/The Image Works; page 317: Ned Skubic; page 319: Mimi Forsyth/Monkmeyer; page 322: Pam Hasewaga/Taurus.

Page 326 (Chapter 20 opener): Steve Bourgeois; page 328: Tom Dunham; page 331: Tom Dunham; page 332: Bob Daemmrich/The Image Works; page 334: Freda Leinwand/Monkmeyer; page 335: Norris Clark/International Stock; page 336: Robert Brenner/PhotoEdit; page 338: Bob Daemmrich/The Image Works.

PART ONE

Making Choices

Making Decisions 1

OBJECTIVES

Overview: Although the vignette introduces Liz's ethical dilemma, the situation has economic ramifications. Students can use the decision-making method to analyze both ethical and economic decisions.

This chapter will help you to:

1. Explain the benefits of managing your resources.
2. Classify a decision by the economic role you are playing when you make it.
3. Describe the steps to follow in making an important decision.
4. Choose the alternative with the most benefits and the least costs.
5. Explain why decisions involve risk and need to be evaluated.
6. Identify five benefits of the systematic decision-making method.
7. Analyze how your decisions affect others.

Liz knocked on the door of her sister Ellen's room.

"Come in. Hey, what's the problem? You look really worried."

"I've got to talk to you, Ellen," Liz said as she sat down. "I've got a real problem. I've found out who's responsible for the shoplifting where I work."

"What's the problem? Why not tell Mrs. Carstairs?" Ellen said. "Then she can do something about it."

"No, it's not that easy. It's Steve, her son."

"What! But you really like him."

"I know," Liz said—"that just makes it harder. I couldn't believe it myself at first. Last week I saw Steve walk out of the store with two or three sweaters, including a blue one with white stars. He looked at me strangely, and called out that he was taking them to his mother. I believed him, until I saw him on the other side of town two days ago, with a friend who was wearing the blue and white sweater."

"Oh, come on!" Ellen said. "He probably bought it somewhere else, and Mrs. Carstairs has Steve's sweaters at home."

"No," Liz answered. "This morning Mrs. Carstairs told me she's going to raise prices because the shoplifting was still going on. The latest loss was three sweaters! Steve wasn't there, and I said, 'You mean that blue one?' She asked how I knew, and I just said that I'd liked it and noticed it was gone. She saw I was embarrassed. In fact, I'm afraid she suspects me now."

"That is difficult," said Ellen. "What are you going to do?"

"I don't know, I really don't," said Liz. "This afternoon I actually saw him put some running shoes in his backpack when he thought no one was looking. But I couldn't bring myself to say anything. And Mrs. Carstairs told us to tell the police if we knew anything about the stealing. But I feel that I can't tell them about Steve unless I have more solid proof—and for that I need to follow him around or something. But it seems easier to quit. Only then how will I earn the money for college next year?"

Note: Our limited resources and unlimited wants force us to make decisions. Ask students if they would have to make decisions if there were unlimited resources.

MANY OF THE CHOICES we make are easy—we can quickly decide whether to pack a lunch or buy one in the cafeteria. Some decisions—like the one Liz faces—are very complex and very important. In this chapter you will examine decisions in greater depth and learn a systematic way to make important ones.

WE USE RESOURCES IN OUR ECONOMIC ROLES

This book is about decision making—in particular, about economic decision making. **Economics** is *the study of how people manage their resources to achieve their goals.* Thus, an economic decision involves choosing how we use our resources to get what we want.

Managing Resources

Resources include more than money. Each of us has many personal **resources**—*the money, time, skills, and energy we possess.* Our aim is to manage these resources to get the most out of them. You'll learn later that a manager is someone who translates the goals of an organization into directions people can follow to achieve those goals. It's the same with managing personal resources. Each of us tries to find the best way to use our money, time, skills, and energy to meet our goals.

Sometimes we can draw on more resources than just our own. Families often pool their resources to use them more effectively. For example, you could ask a skillful brother or sister to make a sweater for you. Someone who is ill may ask a family member to use time and energy to go to the store for medicine.

We can also use **public resources** — *the services that the government provides with the taxes we pay.* Before buying a used car, for instance, we can read books and magazines in the public library to learn which cars are more reliable. We could use a public bus to get to school or work rather than buying a car.

Critical Thinking: Our society is becoming increasingly mobile. Ask your students what resources they would miss by moving to another town or another part of the country.

List: Ask students to list their personal resources. Do they have musical or artistic talents? Are they organized and efficient? Can they type, repair cars, or work well with other people?

Clarify: Economists use the terms **economic resources, productive resources,** or **factors of production** to refer to land, labor, capital, and entrepreneurship. These economic resources are used by the economy as a whole to produce the goods and services needed. The **personal resources** introduced here do not refer to the economists' term **economic resources**.

Note: Chapter 5 contains a complete discussion of public goods and services. This introduction of public resources is designed simply to expand the student's awareness of available resources.

These parents share the responsibility of meal preparation.

Our Three Economic Roles

We make economic decisions in three roles: worker, citizen, and consumer.

Activity: Have students keep a diary of all the decisions they make in one day (whether or not those decisions involve economics). Discuss diaries in class the next day. Allow students to leave out entries they feel are too personal to share.

Worker In our **worker role**, *we decide how to use our time, skills, and energy to earn money*. These decisions include choosing a career, deciding how to train for it, selecting a job, and deciding how to perform the job. As a worker, Liz took the job at Mrs. Carstairs's clothing store because she liked the work and the pay. Now she has other decisions to make that will affect her worker role.

Citizen In our **citizen role**, *we decide how to contribute to and use public resources*. When we vote in an election, we help select the people who spend tax dollars and direct the other resources of government, from police and fire departments to parks and libraries. In addition, we may take other actions as citizens—attending and speaking at town meetings, contributing money and time to political causes, making decisions on the basis of what we feel is the public good. In taking a stand against shoplifting, Liz would be acting in her role as citizen, even though her decision affects her in the other two roles as well.

Critical Thinking: Ask students to give additional examples of multiple roles. Lead them to the conclusion that making decisions affects multiple roles and that this makes decision-making even more difficult.

Consumer In our **consumer role**, *we decide how to use our money, time, energy, and skills to get what we want*. Liz saves the money she earns from Mrs. Carstairs in order to pay for her college education. She could have decided instead to use her resources for a new car, or for clothes or sporting goods. Consumer decisions involve more than just money, however. Liz could choose to spend her time making clothes. She could also trade with a friend, for example, exchanging a sweater she no longer wanted for a blouse.

Multiple Roles Many economic decisions involve only a single role. When we spend money to play a video game, it doesn't much affect our lives as workers or citizens. However, other choices involve aspects of all three roles. Liz faces a decision that could cost her a job (worker role). It could also hinder her from buying an education (consumer role) and compromise her principles (citizen role). It affects some of her noneconomic roles, too, in which resources are not involved—her friendship with Steve, for example.

HOW WE MAKE DECISIONS

We each decide in different ways, depending on how important or hard the decision is. For simple choices—like what to eat or what to wear—we decide quickly. For more important decisions involving the way we manage our resources, a more careful method often helps produce more satisfying results.

Clarify: Business owners, entrepreneurs, and employees make economic decisions in worker roles.

We Use Shortcuts to Make Simple Choices

We make many routine choices so easily, we're not always aware of how we decided. Soon after we wake up, we decide what to wear, what to eat for breakfast, when to leave for school or work, and how to get there. All day long we make more choices, finally deciding when to go to bed and, by setting an alarm, when to get up the next morning. Clearly, if we went through a complex process for each decision, we would never have time to do anything.

Each of us plays three different economic roles: worker (top left), consumer (top right), and citizen (bottom). These roles often overlap.

Instead we make these choices by using four shortcuts. We may decide on the basis of experience. For example, we've learned that one brand of recording tape is better than the rest. We make other decisions by habit — taking the same route to school each day, or going to bed at a set hour. Sometimes we decide by following another person's example. We may go to a movie a friend recommends. We also decide on impulse, choosing chili instead of a sandwich for lunch.

Emphasize: The first step in the decision-making process is probably the most critical step. If students define the problem too narrowly, they unnecessarily limit the alternatives available. If students define it too broadly, they will not be able to focus on the question.

These ways of reaching a decision may be quite satisfactory. They take up little time and may produce satisfactory results, but important choices such as Liz's can best be made after careful thought.

Systematic Decision Making Helps Solve Problems

To help us solve more difficult problems, we can use the **systematic decision-making method**, *a step-by-step way of identifying, analyzing, and choosing among your alternatives, then later evaluating your choice.* The seven steps are:

Explain: Relate the cost of making a decision to the cost of the item. It would not be efficient to use the decision-making model to decide where to buy milk or bread since the costs are small. However, shopping for a house or a car definitely suggests using the decision-making model because of higher costs.

Step 1. Define your problem.
Step 2. Identify and rank your goals.
Step 3. Determine your alternatives.
Step 4. Analyze the consequences of each alternative.
Step 5. Choose the best alternative for achieving your goals.
Step 6. Put your decision into action.
Step 7. Evaluate your decision.

Let's study each step more closely, seeing how Liz might use the method to solve her problem.

Step 1. Define Your Problem The first step, defining the problem, seems easy. Liz's problem is how to tell Mrs. Carstairs about Steve's shoplifting, right? Wrong. That is one of her alternatives — focusing on it skips ahead to step three. Liz's problem is simply that she doesn't know what to do about her suspicions. She feels she must do something — the stealing bothers her, and by asking Mrs. Carstairs if it was the blue sweater that was stolen, she may have drawn suspicion to herself.

Activity: Encourage students to list items they usually purchase using each of the shortcuts (experience, habit, by example, and impulse), and then analyze if this is appropriate or if the use of the seven-step model is justified.

In taking the first step, take care to define the problem correctly. Don't focus on alternatives, but try to find the basic problem that needs solving. We're often better off if we define the problem as broadly as we can. By doing so, we'll be able to identify more alternatives later. Suppose you need a way to get to school. If you define your problem too narrowly as the need for a car, you've already limited yourself to one alternative—you have to get a car. By defining your problem more generally as a need for transportation, you allow more possible solutions. You can solve the problem by walking, buying or renting a bike, buying or borrowing a car, getting a ride from a friend or a member of your family, or taking public transportation. With more alternatives to choose from, you're more likely to find one that solves the problem in a satisfactory way.

Step 2. Identify and Rank Your Goals Next, Liz determines what her goals are. **Goals** are the target, *the results we want from our decisions*. Goals give us direction—they give purpose to our actions.

Define: Make sure students understand the term **criteria** (standards or rules by which something can be judged). When evaluating your alternatives, the criteria could include your goals as well as other standards you think are important.

Liz wants to be honest and uphold the law. She also wants to keep her job and protect her own good name, and she wants both to obey Mrs. Carstairs and to make as little trouble for Steve as possible. Liz wants to achieve all five goals, but they may conflict. She needs to rank them to see how important they are when compared with one another. Then, if only a few are possible, she'll know which ones she most wants to attain.

This step is often difficult and requires us to identify our values. **Values** are *our beliefs about what is important in our lives*. Liz must think about whether she values upholding the law more than protecting her friend. Is it more important to keep her job and pay for her education, or to obey Mrs. Carstairs? Where would she put protecting her own good name? Let's suppose she decides that upholding the law and keeping her job are her two most important goals. Obeying Mrs. Carstairs and protecting Steve tie for second place. Last comes protecting her own name. Now Liz knows which goals to weigh as most important.

Emphasize: Goals and other criteria for evaluating alternatives must be ranked in order of importance. Seldom does any alternative meet all the desired criteria. Therefore, it is important for individuals to identify which goals are most important and which are least important.

Two people may rank their goals differently, even if they are making the same decision, because their values are different. One person shopping for a car may rank gas mileage over appearance. Another may emphasize appearance and be less concerned about mileage.

Step 3. Determine Your Alternatives The third step is to think of possible ways to solve the problem. Liz knew she had two alternatives before she talked to her sister Ellen. She could collect more evidence against Steve to prove to Mrs. Carstairs that he was the shoplifter, or she could quit her job to avoid the problem. By talking with Ellen, Liz saw two more solutions. She could confront Steve with her suspicions and persuade him to stop, or she could go to the police.

A course of action is only an **alternative** if it *will at least partly fulfill our goals and requires resources we have or can get*. If Liz is so busy that she has no time to collect evidence against Steve, then that isn't a real alternative. Suppose you need transportation to school. Buying a car is only an alternative if you have the necessary cash or credit. Remember, though, that you can sometimes rely on resources besides your own. Perhaps Liz could get Ellen to do her detective work for her.

Discuss: Ask students to brainstorm alternative methods of transportation and list them on the board. Analyze whether or not these alternatives are feasible.

Finding alternatives often takes time and energy, and we usually need to get information. You can look for transportation alternatives in the Yellow Pages, for instance. As Liz found, brainstorming with a friend can also be a good way to find more solutions.

Step 4. Analyze the Consequences of Each Alternative To evaluate each alternative, Liz must determine how well it will meet her goals. Each alternative has benefits and costs. The **benefits** are *the goals that are met by an alternative*. The **costs** are *what we must give up in order to have an alternative*. (Benefits and costs can also be called *advantages* and *disadvantages* or *pros* and *cons*.) This "cost-benefit analysis" is the most time-consuming step of the method, but it must be done if the process is to work.

Research: Ask students to research one of the transportation alternatives in which they are interested. Possible resources include: want ads in the newspaper, Yellow Pages, retail stores, Better Business Bureau, library, and consumer periodicals such as *Consumer Reports.*

Locating alternatives often requires us to gather information.

Activity: Have students identify the costs and benefits of the decisions listed in their diaries.

Illustrate: Provide additional examples of cost-benefit analysis, such as comparison of production techniques, comparison of refrigerators leading to a purchase decision, or methods of funding the federal government.

Liz considers her alternatives. If she can collect solid evidence and prove to Mrs. Carstairs that Steve is the thief, her own name will be cleared and she'll have done what Mrs. Carstairs asked. However, there are costs: simply stopping the shoplifting isn't the same as upholding the law. Mrs. Carstairs may punish Steve but still protect him from the police. Liz thinks that she wouldn't feel comfortable working in the store anymore, so she would probably quit. These consequences are shown in the top row of Table 1.1.

If Liz quits her job, Steve won't get into trouble. Quitting will draw more suspicion to Liz herself, and of course, she'll lose the income she earns. Also, quitting isn't exactly doing what Mrs. Carstairs asked, and it doesn't help to uphold the law.

If Liz confronts Steve, he'll probably stop shoplifting and therefore avoid getting into trouble. Liz will be able to protect her good name and keep her job. She'll be keeping the truth from Mrs. Carstairs and, once again, stopping the shoplifting isn't the same as upholding the law.

Finally, if Liz tells the police, she feels she'll be upholding the law, obeying Mrs. Carstairs, and protecting her own name. Steve will be in trouble though, and she certainly won't feel comfortable enough to stay on the job after telling the police about her boss's son. This alternative is shown along with the others in Table 1.1.

Step 5. Choose the Best Alternative for Achieving Your Goals The first four steps make choosing an alternative much easier, especially if you are able to diagram them as shown in Table 1.1. Step 5 involves following the **principle of least cost**, which means *choosing the alternative that offers the most benefits for the fewest costs.* Least cost doesn't mean the *cheapest*

Extension: We usually have to trade off one alternative to obtain another. The federal government might want to maintain a large national defense and a large social welfare program. However, the government does not have enough resources to do both. Therefore, there is always a trade-off between "guns and butter."

Student Motivator: Ask students to identify trade-offs their school district must make. Invite your district financial director to speak to the class regarding this issue.

Illustration: The time element of decisions should be illustrated by referring back to the individual roles: consumer (interest rates may change while deciding to buy a house); worker (the job may be offered to someone else while deciding whether or not to take it); and citizen (deaths may occur while deciding if safety equipment should be required).

Table 1.1 How Liz Compared the Costs and Benefits of Each Alternative

	Goals				
	Tied First		Tied Second		Third
Alternatives	Uphold the law	Keep her job	Obey Mrs. Carstairs	Protect Steve	Clear her name
Collect evidence and tell Mrs. Carstairs	−	−	+	+	+
Quit the job	−	−	−	+	−
Confront Steve	−	+	−	+	+
Contact the police	+	−	+	−	+

\+ Contributes to this goal, a benefit
− Blocks this goal, a cost

alternative, because cost includes more than money—it means anything we must give up to get an alternative.

For Liz the *greatest* cost is clearly quitting her job, because this alternative only has one benefit. The other three alternatives seem equal, however, each with three benefits and two costs. How can Liz decide which one to choose? If she considers how she ranked her goals in Step 2, she'll see that the first alternative – telling Mrs. Carstairs – doesn't meet her two most important goals. The last two alternatives each achieve one of her major goals, so confronting Steve and going to the police seem to be better options.

Still, Liz has no way of deciding between these two options. She must figure out which of the tied goals she wants more—then she'll know which choice to make.

Liz has found that she must *give up something she wants in order to get something she wants more.* This is making a **trade-off**. Suppose you want to buy a used car that gets good mileage, has AM/FM stereo, and costs $1,250. One car has the price you want and gets the mileage you want, but has only an AM radio. Another car costs the same and has the radio but does not get as good mileage. The one you choose depends on which benefit—good mileage or an AM/FM stereo—you'd rather give up to meet the goal that's more important to you. Many choices we make require us to trade off in this way.

Step 6. Put Your Decision into Action Decisions solve problems only when we act upon them. Once she decides, Liz needs to do something. If we delay putting a decision into action, circumstances may change and the alternative we picked may no longer be the best one.

Step 7. Evaluate Your Decision The final step is to evaluate the decision, which helps us to reduce the risk of making an unsatisfying one. All decisions involve **risk**, which is *not knowing for sure whether the alternative*

Stress: The decision-making process is not completed once you have made the decision. The decision should be evaluated in order to improve future decisions. We will not always make satisfactory decisions, even using the seven-step process. However, identifying our mistakes will help us avoid them next time.

Many decisions require us to make trade-offs; that is why it is important to have a goal in mind.

Critical Thinking: Is it possible to eliminate risks entirely?

we choose will have the benefits and costs we expect. This risk results from two causes. First, we cannot know for sure what all the costs and benefits of an alternative are. Second, something unexpected may occur to change our situation. Risk affects all decisions because the future is always uncertain.

Still, there are three ways we can reduce this risk:

Discussion: Explore whether or not elected officials evaluate past decisions. If not, could this affect the quality of future decisions? Is this important for decisions made at the local, state, and federal government levels?

- *Spend time and energy thoroughly investigating the alternatives.* The more you learn about the options beforehand, the less uncertain you will be. Of course, you can't learn everything you need to know before deciding, so you also rely on the second way to reduce risk.
- *Evaluate the results of decisions.* Were the goals met? Were the costs and benefits what you had anticipated? If the benefits were greater or the costs were lower, there's no problem. If the costs were more or the benefits less, you may want to change the decision, perhaps trying another alternative.
- *Evaluate how the decision was made.* Was the problem defined too narrowly? Did you overlook any options? Did you fail to see all the costs and benefits of each alternative? Did you take too much time to decide? By evaluating how well you decided, you can help yourself make better decisions in the future.

Making Systematic Decisions Has Benefits

Using the systematic decision-making method takes time and effort. When we have to make a very important decision, though, this method offers five benefits that are well worth the time and effort. By making systematic decisions:

Stress: Emphasize that others are affected by our actions. A business can succeed or fail based on the work of its employees. The U.S. political system is supposed to represent the views of the people. This can only happen if we all make our views known.

1. *We can use our resources wisely.* By planning, we can manage our resources to get the most out of them.
2. *We avoid being too influenced by others.* We are all affected by family, friends, and the world around us, but systematic decision making lets us set our own goals so that outside influence is not too great.
3. *We can see new alternatives.* The more alternatives we have, the more likely we are to find a good one.
4. *We can make our decisions more easily.* By ranking our goals and alternatives, we may find it simpler to choose a course of action.
5. *We avoid future problems.* By seeing the results of each alternative, we can predict possible trouble. Because we evaluate our decisions, we can act before a problem becomes too serious.

These five benefits of the systematic decision-making method help us to achieve greater satisfaction. We are more likely to make the best choice for us if we take our time and carefully follow this method.

OUR DECISIONS AFFECT OTHERS

Liz's decision affects Steve, Mrs. Carstairs, and people who shop in the store. Our decisions often affect other people. We all live within many groups. Each of us is a member of a family, a resident of a city, town, or village and a state, and a citizen of a nation. We belong to other groups, too—people we work with, volunteer groups we join, and churches we attend. The choices we make affect other members of these groups.

Activity: List a series of decisions ranging from the very simple to the highly complex and ask the students to rank order these decisions according to whether or not the seven-step decision-making process would be beneficial.

Our decisions affect other members of our family. Whether we live with our parents or move to a place of our own, get married or live alone, have children or not, we consider the wants and needs of other people. As we grow older and take on more responsibility, others play a greater part in our decisions. We can help ourselves—and them—by remembering that our choices will affect them.

Society at large is also affected by our decisions—especially our economic choices. How we work affects our co-workers. For example, someone who is lazy at work forces other workers to do his or her job. Steve, by shoplifting, casts suspicion on Liz. How we work also affects the consumers who buy what we make or sell. Sloppy work may mean that someone is hurt when a product breaks down.

Our citizen decisions affect others, too. The candidates we vote for will govern others, as well as ourselves. The taxes we pay support services that all citizens benefit from the stands we take on important issues can influence the future of the nation and even the world.

Our consumer decisions also affect others. Whether we buy this product or that may seem unimportant to strangers, but our purchases really act like dollar votes. They support one business or another, just as our political votes support one candidate or another. Businesses succeed when consumers

Summary: Because of limited resources and unlimited wants, we all must make choices between alternatives. Our satisfaction with the decisions we make can be improved by using the seven-step decision-making process. Because of our interdependence, our economic decisions affect each other.

As we have families of our own, we have more decisions to make.

Note: Personal decision making does not take place in a vacuum. We are all part of an economic system.

Critical Thinking: Do citizens in other countries make decisions the way we do?

buy what they produce, and successful businesses produce more. If we and others don't complain about a product we know is unsafe, we encourage production of poor quality goods that may endanger others. Also, successful businesses often hire more workers. Failed businesses lay people off. To those workers, then, our purchases provide their livelihood.

Just as our decisions affect others, theirs affect us. We depend on others for the food we eat, the clothes we wear, and the houses we live in. The total of all personal economic decisions helps to determine how our economy performs. The economy, through prices, employment levels, and production decisions, affects our personal hopes and plans. Understanding how we interact with the economy is a key to responsible decision making.

SUMMARY

- We manage our personal resources to achieve our goals. We often draw on family and public resources.
- In making economic decisions, we play one of three economic roles: worker, citizen, or consumer. Some choices involve more than one role at the same time.
- We make simple choices in one of four ways: by experience, by habit, by following someone else's example, or on impulse.
- When a decision is important or complex, we can use a systematic method of identifying and evaluating possible solutions to make better decisions.
- The steps of the decision-making method are these: define your problem, identify and rank your goals, determine your alternatives, analyze the consequences of each alternative, choose the best alternative for achieving your goals, put your decision into action, and evaluate your decision.

- By defining the problem in a general way, we allow more possible solutions.
- To know what we're aiming for, we identify and rank our goals.
- We often gather information to identify our alternatives. Something is an alternative only if we can obtain it with resources we have or can get.
- By ranking our alternatives according to our goals, we can choose the best one. The best alternative is the one with the most benefits and the least costs. Sometimes we must give up one benefit in order to get another we want more.
- We can solve the problem only if we act upon the decision.
- We evaluate the outcome of a decision to see if the results are what we expected. By evaluating how we made the decision we can learn to make better decisions in the future.
- The systematic decision-making method has five benefits: we can use our resources wisely, we can set our own goals without too much outside influence, we can discover new alternatives, we can rank the alternatives to make the decision easier, and we can avoid future problems.
- Because we live in groups, our decisions affect other people and theirs affect us. This is true of decisions in all our economic roles.

Key Terms

Match each of the following terms with the definition that most suits it.

alternative
benefits
citizen role
consumer role
costs
economics
goals
personal resources
principle of least cost
public resources
risk
systematic decision-making method
trade-off
values
worker role

a. how a person decides to use time, skills, and energy to earn money
b. the results a person wants from a decision
c. a method of deciding that involves choosing the alternative that offers the most benefits for the fewest costs
d. the goals that are met by an alternative
e. a step-by-step way of identifying, analyzing, and choosing among alternatives, then later evaluating the choice
f. the money, time, skills, and energy a person possesses
g. the uncertainty that results from not knowing for sure whether the alternative chosen will have the benefits and costs expected
h. giving up something a person wants in order to get something he or she wants more
i. how a person decides to contribute to and use public resources
j. a course of action that will at least partly fulfill a person's goals and requires resources he or she has or can get
k. how a person decides to use money, time, skills, and energy to get what he or she wants
l. what a person must give up in order to have an alternative
m. the study of how people manage their resources to achieve their goals
n. a person's beliefs about what is important in his or her life
o. the services that the government provides with the taxes we pay

Review Questions

1. What resources do we manage? Why is it worthwhile to manage resources?
2. Name two sources of resources other than ourselves. Give an example of how you might use each source to solve a problem.
3. What three roles do we play when we make economic decisions? Give an example of a decision in each role.
4. In what four ways do we make simple decisions?
5. What are the steps in the systematic decision-making method?
6. What is the benefit of defining a problem in a general way? Name three alternatives for satisfying hunger.
7. Why should we analyze the consequences of each alternative?
8. Does cost mean how many dollars an alternative requires? If not, what else does cost mean?
9. What principle do we use to choose an alternative? How does it work?
10. Why do decisions involve risk? In what three ways can we reduce risk?
11. What are the benefits of systematic decision making?
12. Give examples of how your decisions in each economic role affect others.

Projects

1. Discuss Liz's problem. What would you do? Did she overlook a better solution?
2. Think of a service you often require—transportation, recreation, education, health care, or any other. Find out what alternatives you have for obtaining that service using your own resources. Now identify any public resources you could draw on for that service. Compare the two methods—what are the pros and cons of each? Report your findings to the class.
3. Make two columns on a piece of paper, titling one "Systematic Decisions" and the other "Unsystematic Decisions." Write down all the worker, citizen, or consumer decisions you've made in the past three days under the correct heading. Compare the decisions in each column. What do they have in common? Why did you decide the way you did? Now place a check next to any decisions you're not happy with. What could you have done differently that might have led to more satisfying results? Compare your findings with your classmates'.
4. Pretend that you just got a part-time job for after school three days a week and all day Saturday. Suppose you could take public transportation that cost 75 cents each way, but the buses run irregularly on Saturday, so you'd have to leave for work early. You could ride a bicycle, but that would take forty minutes each way. You could use a second car of your family's, but you would have to pay for your insurance and gas and you'd have to take your brother to music lessons two days a week. Use the systematic decision-making method to choose an alternative.

Why You Make Choices

2

Overview: George has to make a decision. As we have discovered, making decisions is difficult—and risky—and does not occur in a vacuum. Chapter 2 examines more closely why we must make decisions and how the economic system influences the decisions we make.

OBJECTIVES

This chapter will help you to:

1. Identify wants that motivate you to act.
2. Show how the conflict between unlimited wants and limited resources forces you to choose.
3. Clarify the opportunity costs of the decisions you make.
4. Explain how and why people exchange goods and services.
5. Explain how producers use resources.
6. Describe the five principles on which the U.S. economy is based.

Julio and George were talking in the locker room after gym class. "I hear you got the lead in the play, George," said Julio.

"That's right," answered George. "But I don't know if I can be in it."

"You're kidding. How come?"

"Well, I want to take the senior trip to Washington in April, and the only way I can afford it is to get a job. If I work in the afternoon, I won't be able to make the rehearsals."

"Can't you work at night?"

"No," George replied. "If I rehearse in the afternoon and work at night, I won't have any time left for homework. I've got to keep my grades up or I can't do either one—I made a deal with my parents."

"That's a shame," said Julio.

"I wish I didn't have to choose one thing or the other. I really wanted this part in the play, especially since last year's show was so great. But I've been looking forward to the trip, too."

"So what are you going to do?" Julio asked.

"I don't know." George said. "I guess I'll have to choose which thing I'd rather do—be in the play or go on the trip."

***Define:* Subsistence** is the very basic means of sustaining life or existing. Any discussion about economic wants must begin with the fact that we need to subsist.

GEORGE MUST DO SOMETHING we all do often. He must choose between two alternatives: getting a job to earn enough money for the trip or giving up the trip so he can be in the play. Why does George have to choose? Why can't he have both things he wants?

We make most choices because a basic economic conflict—between unlimited wants and limited resources—forces us to choose. Also, the principles on which the United States economy is based give us the freedom to choose.

ECONOMIC FORCES MAKE PEOPLE CHOOSE

George must choose because of the basic economic conflict that we all face. He has more wants (going on the trip and being in the play) than he has resources (time and money).

Focus: The basic economic problem of limited resources and unlimited wants forces us to make choices.

We All Have Wants

Wants are *our feelings that we lack something that will satisfy us*. George has many wants besides the two just described—keeping up his grades, for instance. He also has other wants that don't have anything to do with this decision, but which are present every day. He needs food, clothing, and shelter. He wants love from his family and he wants friendship.

We share many of these wants with George. This is particularly true of certain basic wants, called *needs* or *primary wants* because they must be satisfied if we are to survive. We cannot live without satisfying our needs for food, clothing, shelter, air, water, and sleep.

Critical Thinking: Aristotle said, "It is the nature of desire not to be satisfied, and most men live only for the gratification of it." Ask students to interpret this statement.

For most Americans, these bare-minimum needs are satisfied. Once our basic needs are fulfilled we begin to feel other wants. We might desire a portable tape player, a car, a ski trip, a home video game, an evening at the movies, or countless other things. We often feel just as strongly about these secondary wants as we do about our primary wants. If we satisfy them, we think our lives will be more enjoyable or comfortable.

We all have wants, then, but our wants differ. Think of what your classmates plan to do after graduation. Some will work. Others intend to continue their schooling. Still others may join the armed forces. Each decision results from a complex set of wants that is unique to the individual. These wants are formed by our past experiences, what we've learned in school and from our families, what our friends and acquaintances want for themselves, and what we hear and see in the mass media. Because these influences vary for each of us, our wants differ. You might like to have a car to get to school, while your friend may prefer to walk. Neither choice is right or wrong: you and your friend simply want different things.

World Economy: Compare our standard of living to that in less developed countries. Two-thirds of the world's population are illiterate and malnourished and have inadequate housing. If you have an average income in the United States and Canada, you are among the richest 10 percent of the world's population.

Some wants recur—the basic physical needs are the best examples. Eating one meal cannot satisfy our hunger forever, and we must breathe constantly to get the oxygen we need. In other cases, satisfying a want creates new wants. Buying a new stereo is satisfying, but it leads us to want tapes or compact discs to play on it. Our lives, then, are marked by a constant cycle of wanting, satisfying our wants, and wanting again.

Illustrate: The cycle of wanting, satisfying our wants, and wanting more can be examined through public policy. Choose a specific program, such as social security, and examine how the demands on that program have evolved from basic assistance to today's retirement program, medical assistance, survivors' benefits, etc.

Each of these people is choosing to satisfy his or her wants in a different way.

To Satisfy Our Wants, We Use Personal Resources

Activity: Encourage students to examine their most recent choices to see if they traded off a more costly alternative for the least costly. Did they eat a muffin for breakfast because it was faster than fixing bacon and eggs? Did they stop by a convenience store to buy a more expensive bottle of cola because it was faster than going to a full-service grocery store? Have students provide additional examples.

Unsatisfied wants bother us until they are satisfied. For that reason, they motivate us to act. Think of how grumpy you are when you're hungry or sleepy, or how frustrated you get when you have to finish washing the dishes before you can go to a movie. To satisfy a want, we must do something—eat, sleep, go to the movies. The discomfort we feel disappears when the want is satisfied.

To satisfy our wants, we must use some of our personal resources—our money, time, skills, and energy. Sleeping takes time; making our own lunch uses all four personal resources. George needs money to go on the school trip, and he needs time to rehearse for the play.

To decide what resources to use and how to use them, we follow the principle of **substitution**. That means *we replace one way of satisfying a want with another way that uses less of our valuable resources*. Some people believe that using time, skills, and energy to make lunch in the morning is worth the money saved by not having to buy lunch at the cafeteria. Others pay more for a cafeteria lunch to save valuable time.

How we each use our resources varies, just as what we want varies. We all make decisions in a similar way though. We usually follow the principle of

Describe: Multiple-income families tend to eat out more; serve frozen meals or convenience foods at home; and hire others to perform tasks they do not have time to do. In other words, they substitute payments to others for their time and energy. However, if family members become unemployed, they tend to cook less expensive meals that take time to prepare and mow their own lawns. They substitute their time and energy for their financial resources.

This teen is using her time, skills, and energy to earn money.

least cost. This means we choose the alternative that uses the least costly resources and offers the most satisfaction.

Define: **Interest** is the cost of money. If we borrow money from an institution or an individual, we must pay interest for the use of that money.

Scarce Resources Make Us Choose Which Wants to Satisfy

We substitute one resource for another because our resources are limited, and substitution helps us get the most out of them. We don't have enough resources to satisfy all our wants. Even if we had unlimited money, skills, and energy, our time is limited, and there aren't many people who have unlimited money, skills, and energy! For all of us, then, resources are scarce.

Scarcity does not mean that something is rare. After all, there are around 250 billion dollars circulating in the United States, but money is scarce because people want more of it than they can get. **Scarcity** exists *when our desire for a specific resource exceeds our ability to obtain it.* If we could have all we wanted of something without paying anything for it, scarcity would not exist. There is more than enough air for all of us to breathe, so it is not scarce.

World Economy: A case of extreme scarcity exists on the island of St. Barthélemy in the Caribbean. This island has absolutely no drinking water available. Water must be shipped in by tanker, or a plant must be built to desalinate the ocean water.

Because scarcity results from a desire for something and the inability to satisfy a desire, it can change from time to time, from place to place, and from person to person. If George didn't want to go on the trip, he would have enough time to be in the play. Once he began to want the trip too, however, he didn't have enough resources to do both. Julio, who does not want to go on the trip, doesn't feel the same scarcity of time that George does, but he has a similar problem. He wants to go to the homecoming football game and to a rock concert, but he doesn't have enough money to do both. Scarcity affects all of us, but in different ways.

Explain: Our goal is to increase the efficient use of our resources; that is, to use our resources in the manner that best satisfies our wants.

There are two causes of scarcity. First, many resources are simply in limited supply, as is the case with the physical energy you have. You can work twenty-four hours a day for one day, and maybe for two, but eventually you will need to stop and rest. The second cause of scarcity is that resources may be available but hard to find or get. This is why money is scarce. Obtaining some of those 250 billion dollars is difficult and requires time, skills, and energy.

Note: Scarcity exists because there are never sufficient resources to satisfy our unlimited wants. Anything that has a price is scarce. Although air is unlimited, clean air is scarce because it has a price.

Scarcity keeps us from satisfying all of our wants—and it's even worse if we don't plan. By managing resources carefully, we can get more out of them. Suppose someone spent all of her weekly pay the day she got it. She already had limited resources for satisfying her wants during the week. Now, because of her lack of planning, she has no resources. Her next paycheck will help, but her problem will return if she doesn't manage her resources more carefully.

The basic economic problem is that wants are unlimited and resources are scarce. We all face this problem, and we all solve it in a similar way—we make choices. We decide which wants we want to satisfy most. This is what George must do in choosing between the play and the trip. One way of trying to make the best possible choices is to use a step-by-step way of making decisions.

Four Factors Help Us Choose

We consider four factors when we choose an alternative:

Note: These four factors expand on themes introduced in the decision-making model. The careful selection of goals and the role of personal values in setting these goals expands Step 2; the examination of benefits and costs associated with each alternative expands Step 3.

1. Our goals
2. Our values
3. The benefits of each alternative
4. The cost of lost opportunities

Suppose Angela is thinking about changing the oil in her car herself instead of paying a mechanic to do it. As with most decisions, Angela will try to achieve more than one goal. Getting the oil changed is most important, but she also wants to get the job done before a weekend ski trip. She'd also like to buy a new sweater for the trip. Angela's values, the things she believes are important, influence how she ranks her goals. Getting the job done is most important, and finishing it in time for the trip is second. The sweater comes last—Angela knows she can wear one she already has. Now she can see which alternative satisfies the more important goals.

Explain: Encourage students to examine Angela's short-run benefits (changing the oil herself may be moro convoniont) and long-run benefits (she will have gained a skill she can use in the future). Often, long-run benefits are ignored because the payoff is not immediately beneficial.

Angela first considers the benefits of each alternative. Whether she pays a mechanic or does the job herself, Angela still gets her car's oil changed. Doing it herself may be more convenient, because she can do it whenever she wants. She may also think about future benefits. If she changes the oil herself now, following the instructions in a repair manual, she will gain a skill that she can use again in the future. A benefit of paying a mechanic, of course, is that she'll have more time to shop for the sweater she wants.

Both alternatives have costs, however. Angela will compare the cost in time of changing the oil herself to the cost in money of paying someone else to do it. Because she ranked her goals, she will know how much weight to give each cost and each benefit.

Angela must also consider another kind of cost. She must recognize that by choosing either alternative she loses the opportunity to do other things. If she pays a mechanic she won't have as much money for a sweater. If she changes the oil herself, she won't have as much time to shop for it.

Illustrate: Encourage students to identify the opportunity costs of their most recent decisions.

Because resources are scarce, all choices involve these lost opportunities. George cannot go on the trip if he chooses to be in the play. Getting a job so he can take the trip will cost him the opportunity to be in the play. *The value of the benefit that is given up when choosing one alternative over another* is called the **opportunity cost**. Table 2.1 shows the opportunity costs of George's and Angela's choices.

Example: If George had decided to go on the trip, what would be his opportunity cost?

Table 2.1 Opportunity Costs for George and Angela

	Choice	Opportunity Cost
George	Go on trip Be in play	Be in play Go on trip
Angela	Pay mechanic Change oil herself	Money to buy sweater Time to shop for sweater

In George's case, only the starring role or the trip can be an opportunity cost. George also loses the opportunity to join the football team, buy some clothes, spend more time studying, and many other things. None of these possibilities counts as the opportunity cost because none is the next most attractive alternative to him.

Because resources are scarce, all choices have opportunity costs. We can make more satisfying decisions if we take time to identify the opportunities we lose by choosing an alternative. If we know not only what we will be getting, but also what we will be losing, we can avoid later disappointments.

BY DEPENDING ON OTHERS, WE CAN SATISFY MORE WANTS

Because our resources are scarce, we cannot satisfy all of our wants by ourselves. Although substitution increases the number of wants we can satisfy, we are still left with some that aren't met. As we want more complex things, we are less able to satisfy them on our own. It would be nearly impossible for most of us to put together a car. The necessary parts and tools would be expensive, and welding together or bolting down the parts would take huge amounts of time, skills, and energy. Therefore, we rely on other people to build our cars. *Our reliance on others and theirs on us,* called **interdependence**, is a major feature of modern life.

Emphasize: **Opportunity cost** is the value of the next best alternative. Students often say, "If I stay home to study, my opportunity cost is going to the movies, going to the game, and watching TV." This is incorrect. The opportunity cost of the decision to study is the one alternative they would have chosen since that is the alternative that was actually given up.

World Economy: Ask students to research the interdependence among countries in our world.

In earlier times, people satisfied all or many of their own wants. Pioneer families grew their own food, built their own homes, and provided their own entertainment. Today such self-sufficiency is rare. The things we want today

By relying on others to produce certain goods and services, we are able to satisfy more complex wants.

are more complex and require specialized labor to produce them efficiently. Another benefit of interdependence is that we can satisfy more of our wants. Because it requires fewer of our resources to buy a car than to build one, we have some left over to use in satisfying other wants.

Enhancement: The United States has been shifting steadily toward a **service economy** since about 1880. What this means is that employment in the service sector has been growing at a rate of about 1.8 percent per year for the last century and is expected to continue at this rate.

To Satisfy Some Wants, We Obtain Goods and Services

To satisfy wants we cannot take care of by ourselves, we depend on other people to produce goods and services. **Goods** are *products that people buy.* Goods include food, clothing, and housing, plus the countless other products we use every day—toothpaste, pens, gloves, paper, eyeglasses, footballs, soap. **Services** are *actions of value that people pay others to perform.* Services include the work of hair stylists, job counselors, teachers, mechanics, doctors, chefs, and bus drivers like the one who will take George and his classmates to Washington.

People who purchase goods and services for personal use are **consumers**. We are all consumers—you and your family, neighbors, friends, classmates, and everyone you don't even know. **Producers** are *those who provide goods and services for consumers.*

Definition: **Productivity** is decreasing the amount of resources needed for a given output, or increasing the output obtained from a given amount of resources.

We Obtain Goods and Services Through Exchange

We must give up something in order to get a good or service. Sometimes goods and services are exchanged directly for each other. This was true in the early days of this nation when trappers exchanged fur pelts for the supplies they needed. Even today, neighbors may exchange goods—one person's unused bicycle for another's extra lawnmower. They may exchange services—one person driving another to work in exchange for babysitting. This *direct exchange of goods and services* is called **barter**.

Emphasize: **Specialization** allows us to be more productive.

These transactions are also **voluntary exchanges**—*trades that are made between willing participants who both think they will benefit.* Without expecting some benefit, neither person would be willing to make the exchange.

Barter is not always an effective way to make an exchange, however. First, people are often unable to match their needs to the needs of another. Second, people aren't always able to agree on the value of what is being exchanged. Third, the goods or services to be traded may not be easy to transport. People need an easier way to make voluntary exchanges, so they use a **medium of exchange**, *an object that is generally accepted as payment for goods and services.* A useful medium of exchange is not perishable, can be carried and stored easily, and can be divided conveniently into exact amounts without losing its value.

Note: *The Curious History of Money* is an excellent film available from the Education Department of your regional Federal Reserve Bank.

Money, which has all of these characteristics, is used by modern societies as the medium of exchange. Because it keeps its value, money can be stored for use in the future. Because it is not perishable and is carried and divided easily, money makes exchanges easier. In fact, money lets us conduct more exchanges than we could if we used only barter. This increases the flow of goods and services between producers and consumers. Producers accept money in payment for the goods and services they sell. In turn, they use money to pay their workers—the people whose time and effort go into providing those goods and services. The workers then use the money they earn to purchase the goods and services they want. Behind each of these transactions is the mutual benefit of voluntary exchange.

Enhancement: Chapter 2 states that wages depend on the need for and the availability of workers who can do a particular kind of work. Demand for workers is derived from the demand for the good or service they produce. If the demand for steel falls, then the **derived demand** for steel workers also falls. If the demand for professional sports rises, then the **derived demand** for professional athletes also rises.

Money also helps people assign value to goods and services. Every good and every service has a price. That **price** indicates *how much money it costs to obtain the good or service and what it is worth compared to other goods or services.* Price is determined by the desirability and availability of the good or service. When many people want oil but there is little of it, its price will be high. If fewer people want it or if a large, easily obtained supply is found, the price will go down.

Work has a price too. A **wage** is *how much producers are willing to pay and workers are willing to accept for their time and skills.* Wages depend on the need for and the availability of workers who can do a particular kind of work. If few people are available to do a certain kind of work, a producer will be willing to pay higher wages for it. The best professional athletes are paid high salaries. The public wants to see them, but few people have enough talent. If more people were qualified or there were less demand for professional sports, team owners would be able to pay lower wages.

Producers Use Resources to Produce Goods and Services

Just as we must use personal resources to satisfy our wants, producers must use productive resources to produce goods and services. One productive resource is labor. *The workers whose time, skills, and energy are used in the production of goods and services* are **human resources**. No goods or services would be produced if people did not voluntarily exchange their personal resources for money.

Clarify: Productive resources include human resources (labor), natural resources (land), capital resources (produced means of production), and entrepreneurship. **Money** is not a productive resource although at times it is called a financial capital.

There are two other kinds of resources that people work with. **Natural resources** are *the resources of the earth used in the production of goods and services.* They include such things as wood, land, and water, and minerals like iron and gold.

Capital resources are *the machines, equipment, and buildings used in the production of goods and services.* In factories and on farms, these capital resources shape natural resources into goods and services. Capital resources increase the number of goods and services that can be produced. Farmers can farm more land with tractors, for example, than they could by hand. Some people believe that information is a capital resource because having it increases the amount that can be produced.

Explain: Price is the point at which supply (availability) and demand (desirability) intersect.

Producers decide what resources to use by using the principle of substitution. If a machine can perform needed work less expensively than human labor, the producer uses the machine. Sometimes the reverse happens, and a producer replaces a costly machine with less costly human labor.

Producers use money to obtain resources. They pay money in wages to workers. Similarly, they use money to buy natural and capital resources. Money makes these transactions easier, just as it makes exchanges between

Critical Thinking: Would the **relative** scarcity of a good change with the price? If the price of oil rises, would more oil become available (and oil become relatively less scarce)?

Elaborate: Businesses substitute one productive resource for another in their production process. When the relative price of a resource becomes higher than a substitute, the producer will use the substitute.

Example: It was once thought that the only way to pick cherries was by hand. Cherries are small. They bruise easily, and they are hard to pick. However, as the wages for farm labor rose, the cherrypicker was invented and came into widespread use. The cherrypicker spreads a tarpaulin under the tree, then a claw grabs the trunk of the tree and shakes. All the ripe cherries fall off onto the tarp and are poured into a bin. The higher price of labor made it feasible to use capital (cherrypicker) as a substitute.

Businesses use human resources (the workers), natural resources (the land), and capital resources (the tractor).

producers and consumers easier. Money is sometimes called *capital,* but it should not be confused with capital resources. As a medium of exchange, money is used to obtain all types of resources.

Human, natural, and capital resources are used in combination by businesses to produce all goods and services. For example, in a gas station the human resources are the workers, the natural resources are the oil products being sold, and the capital resources are the building, the gas pumps, and the tools. Money is used to obtain all of these resources.

Scarcity Limits Production and Consumption

Like personal resources, productive resources are scarce. The amount of goods and services produced and consumed is limited by the amount of available resources. A gas station can pump only as much gas as the oil company supplies. The oil company can supply only as much gas as it is willing to obtain and refine at the going price. Drivers who stop at the gas station can buy only as much gas as they have money and room in their tanks for. The gas station (the producer) and the driver (the consumer) both face the problem of scarcity.

Because of scarcity, producers must choose what to produce. If you owned a hen, you could use it to produce eggs or to provide meat. Once you used it for meat, you could not have eggs.

In deciding whether to produce eggs or meat, you'd consider the same factors Angela used in deciding whether or not to change her car's oil herself. You rank your goals according to your values. Let's say that first you want a steady supply of food and second you want a variety of food. Producing eggs has two benefits: you'll have eggs often, and, when you're tired of eggs, you can trade them with your neighbor for vegetables. The opportunity cost of keeping the hen to lay eggs is that you cannot eat roast chicken. But since the opportunity cost of eating the hen is having less food, you'd decide to produce eggs.

Focus: Producers also use the decision-making process.

World Economy: East and West Germany have merged into an economy that allows free choice. What adjustments will East German citizens have in making their own choices?

Most producer decisions are not all-or-nothing choices like this one. Automakers do not have to select only one type of car to produce; they decide what combination of luxury cars, sports cars, and subcompacts to make. Still, the total number of cars of all kinds that they can produce is limited by scarcity.

Because our personal resources are scarce, our consumer choices are also limited—we cannot satisfy all of our wants. Nevertheless, depending on others to produce goods and services lets us satisfy more wants than we could on our own, and this great variety of goods and services that is produced gives us many alternatives to choose from. Of course, we must also have the right to choose, and our society gives us that right.

SOCIAL PRINCIPLES ALLOW US TO CHOOSE

The economic system of the United States is based on five principles:

- Free choice
- Self-interest
- Free competition
- Private property
- Limited government

Critical Thinking: Adam Smith suggested that individuals, making decisions in their best interest, would benefit society as a whole as if "led by an invisible hand." "By pursuing his own interest he frequently promotes that of the society more effectually than when he really intends to promote it." (*Wealth of Nations,* 1776) Ask students to evaluate this process and determine why this occurs.

In the next few pages, we'll describe how, according to theory, the United States economy works by following these principles.

Free Choice

Our society establishes our right to choose for ourselves. Some societies limit that right more than others, but our limits are few. Economic life in the United States is based on the many choices we make: what careers to enter, what products to buy, where to live, what to eat, whom to associate with, where to go on vacation, and countless other choices we make every day and throughout our lives.

Our society gives us this freedom out of a belief that people will be most satisfied if they make their own choices. Remember George, who needed to choose between going on a trip and being in a play? Someone else choosing for George might not pick the alternative that George would pick. That's why the principle of free choice is so important.

Focus: The concept of **self-interest** is the basis of Adam Smith's "invisible hand" theory.

Emphasize: Competition is the consumer's best protection. Producers are restrained in their price increases, consumers have a wider choice of goods and services, and resources are used more efficiently because of competition.

Discussion: How does self-interest play a role in voting on a school levy issue?

Self-Interest

We exercise our right to choose out of self-interest—our concern for our own well-being and for the satisfaction of our wants. As consumers, we act in our self-interest to satisfy as many of our most important wants as possible by using as few resources as possible. A business's self-interest is to satisfy consumers in order to increase its profits—the money it makes.

You might think that all of this competing self-interest would produce chaos and confusion. Such chaos does not rule, however. According to the principle of voluntary exchange, a producer and a consumer willingly exchange goods or services for money because both feel they will benefit. When each of us pursues our own benefit, society as a whole seems to benefit. Each of our actions works as a check on the actions of others. For instance, if a business was too selfish in its desire for profits and made inferior products, it would fail. Customers have free choice; they are not forced to buy things. Because of that freedom, they will avoid buying a product they don't think will satisfy their wants—it would not be in their self-interest. In order to survive, then, the business must provide products that the public will buy. It's true that some unhealthy or unsafe products are sometimes produced. For this reason, the government has taken action to limit these abuses by passing laws and regulating business. Generally self-interest leads businesses away from producing things that people don't want.

Free Competition

Self-interest does not produce chaos, but it does produce competition. The principle of free competition means that anyone who has the necessary

In our society, we have free choice to satisfy our wants as we wish.

resources can start a business and provide goods and services. The large numbers of stores show how great this competition is.

Critical Thinking: Some economists suggest that limits to competition are almost always the result of government action, not market forces. How does government limit competition?

Enhancement: The cost of doing business includes payments to productive resources. **Wages** are the return to labor; **rent** or **interest** is the return paid for land and capital; and **normal profits** are the return to entrepreneurship. These returns to productive resources provide an incentive to use the resources in producing a particular good or service instead of a different product.

Expansion: Why do businesses fail? What impact does this have on workers, consumers, and other businesses?

Emphasize: Although there is disagreement over how extensive a role government should have in the economy, there is general agreement that government does have a role in making sure the market functions smoothly.

Free competition also provides another check on business's ability to do harm in its pursuit of self-interest. The business that makes poor products or sells them for high prices must worry about competitors who make better products or sell them at lower prices or both. Those competitors, in turn, must watch yet other competitors whose products might perform even better or cost even less. All consumers benefit from this competition, because they are able to get a more satisfying product for a more satisfying price.

Free competition, then, is a result of free choice and it also allows free choice. It results from free choice because anyone who wants to, and who has the necessary resources, can start a business. It allows free choice because it results in many different alternatives for consumers to choose from. By creating more alternatives, competition is one of the best forms of consumer protection.

Competition is another area in which the economy doesn't always work the way it should. Some businesses grow to be so large that they can restrict the ability of others to compete. Here again, the government may decide to reduce the power of those giants and bring competition back. In some cases, though, the government believes that only a huge firm could afford to provide a good or service. It may decide that limited competition by such a firm is acceptable.

Private Property

The fourth principle of our economy is private property—our right to own our labor, land, money, and goods. Like our right to pursue our own self-interest, our right to property allows us to try to satisfy our wants in the way we prefer. The business owner's right to keep profits provides the incentive for entering business. The right to make money makes it worthwhile to spend the time, energy, and skills involved in operating a business. The paychecks that workers receive offer similar incentives. They allow workers to satisfy their wants by providing money for them to spend on goods and services.

Limited Government

According to theory, the role of the government is limited to four actions. First, it should provide services that businesses can't or won't provide. Second, it should act to promote competition, as we mentioned earlier. Third, the government should make and enforce laws to ensure that people and businesses, in pursuing their own self-interest, do not infringe on the rights of others. Fourth, government should try to protect us in our right to own property. To do these four tasks, government uses the taxes it collects from producers and consumers.

People disagree over exactly what government should do to fulfill these four roles. Consumer groups, for example, might ask government to pass strict rules concerning, say, environmental protection. Businesses,

Analytical Writing: The number of eligible voters who actually vote in elections is decreasing each year. Have students research the reasons for this drop-off in voting and write an essay including their opinions of why people are not voting and what can be done to increase participation.

Critical Thinking: Review articles from periodicals relating to the last national election, then ask students to report on the major economic issues. Who is affected by these economic issues? Who will pay the costs? Who will benefit? What effect will alternative solutions have on the economy?

Summary: The economic environment affects our ability to make personal decisions. This interaction also affects businesses and their decision making.

Governments make choices through representatives who are elected by voters.

on the other hand, may argue that they can't operate effectively with too many controls on their production methods. They may say that the rules are unneeded and charge that the government is overregulating.

In the end, each of us helps decide how involved the government should be in the economy. We influence government decisions through our power of voting. If some people feel that the government is interfering with their right to private property by making taxes too high, they can vote for candidates who agree with them. The same is true if people think that government is not doing enough to promote competition or is making the wrong choices for the public good.

SUMMARY

- We all have wants that we must use our personal resources to satisfy. We decide to satisfy our most important wants in such a way that we use the least of our resources.
- Scarcity results when our desire for a resource exceeds its availability, because the resource is available but hard to obtain, or simply because it is limited.
- The basic economic problem of unlimited wants and limited resources forces all individuals and societies to make choices.

- In choosing which wants to satisfy, we consider our goals, our values, the benefits of each alternative, and the cost of lost opportunities.
- Because of scarcity, choosing to satisfy one want means being unable to satisfy others.
- We can satisfy more wants—and more complex wants—by depending on others to produce goods and services. We exchange goods and services willingly with others.
- We can exchange goods and services directly by bartering for other goods and services or indirectly by using money.
- Money lets us obtain more goods and services than direct exchange does. It also gives us a way to measure the value of goods, services, and our time, skills, and energy.
- Producers use natural, human, and capital resources to produce goods and services.
- Production and consumption are limited by scarcity.
- Five principles underlie the United States economy: free choice, self-interest, free competition, private property, and limited government. The economy doesn't always work as smoothly in reality as theory says it should.

Key Terms

Match each of the following terms with the definition that most suits it.

barter	interdependence	price	substitution
capital resources	medium of exchange	producers	voluntary exchanges
consumers	natural resources	scarcity	wage
goods	opportunity cost	services	wants
human resources			

a. machines, equipment, and buildings used in the production of goods and services

b. those who provide goods and services for consumers

c. products that people buy

d. the direct exchange of goods and services

e. the resources of the earth used in the production of goods and services

f. our feelings that we lack something that will satisfy us

g. a situation in which the desire for a specific resource exceeds the ability to obtain it

h. people who purchase goods and services for personal use

i. the workers whose time, skills, and energy are used to produce goods and services

j. replacing one way of satisfying a want with another that uses less of valuable resources

k. the value of the benefit that is given up when choosing one alternative over another

l. our reliance on others and theirs on us

m. an object that is generally accepted as payment for goods and services

n. trades that are made between willing participants who both think they will benefit

o. actions of value that people pay others to perform

p. how much money it costs to obtain a good or service and what it is worth compared to other goods or services

q. how much producers are willing to pay and workers are willing to accept for their time and skills

Review Questions

1. How do our wants affect us? What resources do we use to satisfy our wants?
2. What principle helps us decide how to use our personal resources? How do we follow that principle?
3. What is scarcity? How can you prevent scarcity from becoming worse?
4. What does scarcity force us to do? Why?
5. What factors do we consider in making choices?
6. What is opportunity cost? How can this idea help us to make choices?
7. How does interdependence increase our ability to satisfy our wants?
8. Describe the relationship between producers and consumers. Why do they make exchanges?
9. What characteristics of money make it useful?
10. What two factors determine prices? What two factors determine wages?
11. What resources are used to produce goods and services? Give examples of each resource for a particular business.
12. What are the five principles on which the United States economy is based? Does the economy really work the way theory says it is supposed to?

Projects

1. Make a chart of the decisions you make during an entire day—where you go, whom you see, what you eat, what you do. In the first column, list the decision. In the second, write what want each decision was meant to satisfy. In the third, show whether the want was satisfied. Finally, write down whether satisfying any of these wants created a new want. Compare your findings with your classmates'.
2. Make a chart listing all of the goods and services you obtained or used during one day. In one column, indicate what wants each one satisfied. In the next column, estimate how much each one cost in money, time, skills, and energy. Discuss the charts in class: what other ways might you have used resources to satisfy the same wants?
3. Pick one good or service you identified in the previous project. Visit the place where you bought it or where it was made, and observe all of the tasks that are required to produce it. Take notes on what you see and make a chart showing the tasks and the order in which they are performed. Try to think about necessary functions that you cannot see (for example, flour must be milled and transported before pizza dough can be made). Then go to the library and do some research to see how accurate your chart was. Make a list of all the different jobs that are involved in providing that good or service.
4. Conduct a class poll on decision making. Each student should interview parents or close friends about a major economic decision they made recently. Questions to ask may include these:
   What were your alternatives, and how did you choose among them?
   What resources did you have to use?
   What were the opportunity costs of your decisions?
   If you had to make the same decision today, would you select the same alternative? Why or why not?
   You could also ask these questions of a local businessperson about a recent business decision he or she made. Now put the answers together. What do the answers show about the way people make decisions? Could the results be more satisfying if they decided differently?

PART TWO

You and the Economy

The Marketplace in the United States 3

Overview: Participants in the U.S. economy interact with each other to supply the goods and services demanded in the market. We have a mixed-market system that is disorderly, chaotic, turbulent, and successful. To thrive in this system, students must understand how our system differs from other economic systems, and how they can play a role in this system.

OBJECTIVES

This chapter will help you to:

1. Distinguish between the major economic systems.
2. Identify seven goals of an economic system.
3. Diagram and explain the circular flow of goods and services.
4. Explain how supply and demand determine prices and wages.
5. Discuss how imports and exports affect the economy.

Anna needed a car. "Not a fancy one," she told her friend Stanley. "Just a little, ordinary, sturdy car that gets good gas mileage. I'd like to get around 35 miles a gallon."

"Plenty of cars get that kind of mileage nowadays," Stanley assured her.

Anna made a face. "Yeah, but some of them are so ugly. I mean *ug-ly!*" They both laughed. "Anyway, it's not just mileage I'm after. I need a car that I can rely on—one that won't get recalled and that won't break down."

"That makes sense," Stanley agreed. "You can't afford to buy a car that you can't use."

"You know what I've been looking at? A couple of those Japanese models. They have real good repair records. I think they—"

"You'd buy a foreign car?" Stanley interrupted. "How could you? American auto workers are out of work. American car companies are hurting. Don't you realize what you'd be doing to our economy by giving your business to foreign competitors?"

Anna looked down at the ground. "I was afraid you'd say something like that. But my parents have had two American cars in the past five years, and they were nightmares. I don't want to take any chances. Besides, a Japanese car looks like the best deal for me. Maybe buying an American car would help *our* economy, but don't I have to think about *my* economy? Anyway, does it *really* hurt our economy?"

Focus: Production provides the goods and services we demand. Neither production nor consumption could function without the other.

HOW DO ANNA'S ACTIONS affect "our economy"? How does the state of our economy influence Anna's actions? What is this thing we call "our economy," anyway? In this chapter, you'll learn about the various ways that groups make economic choices and the goals they try to achieve. Then you'll learn about the participants in our economy and how they work together. Finally, you'll see how imports and exports affect our economy.

ECONOMIC SYSTEMS ORGANIZE PRODUCTION AND CONSUMPTION

An economic system is a framework for determining how a large group of people makes economic choices. These choices involve *production*—what goods and services we make and at what price we sell them. They also involve *consumption*—what goods and services we buy from other producers and at what cost.

Creative Writing: Ask students to write an essay on how production and consumption decisions are made in the United States.

Economic Systems Determine the Economic Choices of Groups

Each of us makes choices because of a basic problem: we do not have enough resources to satisfy all of our wants, but no one acts alone. We are all part of a group called *society*. A society makes economic choices, too. These group choices determine how the members of society can make their own personal choices. Society's choices answer three basic questions: what is produced, how much is produced, and for whom it is produced. The answers to all three questions, though, are limited by the scarcity of resources.

What is produced depends first on what resources a society has. People who live on rocky land may raise sheep, those who live on plains may raise cattle, and those who live on a small island are likely to fish.

How much is produced is a trickier question. If it takes the same resources to build ten cars as it does to make three trucks, how many of each should the society make?

For whom it is produced is another difficult question. How does a society decide who gets what is produced?

All societies answer those three questions, but each one answers them differently. *The institutions and principles that determine how a society answers the basic economic questions* form that society's **economic system**. Those answers will affect the choices individuals can make. Suppose a society raises sheep but not cattle. People can eat lamb and wear wool, but they won't be able to eat beef and wear leather unless they can get them from another society. Let's look at the kinds of economic systems there are.

Clarify: Often the terms capitalism, socialism, and communism are used to identify economic systems. This is incorrect; these terms are actually classifications used to describe political systems. However, a correlation can be made between political systems and their economic systems. Capitalism encourages a market system or a mixed-market system. Socialism and communism usually adopt a command economy since the centralized political authority generally also wants centralized economic decision making.

World Economy: During 1989 and 1990, what were Eastern European countries actually rebelling against? Did they want to end the personal repression of their political systems? Or did they want to adopt a new economic system?

Discussion: Encourage students to list countries that have predominantly traditional, command, and market economic systems.

Four Systems Offer Four Ways to Choose

Societies have developed four basic types of economic systems: traditional, command, market, and mixed. What separates one system from another is how economic choices are made.

The **traditional system** is *one in which economic choices are based on the customs or habits of the group.* The wants and needs of individuals are generally not considered. Society produces what it has always produced. It tends to produce the amount it has always produced because a traditional system is not likely to develop more efficient methods. Members of the group receive goods based on their traditional roles.

In a **command system**, *economic choices are made by one or a few individuals who represent a central authority.* Again, little attention is paid to the individual's wants—unless, of course, that person is one of the decision makers. Leaders decide what is produced, how much is produced, and for whom it is produced. People then satisfy their wants as best they can within the limits the leaders set.

A **market system** is *one in which group economic choices are determined by the decisions of many individuals.* Each person's decisions contribute to the group decisions, although no one person is powerful enough to influence group choices alone. For example, a person may love a certain TV show, but that show will be cancelled unless enough other viewers like it too. In the market system, then, what is produced is determined by what most people want and are willing to pay for. How much is produced is decided by how many people want it. Who gets what is produced depends on who has the money to buy it.

The fourth type of economic system is the most common kind—the **mixed system**. A mixed system *combines features of the traditional, command, and*

Table 3.1 Another Way of Looking at Economic Systems. We often hear the terms *capitalism, socialism,* and *communism*. Let's compare these systems.

	Free Choice	Free Competition	Self-interest	Private Property	Limited Government
Capitalism	People have very free choice.	People are free to open most types of businesses.	People act in their self-interest as long as they don't infringe the rights of others.	People have the right to own property.	The government plays a limited role.
Socialism	People have fairly free choice.	People are free to own small businesses, but the government controls major industries.	People act in their self-interest, though the government makes many decisions in the public interest.	People have the right to own some property, but the government owns much.	The government plays a major role.
Communism	People have very little free choice.	People cannot own businesses; the government does.	Self-interest is second to the public interest.	People have a limited right to own property.	The government controls the economy.

market systems. No society has a pure command or market system. In all societies, for instance, traditional roles of men and women influence the choices that particular men and women make. There is no pure command system because all societies allow some degree of freedom of choice. Every system has some command elements — laws that forbid some economic actions. (Table 3.1 shows another way to define economic systems.)

***Expansion:* Privatization** is the process of transferring from public or government control or ownership to private ownership. Great Britain and many developing countries in Latin America and sub-saharan Africa have been actively privatizing many of their state-owned enterprises.

World Economy: Why have Great Britain, Mexico, and Eastern European countries become so active in the privatization of their state-owned enterprises?

Different Societies Have Different Goals

Societies, like individuals, make their economic decisions on the basis of the goals they want to pursue. Not all societies pursue the same goals, and even if they pursue the same ones, different societies will emphasize different goals. For example, a command society that values security the most will downplay freedom to choose. Among the goals that our society pursues are the following seven:

- *Freedom to choose*—to work, to spend, and to save according to one's own wants
- *Equity*—to see who gains and who loses from an economic choice
- *Security*—to protect against economic risks like unemployment, poverty in old age, business failures, and natural disasters
- *Full employment*—to ensure that each worker's labor is fully used
- *Efficiency*—to get the most out of available resources or to produce goods using the fewest resources

- *Price stability*—to prevent sudden large increases or decreases in price
- *Growth*—to increase incomes, profits, and other benefits

Research: Assign each student one of the five principles of a market system. Ask them to research this principle and analyze the deviations that appear in the U.S. economy. (Free choice—Can we purchase automobiles without the added expense of seat belts? Can we use our home for any legal purpose we choose? Can our schools hire teachers without state certification?)

The emphasis placed on these goals may vary from group to group within our society. The Chamber of Commerce (a group of business people) may stress different goals than the Gray Panthers (a group of retired people). The emphasis has also varied within our society over time. In the 1800s the United States placed the highest value on freedom. After the high unemployment of the Great Depression of the 1930s, however, people became more concerned with security. As a result, government involvement in the economy (and government spending) increased. In a sense, the government determined how much freedom its people would give up in exchange for how much security.

Choosing more of one goal may mean having less of another. Societies—and the people who live in them—must remember this fact when they make choices. Increasing efficiency by using machines to do work may mean fewer jobs. Increasing security by ensuring a minimum income for all people may make prices increase.

The United States Has a Modified Market System

Critical Thinking: Ask students to evaluate the goals that are affected by recent government decisions.

As we have seen, there are no pure economic systems. All are to some extent mixed. In the United States we have a **modified market system**. This is *a mixed system based on the principles of the market system but having features of command and traditional systems.*

We can see how the pure market system has been modified in the United States by comparing our economy to the five principles of a market economy. These five principles are free choice, self-interest, free competition, private property, and limited government.

Focus: Trade-offs between goals are important in evaluating societal decisions. If our society supports the freedom to choose, then constraints on that will weaken the goal. If we encourage businesses to produce efficiently, but limit their ability to adjust the number of employees they have in order to provide employee security, then we have increased security at the cost of efficiency and freedom of choice.

Do we have *free choice?* Yes, mostly. However, laws prevent us from buying some goods and services — hard drugs, for instance. In the past tradition restricted the freedom of some people, like women, to enter certain careers, but that is not the case today. Basically we are free to buy what we want and work where we want.

Can we act in our own *self-interest?* Again, the answer is a qualified yes. For example, out of a concern for the public interest, society has passed laws to punish people who drive while drunk. People believed that the benefits of protection for everyone were more important than the cost of lost freedom to a few.

Do we have *free competition?* Not exactly. This is one of the greatest changes from the pure market system. Free competition requires two conditions. First, anyone must be easily able to begin to produce a good or service. Second, there must be enough producers so that no one producer or group of producers can dominate the market. Three variations from this second point are found in our economy.

The purest kind of domination of the market is the **monopoly**. When a monopoly exists, *only one firm provides a product or service and thus controls* *the entire market.* We seldom find a monopoly today. The government has the power to break up monopolies to promote competition.

One special kind of monopoly does exist, though. A **public monopoly** is *a single producer that controls a market through a right granted by a government to ensure that essential services are provided.* Local utility companies are the best examples of such monopolies. The service is so important and the equipment so costly that it is more efficient to allow only one supplier. Still, the government closely watches the practices of a public monopoly to ensure that the public is not harmed by its decisions.

Clarify: **Public monopolies** are also called natural monopolies. A natural monopoly results from an industry in which **economies of scale** are so great that one firm can produce at an average cost that is lower than if there were more than one producer.

The second kind of noncompetitive market is the oligopoly. An **oligopoly** exists when *a few large firms produce most or all of a given product or service and control a market.* Oligopolies control many large industries in the United States. We hear and read about the "big three" automakers and the "seven sisters" oil companies. Companies in an oligopoly are highly interdependent. If one firm raises or lowers its prices, the others often follow.

Example: Breakfast cereals is an example of a oligopoly since three or four companies produce most of the cereals. However, this depends on how you define the market. If you define the market as *breakfast cereal,* then the cereal industry is oligopolistic. If you define the market as *foods eaten at breakfast,* cereal firms compete with muffins, peanut butter sandwiches, bacon and eggs, bagels, maybe even cold pizza. The latter market would be quite competitive.

Slightly different is **monopolistic competition**. This is *a market in which there are a few sellers, but each sells primarily to a specific group of buyers.* Each seller can act more independently than with an oligopoly without fear of losing its group. For example, there are many brands of toothpaste, but each one tries to create a different image that appeals to different people. Some say they are better at preventing cavities; some claim that they make the user more attractive. Because consumers tend to be loyal to their favorite brand, the company can raise prices to a certain extent without worrying about losing customers. If it raises prices too high, though, consumers will begin buying other brands.

Why do markets become uncompetitive? First, successful businesses grow larger, but unsuccessful businesses fail. Second, as businesses get bigger, they tend to get better at making and selling goods. That can drive out competitors. Third, it may cost too much for a new firm to start up. Finally, as long as no one firm has the power of a monopoly, the government may permit limited competition to exist.

What about the other two principles of a market economy? *Private property* is the rule in the United States, but there are exceptions. Federal, state, and local governments own property that they use to govern and to defend the nation. Governments also own property that is used by the public, like highways and forests.

Finally, *limited government* is not the case. Since the depression of the 1930s, the federal government has taken many economic actions to provide jobs and services and to regulate business. Whether government plays too great a role in the economy is often debated.

List: Ask students for examples of industries with different market structures.

WE INTERACT IN OUR MODIFIED MARKET SYSTEM

An economic system is a framework in which decisions are made, but who makes these decisions? In a command system, they are made by a few people who can be identified easily. In a market system, however, everyone contributes to the economic decisions, but in a way that is hard to define.

Review: Earlier we discussed the market for breakfast cereals and foods for breakfast. Returning to this discussion may help the students' understanding about markets.

Critical Thinking: How does government determine what is for the public good?

Clarify: It is important that students understand that the "three actors in our economy" are really one actor, in three different roles. They know individuals are consumers, workers, and citizens. Businesses are merely legal organizations that carry out production and are owned and operated by individuals. Government is the system of rule and control determined by individual citizens. Thinking of business and government as separate actors leads to mistaken conclusions such as we should tax business more (assuming that means less tax on individuals), or that we, as individuals, are powerless to affect change in government. In the United States, individuals are the key actors no matter what role we are playing.

Our Economic System Has Three Actors

There are three kinds of actors in our economic system: individuals, businesses, and governments. Each acts differently. Individuals try to manage their personal resources (money, time, skills, and energy) to satisfy as many wants as possible.

Businesses use land, labor, and capital to make goods or services that consumers will buy. They do this in order to earn as much profit as they can.

Governments regulate the actions of the other two. They tax the other two actors to provide services. They also try to promote the public good, as we saw in the case of drunk driving laws.

The Three Actors Interact in a Market

All three actors make exchanges in a market. A market is not a single place. It could be anywhere from a door-to-door seller's route to a corner store to an office to the New York Stock Exchange. In fact, in some transactions the actors don't even meet. Someone buying through mail order may never talk to the seller, and few people meet with the government workers who handle their taxes. A **market**, then, is *a way by which goods and services are exchanged, usually for money.*

A market is not always a place—it is any way people exchange goods and services.

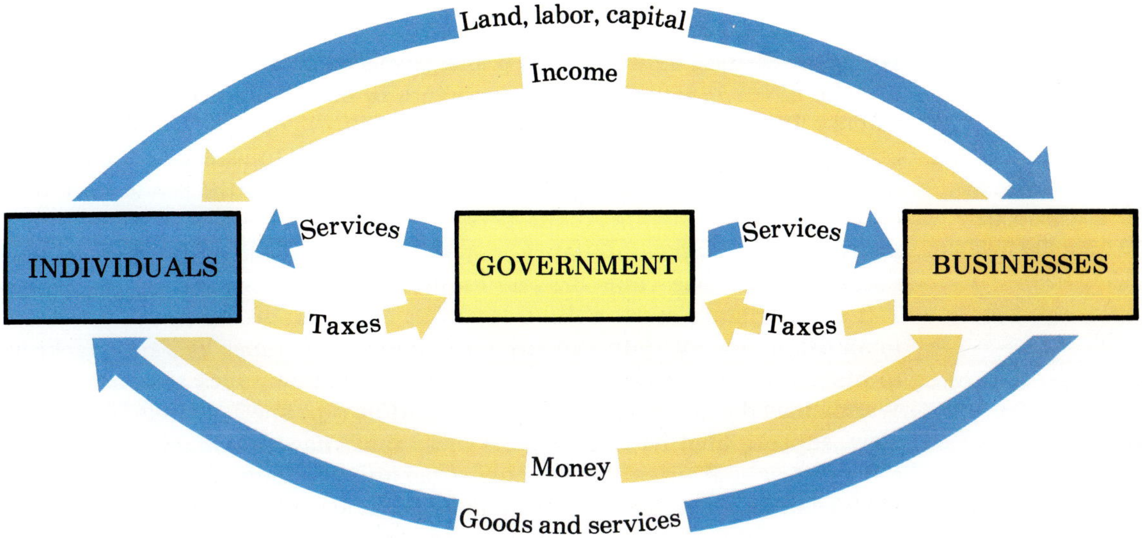

Figure 3.1 The Circular Flow of Goods and Services

Focus: The circular flow model helps students visualize economic activity. Emphasize that individuals are the actors throughout the circular flow model.

How do these three actors interact? Individuals, as workers, sell their labor to businesses in return for wages. Then they act as consumers to buy goods and services from businesses, which are *producers*. These actions make a circle. (See the circular flow in Figure 3.1.) Governments enter the scene when they tax individuals and businesses and use these taxes to provide services. Money serves as a medium of exchange to make all these transactions easier.

Supply and Demand Reveal How Economic Actors Interact

To decide what actions to take—whether to sell and when to buy—all three actors watch *prices*. If the price of a product seems too high, consumers will not buy it. On the other hand, if they feel the price of a product is too low, producers will not make it. If the price of labor seems too high, producers will stop hiring. If the price of labor is too low, workers will work elsewhere.

Clarify: Individuals not only sell labor to business; they also own businesses, sell other resources they own (land or capital) to business, and loan their money to business.

What makes a price too high or too low is not its dollar cost. A $30,000 car is not "too high" if consumers will buy as many as are built. A 75¢ candy bar is "too high" if nobody will buy it. When we say that the price of a product is "too high" or "too low," we aren't comparing it to the price of other products. Rather, we're simply saying that at a "too high" price, people aren't willing to buy as much of a product as producers are willing to make.

Before a price is set, a good or service actually has a range of possible prices. Some prices in that range will be higher than consumers are willing to pay. Others will be lower than producers are willing to accept. At some price in the range, though, consumers will buy as many products as producers will produce. This price is arrived at by studying supply and demand.

Define: The **Law of Demand** states that, holding everything constant, as price falls the quantity demanded rises. Likewise, as price rises the quantity demanded falls.

Demand Shows Consumers' Willingness to Buy Supply and demand are the forces that move economic actors to act. **Demand** motivates consumers. It is *a consumer's willingness and ability to buy a product at various prices over a given time.* If a music store sells all its tapes for $8.98, Andrea may limit herself to buying one tape every other month. David may buy only new tapes by Paula Abdul, perhaps one a year. Jesse may happily buy anything that strikes his fancy, say two tapes a month. Wanda may buy nothing at all. (See Table 3.2 and Figure 3.2.)

Expansion: Economists often use the phrase *ceteris parabis,* other things being equal. Many factors affect the demand for a good.

If another store starts selling tapes for $6.98, Andrea may treat herself to an extra tape every few months. David may add tapes by Janet Jackson to his collection. Jesse may start buying three new tapes a month. Even Wanda may decide to buy that classical guitar tape she's wanted for so long. Now, suppose another store marks these tapes down to $3.98 for a special clearance sale. Andrea may go on a spree and buy four or five at once. The others may also increase their demand. (David probably won't. Somehow, tapes by Paula Abdul and Janet Jackson don't seem to get marked down for clearance.)

Demand has two features. Willingness is the obvious one. Demand shows a consumer's aim to satisfy a want. Ability, however, is just as important.

Table 3.2 Yearly Demand for Records

Price	Number of Records Consumers Are Willing to Buy				
	Andrea	David	Jesse	Wanda	Total
$10.98	1	0	4	0	5
$ 8.98	6	1	24	0	31
$ 6.98	9	2	36	1	48
$ 3.98	13	2	50	3	68

Math Activity: Develop a demand schedule for doughnuts using real-world data.

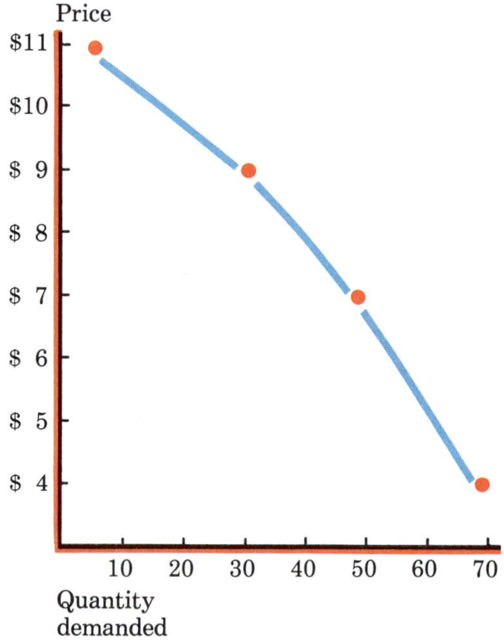

Figure 3.2 Demand Curve for Tapes

There has to be money to back up that willingness. Demand does not mean actual purchases. It only indicates consumers' willingness and ability to make a purchase at a given price.

Define: The **Law of Supply** states that, holding everything constant, as price falls the quantity supplied falls. Likewise, as price rises the quantity supplied rises. This direct relationship develops the upward sloping supply curve.

The demand of all consumers for a product is called the **market demand**. This is *the sum of all the individual demands for a product in a market.* The market demand for tapes at $8.98 would be the total number of tapes people were willing and able to buy at that price. As we've seen, the market demand at $6.98 would be higher and at $3.98 higher still. The market demand for tapes at various prices is shown in Figure 3.2.

Supply Shows Producers' Willingness to Sell The other side of the coin is **supply**. It is *a producer's willingness and ability to sell a product at various prices over a given time.*

Critical Thinking: Do the laws of supply and demand work the same way for productive resources?

Again, both features are important. A music store owner might want to see how demand would change if he or she sold tapes at $5.98 each, but consumers would have to buy a lot more tapes to make this $3.00 price cut practical. Unless the purchases add up to cover all the owner's costs—including rent, electricity, and wages, as well as what the tapes cost—he or she will lose money. Another store might try to sell tapes at $9.98. If competitors are selling the same products for less, however, that store would be unable to sell at the higher price for very long.

The number of tapes producers are willing to supply at various prices is shown in Table 3.3 and Figure 3.3. As you can see, supply goes up as price goes up.

Table 3.3 Yearly Supply of Records

Price	Number of Records Producers Are Willing to Sell		
	Store A	Store B	Total
$10.98	22	15	37
$ 8.98	19	12	31
$ 6.98	13	9	22
$ 3.98	3	2	5

Stress: To be an actual part of the demand, the consumer must be able to purchase the product at a given price.

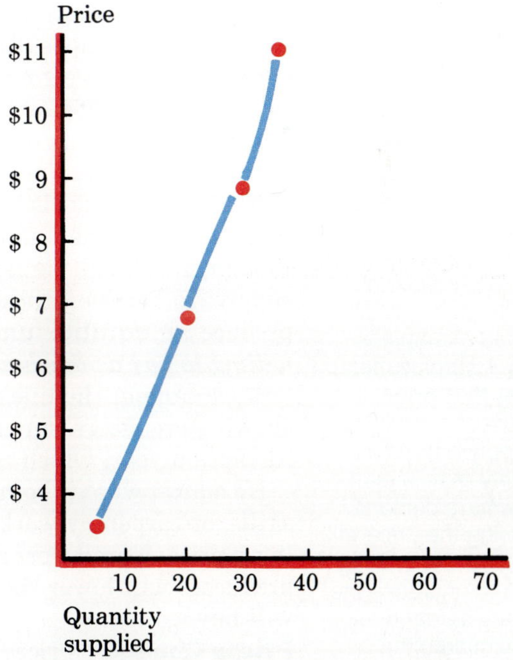

Figure 3.3 Supply Curve for Tapes

Emphasize: The equilibrium point is the point at which everyone is satisfied. Everyone who is willing to produce at that price can sell their product. Everyone who is willing to consume at that price can buy all they want.

Expansion: If a price ceiling below the market price is enforced, then we will have a shortage. (A good example is gasoline in the late 1970s.) A shortage means that **at that price** consumers demand a larger quantity of gasoline than producers are willing to supply. Raising the price will increase the quantity supplied, decrease the quantity demanded, and eliminate the shortage.

Expansion: If a price floor below the market price is enforced, then we will have a surplus. (A good example is milk.) A surplus means that **at that price** producers are willing to supply a greater quantity of milk than consumers demand. Lowering the price will decrease the quantity supplied, increase the quantity demanded, and eliminate the surplus.

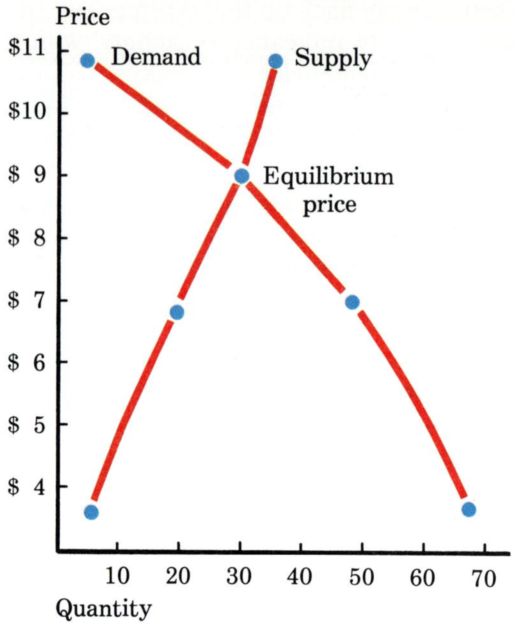

Figure 3.4 Supply and Demand Interact to Produce Price

Supply and Demand Interact to Set Price As we have seen in the example of the tapes, the quantity demanded generally increases as price goes down. This is a simple matter of people acting in their own self-interest. When the price of tapes is lower, people have more money left over to buy other products, even other tapes.

The quantity that producers supply, on the other hand, increases as price increases. This, too, is because of self-interest. If producers sell a product at a higher price, they make more profit on each sale. Above a certain price, though, there will be no demand. Below a certain price, there will be no supply. In between those two prices, though, supply and demand meet to produce an **equilibrium price**. This is *the price at which consumers are willing to buy as much as producers are willing to supply*. Figure 3.4 shows how we can put the line showing consumers' demand together with the line showing producers' supply to find that price. At $8.98, producers will supply 31 tapes a year, which is the same number consumers will buy.

No matter what is being sold—airplanes, movie tickets, hamburgers, legal skills, or carpentry work—supply and demand will work together to establish a price. If producers are charging too much and consumers aren't buying, producers will lower their price. If the price comes down, more consumers will buy.

Prices Change Prices don't stay the same over time. Tapes that are $8.98 today may cost $6.98—or $10.98—tomorrow. A number of factors change prices. All of them are related to the basics of supply and demand.

Prices tend to go *up* when:

- *People's incomes go up.* With more money, people will be willing to buy more. When demand goes up, price goes up.
- *Producer costs rise.* If their costs go up, producers will raise prices. How far they can raise prices is determined by demand.
- *Demand for complements goes up.* **Complements** are *related products.* If people buy more compact discs, they will also want more compact disc adapters, cleaning kits, and stereo equipment. With increased demand, the prices for these related goods may increase.

Critical Thinking: How does business know what the market price for the good or service should be?

Explain: The determinants of demand are: (1) consumer tastes and preferences; (2) market size; (3) consumer income; (4) the price of related goods (substitutes or complements); and (5) what consumers expect prices and their income to be in the future.

Explain: The determinants of supply are: (1) change in the price of productive resources; (2) introduction of new technology; (3) change in taxes or subsidies; (4) the price of other goods; (5) market size; and (6) expectations about future prices.

Extension: If consumers become willing and able to buy a larger (or smaller) quantity of CDs at every price, then there is a **change in demand** and the entire demand curve has shifted. This shift is not price related (meaning movement along the demand curve because of price); it means that one or more of the determinants of demand has changed.

Prices tend to go *down* when:

- *Supply increases but demand stays the same.* If more products are available than people are buying, producers must lower the price until they can sell them.
- *Competition increases.* Competition drives prices down in two ways. First, sellers sometimes try to increase their own sales by undercutting the prices of competitors. Second, competition lowers prices simply because it increases supply.
- *Substitutes are introduced.* **Substitutes** are *products that replace existing ones.* The availability of compact discs drives down the demand for tapes, which would reduce the price of tapes.
- *Producer costs decrease.* If new technology makes it cheaper to make a good, producers will be able to sell it for less.

Other circumstances can influence prices. Governments can raise the price of foreign goods by limiting their supply. Governments or other groups can also set price limits. The Organization of Petroleum Exporting Countries (OPEC) sets the price of the oil its members export. The United States government sets a minimum price for dairy products—none are sold at a lower price.

All prices in an economy may change. When prices are generally rising, it is called *inflation.* When the general level of prices decreases, we call it *deflation.*

Supply and Demand Also Set Wages Supply and demand also set workers' wages. After all, wages are the price workers charge for their labor. When workers with a special set of skills are scarce, those skills will bring a high wage. When workers of all types are scarce in a region, wages for all jobs will be higher in that region. As the number of workers—the supply—increases, the price of labor will decrease. *The equilibrium price of labor* is known as the **prevailing wage**.

The prevailing wage, like the equilibrium price of goods, can change. Both the demand for labor and the supply of labor are affected by other circumstances. A new machine might do the work of five people in a factory. This would reduce the demand for workers with those skills and drive down the wages for that job, but the company might need a trained operator to run the new machine. If there aren't many people with that training, the wages for that job will rise.

YOU INTERACT WITH THE ECONOMY: BUYING IMPORTED GOODS

Critical Thinking: Students should examine the growth and influence of multinational corporations. What effect do multinationals have on the domestic and foreign economies?

Research: Ask students to research the domestic industries that rely on exports and those that rely on imports.

Research: Ask students to locate and graph data on U.S. merchandise imports, exports, and the trade balance over a period of time.

World Economy: Increasingly, we are participating in a global economy. The United States has signed a free trade agreement with Canada and is negotiating an agreement with Mexico. Europe is attempting to eliminate trade barriers between European countries and to establish a common currency. The Soviet bloc is attempting to become a participant in world trade. Meanwhile, special-interest groups call for increased trade barriers.

At the beginning of this chapter, Stanley was trying to talk Anna out of buying a foreign-made car. He told her that doing so could be bad for the American economy. Anna told Stanley that a Japanese car would be a good personal economic choice for her. Anna and Stanley are discussing one of the most difficult questions facing an economic system: the role of imports and exports.

Imports are *products brought into one country from another country*. **Exports** are *products sent out from one country to another country*. Any product that is one country's import is another country's export.

Some people argue that imports should be restricted to protect domestic industries, that is, industries in their own country. Other people argue that free trade is best because it promotes happy consumers and efficient markets. How does each of us decide what to do about buying imports?

Where Do Imports Fit In?

The circular flow of goods and services described earlier in this chapter was a closed system. The amount consumers spent on products was the amount they received for selling their labor, minus what they saved and paid in taxes. The amount producers received for selling goods was the amount they spent making them, plus profits and taxes.

Imports and exports break this circular flow, as we can see in Figure 3.5. Imports send dollars outside the circle. The wages paid by domestic producers to domestic workers are no longer used to buy domestic goods. Instead, they're used to buy goods made by foreign producers. Exports work in the opposite way. The wages foreign producers paid to foreign workers are used to buy goods made by domestic producers.

If exports and imports are equal, the circular flow is restored, with a few more stops along the way. If exports are greater than imports, we say there is a *trade surplus*. That means money is coming into the country. If imports are greater than exports, we say there is a *trade deficit*—money is leaving the country. The United States exports huge amounts of food and other products. It imports large quantities of oil, raw materials, and consumer goods. In most recent years, the United States has had a trade deficit.

Do Imports Harm the Economy?

Is Stanley correct in saying that buying a foreign car hurts our economy? Many people think so. Domestic producers cannot sell all they make if consumers buy foreign goods instead. To increase sales they will have to lower their prices, but that lowers their profits. Producers will begin to make less, which leads to the second problem people blame on imports: unemployment. Lower production means fewer jobs.

Others argue that imports are a good thing. They say that competition from other countries will force domestic producers to make better products at lower prices. These people also say that the dollars sent to other countries

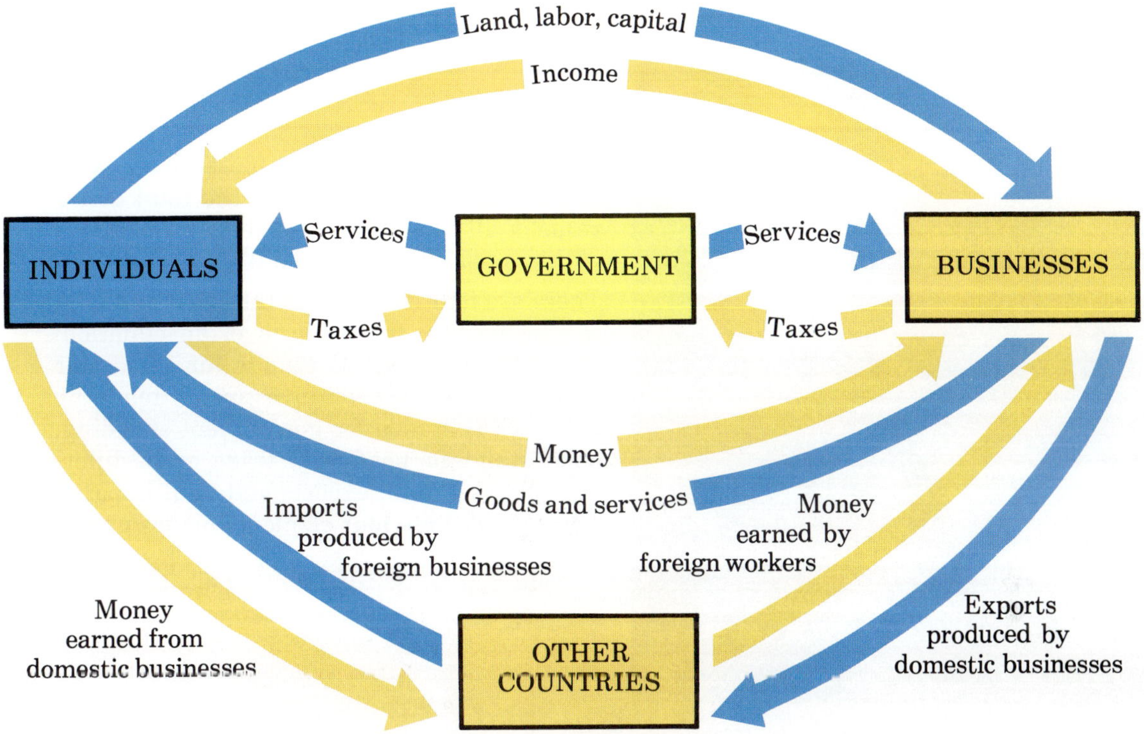

Figure 3.5 How Imports and Exports Affect the Circular Flow of Goods and Services

World Economy: Trade barriers seek to limit the import of foreign products. If the United States raises trade barriers, foreign countries tend to react by increasing their barriers against U.S. products. These trade wars have negative consequences to producers as well as consumers in both countries.

can be returned. Foreign consumers may buy our exports, or foreign investors may invest in our industries. Those who favor trade also argue that by setting limits on imports, a country is asking for trouble. Other countries will simply answer by limiting that country's exports to them.

Both opponents and supporters of trade agree that it can be harmful to an economy if imports exceed exports for many years. In that case, the money that leaves the circular flow is not coming back. The result can be a weaker economy.

Do Imports Help or Hurt Consumers?

The effects of imports on consumers can be seen from their effects on the economy as a whole. Competition from imports can lower prices. This is clearly good for consumers. Too many imports *do* cause domestic firms to lose sales, and those firms *do* respond by laying off workers. These workers are also consumers.

One other point in favor of imports is that they can add richness and variety to our lives. They give us more goods—and more *kinds* of goods—to choose from. According to economist Milton Friedman, "We cannot eat, wear, or enjoy the goods we send abroad," because they are surplus goods—more was produced than consumers want to buy. On the other hand, says

The United States sends billions of tons of food to other countries every year.

A Word About GNP

Have you ever heard a TV anchorperson talk about the "GNP"? Do you know what the GNP is?

The GNP means gross national product. It is an economic statistic we use to measure the state of our economy. The GNP is the total dollar value of all final goods and services produced within a period of time, usually one year.

There are four elements to the GNP, and they can be written in the form of an equation: $C + I + G + F = GNP$. C stands for consumer spending; I stands for investments made by business; G stands for government spending; and F stands for net foreign trade, or the difference between total exports and total imports. The sum of these four elements makes up the GNP.

Summary: Societies form economic systems to decide what shall be produced; how it shall be produced; and for whom it shall be produced.

Friedman, "We eat bananas from Central America, wear Italian shoes, drive German automobiles, and enjoy programs we see on our Japanese TV sets. Our gain from foreign trade is what we import. Exports are the price we pay to get imports."

Anna will think about all of this before she decides what car to buy, and maybe Stanley will think about it, too.

SUMMARY

- An economic system is a framework for determining how a group of people makes economic choices. It determines how a society decides what is produced, how much is produced, and for whom it is produced.
- There are four kinds of economic systems: traditional, command, market, and mixed. To some extent, all systems are mixed, containing elements of the first three types.
- There are seven basic goals our economic system pursues: freedom to choose, equity, security, full employment, efficiency, price stability, and growth. Different groups emphasize different goals, and the emphasis on these goals has changed over time.
- The U.S. has a modified market system. It follows three principles of a market economy with few changes: free choice, self-interest, and private property. The U.S. system doesn't follow the other two principles—free competition and limited government—as closely. Some markets are fairly

uncompetitive, and the government plays a more prominent role in the economy than theory suggests.

- Individuals, businesses, and governments interact in the market in a circular flow.
- Supply and demand determine prices. Demand increases as prices decline. Supply increases as prices rise. At the equilibrium price, supply and demand are equal. Anything that affects supply or demand can cause prices to change.
- Wages—the price of labor—are also determined by supply and demand.
- No economy is independent. Consumers import goods from foreign producers. Producers export goods in foreign markets. Some critics say that too many imports hurt our economy. Other people say that imports keep our economy competitive and are good for consumers.

Key Terms

Match each of the following terms with the definition that most suits it.

command system	exports	mixed system	prevailing wage
complements	imports	modified market system	public monopoly
demand	market	monopolistic competition	substitutes
economic system	market demand	monopoly	supply
equilibrium price	market system	oligopoly	traditional system

a. an economic system that combines features of traditional, command, and market systems

b. products sent out from one country to another country

c. the price at which consumers are willing to buy as much as producers are willing to supply

d. a single producer that controls a market through a right granted by a government to ensure that services are provided

e. an economic system in which economic choices are based on the customs or habits of the group

f. a producer's willingness and ability to sell a product at various prices over a given time

g. a consumer's willingness and ability to buy a product at various prices over a given time

h. the institutions and principles that determine how a society answers the basic economic questions

i. a situation in which a few large firms produce most or all of a given product or service and control a market

j. an economic system in which group economic choices are determined by the decisions of many individuals

k. products brought into one country from another country

l. the sum of all the individual demands for a product in a market

m. a way by which goods and services are exchanged, usually for money

n. products that replace existing ones

o. a mixed economic system based on the principles of the market system but having features of command and traditional systems

p. an economic system in which economic decisions are made by one or a few individuals who represent a central authority

q. related products

r. a situation in which only one firm provides a product or service and thus controls the entire market

s. a market in which there are a few sellers, but each sells primarily to a specific group of buyers

t. the equilibrium price of labor

Review Questions

1. What are the three basic decisions an economic system enables a society to make?
2. What are the four types of economic systems? Are there any pure examples of economic systems?
3. List the seven basic goals our economic system pursues. Do all people within our system agree about their relative importance? Give an example of people or groups within our system who might disagree. Why would they disagree?
4. Why is the economic system of the U.S. called a modified market system? How does it differ from a pure market system?
5. How does a monopoly differ from an oligopoly? How are they similar? Give an example of each.
6. Who are the three actors in our economic system? Briefly describe the role of each actor.
7. What are the two important features of demand?
8. Why do tapes by Paula Abdul and Janet Jackson usually not get marked down for clearance?
9. What is equilibrium price? What happens to goods priced higher? What about goods priced lower?
10. Name three factors that can make prices go up. Name three factors that can make prices go down.
11. What is the circular flow of goods and services? Discuss some of the ways imports and exports affect this flow.

Projects

1. Take a poll of attitudes in your community. Describe to people the seven economic goals explained in this chapter and ask them to rank the goals in order of their importance. Note the interviewee's age and sex and his or her occupation. Put your answers together to see what your community thinks about these goals.
2. Choose another nation or culture and try to determine what kind of economic system it has. Who are the decision makers? What are the goals and values of the system? How are the goals achieved? How successful is the nation in using this system? How do you rate that success? Report what you've found to the class.
3. The federal government has many antitrust laws that it can use to ensure free competition. Around the end of the nineteenth century and in the beginning of the twentieth, many businesses were broken up into smaller units. Go to the library and do some research into monopolies and trust busting. Choose one of the following:
   a. Make a time line showing the history of monopolies in this country, with the names of companies and the actions taken by the government.
   b. Have any companies been able to resist the government's attempts to break them up? List and discuss these cases.
   c. Write a report about a recent antitrust case, describing the effects of the government's decision on the company and on consumers.
4. Research the supply and demand history of home computers. Make a table showing the price and number of units sold for the top five home computers over the years. Then draw a curve showing how the price and the number purchased changed over that time. What caused those changes?
5. Have a class debate on imports and exports. Do imports hurt our economy and should they be restricted? If so, how?

What Business Is All About

4

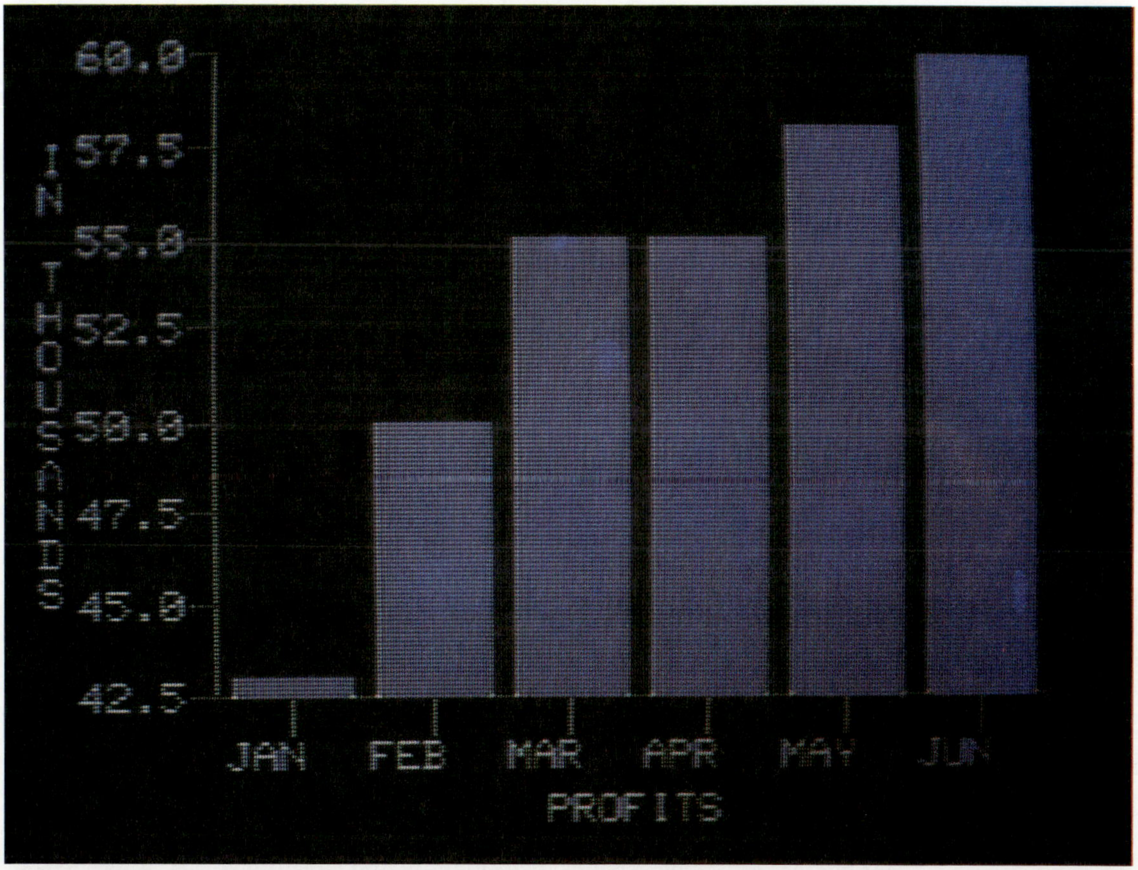

Overview: Randy has been running a business part-time with minimal investment and minimal return. Although expanding this business is attractive, additional investment and risk is necessary.

OBJECTIVES

This chapter will help you to:

1. Explain how going into business is a decision involving risk and reward.
2. Describe how businesses combine resources.
3. Outline the four roles a person may play within business.
4. Classify businesses by what they do.
5. Identify the major forms of business and describe the advantages and disadvantages of each.
6. Evaluate the importance of small business to the economy.

Randy paints houses. He got started last summer. Once school ended, he spent ten days painting his parents' house. When he was almost finished, a neighbor asked if he would paint her house, too. They agreed on a price, and Randy was in business.

Other neighbors, and even complete strangers who passed by, noticed Randy's work and asked him to do their houses. They recommended Randy's work to others, and calls began to come in. Before long, Randy had more work than he could handle. He asked his friend, Otis, if he wanted to make some money. Otis agreed to work for an hourly wage.

Once school began, they worked after school as long as the weather was good. In the spring they started again.

Randy and Otis will graduate in the summer, and Randy wants to go into the painting business full time. "But to do it right," he told Otis, "I'll need some money. I've got the brushes, work clothes, drop cloths, and paints. But I need a truck—we can't keep using the car. And I'll need to take out an ad in the Yellow Pages and hire an answering service. But I haven't been able to save enough yet."

Otis had an idea—"I've got some money. Why don't we both put some in. Then we can be partners!"

But Randy wasn't sure he wanted that. "We could do that," he said, stalling for time. "Let me think about it." Randy liked owning his own business. He wasn't sure he wanted a partner. But where would he get the money?

Define: Profit is the amount by which a business's income exceeds its costs.

IN THIS CHAPTER, you'll learn about business—what it does, what the people in a business do, and the different ways businesses are organized.

BUSINESSES PRODUCE GOODS AND SERVICES FOR PROFIT

Stress: Individuals form businesses to produce goods or services for profit.

We encounter many businesses every day—restaurants and movie theaters, car dealers and bicycle shops, dry cleaners and clothing stores. What do they all have in common? Each is a **business,** or *an individual or a group of individuals who produce goods or services for profit.* The key word here is *profit.* Randy was producing a service when he painted his parent's house. We all produce goods and services every time we do such things as cook dinner or build shelves. Governments also provide services. Among other things, they deliver the mail, run schools, and publish pamphlets full of information for farmers and small business owners.

People who cook and governments that deliver mail are not businesses, however. The difference is that businesses *sell* their goods and services for a profit. **Profit** is *the amount by which a business's income exceeds its expenses.* The desire for profit is the reason people start a business.

Randy wasn't in business when he painted his parents' house. When he painted other people's houses for a fee, though, he was in business.

Profits Reward Risk-Takers

Profit is the goal of any business. The owners of a business want profits so they can use the money they earn to satisfy their own wants. Randy wants to earn enough profits to take a trip. He also wants to make sure his business grows. Otis agreed to work for Randy for a similar reason—he wants money to satisfy his wants, too. Otis's wages, however, are different from Randy's profits. What makes them different is that Randy takes a greater risk. Let's see why.

Expansion: Many charities are not-for-profit corporations. Why would a business organize in a way in which it could not make profits?

Business owners invest their time and money to start a business. In doing so, they are taking a risk. The business may not take in as much money selling a product as it cost to produce it. Then the owners suffer a loss. A **loss** is *the amount by which a business's expenses exceed its income.* The business may not sell anything at all. Then the owners will come up empty-handed, losing the money and time they invested. What if Randy underestimated how much time and paint it would take him to finish a house? By agreeing to be paid less than it cost him to do the job, he would suffer a loss. Otis, on the other hand, took less of a risk—Randy owes him wages for the work he's done.

World Economy: Do command economies have profits? If so, who receives them? If not, what is the incentive to begin a business?

Risk doesn't just apply to small businesses. Even giant corporations take risks—they have no guarantee of a profit. Sometimes a new product they introduce fails, like the famous Edsel of the 1950s. Other times the business itself may collapse, no matter how large. B. Altman and Company, the department store chain, went out of business in 1989.

Expansion: A market economy is a growing, dynamic system. Entrepreneurs have been described as market builders and market destroyers. They identify wants that are not being met or could be met better and form a business to satisfy those wants. In doing this, they may destroy the markets of firms with products they are replacing. Rotary calculators used to be common machines in U.S. offices. With the growth of the calculator industry, rotary calculators were replaced and are now out of business. This reflects the dynamism of the market.

Why would anyone accept *this* risk? The reason is the possibility of profit. If the potential profit is high enough, and the chance of attaining it is reasonable enough, some people will accept the risk and start a business.

Profits Offer Benefits to Society

The desire for profit leads to the great variety of goods and services we can choose from. Without the reward of profits, no one would be willing to take the risk of starting a business. If there were no businesses, few goods and services would be produced.

Profits benefit us as individuals. Corporations (which we'll discuss in detail later) may be owned by thousands of people. Each owner's share of the profits is used to satisfy his or her wants. The desire for profit leads businesses to produce more, better, and less costly goods and services, especially if there is much competition. This benefits consumers. Business owners often use profits to make their businesses grow, which also means more and more affordable goods and services. They also create new jobs, and so provide wages for more people. Finally, governments tax profits and use these taxes to help provide services.

Are Profits Too High?

Some people feel that businesses' profits are too high. Is this the case? The question is difficult to answer. One problem is the difficulty of generalizing. As Figure 4.1 shows, profits vary from industry to industry.

Explain: Are profits too high? How do we determine that profits (or wages, rent, interest) are too high? Incentives must be high enough to cover opportunity costs. The business owner has skills, abilities, and/or funds that are needed by a wide variety of firms. Therefore, in order to maintain interest in producing a given product, the expected profit must be larger than he or she could earn by producing or investing in a different product.

Math Activity: Ask students to examine the current rate of return on savings bonds, certificates of deposit, blue-chip stock, or government securities. Note that these all entail less risk than the average new business enterprise. Point out that the profit of investing in a new business must be greater than the highest return found in the investigation. The opportunity cost of investing in a new enterprise would be the next highest investment opportunity and must cover risk-taking as well.

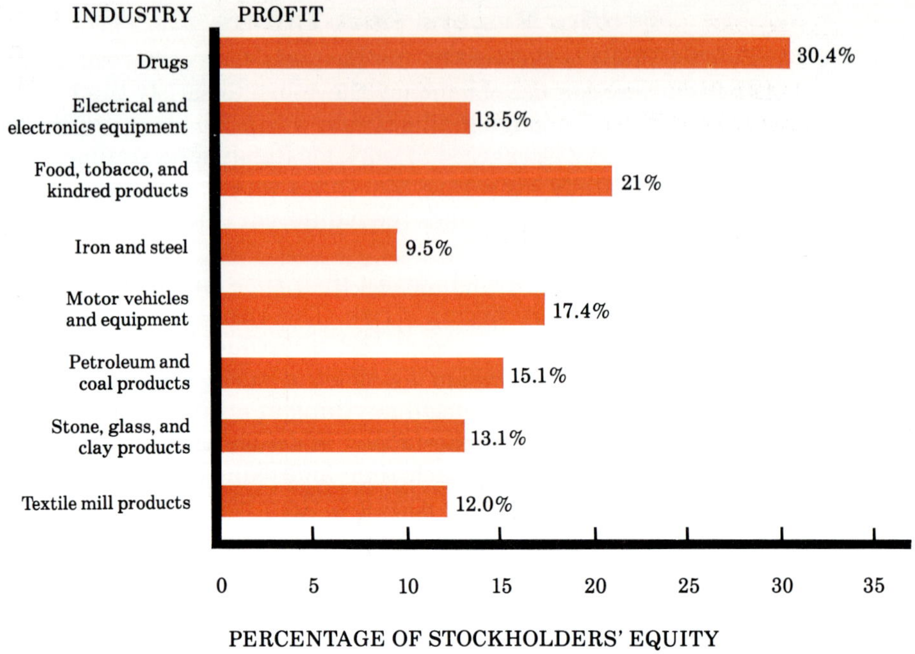

Source: U.S Bureau of the Census

Figure 4.1 Profits for Some Manufacturing Industries. Bars show profits after taxes as a percentage of stockholder's equity—the amount owners invest in the business. Figures are from the last quarter (or three months) of a recent year.

Another difficulty is knowing what is meant by *profits*. Some people think profits are high because they confuse profits with markup. Hearing that a department store paid $10 for a pair of pants that it sells for $20, they conclude that the $10 difference is all profit. That isn't true. The difference (called *markup*) must cover the store's other expenses—salaries, electricity, advertising, and the cost of offering credit and other services. The profit on that sale is much smaller, perhaps under 15 cents.

Profits are the return on money invested. The question becomes, What rate of return is too high? We need to compare how much the investor could earn by using the money differently—buying bonds, say, or lending the money out at interest. Profits often are lower than the income from these other investments. If profits are higher, it's usually because the business involves more risk. Profits are not guaranteed. Figure 4.1 shows industries making money. Sometimes, however, industries lose money.

Businesses are sometimes criticized for harming consumers or the environment in their pursuit of profit. Critics charge that businesses pollute the air or water rather than build costly antipollution devices, for instance. In response to this concern, the government has taken action. By passing and enforcing such laws as the Clean Air Act and the Consumer Product Safety Act, it tries to protect the environment and consumers from harmful actions.

BUSINESSES COMBINE RESOURCES TO PRODUCE GOODS AND SERVICES

World Economy: Ask students to research recent efforts to develop private enterprise in command economies.

Producers use three kinds of resources. *Human resources* are people who use their time, energy, and skills to produce the good or service. *Natural resources* are the raw materials found in or on the earth. *Capital resources* are tools, machines, and buildings. To get these resources, businesses use money. Money is sometimes called *capital*, but it shouldn't be confused with capital resources. Money is used to get *all* resources.

All businesses, even the smallest and simplest, use these three kinds of resources to produce their goods and services. The human resources in Randy's housepainting business are Randy and Otis. Capital resources are their equipment—brushes, drop cloths, ladders. Natural resources make up the paint they use. Bigger businesses use more resources, but they all fall into one of these three categories.

Critical Thinking: Encourage students to debate whether or not the following are entrepreneurs, and why: the originator of Apple Computer; the franchiser of a new McDonald's restaurant; the president of AT&T; the owner of the new neighborhood grocery; Randy.

Entrepreneurs Combine Productive Resources

A business doesn't exist until someone puts these three resources together. *A person who has an idea, is willing to take risks, and is able to combine resources to produce goods or services for profit* is called an **entrepreneur**. What moves the entrepreneur to start a business is the desire for profit.

The ideas of successful entrepreneurs can grow. In 1975, Liz Claiborne started designing and selling women's clothing. By the end of the first year, her company had sold over $2 million worth of goods. Just over a decade later, Liz Claiborne, Inc., had grown into a billion dollar business with 3,000 employees. Michael Dell is a successful entrepreneur too. He knew he could sell a computer that was just as good as some of the leading brands, but less expensive. After some ups and downs, Dell Computer Corp. recently reached over $300 million in sales.

Activity: Require that students conceive and present to the class a new product or service. Analyze the market, competition, resource needs, and possibilities for success of this product/service. After the presentations have been made, let the market (class) vote on the product/service with the best chance for success.

All entrepreneurs share three features. The first is the *willingness* to take a risk. There is no guarantee that enough consumers want to buy housepainting, skin-care products, or word processors—or anything else. The people who go into business, however, feel that if they plan carefully and work hard, they will find people who want their good or service.

The second feature these entrepreneurs have in common is the *ability* to combine human, natural, and capital resources. This ability requires having knowledge and money. Entrepreneurs must know how to combine the resources to make a good or service that people will want. Randy must be good at housepainting or people won't buy his service. An entrepreneur must also have the money—or know how to raise the money—to get the resources he or she needs.

The third feature of an entrepreneur may be the most important: the *idea*. An entrepreneur has an idea for a good or service that people will want to buy and believes that he or she can produce and sell it at a profit. Sometimes an entrepreneur simply recognizes that opportunity exists because no business yet offers a good or service. Randy may have seen that there weren't

Research: There are periodicals that concentrate on franchise opportunities. Use these periodicals to determine costs for starting a business. Students will develop an appreciation for the amount of risk an entrepreneur undertakes.

Focus: The primary mistake entrepreneurs make is a lack of adequate initial investment. Students may think that all they need is their time and some skills. However, inadequate levels of investment mean that the possibilities for growth are limited, and that the entrepreneur has a limited amount of time for the business to be successful. Both of these consequences can lead to business failure.

Activity: Ask students to develop a matrix and use the decision-making process to decide what they think Randy should do about Otis' offer. Discuss their decisions in class.

Trish Cronan is an entrepreneur whose dream—a yacht chartering company—became a reality worth millions of dollars.

enough housepainters in town to paint all the houses that needed painting. Other times the entrepreneur sees a new solution to an old problem. Michael Dell, for instance, saw that his machines could help businesses work more efficiently.

People Play Three Other Roles in Business

Any business includes other people besides an entrepreneur. Let's see what they do.

Owners are *people who have invested money in a business.* Entrepreneurs often own the businesses they start, as Randy does, but to grow, a business may need more money than the entrepreneur alone can provide. If others invest their money in the business, they become part-owners. They are entitled to share in the profits. They are also liable to share in any losses. Otis's offer to Randy was to become a part-owner. (If a business borrows the money it needs, the lender is *not* a part-owner.)

Another part of each business is the manager. **Managers** are *the people who turn a business's goals into directions for the workers.* They perform four functions: planning, organizing, directing, and controlling. Keep in mind that though we describe these functions separately, managers may do more than one at a time.

Emphasize: The quality of work is very important to the success of the business. Many of your students will become workers rather than business owners. They should realize that their efforts are the basis of a successful business, or they could be the reason for a business failure.

Note: Many entrepreneurs are good at innovating but are not good at managing. The required skills are quite different. Many enterprises fail when the entrepreneur tries to expand the business without the skills needed to manage the expansion.

Expansion: Marketing is not covered in this text. Randy may decide he has to paint three houses a month to make a profit. But how will he find three houses a month that need painting and convince the owners that they should pay Randy to paint them? This effort could be undertaken by Randy (at the cost of painting) or by the manager (who may want a higher salary for increased responsibilities).

- *Planning* is finding the best way to meet the business's goals. Randy must decide how many houses he needs to paint each month and how quickly he and Otis must work to get that number done.
- *Organizing* means arranging resources to carry out these plans. Randy must answer such questions as, How do we use our resources to paint those houses? How do I divide the tasks between Otis and me, or should I hire new workers? How do I get the paint I need on time?
- *Directing* is coordinating how the different resources—especially the human resources—are used. Randy must show Otis how to perform his tasks. Randy must also motivate Otis—make him *want* to do his job well.
- *Controlling* means examining results and answering such questions as, Are we meeting the goal? Can we do better? Randy must see that enough houses are being painted—and are being painted well.

The last business role we will examine is that of the worker. The **worker** *makes the product or provides the service that a business sells.* Though we look at the worker's role last, it's hardly the least important—far from it. Workers determine whether a business will meet its goals.

Among the qualities businesses look for in workers are these:

- *Quality*—doing the work well
- *Reliability*—being at work on time and working well consistently
- *Productivity*—doing as much work as possible
- *Efficiency*—using resources wisely and not wasting time
- *Safety*—using equipment properly and carefully
- *Initiative*—being willing to learn new tasks

Like all managers, this coach directs workers to do their jobs more effectively and efficiently.

- *Adaptability*—being open to new tasks and new ways of working
- *Cooperativeness*—working well with others
- *Honesty*—dealing truthfully with the employer

Focus: Most businesses grow over time as business expands enough to cover the increased costs.

Because the worker's role is so important, we will examine it in detail in Part III of this book.

These four roles—entrepreneur, owner, manager, worker—often overlap. Owners usually manage. Managers also work. In a new company, the entrepreneur is almost always the owner and usually the top manager.

WHAT BUSINESS DOES

Businesses provide many different goods and services. Still, all businesses can be placed into one or another of three broad types: producers, distributors, and services.

Discuss: Many communities have box stores or food cooperatives that sell food at reduced prices. How are they able to do this? Food co-ops are composed of a group of consumers who are willing to substitute their time and effort for that of the go-between. Box stores offer a limited selection of items and sell these items in bulk form while providing limited services for the customer.

Producers are *businesses that produce goods.* There are three kinds of producers. *Extractors* take raw materials from the earth, air, or water. This type includes miners digging for iron ore, farmers raising wheat, and oil riggers drilling for oil.

Processors convert these raw materials into usable form. A steel mill turns iron ore into bars, sheets, and rolls of steel. Another kind of mill grinds wheat into flour.

Manufacturers use raw materials and processed goods to make finished goods. Automakers use steel, glass, plastic, and other processed goods to make their cars.

Distributors are *businesses that help consumers and producers exchange goods.* Some distributors help two producers make exchanges. They may buy feed grain from farmers and sell it to cattle ranchers.

Other distributors work between producers and consumers. A tire store buys tires from the maker and sells them to the general public. This kind of selling to consumers is called *retailing.*

Another kind of distributor, a *wholesaler,* helps producers make exchanges with other distributors. For instance, a compact disc wholesaler buys large numbers of discs from all the compact disc makers, large and small. It then resells them to retail stores.

Activity: Ask students to identify local firms that perform the functions described in the section "What Business Does".

Services are *businesses that perform actions of value for consumers or for other businesses.* Businesses' services include research and information (like reports on consumers' habits), transportation (trucking and air freight), communication (telephone repair and copying machines), and finance (raising or lending money). Services to consumers, or pure services, include a variety of things from cutting hair to cleaning teeth to painting houses.

BUSINESSES ARE ORGANIZED IN FIVE WAYS

There are five ways of organizing a business. Each kind has its own legal definition and its own advantages and disadvantages.

Businesses can be grouped into types according to what they do. The farmer is a producer, creating goods. The store that employs this salesperson is a distributor. The lawyer provides a service.

Sole Proprietorships Are Owned by One Person

Discuss: Have students brainstorm additional sources of financing for Randy's business.

Critical Thinking: Encourage students to interview a banker for insights on Randy's ability to obtain a loan for his new business.

Emphasize: Compare the forms of business organization according to their advantages and disadvantages. Refer to Table 4.1 as you discuss each form.

A business owned by one person is a **sole proprietorship**. Randy is a sole proprietor. There are no legal requirements for forming a sole proprietorship—no contracts need be drawn up or official papers signed. Some local governments do require sole owners in some businesses—those selling food, for instance—to get a license.

Sole proprietorships have many advantages. They are easy to form. All Randy really needs is paint, brushes, and a ladder. Often only a little money is needed to start one. The profits equal the owner's income, so they are taxed at the rate for personal income. This rate is usually lower than the tax rate for corporate income. The owner is free to make all decisions and to enjoy all the profits.

There are disadvantages. Sole owners may have a harder time raising money than owners of the other types of business. The firm's success is limited by the owner's abilities, and the company ends when the owner dies or abandons it. The biggest disadvantage is that the owner has **personal liability.** *The owner is responsible for all of a business's debts.* If the business fails, the owner's personal car or house or bank account can be used to pay its bills.

Partnerships Are Owned by More Than One Person

A **partnership** is *a business owned by two or more persons, at least one of whom has personal liability for the firm's debts.* Partners usually have a legal agreement that spells out the terms of their partnership. The agreement might state exactly how much money and work each partner will give to the business.

Partnerships have their advantages. They, too, are easy to form, and their earnings are also taxed at the individual rate. Partnerships can draw on the skill of more than one person. Partners may be able to raise more money than sole proprietors, since more than one person is investing.

Partnerships have disadvantages, too. As Randy realized when Otis made his offer, partners don't have complete control of the business and have to share profits. Though partners can raise more money than sole owners, they still cannot raise as much as corporations. Partnerships can also be fragile. A major disagreement between partners can paralyze the business. Finally, like sole proprietors, owners of a simple partnership have personal liability for the business's debts.

A **limited partnership** solves this problem in some cases. In this form, *the liability of some partners is limited to the amount they invested in the business.* Their personal property cannot be used to pay the firm's debts. Still, at least one partner must have unlimited liability.

Randy has thought about Otis's offer and about the pros and cons of these two forms. He's decided he'd prefer to keep control of his business for now. Rather than take Otis on as a partner, he'll make do with less money. Perhaps he'll try to borrow the money he needs from a bank.

Corporations Are Owned by Stockholders

A **corporation** is *a business owned by stockholders.* The corporation is run according to its **charter**, which is *a legal document that states the corporation's name, its business, and its procedures.* The charter is filed with the state where the business is incorporated.

Enhancement: Invite a local entrepreneur to class to share insights regarding the start-up of an enterprise. Ask him or her to identify the form of business adopted and to explain why that form was chosen.

A corporation issues and sells stock to raise the money it needs. **Stock** is *a share or shares of ownership in a corporation.* These shares can be bought and sold, or otherwise transferred from one owner to another. *People who purchase shares of stock in a corporation* are called **stockholders**. They are the corporation's owners. Stockholders elect a board of directors, who oversee the business. The directors appoint managers to run the company. Figure 4.2 shows these connections.

Critical Thinking: Have students research the process of changing from a privately owned to a publicly owned corporation. What is the success rate for this process? Can a publicly owned corporation become privately owned?

Stockholders may receive dividends based on the number of shares they own. A **dividend** is *a part of the profits of a corporation that directors decide to pay to stockholders.* Dividends are paid after the corporation pays its taxes and often after part of the profits are reinvested. Corporations do not always pay dividends. Some reinvest all profits. Others don't make a profit. That's the risk people take when they buy the company's stock.

Two kinds of corporations are in business to make a profit. The stock of a *public corporation* is traded on the open market. Anyone can purchase shares, either in a stock exchange or "over the counter." Stockbrokers usually do the buying and selling for people, acting on instructions and charging a fee. Most major corporations, such as AT&T, Exxon, and IBM, are public.

Enhancement: Introduce students to the markets where stocks of publicly held companies are traded. Contact the New York Stock Exchange and the Security Industries Foundation for Economic Education for information.

The stock of a *private corporation* is held by only a few people, often by members of a family or by the founder of the company and a few original employees. These shares are not sold to the general public. Well-known private corporations include Estée Lauder, the cosmetics firm, and Jordache, the sportswear maker. A business can start as a private corporation and then become a public one. This happened with the Ford Motor Company. (In fact, a business can begin as a partnership and then become a public corporation, as Sears, Roebuck did.)

Corporations have disadvantages. Stockholders of a huge public corporation have little control over the company's actions. Profits are taxed twice—first as corporate income and then again as personal income. Corporations must meet many legal restrictions and reporting requirements.

Discussion: Under what conditions might Randy want to change the form of his business to a partnership? to a corporation?

Of course, corporations have advantages, too. They are able to raise far more money than the other two forms. For this reason, most of the largest businesses are corporations. Also, the other two forms have limited life. When sole proprietors or partners die, the firm legally ends. This isn't true of corporations because the shares of a stockholder who dies can be transferred to someone else. Perhaps most important, stockholders have only *limited liability* for the company's debts. If the business fails, stockholders lose only the amount they invested. Their personal property is safe.

Table 4.1 compares the advantages and disadvantages of the three main forms of business.

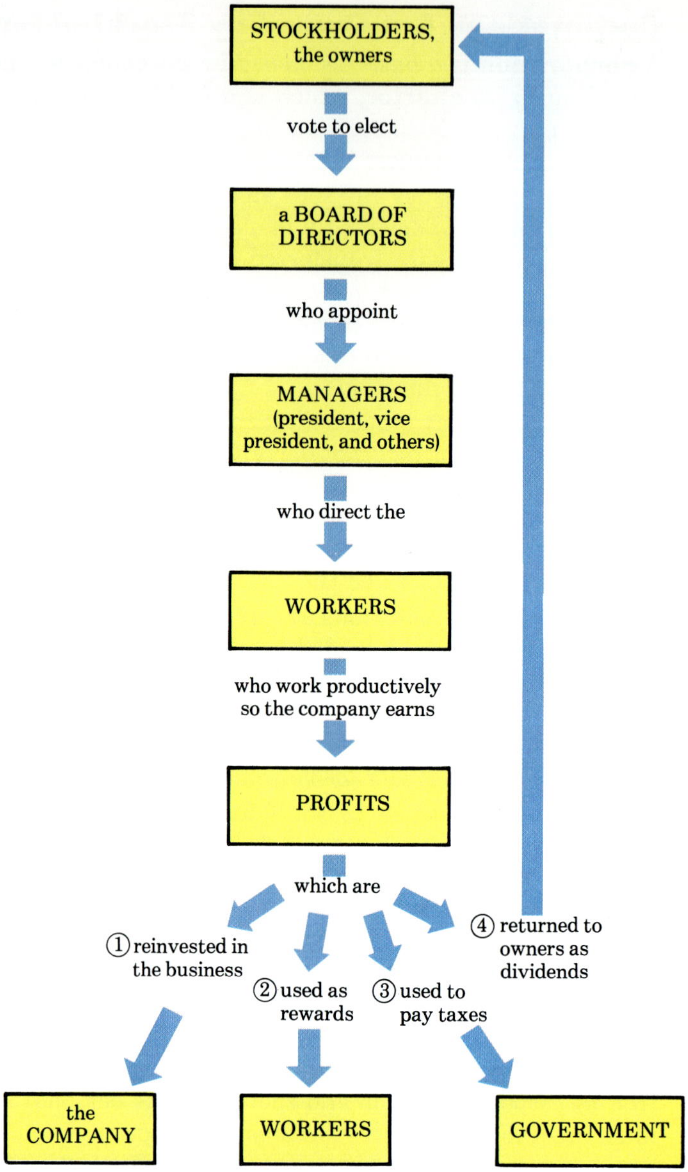

Figure 4.2 How a Corporation Operates

Two Other Ways of Organizing a Business

A **cooperative** is *an enterprise owned by more than one person or business, which acts for the benefit of its members.* There are two kinds. Many small businesses may form a *selling cooperative* to try to compete with larger firms and sell their goods for higher prices. Sunkist Growers, a group of citrus fruit farmers, is one example. *Buying cooperatives* join many businesses or

Activity: Ask students to interview franchise owners about benefits or problems they encountered in owning a franchise. Interview a lawyer about the cost of obtaining legal advice in beginning a franchise operation.

Activity: Ask students to interview organizers of a local cooperative about benefits or problems they encountered in the operation of the co-op.

Critical Thinking: Many small-business owners are critical of the competition of not-for-profits. Identify examples of this competition. Why might this competition be unfair?

Expansion: Research state and federal laws regarding the formation of a not-for-profit; survey the types of goods or services not-for-profits provide; and invite a director of a not-for-profit to class to discuss the advantages and disadvantages of this form of business.

Table 4.1 Comparing the Three Main Ways of Organizing a Business

	Sole Proprietorship	Partnership	Corporation
Ease of formation	Very easy	Fairly easy	Fairly complex
Money needed to form	Very little	Fairly little	Large amounts needed
Ability to raise money	Can raise little	Can raise more	Can raise large amounts
Ease in making decisions	Very easy	Fairly easy	Fairly easy
Owner controls business	Complete control	Partial control	Little control
Number of people whose skills can be used	One	Few	Many
Possible lifespan of company	Limited to owner's life	Limited to owner's life	Unlimited
Extent of owner's liability for business debts	Unlimited personal liability	Unlimited personal liability for at least one partner	Limited for all owners
Taxes due	Personal income	Personal income	Corporate and personal income

consumers to buy products in bulk. That way they can often buy at lower prices.

In a **franchise**, *one business sells another business the right to use its name and sell its products in a certain area.* The buyer of this right is called the *franchisee*. The seller is the *franchisor*. The franchisee pays the franchisor a fee, or a percentage of its sales, or both. A legal contract defines the terms of the agreement and the duties of each party.

Franchises are among the most well-known businesses. Many gas stations are franchises, and you can probably name at least five fast-food franchises. Franchises are as varied as auto products dealers (AAMCO and Midas) and temporary employment companies (Kelly Services and Manpower).

Franchises are a good way for a person with limited money to get some of the advantages of running his or her own business. Also, the franchisor can provide training and advice. The main disadvantage of franchises is that the franchisee isn't entirely free to act as he or she wishes. The franchisor will require certain procedures and standards. Franchise contracts are complex. Anyone thinking of entering into this kind of agreement should get sound business and legal advice first.

YOU INTERACT WITH THE ECONOMY: SMALL BUSINESSES

Small businesses like Randy's are a vital part of our economy. More than 95 percent of businesses in the United States are small businesses, and they produce over 45 percent of the nation's goods and services. What exactly is a small business?

The **Small Business Administration** (SBA) has an answer. The SBA is *an agency of the federal government that provides loans, advice, and information to small businesses.* The SBA defines a small business as any firm that employs fewer than 500 people. As Figure 4.3 shows, more small businesses are in the service industry than in any other industry.

Most businesses start small. The Coca-Cola Company started when a pharmacist mixed a new medicine. Polaroid started when a scientist experimented with lenses and light in a lab in his home. Each example in this chapter, real or not, is a small business, or was when it got started, like Liz Claiborne's and Michael Dell's.

We buy many goods and services from small businesses. Small service firms include travel agents and dry cleaners. Small retailers include bookstores, corner grocers, and car dealers. Small construction companies build new homes and offices. Small manufacturers often sell parts to larger ones—headlights to an automaker or electric cables to a shipbuilder. Even a babysitter or a person who mows lawns is a small business.

Because small businesses are such a large part of our economy, they create a lot of jobs. Almost 60 percent of all jobs are provided by small businesses. Small businesses also create more competition. That means consumers can choose from more goods and services and buy at lower prices.

Enhancement: In order to increase efficiency, large corporations today are "outplacing" work with small businesses. For example, instead of operating a manufacturing division to make headlights, many auto manufacturers buy headlights from an outside supplier. Thus, if demand falls, the auto manufacturer is not constrained by an existing work force.

World Economy: In command economies, the best example of entrepreneurs and small business is the very active black market. Students could discuss the role of the black market and determine why it has such an important role in the command economy.

Discussion: Why do small businesses represent over 95 percent of the businesses in the United States and employ almost 60 percent of the workers yet produce only 45 percent of the nation's goods and services?

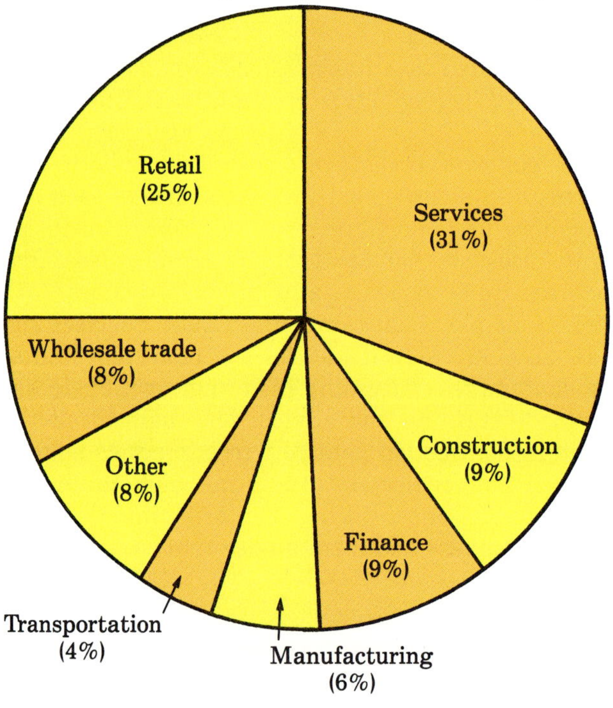

Source: U.S. Bureau of the Census

Figure 4.3 The Proportion of Each Type of Small Business

Summary: Forming a business requires many complex decisions. What should the business produce? What form should the business take? How large should the business become? What resources will the production require? All of these decisions have opportunity costs that must be considered.

Small businesses introduce innovations. They have produced much exciting new computer software—from complex programs used by large businesses to the video games that gobble up quarters. Small businesses can add a special touch that gives extra satisfaction. Think of the helpful service of a small local retailer or the special care taken by a dedicated craftsworker.

To keep this important part of the economy working smoothly, the government set up the SBA. The agency gives three kinds of help to small business owners:

- The SBA guarantees bank loans that small business owners obtain or makes direct loans.
- The SBA provides information and advice on running a business.
- The SBA connects owners with active or retired business people who give advice on successful practices.

The SBA has 110 field offices to make this help available in every state.

SUMMARY

- Businesses produce goods and services for profit. Profit is the business owner's reward for taking the risk of investing in the business. If the business doesn't succeed, its owner suffers a loss.
- Businesses combine human, natural, and capital resources to produce goods and services. An entrepreneur is a person who has an idea that these resources can be combined to make and sell a product or service, and who is willing and able to act on that idea.
- Individuals play four roles in business. Entrepreneurs start the business. Owners invest money in the hope of making a profit. Managers plan, organize, direct, and control the work of the business. Workers produce the business's products or provide its services.
- Businesses can be divided into three general categories. Producers produce goods. Distributors help consumers and producers exchange goods. Services perform actions of value for individuals and for other businesses.
- There are three main kinds of business ownership. Sole proprietorships are owned by one person. Partnerships are owned by two or more persons, at least one of whom has personal liability. Corporations are owned by stockholders. Each way of owning a business has its advantages and disadvantages.
- Two other forms also exist. Cooperatives are groups of people or businesses who band together to sell more products or buy goods for less. Franchises are agreements by which one business pays to use the name and sell the product of another business.
- Small businesses are a vital part of our economy. They account for 95% of all businesses, provide almost 60% of all jobs, and produce over 45% of the nation's goods and services.

Key Terms

Match each of the following terms with the definition that most suits it.

business	franchise	producers	stock
charter	limited partnership	profit	stockholders
cooperative	loss	service	workers
corporation	managers	Small Business Administration (SBA)	
distributor	owners	sole proprietorship	
dividend	partnership		
entrepreneur	personal liability		

a. a business owned by two or more persons at least one of whom has personal liability for the firm's debt

b. the people who turn a business's goals into directions for the workers

c. a type of business that performs actions of value for consumers or for other businesses

d. an enterprise owned by more than one person or business, which acts for the benefit of its members

e. the amount by which a business's expenses exceed its income

f. the principle that an owner is responsible for all of a business's debts

g. people who purchase shares of stock in a corporation

h. a person who has an idea, is willing to take risks, and is able to combine resources to produce goods or services for profit

i. a type of business that helps consumers and producers exchange goods

j. the people who make the product or provide the service that a business sells

k. a legal document that states a corporation's name, its business, and its procedures

l. an individual or a group of individuals who produce goods or services for profit

m. people who have invested money in a business

n. a share or shares of ownership in a corporation

o. an arrangement in which one business sells another business the right to use its name and sell its products in a certain area

p. the amount by which a business's income exceeds its expenses; the reward for taking a risk

q. a part of the profits of a corporation that directors decide to pay to stockholders

r. a type of business that produces goods

s. a business owned by stockholders

t. a business owned by one person

u. a form of business in which the liability of some partners is limited to the amount they invested in the business

v. an agency of the federal government that provides loans, advice, and information to small businesses

Review Questions

1. What is profit? How is it related to risk?
2. What are the three characteristics of an entrepreneur? Explain each briefly.
3. What are the four roles people play in business? Might these roles overlap?
4. What are the four functions of managers?

5. What are the three types of businesses? Give examples of businesses that perform each.
6. List the advantages and disadvantages of being a sole proprietor.
7. List the advantages and disadvantages of a partnership.
8. List some of the advantages and disadvantages of organizing a business as a corporation.
9. What is a franchise? What are the advantages and disadvantages of a franchise?
10. What kind of help does the Small Business Administration give small business owners?

Projects

1. Be an entrepreneur. Think of a good or service that consumers or businesses would be willing to buy. Your idea could be a new good or service or an improved version of an old one. Now identify what resources you'd need to produce that good or service. Report to the class about your product, what you'd use to produce it, and how you'd organize the business.
2. Pick a well-known business. Go to the library and find out what entrepreneur started the business. What was his or her idea? What risk did he or she take? How has the business changed over time? Compare your findings with your classmates'.
3. Interview a local small business owner and ask how he or she got started in the business. What was the idea that got the business started? What risk did the owner face in starting the business? What roles does the owner play in the business today? What kind of business is it? How is it legally organized? Is the current owner the founder? Is the business today what the owner thought it would be when he or she started it? Tell the class what you learned.
4. Do some research into the Small Business Administration. What sort of aid does it offer small business owners? How do they get this help?
5. Some people charge that profits are too high. Others reply that profits mean growth and jobs. Have a debate on profits: are they too high, too low, or about right? If there were no profits—or if profits were lower—how would our economy be different?
6. Many businesses issue annual reports to their stockholders. Annual reports tell you the company's financial position, expanding markets for the business, and corporate contributions to social programs. In small groups, select a company you want to know more about and request an annual report from the company. Plan a group presentation discussing the contents of the annual report to the class. How does the company view its business? Did the company do well that year? What is the business outlook for the next year?
7. Find out if any businesses in your area are owned and run by families. Arrange with your teacher to invite family members who are active in the business to class to discuss the pros and cons of working with family members. How are responsibilities divided among the family members? How are problems resolved? If the business has been in the community for many years, you might ask them to discuss the history of the business and how it has changed through time.

The Government and the Economy 5

Overview: Chapter 5 expands on methods of raising money for government and on the ways in which government spends that money.

OBJECTIVES

This chapter will help you to:

1. Explain why government's economic policies have changed over time.
2. Categorize the services governments provide.
3. Identify five ways that governments regulate economic activity.
4. State examples of three types of government spending.
5. Classify and evaluate the taxes governments collect.
6. Determine your ability to affect government decisions.

Kim was on her way into the supermarket when she heard a familiar voice from the other side of the parking lot. "Hey, Kim!"

Kim looked up and saw her friend Cora standing behind a folding table. A sign was attached to the table. Kim walked over.

"Do you want to sign our petition?" Cora asked.

"What does it say?"

"We're protesting because they're going to start charging people $10 a summer to use the community pool," Cora replied. "We want it to stay free."

"Oh yeah. I heard about that." Kim thought for a minute. "Aren't they going to start charging for a lot of city services? Won't they charge when we have a dance in the high school gym or use the auditorium?"

"That's right," Cora said. "And tuition is going up at the city college. Isn't it terrible? Sign here. You can even be part of the group that brings this to city hall when we get enough signatures."

"I don't know," Kim replied. "My parents told me that if they *don't* start charging all those fees, property taxes will go up. And if taxes go up, we won't be able to afford our vacation at the beach this year. That's more important to me than keeping the pool free."

"But that's just two weeks. The pool's open all summer!"

"Sure. But I can afford $10. I don't know if I want to give up my time at the beach for all those other things."

Assignment: Assign students to research a regulatory agency or a department and report on its origin, responsibilities, and current level of activity.

KIM AND CORA are discussing the pros and cons of how governments pay for the services they provide. They're also thinking about the whole question of government's role in the economy—as we will do in this chapter. In this chapter you'll learn what services governments provide and how they tax people to raise money to pay for those services.

GOVERNMENT'S ROLE IN THE ECONOMY HAS CHANGED

In theory, the role of government in a market economy is limited to three functions. First, it keeps law and order, so people and their property are safe. Second, it enforces contracts among producers and consumers. Third, it makes sure there are no barriers to free competition.

Focus: Highly defined roles for government are needed to ensure that markets function efficiently and that citizens are safe.

In theory, a market economy relies generally on the forces of supply and demand. Businesses decide what to produce (supply) by seeing what people wish to buy (demand). This results in competition. All actors will follow their own self-interest. People will buy goods and services to satisfy their wants. Businesses will produce what people want so they can earn profits. What is called "the invisible hand" of supply and demand will ensure that this works out to be in the best interests of all.

Focus: In 1929, U.S. government purchases of goods and services were $8.9 billion (out of a total gross national product of $103.9 billion—about 8.6%). By 1988, U.S. government purchases had grown to $936.3 billion (out of total gross national product of $4,861.8 billion—about 19.3%).

Research: Identify your local elected officials and the years in which they will be up for reelection. Maintain a file on local government activities to refer to during the unit.

The free market can be unstable, however. Cycles of prosperity are often followed by periods of unemployment and business loss. After the worst of these times of economic trouble—the Great Depression of the 1930s—the federal government acted to promote more stability. Since the end of the Great Depression of the 1930s, it has run spending and job programs to support the economy. Some people feel that these actions have met with some success: we have had few severe depressions since. Of course, there have been costs, too. Prices have increased steadily, and critics say that higher federal spending means inefficiency and waste.

Governments also act because people see a need to deal with problems that a free, competitive market cannot solve. For instance, governments put tariffs on imported goods to protect our industries from foreign competition. Governments pass laws and issue rules to protect consumers. The federal government, for instance, tests all drugs for safety before they can be sold.

Governments act in four ways: they *provide* services, they *regulate* economic activity, they *spend* money, and they *tax* to pay for their actions. We shall examine each of these actions.

When we speak of *government,* we are not speaking of one giant organization. There are three levels of government in the United States. Guiding the nation is the federal government, made up of the president and the executive agencies, Congress, and federal courts. It is based in Washington, D.C., but is at work all over the country. Each of the 50 states has its own government, which is in many ways a smaller version of the federal government. Finally, there are about 80,000 local governments in cities, towns, and counties. These range from small town councils to the huge governments that run cities like New York City and Los Angeles.

GOVERNMENTS PROVIDE SERVICES

Research: Identify your state and federal politicians, their policy stance, and the committees they serve on.

Math Activity: Ask students to calculate U.S. government expenditures as a percentage of gross national product for the years between 1929 and 1988, then develop a line graph.

All three levels of government provide services to the people. These services can be divided into two groups.

Public services are *services that only government can or will provide because the service must be provided for everyone, regardless of any person's inability or unwillingness to pay.* Businesses, which sell services for a profit, will not produce these services. Imagine the result if a business built and controlled the sidewalks in a city. How could it make everyone who used the sidewalk pay for that use? It's easier for the city government to build the sidewalk and make it open to everyone.

Public services include the protection provided by local police, state national guard units, and the national armed forces. They also include courts and streets and roads provided by governments at all levels.

The second type of government services is **merit services.** These are *services a government decides it should provide out of a belief that businesses cannot or will not provide enough of them for all people.* Businesses may be willing to produce these services and sell them only to people who will pay for them, but a government decides that more people ought to have them.

Activity: List the goods and services provided by your local government and evaluate whether these are pure public goods and services, or merit goods and services. Compare your local area to a neighboring area. Are the goods and services provided the same?

Critical Thinking: If government did not maintain a park system, does this mean that we would have no parks?

Clarify: In order to be a pure public good or service, several criteria must be met: (1) public goods cannot be broken up into smaller lots and sold to individuals; (2) there is no effective method of excluding individuals from using the good or service; and (3) there are large spillover benefits, which means the market would not allocate enough resources to the production of that good or service.

Police services are public services—provided only by governments and provided for all people.

Local governments provide many merit services. Free libraries, public schools, and museums are services of this type, so are city parks, hospitals, bus and subway systems, and water and sewer lines. States also provide parks, as well as bridges, airports, and tourist information, and state colleges educate people for less tuition than private colleges charge. The federal government offers merit services like information for producers and consumers, medical and scientific research, highways and parks, and space exploration.

All governments do not provide the same merit services. Some public utilities are owned by cities or states; others are privately owned. Many cities have public mass transit systems; others leave it to private companies. Some states allow liquor to be sold only in state-owned stores; others let private stores sell it. In some localities, no liquor is sold. Because merit services are services a government *chooses* to provide, there will always be some differences from time to time and from place to place in the merit services provided.

All voters don't agree on what merit services a government should provide. Some people may believe that a city government should stop running a mass transit system. Some may say that the federal government should publish fewer information booklets or spend less on research. Voters and elected

Public transportation is a merit service—it isn't provided by all governments.

officials are always debating what services a government should provide — and how much of each service.

GOVERNMENTS REGULATE ECONOMIC ACTIVITY

Another way the government acts in the economy is to regulate economic activity. Some of this regulation comes from local governments. More comes from state governments, which oversee all business that takes place within the state. The federal government does the most regulation because it oversees *interstate commerce*—business that occurs between states. Let's see why governments take these actions.

Define: **Trademarks** are a registered name, symbol, figure, word, or mark which distinguishes a product from its competition. A **patent** is the exclusive right of an inventor to produce, use, or sell the invention for a period of time.

Governments Regulate Competition

Some regulation is meant to make sure that competition is free and fair. The most important rules for this purpose are *antitrust laws.* **Trusts** exist when *one or a few businesses control an industry.* (The industry could be controlled by a *monopoly*—one firm—or an *oligopoly*—a few firms.) By controlling an industry, a trust has the power to restrict the supply of goods and to fix prices. Many federal laws, beginning with the Sherman Antitrust Act of 1890, have been passed to prevent trusts from being formed. These laws are summarized in Table 5.1.

A government may decide that people will benefit most if there is no competition. In that case, it allows a *public monopoly* to exist. The best examples of these are utilities—power companies and cable TV companies.

Table 5.1 Major Antitrust Laws

Name of Law	What It Does
Sherman Antitrust Act (1890)	Forbids businesses to join together or make contracts to restrain trade.
Clayton Act (1914)	Forbids businesses to cut prices, sign contracts for exclusive dealing, acquire another business, or be run by the same directors who oversee a competitor, if the effect is to lessen competition.
Federal Trade Commission Act (1914)	Forbids businesses to practice unfair competition. Creates the Federal Trade Commission (FTC) to enforce this and other laws.
Robinson-Patman Act (1936)	Forbids businesses to charge one business more than another.
Wheeler-Lea Act (1938)	Forbids unfair competitive practices that harm the public. Extends FTC power to include consumer protection.
Celler-Kefauver Act (1950)	Forbids two or more companies to merge together if the result will lessen competition.

Critical Thinking: Ask the class to debate the following: Some detractors disagree with the strict U.S. regulation of the drug industry arguing that the negative 'second round effects' of the difficult approval process cancel out the benefits of this process. 'Second round effects' emphasize the number of people that could be helped (or lives that could be saved) by a new drug which has been awaiting approval for years.

They are allowed to control a local industry out of a belief that they can provide their service more efficiently that way. Even though governments allow this control, they often oversee the firm's actions. For instance, a government agency may have the power to decide whether a public monopoly can raise prices or change its services.

Clarify: The courts recently have found that local communities cannot regulate the rates of cable TV companies.

Some Government Agencies Regulate Specific Industries

Sometimes governments believe that it is necessary to regulate a particular industry. There are three reasons why.

First, government may regulate an industry that uses public resources—those that belong to all the people. Radio and television broadcasting make use of the airwaves. When these industries were new, the courts decided that the airwaves were public property. Thus, the Federal Communications Commission (FCC) was created in 1934 to regulate use of the airwaves.

Second, industries are regulated if they affect public safety. The Food and Drug Administration (FDA) was created in 1931, although an agency begun in 1906 had a similar task. It protects consumers by enforcing laws and rules to prevent the sale of adulterated, misbranded, or unsafe foods, drugs, and cosmetics. This can pay off. The drug Thalidomide was sold in western Europe in the early 1960s. Hundreds of pregnant women who took this tranquilizer later gave birth to babies with severe birth defects, but the drug had never received the FDA's approval. No Thalidomide was ever sold in the United States. Critics, however, say that while the FDA acted well in this case, the public is sometimes harmed by its slowness in approving helpful drugs.

Third, governments regulate industries that are important to the economy. The Securities and Exchange Commission (SEC) was created in 1934

Critical Thinking: Recently government has considered mandating new employee benefits that must be provided by businesses (parental leave, health care, etc.). This means that the cost of these benefits is borne by individuals and businesses rather than the government. Why is this attractive? What are the ramifications of this policy change?

Expansion: Invite an employee relations specialist from a local firm to discuss the changes in business policy and actions resulting from government policies on discrimination.

Critical Thinking: With the protection of the Securities and Exchange Commission in place, how could the recent **insider trading** and other Wall Street manipulations take place?

Research: Encourage students to research the antitrust exemptions for unions and their impact on employer/employee negotiations.

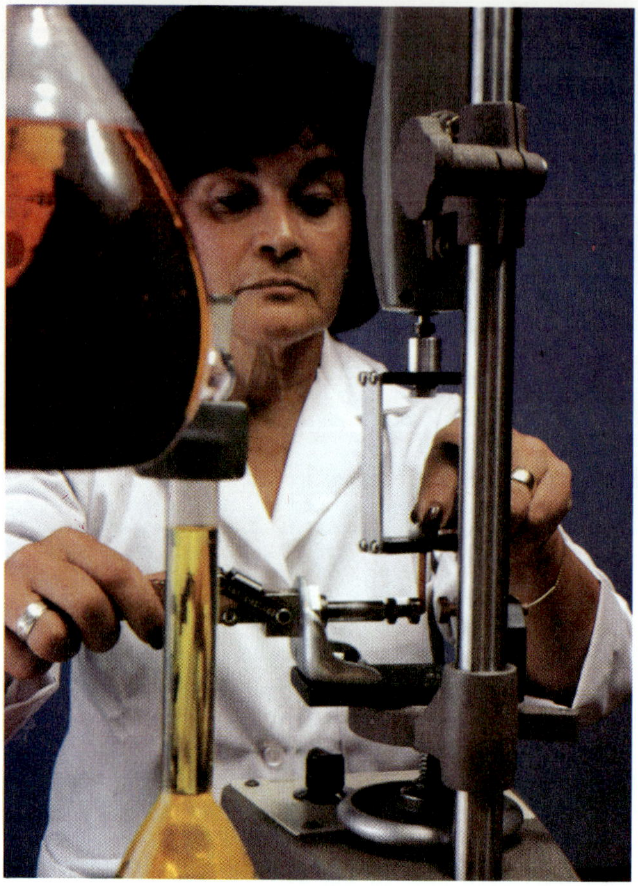

The Food and Drug Administration requires all drugs to be tested before approving them for sale.

in response to the stock market crash that marked the start of the Great Depression. It oversees the buying and selling of *securities,* which are the stocks and bonds of corporations. Some critics, however, argue that the SEC has created so many rules that its actions cost too much and provide too few benefits.

Governments Regulate the Workplace

Governments regulate the relations of employers and workers in several ways.

Laws give workers the right to form a union if they wish. When businesses and unions bargain for a contract, they must obey various laws. Other actions of the unions are regulated, too, such as how they manage retirement funds. Governments also prohibit employers from discriminating against workers because of race, color, sex, religion, age, or physical handicap.

The Occupational Safety and Health Administration (OSHA), formed in 1971, tries to make workplaces safe. OSHA made many complex and con-

Define: Pollution is referred to as a **spill-over cost.** This means that some of the costs of producing a good or service "spill over" onto others. If a plant spews pollutants into the air or water, then the costs of cleaning up that air or water are not being added to the costs of production of that plant. This means that too many resources will be allocated to that production process.

Research: Ask students to research the costs of the Clean Air Bill passed by Congress in 1990.

Explain: Opinion varies on the effects of the minimum wage. However, one outcome has been reduced employment for youth. We have determined that supply and demand interact in the market for labor. Therefore, if the minimum wage is set to a level above equilibrium (a price floor), then there will be a larger quantity of labor supplied than quantity of labor demanded. Workers who have fewer skills—youth and the disadvantaged—will not be hired.

flicting rules in its early years. Since 1977, though, it has cut the number of its regulations in an effort to focus on what it sees as basic protection. Still, OSHA's rules are much debated. Many critics argue that they are too strict and costly to meet and that they provide too few benefits.

Finally, government regulates income by setting a minimum hourly wage. It also provides some income security by taxing employers to provide an insurance fund that will pay benefits to unemployed workers and workers injured on the job.

Governments Regulate for Public Safety

Many government regulations are meant to ensure the safety of the general public. Some apply to certain industries, such as nursing homes and nuclear power plants. Others, like OSHA, affect almost every kind of business. One such agency is the Environmental Protection Agency (EPA), which was formed by Congress in 1972. The EPA issues rules meant to control and clean up pollution of the environment.

Regulation Is Decreasing

Since the late 1970s, the rate of federal regulation has been reduced somewhat. Critics argued that too many rules meant too little competition. It was time to give the market a chance to work, they said. In response, many federal agencies began reducing the number of their rules. As we have said, OSHA began cutting back on its rules in 1977. The Civil Aeronautics Board (CAB) began phasing out its control of passenger airline fares and routes in 1978 and was abolished at the end of 1984. In addition, as you will learn in a later chapter, government control of banking practices has been reduced.

While people generally approve of reduced regulation, critics argue against some of the cutbacks. Some people, for instance, feel that the EPA should watch more carefully to prevent pollution. The debate arises because regulation is a merit service—people disagree on how necessary it is.

Government Regulates the Economy

In a broad sense, all the economic actions of government "regulate" the economy. Increased government spending puts more money in the hands of producers and consumers. This stimulates producers to make more and consumers to buy more. Tax cuts, which leave more income in the hands of the people who earned it, can do the same thing. Governments also encourage certain types of spending by giving producers and consumers tax credits for certain investments.

The federal government also controls the amount of money in the economy. The **Federal Reserve System,** formed in 1913, is *a federal agency that controls the money supply and oversees the practices of its member banks.* The system is led by a board of seven governors who are appointed by the president. The system also includes twelve regional banks with twenty-four branches. Over 35 percent of the country's banks are members of the system. They hold over 70 percent of all deposits.

World Economy: Research the differences between our central bank (the FED) and central banks in other countries.

"The Fed," as the board is called, controls the money supply by setting the amount of money that member banks must keep on hand as reserves. This affects the amount of money these banks are able to lend. A decrease in the money they can lend will reduce demand. This can drive prices down, thus curbing inflation. A rise in the money being lent can help build demand, which encourages production. The Fed acts to increase the money supply when the economy is not performing well and needs to be stimulated.

GOVERNMENTS SPEND MONEY

Critical Thinking: Should the Federal Reserve system remain independent, or should it be held accountable to elected officials?

To provide services, governments must spend money. The 1989 federal budget provided for spending 975.5 billion dollars. Spending at all levels of government passed a *trillion* dollars in the early 1980s. The federal government spends over half of this total, local governments about a third, and the states the rest. Figure 5.1 shows how federal spending has grown over the years. Figure 5.2 shows how the money is spent. The percentages for state and local governments are averages.

Emphasize: During the 1980s President Reagan reduced the role of the federal government. Yet during the 1980s federal spending almost doubled. What occurred in the 1980s was a **reduction in the rate of growth** of the federal government (since federal spending increased by more than 600 percent in the 1970s).

Government Acts as an Employer

Governments hire and pay millions of workers. In a recent year, about 17.2 million people worked for government at all levels. These workers included

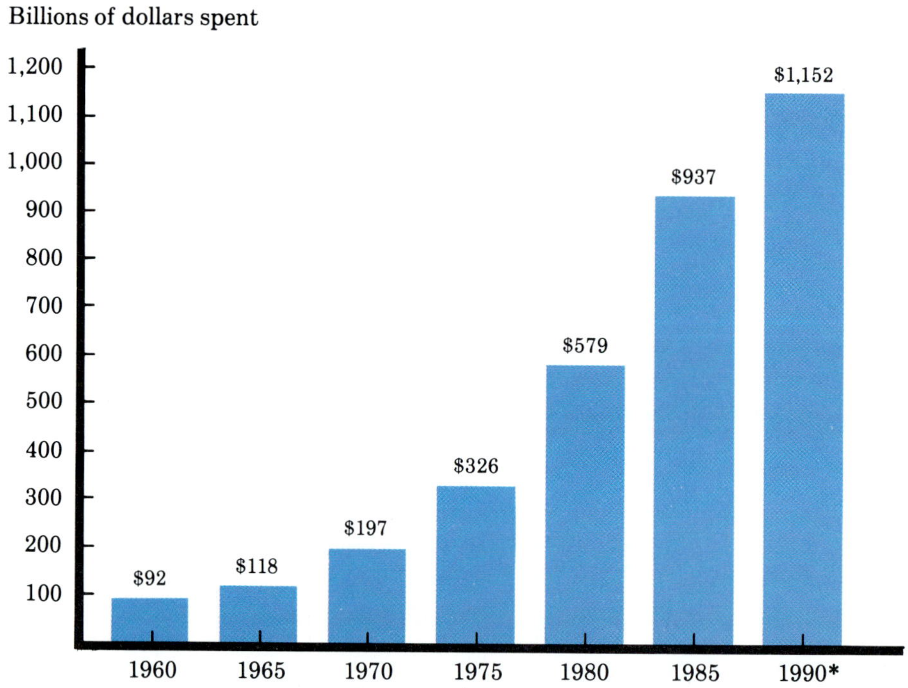

Sources: Department of the Treasury and U.S. Office of Management and Budget

Figure 5.1 Rise in Federal Spending Since 1960

*estimated

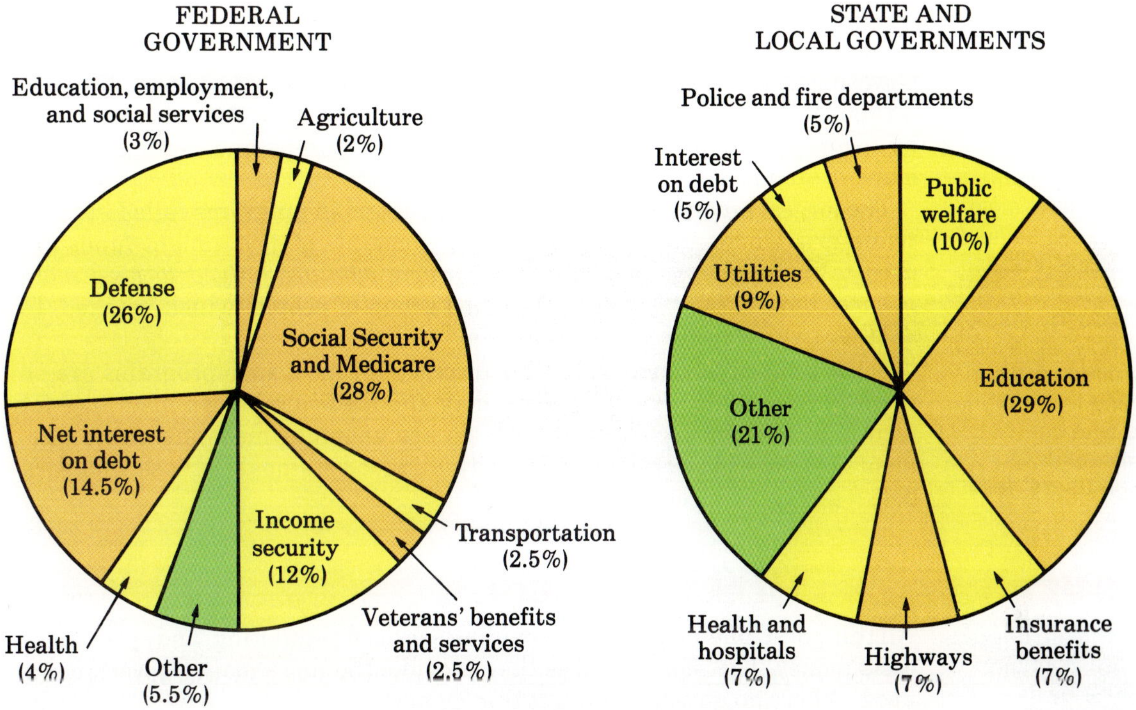

Sources: U.S. Office of Management and Budget and U.S. Bureau of the Census

Figure 5.2 What Governments Spend Money On

Emphasize: Examine expenditures of the three levels of government. Federal government expenditures are primarily (1) income security; (2) national defense; and (3) interest on the national debt. The major expenditures at the state level are (1) education; (2) public welfare; (3) health and hospitals; and (4) highways. At the local level, the major expenditure is education.

lifeguards at community swimming pools and the chief justice of the Supreme Court; license examiners in state motor vehicle bureaus and the president of the United States. In short, the total included anyone who provided government services. About 3 million people worked for the federal government, 4.1 million for the states, and 10.1 million for local governments.

Governments also spend money on pensions to retired government workers. From high school teachers to admirals, government workers receive benefits when they retire. In a recent year, the federal government paid out more than 30 billion dollars in pensions for former government workers. State and local governments also spend billions of dollars on benefits for retired workers.

Governments Buy Goods and Services

Governments must also buy many goods and services so that all these workers can do their jobs. Police officers need police cars, park rangers need uniforms, and soldiers need guns. Nearly every government office needs the file cabinets, typewriters, paper, and pens that a business office needs. Governments do not produce these goods themselves. Rather, they buy them from businesses. Government can be an important customer for a business.

Governments Provide Aid

Clarify: Government gains revenue through taxation only. The basic sources of revenue at the state level are sales and income taxes. Local revenue is primarily from property taxes. Increasingly, all levels of government are attempting to directly tax those who benefit from specific services through **users' fees.**

A third type of government spending is aid to businesses and consumers. Governments help small businesses with loans and loan guarantees. They aid farmers by buying surplus goods and setting price limits. They aid consumers by insuring low-interest home mortgages to veterans and making college loans to students.

The largest amount of government aid is found in programs called **income transfers.** Under these programs, huge amounts of government funds are used to make *payments to groups of people who are judged to need more income.* Income is transferred from one group of people (which is taxed) to another (which receives the payments).

Some local governments transfer income, but most such programs are on the federal or state level. Social security and Medicare health insurance for retired people are income transfers. So are unemployment insurance payments to those temporarily out of work and food stamps for those who earn below a certain income.

GOVERNMENTS COLLECT REVENUE

Note: Private transactions are voluntary decisions by individuals; public transactions are compulsory. Government taxes are not voluntary. Likewise, some government programs, such as education, are also compulsory.

All this government activity—providing services, regulating, and spending—costs money. The more services they provide, the more money governments need. Where do governments get this money?

Four ways governments raise revenue are directly related to the service provided. **User fees** are *charged to those who benefit from specific services.* The swimming pool charge Cora was protesting at the beginning of this chapter is a user fee, so is tuition at a state or city college. **Fines** are *penalties. paid by those who break a law.* If you've ever paid a parking ticket, you know about fines. **License fees** are *charged to those who want to perform certain actions, including many that the government oversees.* You must pay for a driver's license if you want to drive your car on public roads. Someone wanting to start a restaurant must get a license to be able to cook and serve food. Governments also sell bonds to raise money. Some bond issues pay for specific projects, like building a bridge. Others are used to cover general expenses.

To provide such a great number and variety of services, governments need a more general source of revenue. The biggest source of government money is taxes. **Taxes** are *contributions required by a government, which uses them to provide services.* Let's look at the different kinds of taxes.

Governments Levy Three Kinds of Taxes

Governments collect taxes on income, on the sale of goods and services, and on wealth. Figure 5.3 shows how much each type of tax contributes to government revenue.

An **income tax** is *a tax on the income that people and businesses earn.* The personal income tax is the federal government's largest source of rev-

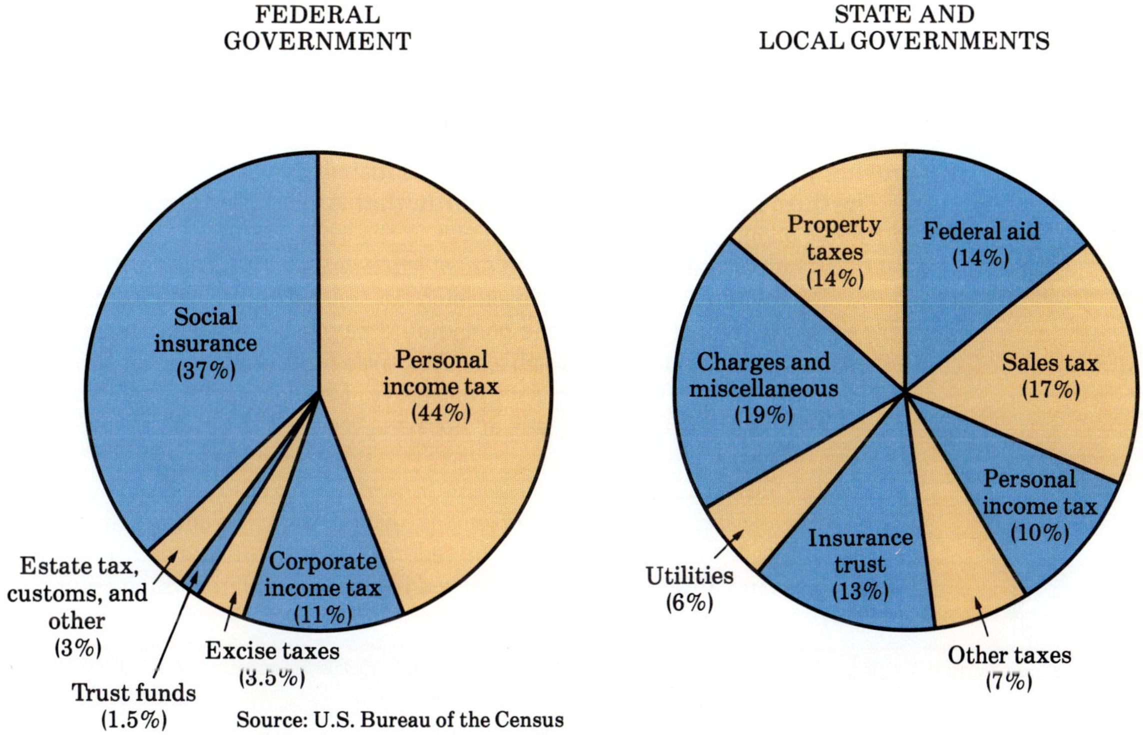

Source: U.S. Bureau of the Census

Figure 5.3 How Governments Raise Money

Math Activity: A social security payment of 15.3 percent is paid on all wages up to $51,300. This is the maximum payment whether you are making $51,300; $151,300; or $251,300. Ask students to figure the amount and the percent of total income paid to social security at these three income levels.

enue. Many states and some local governments also have income taxes, but they rely more heavily on other taxes. The federal personal income tax is a *graduated tax*. This means the tax rate goes up as income rises.

The federal government levies another kind of personal income tax. This is the **social security tax,** *a required contribution most workers make to the federal government's pension system*. Unlike the personal income tax, the social security tax applies only to income earned on a job. It does not apply to income from savings and investments. Also unlike the personal income tax, the social security tax takes the same percentage of almost everyone's income. In 1990 it took 7.65 percent of all wages and salaries up to $51,300. Employers match amounts paid by their workers. Self-employed people pay 15.3 percent, which is equal to the tax both workers and employers pay. Some government workers and others do not pay this tax.

A **sales tax** is *a tax paid by a consumer when he or she buys a good or service*. There is no federal sales tax, but this kind of tax is the biggest source of revenue for most states. The rate varies by state, but generally is between 2 percent and 7 percent. Some cities and towns also charge a sales tax. Many states do not charge a sales tax on purchases of items they believe are essential, such as food and clothing.

Discussion: Should charities, schools, churches, and other not-for-profits pay property taxes? Why or why not? Examine the costs and benefits of their tax exemption.

An **excise tax** is *a sales tax on a specific product.* The federal government levies excise taxes on tobacco, liquor, gasoline, new tires, phone calls, and other products. Many states also charge gasoline taxes.

A **tariff** is, in a way, a tax the government hopes it will not collect. It is *a fee charged on imported goods.* The purpose is to discourage people from buying imports and to protect domestic industries.

The third kind of tax is a tax on **wealth,** that is, on *the money and property a person owns.* The most common form is the **real estate tax,** *a tax based on the value of land, buildings, and other real property a business or consumer owns.* Recall Kim and Cora's discussion at the beginning of the chapter. They were debating whether the pool should be paid for by their town's real estate tax. This is the biggest source of revenue for most local governments. Some also collect a tax on personal property. Charities, churches, schools, and other nonprofit organizations do not have to pay real estate tax in many places.

Another form of tax on wealth is the *inheritance tax,* a tax levied against a person's estate, or property, after his or her death. Federal and state governments levy such taxes, but the federal tax only affects estates larger than a certain value. That limit increased from $225,000 in 1982 to $600,000 in 1987.

Religious or educational institutions are often not required to pay real estate tax.

Taxes Can Be Measured Against Four Standards

Four tests can be used to measure how effective and fair any tax is.

Emphasize: Taxes can be evaluated on the basis of fairness, directness, ease of collection, and economic effects.

The first test is *fairness*—is the tax paid by those who should pay it? People measure fairness in two ways. The first measure, the **benefits-received standard,** is *the principle that people should be taxed according to the share of government services they receive.* For instance, federal gas taxes are used to build and repair highways. Thus, the people who pay the tax (those who buy gas so they can use the highway) reap the benefits (they drive on better highways). This kind of tax is similar to a user fee, but not all taxes can conform to this standard. A lighthouse must shine its light to all ships that pass, not only those willing to pay for its light.

Critical Thinking: Ask students to examine the role of **special interest groups** in determining revenue and expenditures policies.

The second measure of fairness is the **ability-to-pay standard.** This is *the principle that people with more money should pay more in taxes than people with less money.* Economists divide taxes into two groups. A **progressive tax** *sets a higher rate for people with high incomes than for people with low incomes.* The federal personal income tax, which is graduated, is such a tax. On the other hand, a **regressive tax** is *a tax that takes a higher percentage of money from people with low incomes than from people with high incomes.* A sales tax is such a tax. Everyone must pay the same price for a chicken or a pair of pajamas (assuming they buy the same pajamas). Thus, they pay the same amount in sales tax. This is a much smaller percentage of a $40,000 income than it is of an $8,000 income. States that exempt food and clothing from sales tax do so to make the tax less regressive. They believe that purchases other than food and clothing are more likely to be a matter of choice. For this reason, the tax affects people with high incomes more because they make more optional purchases.

Explain: Most of the fees discussed earlier are based on the benefits-received principle. User fees and license fees are both taxes on individuals who will benefit.

A second test is *directness.* Is the tax levied on the person who actually pays it? Some people have argued that there really is no such thing as a "corporate income tax." Businesses, they say, just pass the tax along to consumers in the form of higher prices or to workers as lower wages. The personal income tax is perhaps the most direct form of taxation.

A third test is *collectibility.* Most tax collections depend on cooperation from the taxpayer. If people hide income, or businesses conceal sales, the system can break down.

The fourth test is the effect a tax has on the economy. When all is said and done, no amount of talk about fairness or ease of collection can keep people or businesses from moving elsewhere if they think their taxes are too high. If they move away, their tax revenues—or the jobs they provided—are lost.

YOU INTERACT WITH THE ECONOMY: YOU AFFECT GOVERNMENT

At least in theory, all government actions are taken to benefit the people, and they are all paid for by taxes and other fees that are paid finally by the people. Decisions about government actions are made by voters or by elected

Responsible citizens make their voices heard and try to influence decisions about how public resources are used.

Critical Thinking: What does the declining voter turnout say about politics in the United States? What does the 97 percent reelection rate in the United States say about politics? What can be done to make the political system more responsive to the public, and to encourage the public to be more active in the political process?

Writing Assignment: Encourage students to share their opinions with the elected representatives from your area. Emphasize that representatives are aware of their constituents' attitudes.

Debate: Campaign reform laws are a hot topic. Many criticize the preferential treatment given some large campaign contributors and the constant fundraising. Those in public office argue that campaigns are expensive. The class can debate strategies for reforming political campaigns and their financing.

officials or the people they hire. Can one person affect the decisions those officials make?

You've probably heard all the cynical answers. Millions of people vote, they say. No vote can be seen as *the* decisive one.

Cynics have another argument. In politics as in any other walk of life, they say, money talks. An elected official listens to voters, but he or she listens more to lobbyists and interest groups. They have more money, control more votes, and make more noise.

Cynics offer a third argument. Governments make decisions all the time, but elections are held only every two or four years. If some official's decisions make you unhappy, you can protest all you want. If the next election is two years away, he or she will be making a lot more decisions. Even then, you won't find a candidate whose ideas you agree with all the time.

That's what the cynics say. They ignore the fact that government decisions are based on many people with different ideas agreeing on a common goal. No one person can *control* the government, but each of us surely can *influence* it. We have many ways of showing that influence.

You can vote. More than 75 million people who could have voted *did not* vote in the 1988 presidential election. Seven million of these votes could have changed the outcome. On the local level, your odds are even better because the number of voters is smaller. More than a few local elections have been decided by one or two votes.

If you feel that groups are more effective than one person alone, you can join a political party or a group that supports something you care about. Groups, after all, are made up of individuals.

Summary: Governments at all levels conduct a variety of activities having a direct impact on individuals. With almost one-third of our individual incomes being used to pay for government activities, we all should take an active interest in government.

You can draw up or sign a petition, as Cora and her friends did about the new swimming-pool fee. Elected officials know that the voters they hear from on an issue are likely to be informed voters. They also know that these voters will remember how they responded to the voters' wishes. In many states, voters can petition to have a question put on the ballot at election time, so the people themselves can decide an issue.

You can campaign for a candidate you agree with, and try to convince other voters to vote your way.

You can go to public hearings that government agencies or legislative committees hold when they are considering some action, and speak your views. Many local governments hold open hearings when they're deciding on the year's budget. That gives all people a chance to comment on the government's policies and programs.

You can just write a letter or make a phone call to your representative's office. You'd be surprised how few people do this. The voice that speaks is louder than the voice that remains silent.

Any of these actions can be taken by anyone, and they can make a difference. All of the millions of people who vote are individuals, with personal reasons for voting as they do. Smart politicians know this, and they listen.

Kim may sign Cora's petition. She also may decide to draft another petition, urging the city to charge *more* user fees and lower taxes. Whatever she decides, after she thinks the issue through, she's going to make *her* voice heard.

SUMMARY

- In theory, government in a market economy has only a limited job: to keep law and order, to enforce contracts, and to ensure competition. Our government's role has increased over time as people wanted to meet other economic goals, such as stability and security.
- Federal, state, and local governments provide services, regulate economic activity, spend, and tax.
- Governments provide public services—essential services only they can provide. They also supply merit services, which they have determined should be made available to the public. People may disagree over whether a merit service should be provided.
- Governments regulate economic activity to ensure free and fair competition. They also oversee industries that use public resources or affect society as a whole. They regulate to ensure fairness and safety in the workplace and to ensure public safety. The federal government controls the amount of money in circulation.
- The amount and scope of federal regulation has been shrinking since the late 1970s.
- Governments provide services by spending money to employ people, who in turn buy goods and services. Governments also give financial aid to businesses and consumers.
- To provide services, governments must collect revenue. Governments collect user fees, fines, and license fees and sell bonds, but the biggest source of revenue is taxes.
- Governments raise money with income taxes, sales taxes, excise taxes and tariffs, real estate and property taxes, and inheritance taxes.

- A tax can be evaluated four ways—how fair it is; how direct it is; how easy and practical it is to collect; and how it affects the economy.
- Individuals can affect government actions. They can do this by voting, by joining or forming groups, by drafting and signing petitions, by campaigning for candidates for public office, by speaking at public hearings, or by writing or calling their elected officials.

Key Terms

Match each of the following terms with the definition that most suits it.

ability-to-pay standard	income tax	public services	tariff
benefits-received standard	income transfers	real estate tax	taxes
excise tax	license fees	regressive tax	trust
Federal Reserve System	merit services	sales tax	user fees
fines	progressive tax	social security tax	wealth

a. penalties paid to a government by those who break a law

b. a tax based on the value of land, buildings, and other real property that a business or consumer owns

c. the principle that people with more money should pay more in taxes than people with less money

d. services a government decides it should provide out of a belief that businesses cannot or will not provide enough of them for all people

e. a required contribution most workers make to the federal government's pension system

f. a tax paid by a consumer when he or she buys a good or service

g. a tax that takes a higher percentage of money from people with low incomes than from people with high incomes

h. the money and property a person owns

i. a sales tax on a specific product

j. payments a government makes to groups of people who are judged to need more income

k. fees charged by a government to those who benefit from specific services

l. a tax that sets a higher rate for people with high incomes than for people with low incomes

m. a fee charged on imported goods

n. contributions required by a government, which uses them to provide services

o. services that only a government can or will provide because the service must be provided for everyone, regardless of any person's inability or unwillingness to pay

p. a tax on the income that people and businesses earn

q. a federal agency that controls the money supply and oversees the practices of its member banks

r. the principle that people should be taxed according to the share of government services they receive

s. fees charged to those who want to perform certain actions, including many that the government oversees

t. a situation in which one or a few businesses control an industry

Review Questions

1. According to theory, what are the three functions of government? How and why has the role of government in the United States changed over the years?
2. What are the three levels of government in the United States? How many governments at each level are there?
3. What is the difference between public services and merit services? Give examples of each kind for each level of government.
4. List five reasons governments regulate business activity.
5. Give three examples of recent moves to ease federal rules. What is the reason given for the changes?
6. What are the three things governments spend money to do?
7. Why are payments to certain groups of people called *income transfers*?
8. What are the three factors on which governments base taxes? Give an example of a tax based on each factor.
9. What are the four standards for evaluating taxes?
10. List six actions individuals can take to influence government decisions.

Projects

1. As a class, identify a merit service offered by your local or state government or by the federal government. Stage a debate about whether that service should be provided. (You could also choose a service the government does not provide and argue whether it should.) Debaters in favor of providing the service should explain how to pay for it—by raising taxes or by reducing some service already provided.
2. Choose a government rule that affects your life in some way. Do some research to find out the government's reason for issuing it. If the regulation is a local one or if it is a state or federal one that has a local administrator, you might interview someone who is responsible for issuing or enforcing it. Now look into opposing views—do any individuals or groups argue that the rule should be done away with? Report to the class describing both views and concluding with your recommendation: keep or do away with the regulation.
3. As a class, identify all taxes levied in your town or city or in your state. Apply to these taxes the four standards discussed in this chapter: fairness (benefits received and ability to pay), directness, collectibility, and effect on the economy. Which taxes seem most effective? Why?
4. Find out what bills are being considered in your state or in Congress, or what new laws are being discussed for your town. Pick one that interests you, either because you support it or oppose it. Study the issue—what problem is the proposal meant to solve and how well does it solve the problem? Debate the issue and hold a class vote. Write a letter to your representative in the state legislature or in Congress, or to a member of your local government, explaining the class's stand on the issue.
5. If you are over eighteen, register to vote—and *vote*.

PART THREE
Earning an Income

Planning for the Job You Want

6

Overview: As the vignette illustrates, teenagers have been introduced to only a limited set of career possibilities. Their self-knowledge, likes and dislikes, and their personal desires may be their greatest limitation. Chapter 6 broadens the students' knowledge of career paths, helps them identify their capabilities and desires, and provides basic job-hunting information.

OBJECTIVES

This chapter will help you to:

1. Explain how career and life-style influence each other.
2. Find information on careers that interest you.
3. Match your interests, abilities, and resources to careers.
4. Develop a strategy to get the job you want.
5. Use a résumé, application, and interview to persuade an employer to offer you a job.
6. Find information to help you analyze changing job trends.

Greg and Martha were looking through the career resource center in their guidance counselor's office.

"Look at this," said Greg. "The community college gives a certificate in Restaurant Management."

"Are you interested in that?" asked Martha.

"I think so," answered Greg. "Especially after working as a waiter last summer. The restaurant business is pretty interesting, and I'd like to be the boss. I didn't know you could go to school for that, though. And look here, this says some colleges even offer four-year degrees in Restaurant-Hotel Management."

"Sounds impressive," said Martha. "If you can handle all that schooling, I'd say go for it."

"Maybe—I don't want to decide too quickly," Greg said. "I might want to do more for people than just feed them. You know, summer before last I worked as an aide at the nursing home."

"Oh, I remember that," said Martha. "You were always pretty tired after work. Wasn't it kind of depressing being around sick people all day?"

"The work *was* tough," answered Greg. "But I wouldn't say it was all depressing. It made me feel pretty good to be helping the patients. The other thing I'm thinking about going into is nursing."

"My cousin Joyce is a nurse," said Martha. "I'll give you her number and you can talk to her about it."

"Thanks—that will help," said Greg. "Meanwhile, I'm going to do more reading about both careers."

Activity: Ask students to identify a career cluster and list jobs that fit within that cluster. They should keep this list available.

IN THIS CHAPTER, you'll learn about finding the career you want and getting a job in that career. In the first part you'll see how to focus on a career by looking into careers you find interesting, identifying your interests and abilities, and getting training for the career you want. Then the chapter outlines how you can develop a plan to get the job you want.

CAREER AND LIFE-STYLE INFLUENCE EACH OTHER

World Economy: Ask students to research how career choices are made in the U.S.S.R. or China.

Greg has begun thinking about choosing a career. He wants more than just a job—he wants a line of work he'll pursue for many years. A **career** is *a long-term commitment to a field, industry, or profession.* Within each career are hundreds of **jobs,** which are *the positions at which people work to earn an income.* Law is a career, but jobs in law include lawyer, legal secretary, judge, paralegal assistant, court reporter, and many others. Construction is a career that includes such jobs as plumber, carpenter, electrician, building contractor, and architect.

Entering a career requires investing time and money to get the proper training. Someone entering the legal profession would have to spend at least two years learning how to be a paralegal or six or more studying to be a lawyer. Sometimes the training for a career takes place on the job. Plumbers and carpenters, for instance, learn during four or more years of **apprenticeship.** This is *job training that blends on-the-job experience and classroom study to teach a skill.*

Activity: Using the career cluster and list of related jobs that your students developed earlier, encourage them to rank these jobs on a career ladder.

Investing time and money isn't the only thing that makes career decisions important. A career is one of the major influences on life-style. **Life-style**—*the way we live and how we spend our resources*—is shaped by income, leisure time, family, friends, education, and interests. A career affects all of these areas.

Life-style affects career, too. Interests, friends, education, and family influence career choice. Family can lead us to a certain career. For example, someone brought up on a farm might learn farming there. The income we desire also can guide a career choice. Someone who wants to make a lot of money might choose a career in a business that he or she thinks will offer that opportunity.

Stress: The interrelationship between how we live our life and how we earn our living is an important one. The types of activities we pursue and the people we meet are affected by our career choices.

Career decisions are important for another reason. Most adults spend one-third of their waking hours at work, more time than at any other activity. Thus, happiness can depend to a large degree on **job satisfaction,** *the enjoyment, pride, and sense of accomplishment workers get from their work.*

Because career and job choices are so important, we want them to be good ones. You can help make sure they are by using the method of systematic decision making:

Define: Pursuing further education or training can be called **investment in human capital**. This is any action taken to increase the productivity of labor and includes improvements in health or mobility.

Step 1. Define the problem—you need to work to be able to satisfy your wants.

Step 2. Identify and rank goals—decide what you want from a career.

Step 3. Determine alternatives—learn about careers and look into the ones that seem interesting.

Step 4. Choose the best alternative—match your interests, abilities, and resources to the careers you've looked into.

Step 5. Put the decision into action—get the training you need to enter the career.

Step 6. Evaluate the decision—decide whether your career fulfills your goals.

Critical thinking: Why do some people who are at the top of their profession opt for a career change?

This chapter will show you how to accomplish steps 1 through 5, but the sixth step—evaluating your decision—is important to remember. Some people stay with one career all their lives, but many change to another career they feel offers a greater chance for success and satisfaction. If economic conditions change, it may also be time to change careers.

Part of evaluating a job is looking at the future with a current employer. Try to see how a current job fits into the **occupational ladder,** *the steps up from the lowest job in a career to the highest.* For instance, someone working for a department store can begin as a salesperson, move up to a supervisor, eventually be promoted to department head, and finally become a store manager. Seeing this series of steps, the salesperson has a clear idea of where the present job may lead.

FOCUSING ON A CAREER

Activity: Have each student identify a job from their career cluster in which they are interested and identify where this "target job" is located on the career ladder (entry level, mid-level, or upper level).

Activity: Ask students to write down the names of people who are employed in their "target job" and where these people work.

Activity: Ask the school librarian or guidance counselor to show students how to use career-related reference materials.

Choosing a career involves many steps. In this section, you'll learn how to find out about different careers and what to look for in a career to see if it's for you. You'll see how to learn about yourself so that you'll make the best career choice, and you'll learn how to get the skills you'll need for the career you choose.

Learning about Careers

You've already spent many years in school learning about the great variety of careers you can choose from. As you get closer to making a choice, you need to be able to find more detailed information about the careers you're most interested in.

There are many sources of information on careers, and the best place to find them is in the school library or resource center. Here you can look through many books describing career fields and jobs within each one. Some of these books give facts and figures about the work, salary, and future prospects of a job. Others contain descriptions of jobs by working people who tell us what they do and how they like it.

An important reference book is the *Occupational Outlook Handbook*, published every other year by the Bureau of Labor Statistics. It gives descriptions, earnings, working conditions, and the employment outlook for more than 300 occupations. Two more good resources are the *Handbook of Job Facts* and the *Encyclopedia of Careers and Vocational Guidance.*

You can also get information by writing to trade and professional associations or labor unions. These groups often publish booklets and brochures describing the jobs in their fields, along with important statistics. Names and addresses of these groups are listed in the *Directory of National Trade and Professional Associations of the United States* and the *Directory of United States Labor Organizations.*

You can get expert advice about careers by talking with people who actually work in the career you're interested in. At the beginning of the chapter, Greg's friend Martha suggested that he talk to her cousin, who is a nurse. This is a great way for him to learn about the job. If you interview someone, plan your questions in advance so that you'll get helpful answers about what the work is like, what training is needed, and what related jobs there are. Remember to send a thank-you note after the interview.

One of the best ways to learn whether you like a career is to do part-time work. Greg's summer job as a nurse's aide gave him enough experience to make him think he might like to be a nurse. Part-time work also helps you meet people in the field who can tell you about their jobs.

What to Look for in Careers

We all pursue different goals when we make our career choices. But we can use eight factors to analyze careers to see if they match what we want.

- *Income*—some people want a high income; others may want more free time. All people want some income. Income and benefits are the first things we

Each career contains many different jobs. The workers in these photographs are doing two of the many jobs in the transportation industry.

Activity: Ask the guidance counselor to administer career interest and aptitude tests to your students.

Clarify: The opportunity cost of pursuing further education and training includes more than just tuition and books. You must also consider the income that could have been earned while in school. Thus, if you could have earned $15,000 per year after earning a high school degree, then this $15,000, multiplied by the number of years you will be in school, is an opportunity cost.

ask about when deciding about careers, but we need to consider other factors, too.

- *Training or education*—today, almost all jobs require at least a high school diploma. Many careers call for more schooling or special training. Think about how much training a career requires and how willing you are to invest the time. Like all choices, training has an opportunity cost—how much income are you giving up now by taking the time for training? Still, this time is also an investment for the future. Training now may mean higher income later, as Figure 6.1 shows.
- *Personal and physical characteristics*—each career demands certain traits for success. A jeweler must have patience and an eye for detail. Police officers must meet certain standards for height and weight.
- *Economic future*—the job market is constantly changing. Some changes result from the pushes and pulls of supply and demand; others are caused by new technology making some jobs out of date or creating new ones. For instance, the use of computer phone systems means that fewer operators will be needed. The library has information on job trends. The *Occupational Outlook Handbook* tells whether the number of people needed for a job will grow or decline. News reports and magazines publish similar predictions, often near the end of the school year. Magazines that offer this information include *Changing Times, Consumers' Digest*, and *Money*. The last section in this chapter gives some hints on what skills are likely to be most valuable in the future.
- *Working conditions*—steelworkers should expect a hot, noisy, demanding workplace. Farmers must be prepared to work outdoors in many types of weather. Working conditions also include the number of hours a career calls for. Doctors spend many hours seeing patients, sometimes in the middle of the night. Many health careers offer less leisure time than does a 35-hour-a-week bank teller's job. Some careers, like selling, may require

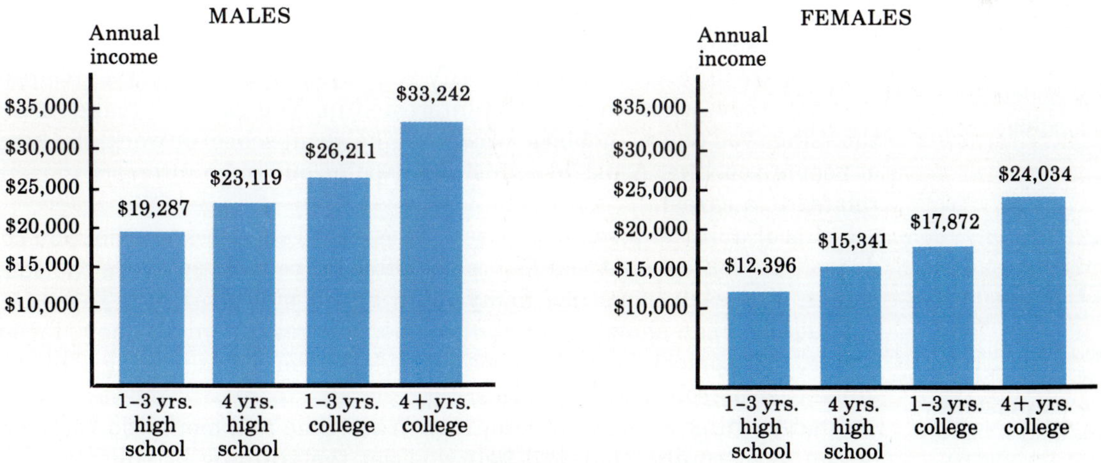

Source: Bureau of Labor Statistics

Figure 6.1 Comparing the Annual Income of Workers with Different Educations

- *Kind of work*—careers are grouped according to whether they involve work with data, people, or things. Of course, most careers include all three, but each emphasizes one or another. A company treasurer, for instance, works primarily with data—reports and tables. Social workers or hair stylists spend most of their time working with people. A potter or machine operator works with things. Each of us prefers one type of work or another, and this affects job satisfaction.
- *Degree of control*—careers differ in how much control workers have over the work they do. Specialists like advertising copywriters or master electricians may have a lot of freedom. Factory workers and receptionists, on the other hand, are often under close supervision.
- *Responsibility*—how much work you are answerable for is another factor. A sales clerk, for example, is responsible only for his or her own work. A headwaiter in a restaurant or an office manager has to supervise a group of people and must ensure that they do their jobs well.

Activity: Have each student rank order the eight career factors with 1 as the most important, and 8 as the least important. When examining their "target jobs," the ranking of these factors becomes increasingly important.

Illustrate: Examine the teaching profession using the eight career factors.

By considering these eight factors, you analyze the careers you're interested in. Of course, each person will rank these factors differently. Some people will emphasize income; others will stress working with people; and still others will emphasize some other factor. Each of us can use these factors to make our goals clear.

Critical Thinking: Explore the trade-offs that may be necessary between career factors. For example, spray painters in auto assembly plants are paid a high salary to compensate for their health risks (inhaling chemicals from the spray). If OSHA requires protection for the workers to decrease the health risks, does the firm need to continue paying higher salaries?

Learning About Yourself

To know what career to choose, you must learn about yourself. You've already learned some things about yourself by identifying what you're looking for in a career, but you also need to know your interests, abilities, and resources. When you combine this knowledge with the research you've already done, you will be ready to choose a career.

Interests, as we've seen, include whether you prefer to work with data, people, or things. They also include hobbies and extracurricular activities, which sometimes lead people into a career. Because athletes and musicians often like what they do, they are willing to put in the long hours of practice needed to sharpen their skills.

There are different ways to identify your interests. Counselors give tests that can show what areas you're interested in. You can also make lists of the things you enjoy—hobbies, what you like about school or work, the kinds of people you like. A list like this might point out some interests that are related to a career.

World Economy: In a command economy, individuals have much less choice in their career path. The central authority identifies what workers are needed and which individuals should be trained for those jobs.

Skills or abilities also affect career decisions. Take stock of what you *can* do well as well as what you *like* to do. Often, of course, these are the same things. But each of us has many abilities we may overlook. Taking an aptitude test can show where abilities lie. The results might show, for example, that someone is good at math but less talented at writing. This can guide that person's career choices.

Finally, think about your resources. What time and money do you have, or can you acquire, that will help you get the training or education you need? Can you manage to go to vocational school or college full-time? Part-time? Could you get a student loan?

Activity: Ask students to research the skills needed for their "target job." Would this job require further education or training? Is the job only available in specific geographic locations? What upward mobility is possible?

Emphasize: Entry-level workers are often faced with the dilemma that they cannot get a job without experience, but they cannot get experience without a job. Volunteer activity is one way of solving this dilemma.

Critical Thinking: The United States has had a volunteer military service for some time. The pay rates of the military rose as an incentive for individuals to join. Advertisements and recruitment materials emphasized the training and careers available. The ultimate need for the military, physically protecting the nation, has been minimized. Would you trade a few years in a war zone for job training?

School guidance counselors can give students valuable help in identifying their abilities, interests, and resources.

You can get help from many people to learn about yourself. You can ask family and friends for their views. People who know you can often tell you valuable things about yourself. School counselors and teachers are very good sources for learning about yourself. Counselors can help by giving the tests we've mentioned, and by helping you interpret the results.

Learning the Skills for the Career You Want

After settling on a career, it's time to learn the skills you'll need. You can learn the tasks required for a particular job by getting experience, training, or education, or a combination of these.

One way to get experience in a career area is to do part-time or volunteer work in that area. When Greg worked as a nurse's aide one summer, he learned skills he will use later if he becomes a nurse. Summer jobs are great for getting different kinds of experience. You can find out about summer jobs in the latest edition of the *Summer Employment Directory of the United States*, which lists 50,000 summer jobs every year, in camps, hotels, resorts, parks, conference centers, and other places.

You can get training for a career at a vocational school, in the military service, or on the job. Training usually results in being certified to perform a specific skill. There are vocational programs in many high schools for specific skills, like welding, trucking, and operating a computer. The armed forces provide good training in many areas. This training is free, although it does cost the few years of time that must be spent in military service. On-the-job training means that you get the job first and are trained by your supervisor as you do the work.

Activity: Using the Sunday newspaper, have students research the want ads. You also may use a newspaper from a large city near you for comparison.

Education after high school includes formal schooling in two-year or four-year colleges, night schools, and graduate or professional schools. Instead of being certified for one particular skill, the student gets a degree when the schooling is complete. The material covered in school may be general and useful for a wide variety of jobs. The course of study can be directly related to knowledge needed for a few related jobs.

Finally, you can combine experience, training and education to learn the skills you'll need. Many people have summer jobs *and* get education or training. Jobs provide some on-the-job training, even for workers who are already certified or have had formal schooling after high school.

PLANNING TO GET THE JOB YOU WANT

Getting a job is not simply a matter of walking into an office and asking for work. Greg's friend Martha has decided on the career she wants—photography. She needs a part-time job to earn some money while she takes photography courses, and she'd like it to be related to photography. To get the job, though, Martha needs a plan. Her method for getting a job is to find a job opening and to present herself to potential employers as the most qualified person for that opening. The tools she will use to persuade someone to hire her are a résumé, an application, and an interview. Let's see how she uses them.

Extension: The term describing the cultivation of contacts is networking. Students will locate a variety of magazine articles that describe benefits and costs of networking and methods of developing these contacts.

Learning about job openings means more than reading the help wanted ads. Contacts—family, friends, teachers, guidance counselors, and former employers—are good sources for finding jobs. People with something in common—like members of a professional group, graduates of the same school, or residents of the same community—often tell each other about job openings. Once they know, they may pass the information on to you. Contacts may also recommend you for a job. If they do, you have a responsibility to live up to the good recommendation.

Focus: Invite a representative from the state employment service to talk with your students about conducting a job search.

You can also use a **private employment agency,** which is a *business that tries to match employers with qualified job applicants*. Many charge a fee, but sometimes the employer will pay it. Some agencies handle only high-level positions. Some also specialize in jobs in certain fields. Many have so many clients that it's a good idea to check with them often to keep your name in their minds. Before using an employment agency, check on its record of effectiveness. Ask to talk to people they've placed in the past. Get all fee terms clearly spelled out in writing.

Research: Ask students to research the medieval guild system.

Public employment agencies run by the state or city government offer information too. They can tell you about government jobs, but they also list openings in private industry. Their services are free.

Activity: Require students to put together their résumé. This may take time and assistance from you.

Extension: Ask a personnel director to assist the class in résumé writing. Send the completed student résumés to the director for review and comments. Give these comments to your students and have them revise their résumés accordingly.

Focus: Invite a guest speaker to speak about civil service positions and to identify how civil-service jobs differ from private-sector jobs.

Activity: Survey businesses in your area to determine how many have help-wanted signs in the window and how many display them in the store.

So far we've looked at some indirect ways of finding a job—relying on contacts or agencies. It's usually more effective, though, to apply for a job on your own. You can do this by talking to an employer, answering a want ad, or acting on information you read or hear about in the news.

Talking directly to employers is a good way to explore job prospects. You could apply directly to the personnel office of an employer you want to work for. Large companies often fill job openings this way. Remember that personnel officers may want to fill the job they have open, rather than another job the applicant is interested in. Make sure your own interests are being considered.

Of course, want ads are a good way to find out about openings, although they aren't the only way. In responding to an ad, be sure to answer promptly and follow the ad's directions exactly.

News reports may reveal present or future needs for workers. The announcement of a new company being formed or a new building being built hints at potential job openings. Watchful newspaper readers can apply to the new company before any jobs are actually posted. By being on the scene so early, these people may persuade the employer to hire them—they show initiative.

Government jobs are a separate area, and there are several ways to apply for them. People who want to join the armed forces will go to a military recruiter. Those who want civilian jobs must complete a civil service application form, called *SF171*. Someone trying to enter the civil service should sign up for a particular type of job. The person should fill out the form a few months before he or she intends to start work. Many state and local government workers are hired on the basis of test results.

Getting an Employer to Consider Hiring You

Getting a job is work. To get that work done, we must use the right tools, including a résumé, an application, and an interview.

A **résumé** *summarizes a job applicant's education, experience, and interests.* It presents such information as the applicant's name, address, employment objective, education, work experience, special interests, achievements, and references. Look at the sample in Figure 6.2 to see what a good résumé looks like.

Here are some hints for what to put in a résumé:

1. *Job objective*—this shows employers what your goals are. Like Martha, you should use it to structure the other information you include. Tailor the other information to fit the objective.
2. *Work experience*—include past employers, dates, titles, and work done. This shows the experience you've gained and what skills you have. Martha's résumé lists all the part-time and full-time work she's done, and it describes briefly how each job fits into her objective.
3. *Education*—you may put this section before work experience if you have not had many jobs. It includes schools, dates, and special activities and achievements, especially if they're related to the job being applied for—

Focus: Before listing someone as a reference on their résumés students should consider what characteristics they would like the reference to address. Maybe a reference could attest to the applicant's honesty or punctuality or their overall character. Maybe the reference is a former employer who can address the applicant's work experience. When asking an individual's permission to be included as a reference, tell the individual why you wish to include them.

Critical Thinking: How can a prospective employer ascertain whether or not the information in a résumé is true?

Discussion: When and how would you use a résumé?

Martha Stone
921 Great Road
Lumberville, NJ 08530

Phone: (609) 555-3867

JOB OBJECTIVE:	Job that leads to further career opportunities in photography.
<u>Work Experience</u>	
September 1990-present	OFFICE ASSISTANT (part-time). Herb Young Studios, Lumberville, NJ. Handled billings and receipts and appointments books. Maintained equipment. Assisted on set-ups for portraits.
September 1989-September 1990	OFFICE ASSISTANT (part-time). Drs. Robert and Joan Driver, Stanton, NJ. Logged appointments, pulled files for patients, helped with billing to insurance companies.
September 1988-September 1989	COUNTER WORKER (part-time). Hamburger Heaven, Stanton, NJ. Took and filled orders, some cooking. Handled cash; in last three months, helped close daily books.
<u>Education</u>	
	STUDENT. MacArthur High School, Lumberville, NJ. Business education curriculum. 3.1 grade point average. Member of Camera Club for 3 years, president 1990-1991. Photographer for MacArthur <u>Centennial</u>, school newspaper, for 3 years.
<u>References</u>	
	Thomas McCormick (sponsor of school newspaper and yearbook), MacArthur High School, Lumberville, NJ 08530
	Drs. Robert and Joan Driver, 731 Professional Plaza, Stanton, NJ 08559

Figure 6.2 Martha's Résumé

like Martha's Camera Club membership and her work on the school paper.

4. *References*—people who know a job applicant's character and work are **references.** Martha listed a teacher and former employers who she knew would speak well of her work and character. She also made sure to ask their permission before listing them. A résumé doesn't have to include references. Martha could have just written, "References will be furnished upon request."

The information in a résumé, of course, should always be the truth, and remember a few points on how to prepare a résumé. One page is generally best, unless there is too much to say to fit in that space. Résumés should be typed, and they should always be neat. They are most effective if their format is clear and logical.

Martha used her résumé to apply for a job at the Camera Store that she saw advertised in the paper. She also included a cover letter, which is shown in Figure 6.3. Notice how she uses the letter to highlight the experience that relates most to the job.

Note: A résumé is helpful in recalling dates, activities, and names while completing application forms.

Most large companies ask applicants to fill out an application form. A **job application** is *a form companies use to keep a record of similar information for all people who apply for work.* Although the application may repeat information on a résumé, companies want it for their personnel records. It must, of course, be filled out neatly and completely.

Activity: Tape students during mock interviews. With students playing the roles of both interviewer and job candidate, the class will be able to examine both sides of the interaction. By playing back the tape, students will be able to evaluate their conduct during the interview.

Employers usually interview all applicants. An **interview** is *a meeting that gives employers and job applicants the chance to talk to each other.* Large companies often give two interviews. The first is with a personnel officer, who checks the facts in the applicant's résumé and determines if the applicant seems willing and able to work. The second is with the person who will supervise the applicant if he or she is hired. This person may ask more detailed questions related to the specific job. He or she may also try to find out how the applicant will fit in with the other workers.

The fact that someone is asked for an interview means that the employer is interested in that person's skills. Whether or not he or she gets the job,

Extension: Ask a personnel director to direct and critique mock interviews in class.

Evaluation: Write a mock want ad for an entry-level position. Require that your students apply in writing for this position. By not specifying what should be included in the application (contents of the cover letter or résumé) you can evaluate their understanding of Chapter 6.

921 Great Road
Lumberville, NJ 08530
June 6, 1991

Ms. Louise Sagan
The Camera Store
Three Corners Mall
Hamlin, NJ 08648

Dear Ms. Sagan:

In response to your ad of June 6, 1991, in the Star, I am applying for your position as a full-time sales clerk. My résumé is enclosed.

My last three jobs have given me much experience working with customers. I have also learned how to take and process orders and handle basic bookkeeping tasks. My experience as a photographer has familiarized me with basic equipment and film types, so I should be able to answer customers' questions knowledgeably.

I am available for an interview any weekday after 3:00. I could start working two weeks after notifying my current employer. My telephone number is 555-3867.

Sincerely,

Martha Stone

Martha Stone

Enc.

Figure 6.3 Martha's Cover Letter

Discussion: Describe appropriate attire and grooming for an interview.

Critical Thinking: Is it hypocritical for an applicant to dress in a way that is not natural, just to conform in the hope of getting a job?

List: List questions that are appropriate to ask during an interview.

Note: Beware of bragging or exaggerating positives attributes. Both behaviors may cause problems later.

Show an interviewer that you're ready for work by dressing neatly and appropriately, being polite, and being prepared to answer questions.

though, will depend on how well the interview goes. To be sure to do well, prepare carefully.

Here are some things to do to prepare for an interview:

- Find out as much as possible about the company or business you're applying to by reading and by talking to other workers or customers.
- Practice for the interview by having a friend ask you some questions the interviewer is likely to ask, like "Why do you want this job?" and "What work have you done that will help you do this job?"
- Check over your résumé just before the interview begins to refresh your memory of what it says.
- Make a good impression by being punctual and polite and by dressing neatly and in a style appropriate for the job you're interviewing for.
- An interviewer's aim is to find out if you're right for the job, but you also need to know if the job is right for you. Be prepared to ask some questions of your own to find out about the kind of work, the hours, the size of the staff, and any other concerns you may have.
- Remember to stress your good side—you're trying to persuade someone to hire you.

After the interview may come a job offer. To evaluate an offer, be sure to get all the information you need to make a choice. Get a clear statement of the job duties, salary, and working conditions. Ask how soon you need to make up your mind.

You can ask for advice from your friends and your family, but be sure to evaluate job offers according to your own goals and values. Other people can help you, but it is your choice to make.

YOU INTERACT WITH THE ECONOMY: OCCUPATIONAL TRENDS

Focus: If offered the job, most applicants feel pressured to decide immediately. There is a trade-off between accepting a position too quickly (and foregoing better job offers that may come later) and waiting too long (with someone else being hired for the position). It is important for students to analyze the benefits and liabilities of a job offer and to know the consequences of accepting or rejecting that offer.

Career choices affect the rest of our lives, so we want to make them carefully. We not only think about our personal interests, but also consider the general condition of the economy. We need to think about how much demand there will be in the future for the career we choose.

Economic trends affect the desirability of certain careers at different times. For example, during the 1970s, the number of students graduating from law school more than doubled. This caused a great deal of competition in the field. The number of law school graduates leveled off in the 1980s, but there are still not enough jobs for all the new lawyers. By the year 2000, however, the number of lawyers should be equal to the number of jobs available.

We are in a world of careers in which two of the key words are *information* and *service*. As Figure 6.4 shows, agriculture, mining, and manufacturing

Critical Thinking: Why did the number of law-school graduates level off in the 1980s? What signaled that the number of lawyers available was greater than the number of lawyers demanded? Ask students for other examples (i.e., engineers, teachers, computer programmers, MBAs).

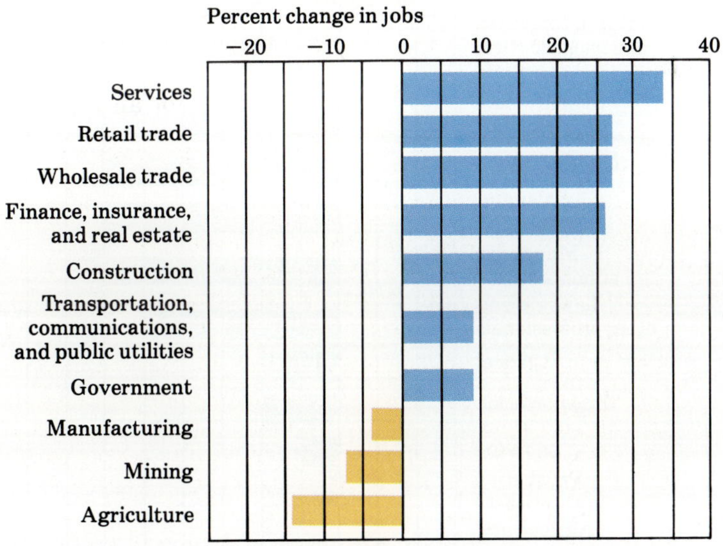

Source: Bureau of Labor Statistics

Figure 6.4 Estimated Growth in Jobs by Industry from 1986 to 2000

Discussion: Many people are critical of our movement toward a service economy. They predict we will become a country of "short-order cooks and hamburger flippers." Actually, the service sector represents jobs with both high- and low-skill levels as well as high and low incomes. Physicians, lawyers, and accountants are included in the service sector. Ask your students to brainstorm all the jobs they can think of in the service sector.

World Economy: The United States is often criticized because for the most part our citizens speak only one language. However, for the past few decades, English was the international language of business. Therefore, if a businessperson in Japan wanted to conduct business in international markets, he or she had to communicate in English. The same was true in Europe and other countries.

are expected to lose jobs through the 1990s. The fastest growing types of jobs now are professional, service, sales, and those in the fields of computer and natural science. (See Figure 6.5.)

Another important feature of today's economy is that the United States is facing stronger economic competition from other countries than ever before. At the same time, the nation depends more on other countries than ever before, especially for natural resources like oil. As a result, employers want workers who know and can use foreign languages. They also need workers who can understand how people live and think in other countries. Those other nations may contain a firm's suppliers or a new market of consumers.

What does all of this mean for you? When choosing a career, keep these trends in mind and try to get the skills that will prepare you for jobs that will grow in the future.

The four basic areas of skills useful in the information and service industries are:

1. *Language and communication skills*—these include the ability to read, write, listen, and speak effectively. They also include the ability to speak foreign languages.
2. *Media skills*—these include the ability to receive and evaluate information from the various media we are exposed to, like radio, TV, newspapers, magazines, and more.

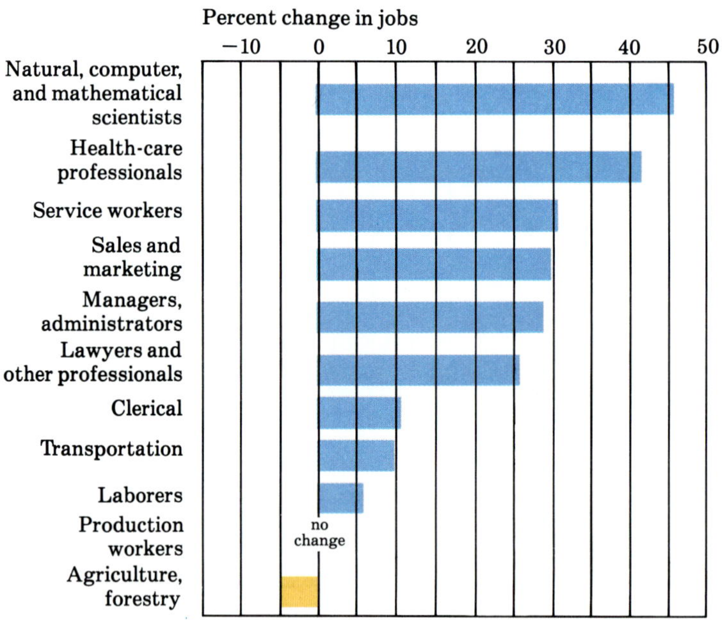

Source: Bureau of Labor Statistics

Figure 6.5 Estimated Growth in Jobs by Occupational Type from 1986 to 2000

Summary: Students have been introduced to the world of the labor force. They have also learned steps to take in order to participate in the labor market. By examining their abilities and what they want from a job, students begin investigating a career path.

Focus: Necessary skills for success in the labor market are the abilities to read and comprehend, to write and communicate, to perform math functions, and to think and make rational decisions.

3. *Computer skills*—because computers play a part in most jobs, we need to know how to use them and how to use the information they provide. This includes knowing how to use a computer's keyboard.
4. *People skills*—service workers need tact, patience, understanding, and friendliness. These can all be grouped under one heading—consideration for others.

These skills will prepare you for future careers in two ways. One is related to the principle of supply and demand, and the other to the advantages of flexibility. First, these skills are in demand. Having them will make you more likely to get a job, better able to do well at that job, and more likely to earn a high income. Remember that the higher the demand for a particular skill, the higher the pay will be. Second, these skills will also make you more flexible. Since most employers will be looking for people with these skills, you will have more freedom to move if you wish and more alternatives to choose from. Adaptability to changes in the job market is essential. Technological advances and the results of supply and demand bring about changes in the job market. Developing skills such as language and communication skills and people skills will help you adapt to any new situations. However, you may also have to learn new skills as well.

SUMMARY

- Careers shape life-style, but career choice is also guided by life-style. Because of the amount of time people spend working, job satisfaction is important.
- Focus on a career by learning about different careers and what to look for in a career; learning about your interests, abilities, and resources; and learning the skills you will need for the career you want.
- To investigate careers you find interesting, talk to people already working in them or do research in the school's career center or in the public library.
- Evaluate careers according to eight factors: income, education and training, physical or personal characteristics required, the future of the career, working conditions, type of work involved, degree of control over the work, and responsibility.
- To learn about your interests, abilities, and resources, you can explore your ideas, talk to others, and take tests.
- To prepare yourself for a career, get the needed education or training. You may also be able to learn by doing part-time work.
- Getting the job you want results from finding an opening and using a résumé, an application, and an interview to persuade an employer that you're the right person to fill the job.
- To identify job openings, use want ads, news reports, contacts, or employment agencies. You can also apply to the employer directly.
- A résumé should be one page long and neatly typed. It should summarize the education and work experience that relate to the job objective.

- In applying for some jobs, include a cover letter with the résumé. Some large companies ask people to fill out job applications.
- Interviews can determine whether an applicant gets a job or not. By preparing well for an interview and making a good impression, you can persuade an employer to offer you a job.
- Career decisions are better if they take the future of the economy into account. Consider which areas will decline in importance and which will grow and what skills those fields require.

Key Terms

Match each of the following terms with the definition that most suits it.

apprenticeship	job	life-style	references
career	job application	occupational ladder	résumé
interview	job satisfaction	private employment agency	

a. the position at which a person works to earn an income

b. a meeting that gives employers and job applicants the chance to talk to each other

c. the enjoyment, pride, and sense of accomplishment workers get from their work

d. a fact sheet that summarizes a job applicant's education, experience, and interests

e. people who know a job applicant's character and work

f. a long-term commitment to a field, industry, or profession

g. the steps up from the lowest job in a career to the highest

h. a form companies use to keep a record of similar information for all people who apply for work

i. the way we live and how we spend our resources

j. training that blends on-the-job experience and classroom study to teach a skill

k. a business that tries to match employers with qualified job applicants

Review Questions

1. How do career and life-style affect each other?
2. How important is it to evaluate your career? Why? Is it likely that every person will have only one career?
3. Where can you get more information on careers?
4. What factors can you use to evaluate careers?
5. How can you learn about yourself in preparing to choose a career? What should you try to learn?
6. Why make a plan for getting a job?
7. In what ways can you learn about job openings?
8. What makes an effective résumé?
9. What can interviewees do to make a good impression?
10. How can we take the future into account when choosing a career? Where can we get information about the economy in the future?

Projects

1. Identify a group of related careers that seems interesting to you. In the library, research six jobs in that group. Make a chart for these jobs showing which require little education and which require much education or training. Add estimates for yearly income and benefits for the jobs. Now try to find information about the future of those jobs. Add another column to the chart, and in it rate the jobs with a good future with a plus and give those with a poor future a minus. Pool your findings with your classmates to create a reference file on promising careers.
2. Pick a job that seems interesting to you. Learn what kind of work it involves and what training it requires. Make a list of questions—things you'd like to know about the job. Set up an interview with someone who has the job and ask him or her the questions. Afterwards, be sure to send the person you interviewed a thank-you note.
3. Write a résumé for yourself with the job you studied in project 2 as your job objective. (If you've changed your mind, find another job you'd like.) Include all your experience that is related to the job. If you are fully trained for the job, fine. If not, for the sake of this project, assume that you have gotten the training you need.
4. Raymond Marlowe wants to be an airplane mechanic. He graduated from Lake Shore High School in 1988. He was in the vocational program for mechanics and took courses in mathematics and science. He had a B average. He also graduated in June 1990 from a two-year school, where he learned airplane mechanics. The school was the Michigan School of Aeronautics in Denton, Michigan. His instructor's name was Randy Jackson. In October 1990 he took and passed the test to obtain an A license, allowing him to work on airplane bodies. (In the future, he plans to take the test for a P license, allowing him to work on airplane engines.) He worked as a gas station attendant and auto mechanic part-time from June 1985 to January 1988. He pumped gas, did engine maintenance and tune-ups, and mounted and balanced tires. The station's name was Berman's Exxon in Laketown, Michigan. He worked as an airplane mechanic's assistant at Detroit Metropolitan Airport from January 1988 to September 1988. His supervisor's name was George Kennedy. Raymond's address is 10608 Hayes, Laketown, Michigan 48170. His phone number is 313-555-2067. Write a résumé for Raymond.
5. Team up with another student. One of you will identify a job you are interested in. While that person prepares a résumé, the other will take the role of an employer with that job opening. Determine what the working conditions, pay, benefits, and tasks are. Decide what you want in an employee—what personal characteristics, experience, and skills you're looking for. Meanwhile, the applicant will prepare for the interview. Now the employer should read the applicant's résumé and interview him or her for the job. Once the interview is done, the employer should say whether he or she would hire the applicant, and the applicant should say whether he or she would want the job. Both should explain why they made this decision.

Entering the Work Force

7

Overview: Chapter 7 investigates the work force, land, labor, capital, and entrepreneurship. As the vignette illustrates, the quality of any of these components in the production process can affect the productivity of the others.

OBJECTIVES

This chapter will help you to:

1. Explain how entering the work force requires you to work cooperatively with others.
2. Relate worker and management rights to the responsibilities of each.
3. Define labor unions and explain what labor and management bargain about.
4. Describe how your status as a worker may change.
5. Summarize how worker productivity affects economic growth.

The supervisor looked at the dozen workers gathered around her before coming to the point of her short speech. "So," she finally said, "the word is that unless there's a big increase in productivity, we're going to have to lay some people off. Maybe three or four, maybe the whole crew. Sorry, but that's the way it is."

Sheila and her friends discussed the situation at lunch. "More productivity!" Dave fumed. "What do they want? We're doing the best we can with these beat-up old machines. Why don't they modernize the plant?"

"Times are tough," Sheila said. "You know how expensive that would be."

"You ever notice how it's always the workers that get the raw deal when times are tough?" asked Carla.

"Oh, don't be silly!" chimed in Ernie. "We *could* be more productive. We *could* get more finished parts out every day. We did last year."

"Last year the machines still worked," Dave grumbled.

"I don't know," Sheila said. "Maybe Ernie has a point."

"Forget it," said Carla. "You know what we should do? We should have a slowdown. Show them how important we are. Make them understand what we contribute to this business."

"That's true, we do work pretty hard," said Sheila.

"But don't you think the owners have a right to expect that we'll do the best we can?" countered Ernie.

Critical Thinking: What must a business do in order to make a profit? Who benefits from profits?

SHEILA AND HER CO-WORKERS have a decision to make. Before they decide, they'll have to think long and hard about their rights and responsibilities as workers. They'll have to consider their employer's rights and responsibilities, too.

HAVING A JOB MEANS WORKING WITH OTHERS

Discussion: What is meant by modernizing a plant? If a firm invests in order to buy new capital equipment, what impact does that have on labor? If the capital equipment is allowed to become outdated, what impact does that have on labor?

Whatever work you do, you will work with others. Even if you open your own business and hire no other workers, you will need the cooperation of suppliers and you must meet the needs of your customers. Chances are, however, you will go to work at first for an organization. An **organization** is *a group of people working toward a common goal.*

All organizations have an objective or goal. For a business, the main goal is to make and sell a product or service at a profit. For a government agency, it might be to clean up polluted waters or to reduce crime. For a nonprofit organization, it might be to find a cure for cancer or to teach children about music. Whatever its goal, all members of the organization will (or should) work to achieve that goal.

Organizations rely on managers to ensure that all work is aimed at meeting their goals. **Managers** are *the people who turn an organization's goals into directions for the workers.* Managers try to ensure that work is effective and efficient.

Define: Productivity is the quantity of output achieved from each unit of input. Increasing productivity could mean increasing the output gained from using the existing inputs; or it could mean producing the same output by using fewer inputs.

World Economy: In the 1980s Japanese production methods were considered to be the most efficient in the world. U.S. industries studied Japanese production methods, especially "Quality Circles." The Quality Circle process gives Japanese workers opportunities to suggest improvements in the production process. Some business experts believe that by adopting this communication process, U.S. firms would increase production and help all workers feel they are an integral part of the process; thus, improving labor productivity.

Communication is two-way: managers must give advice and instructions but also be ready to listen to workers' suggestions and problems.

When an organization meets its goals, everyone gains. Workers get the personal satisfaction that comes from a job well done. They may also receive such rewards as praise, higher pay, or a promotion. Society gains because more goods and services are produced or they are sold at a lower price.

Cooperation is the key to meeting goals. An organization is a *group* of people who must work together. Each person must communicate with others, do his or her job well, and have a considerate personality.

The first requirement is *communication*. Managers must communicate clearly with workers, explaining what must be done and how. Workers must also communicate with managers, requesting more instructions or asking for help. Workers must also communicate ideas they have about better ways to do their jobs. After all, no one knows a job as well as the person who does it. Finally, workers must communicate with each other. For instance, experienced workers can help new ones learn the job.

The second requirement is *performance*. Each worker must do the work that is expected of him or her, or else others may have to work harder. If not, the organization will produce less than its goals require. Workers must also take care that they work their best. Otherwise, the organization will not meet its goals. Finally, workers must be sure to work safely. By using machines carelessly or acting thoughtlessly, workers can endanger others and themselves.

The last requirement is that workers have a considerate *personality*. This does not mean clowning around on the job. Be as careful, polite, and helpful with others as you hope they will be with you. Work with others to help meet the organization's goals, and not just for your own advantage. Be pleasant and friendly with other workers, or else no one will want to work with you.

WORKERS AND MANAGERS HAVE RIGHTS AND RESPONSIBILITIES

Focus: Workers have rights as well as responsibilities in the workplace.

Activity: In 1990, President George Bush vetoed a civil rights bill. Ask students to research the reasons why the president refused to sign it.

World Economy: During the Stalinist era, a coal miner named Stakanivich was able to mine more coal than any other worker because of his size and strength. The central command decided to make him a model for all workers. To increase his production, co-workers were to "feed" coal to Stakanivich. This caused resentment among the workers who slowed down production in order to reduce Stakanivich's (and the mine's) output. Thus, the negative term Stakanivite refers to people who produce more than the norm and make their peers look bad.

For an organization to work smoothly and meet its goals, workers must meet their responsibilities. Managers have a right to expect certain things from workers. Workers also have rights, which management must recognize.

Workers' Rights Are Management's Responsibilities

Many of the rights of workers are spelled out in federal and state laws. These involve many aspects of a job, starting at the point when workers are hired.

People who apply for jobs are protected by **antidiscrimination laws.** *These laws forbid employers from refusing to hire workers because of race, age, sex, religion, or other traits.* The Civil Rights Act of 1964 made it illegal to discriminate on the grounds of race. Other laws, court decisions, and rulings of the federal government have broadened this protection. Employers

The federal government forbids employers from refusing to hire qualified job applicants who are handicapped as long as the handicap won't affect their performance of the job.

Extension: **Taft-Hartley Act of 1947** listed a number of unfair union practices; imposed controls on internal union administration; controlled the collective bargaining process and outlawed the **closed shop** (hiring only workers who are already union members); and allowed the president to obtain an injunction to delay strikes because of health and safety issues. These regulations were extended through the **Landrum-Griffin Act of 1959**.

are now prevented from discriminating on the basis of age, sex, or a handicap that does not affect performance of the job. Another law, the National Labor Relations Act of 1935, forbids employers from refusing to hire union members. This law, sometimes called the *Wagner Act*, also forbids employers from interfering with workers' rights to form a union.

Laws and regulations also restrict the work that can be done by minors. Most states prohibit employers from hiring children under fourteen and require any workers under sixteen or eighteen to get a **work permit.** *This document allows a person under the minimum working age in a state to hold a job.* Special laws also restrict the work allowed under such a permit, but these vary from state to state. A work permit is not required for some part-time jobs that are often done by young people, such as babysitting, delivering newspapers, or caddying at a golf course.

Workers have rights that govern their pay. Federal law has set a minimum hourly wage that most workers must be paid. The minimum was 25 cents an hour in 1938, when the law was first passed. The most recent increases occurred in 1989, when Congress voted to raise the minimum hourly rate to $3.80 in April 1990 and $4.25 in April 1991. There are exceptions to the minimum wage. Food-service workers, earn a lot of their income in tips. Employers are not required to pay them the minimum base wage.

Some critics argue that minimum wage laws hold employment levels down. Businesses would hire more workers, these critics say, if they did not

The federal government requires employers to pay men and women equally for doing the same work.

have to pay as much. There are continuing efforts to exempt workers under eighteen from this protection. This is aimed at creating more part-time job opportunities for teenagers.

Note: Different wages are allowed if they are based on experience or performance. They are outlawed only if it can be proven that they are based on discrimination.

Other laws require that most workers be paid extra—at least time and a half—for *overtime* work, which means any time over forty hours a week. Still others prevent employers from paying different wages for the same job if the difference is based on race, sex, age, or anything other than experience and performance.

Workers have a right to safe working conditions. The Occupational Safety and Health Administration (OSHA) was created by Congress in 1970. This agency sets standards for safety in the workplace. The law also gives OSHA the power to inspect workplaces and to order employers to correct unsafe conditions.

Critical Thinking: What does the phrase "a day's work for a day's pay" mean in terms of pay increases and/or worker productivity?

Some workers' rights grow out of the contract that exists between the worker and the employer. A contract exists even if nothing is written down on paper. Because of this contract, employers are required to pay workers the promised wage for their work at the promised time. Workers can expect employers to explain fully any rules or procedures about how they should behave on the job. Workers can also expect that their performance will be reviewed fairly. This gives them a chance to find out if they don't measure up to their employer's standards and to improve their performance. It also lets them know if they are meeting or exceeding those requirements, and so have grounds to ask for a raise.

Graphic Analysis: Using supply-and-demand graphs, illustrate what will happen if the minimum wage is below the equilibrium (or market) price. What will happen if the minimum wage is above the equilibrium (or market) price?

Management's Rights Are Workers' Responsibilities

Managers have the right to expect workers to work toward the organization's goals. These management rights, then, are workers' responsibilities. Managers expect the following qualities in their workers:

- *Quality work*—making the product or providing the service well enough to satisfy the customer.
- *Reliability*—doing the job the right way all the time and being at the workplace and ready to work at the required time, except in an unusual circumstance.
- *Productivity*—doing as much quality work as possible.
- *Efficiency*—using resources like raw materials or machines wisely and putting in a full day's work.
- *Safety*—using equipment properly and taking care to protect themselves and their co-workers.
- *Initiative*—seeking out new tasks, not just waiting for them to be assigned, and telling managers about ideas for doing a job faster, better, or more safely.
- *Adaptability*—being willing to learn new jobs or new ways of doing a task.
- *Cooperativeness*—sharing special skills or knowledge with fellow workers and doing whatever is possible to make others' jobs easier.
- *Honesty*—respecting an employer's property by not stealing or cheating on time worked.

Extension: In order to remain competitive, a firm must produce a quality product that is in demand at a price that buyers are willing to pay. Competition leads to lower product prices thus forcing firms to continually increase their productivity. Workers play a major role in productivity increases.

Review: Who benefits from profits? If a firm is unable to make a profit, it will go out of business. Thus, one of the beneficiaries is the labor force since a profit is necessary in order to maintain the jobs provided by the firm.

Focus: The phrase "there is safety in numbers" may explain part of the reason why workers initially feel the need to organize. Ask students to discuss this point.

The quality of the work that employees perform is essential to a business's success. Many businesses have rigid quality control programs.

- *Good attitude*—being positive about the job, the co-workers, and the organization. Having a positive attitude also results in a good work attendance record.

Workers who act responsibly do themselves a favor. A healthy organization stays in business, which means it keeps providing jobs. A successful organization rewards the workers who help it succeed. These workers may get raises and promotions.

WORKERS ORGANIZE TO BARGAIN MORE EFFECTIVELY

If the market for labor operated the way theory says it should, workers and employers would bargain as equals. The supply of workers and the demand for their skills would determine the *wage* for different kinds of labor, but workers do not always believe that they can bargain equally as individuals. To have more influence over their working conditions, many workers join together to form an organization of their own, called a *union*.

Clarify: The American Federation of Labor (AFL) was formed to organize specific crafts. Each craft had its own union which was affiliated with other craft unions at the national level. The Congress of Industrial Organizations (CIO) was designed to organize unskilled, assembly-line workers in mass-production industries. In 1955 these two movements merged into the AFL-CIO.

Illustrate: Examine the role of Samuel Gompers and the AFL in the 1880s. The AFL-CIO has print and audiovisual materials pertaining to the formation of unions.

Extension: Collective bargaining usually involves four areas: (1) the status to be afforded the union and management prerogatives; (2) wages and hours; (3) seniority and job opportunities; and (4) procedures for settling prerogatives.

What Unions Are

Labor unions are *groups of workers who join together to bargain more effectively*. Some unions are groups of workers who have the same skill or follow the same craft. Examples include the Newspaper Guild and the International Woodworkers. Others bring together many kinds of workers in a single industry or in a few related industries. The United Auto Workers or the United Mine Workers are this type. The National Labor Relations Act of 1935 (also called the *Wagner Act*) gave workers the right to organize unions if they chose to.

Today, fewer than 20 percent of workers in the United States belong to unions. This is a smaller percentage than at any time since just after the Wagner Act was passed. Still, union membership in some fields is growing. White-collar workers and workers in government and other service jobs are joining unions in greater numbers than before. Figure 7.1 shows trends in union membership since 1935.

How Unions and Management Reach Agreements

Unions engage in **collective bargaining** with employers. This is *negotiation over the terms of employment handled by officials of an employer and a labor union*. The officials bargain until they come up with a tentative contract with terms both sides find acceptable. Then union members vote to accept

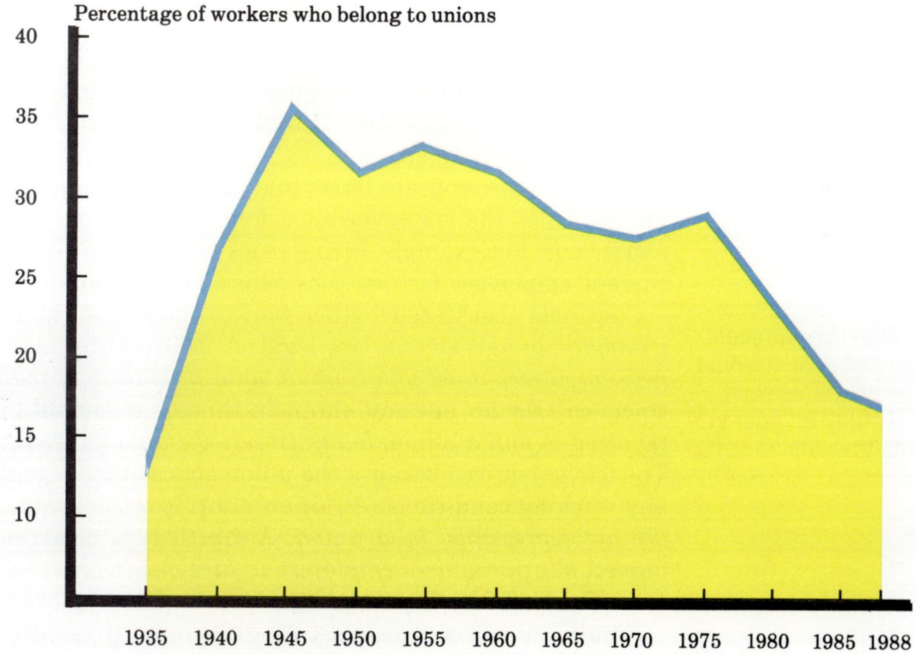

Source: Bureau of Labor Statistics

Figure 7.1 The Percentage of Workers Who Belong to Unions

Critical Thinking: The establishment of a **union shop** decreases personal freedom by requiring union membership to obtain a job. An **agency shop** allows individuals to not join the union but requires them to pay for union representation whether or not they would like the union to represent them. Ask your students to debate the costs and benefits of these limits to personal freedom.

Enhancement: Invite a representative of the teacher's union to discuss collective bargaining and the value of organized labor.

Illustrate: If your school district or a neighboring district has gone through mediation and into arbitration over a recent labor contract, it would provide an excellent case study for your students to examine.

or reject this agreement. Both parties must bargain in *good faith*. This means they must show a sincere desire to reach an agreement. The exact definition of good faith is vague. One party that suspects the other of not bargaining in good faith may ask the courts to decide the case.

When an agreement cannot be reached, the two parties may ask an outside mediator for help. A **mediator** is *an impartial person who joins labor negotiations to help the two parties reach an agreement.* They also may seek help from an **arbitrator.** This is *an impartial person who examines the proposals of the two parties in a negotiation and makes a decision they must accept.* A federal agency has a staff of mediators. This agency also has a list of skilled arbitrators that unions and management can choose from.

Union Contracts State the Terms of Employment

The contracts between unions and management cover pay, benefits, working conditions, and job security. Contracts also set up a method for settling disputes.

With regard to pay, contracts set workers' hourly wages, raises, and overtime rates. They state what benefits workers will receive, such as vacations, holidays, medical insurance, and pensions. A controversial part of some contracts is a **cost-of-living adjustment** (COLA). This is *a periodic automatic increase in wages that is based on the rate of inflation.* It is separate from any other raises that the contract calls for. These increases, though, can help to drive up the very rate of inflation that they are meant to combat. This is because the business may raise prices to cover the higher wages.

Contracts set working conditions. These include the number of hours in a work day, the number and length of breaks, and some safety and health rules. Some contracts state the kind and quantity of work required from workers in various jobs.

Contracts also contain items that protect the job security of workers. They include rules the employer must follow for hiring, promotions, and layoffs and firings. For example, hiring rules might require an employer to consider current employees for new jobs before looking outside the organization.

Contracts also state whether workers must join the union. Three types of membership agreements are legal. A **union shop** is *a workplace in which new employees must join a union within 30 days of their hiring.* Some contracts call for an **agency shop**. In this arrangement, *new workers are not required to join a union, but must pay the union a fee roughly equal to dues.* The fee is required because the union acts as their agent in negotiating pay and working conditions. An **open shop** is *a workplace in which employees are not represented by a union.* A fourth type of arrangement, called the **closed shop,** *requires employers to hire only workers who are union members.* The Taft-Hartley Act of 1947 made this requirement illegal.

Finally, union contracts set up **grievance procedures.** These are *steps workers can follow to protest and appeal any employer decision that they feel violates the contract.* These rules set up an orderly way of settling disputes between workers and managers that occur on the job. The first step usually allows the worker's supervisor and a union official to settle the problem. If they cannot, the matter is referred to higher-level managers and union leaders.

Discuss: Ask your students to imagine they are working at a firm where another union is striking (not a union they belong to). Would they cross the picket line? Why or why not? What cost would they have to bear if they did not cross the line? if they did cross the line?

Unions and Managers Take Action When They Cannot Reach Agreement

Sometimes negotiators cannot agree on a contract. Then both workers and managers use certain tools to influence each other to change their positions or to speed up the agreement.

The most powerful tool unions have is the **strike**. This is *an organized stoppage of work by employees*. Strikes can slow down an employer's production or even stop it entirely. Many unions that go on strike set up picket lines outside the workplace. These pickets often carry signs that state their views. Striking workers may also try to encourage members of other unions and the general public not to do business with the employer.

Illustrate: If a strike has occurred recently in your community, invite a member of the striking union to speak to your class regarding his or her experiences.

Some unions pay strike benefits to their members during a strike. In this way, the loss of their regular paychecks will not create hardships that might make them give up before they are satisfied with the agreement.

Before they go on strike, workers give serious thought to the possible effects of their actions. Are there benefits to be gained from a strike? Will these be greater than the wages they'll lose during the strike? Will the

Illustrate: The mechanics' union strike of Eastern Airlines, the drivers' strike against Greyhound Bus Lines, and the air traffic controllers' strike make excellent case studies.

A strike is the major weapon that unions use to persuade management, but strikes cost union members lost wages and possible damage to the company.

strike or the terms of the settlement endanger the health of the organization, and even its very survival? Will other workers who are not on strike be harmed? For instance, a strike at a plant that makes parts for a product can lead to layoffs at the factory that makes the product.

Discussion: Ask students to discuss the fairness of business actions in response to a strike or threat of a strike. How do these actions affect attempts to compromise in the negotiations between workers and management? How do they affect the economy?

Unions also try to persuade other workers and consumers to **boycott** the employer's products. This *refusal to do business with an organization or to buy its products or services* can put pressure on an employer to settle. Unions can also seek injunctions from the courts if they think employers are taking illegal actions against them. An **injunction** is *a judge's decision ordering a person or an organization to stop an illegal action.*

Employers can also ask for and get injunctions against unions, but they have other ways of trying to influence workers. If workers strike, employers can hire nonunion workers or use supervisors to do the striking employees' work. If they believe workers are going to strike, they can act first by closing down the workplace. This is called a *lockout.* Some businesses buy strike insurance. Then, if a strike occurs, the company receives money that replaces the sales it loses. If a business feels that the threat of a strike is too regular or too severe, it may close down its workplace and move elsewhere.

YOUR STATUS AS A WORKER CAN CHANGE

Your status and your position in an organization can change in several ways. You can receive the rewards of raises, promotions, and transfers. You can leave an employer by resigning, being laid off, being fired, or retiring.

Illustrate: In the 1960s, Cesar Chavez attempted to organize lettuce pickers in California. One of the tools he used to increase the union's strength was a national boycott of lettuce. This effort provides a good example of the difficulties in trying to organize a national boycott.

A **raise** is *an increase in a worker's wage, either as a reward for good work or as called for in a contract.* The employer may review your performance as a worker regularly and decide then whether you deserve a raise. You may need to review your own performance. Be sure to look at your work objectively. Ask yourself whether you're doing your best. Are you doing as much work as others—and as well? If your work is above average, you may have grounds to ask for a raise.

The key word is *ask.* Don't demand a raise. Persuade your employer that you deserve a raise by pointing out what you have done in the past and can do in the future. When you ask for a raise, be reasonable—speak calmly, and don't ask for too much. Give your supervisor a chance to think it over.

Another change in status is a promotion. A **promotion** is *an employer's decision to move a worker to a new job with more responsibility as a reward for working well in an old job.* It often brings a raise with it. The new job may require you to produce more work or to do more complex work. Perhaps the promotion will make you a supervisor.

When you are promoted, be sure your supervisor explains your new job fully, so you can do it as well as you did your old one. He or she should also let others know about your promotion. Then they will know what to expect of you and not keep asking you to do work you did in your old job. If you have been promoted to a supervisory position, you will be more responsible for seeing that the organization meets its goals. Be prepared to explain management's point of view to workers. Be prepared also to handle the difficult task of managing other workers—some of whom may be your old friends.

Emphasize: A job change is one of the most disruptive events in an individual's life. This is because lifestyle and work are inextricably interwoven. Therefore, it is important to consider carefully any job changes and use these points in your career as opportunities to improve your situation and life.

Your employer may transfer you. A **transfer** is *an employer's decision to assign a worker to a job in a different place.* Employers transfer workers to make the best possible use of the human resources they have. Starting to work in a new place is something like starting a new job. You and your fellow workers will be unknown to each other. To make your work easier, you—and they—must follow the guides for working cooperatively.

Many workers these days are part of a two-income family. As a result, some workers are less likely to accept transfers, because of the effect these moves have on their spouses' careers. Before accepting or rejecting a transfer—or any other voluntary change in your status—be sure to evaluate its effects on your life and your family.

Research: Ask your students to investigate your state's unemployment insurance program. How do you qualify for benefits? What is the range of benefit payments? How long will they be paid? What is required to remain eligible?

You may leave an organization. You might **resign**—that is, *leave a job to work somewhere else.* If a job doesn't measure up to your goals, or if another employer offers you more responsibility and better pay, or if you see a chance to start your own business, you may decide to resign. This decision is important and shouldn't be made without thinking carefully. Evaluate the change you are about to make. Remember that the *way* you resign a job can affect your future jobs. Your former employer may be asked for a recommendation. If you leave in haste or anger, that recommendation won't be positive.

Give proper notice when you resign because your employer needs time to replace you. One pay period is standard. You should give more notice if you are leaving a supervisory job or leaving at a busy time. Notify your supervisor, in writing, before you tell your friends. Don't brag about your new employer or downgrade your old one—doing so makes bad feeling. Until you leave the company, be sure to work cooperatively and well.

Enhancement: Some economists argue that unemployment benefits hinder the individual's return to the work force. The theory is that as long as benefits are paid, individuals postpone revising their expectations and accepting a lower-paid job. Once all benefits are exhausted and supporting a family becomes a necessity, individuals begin a vigorous job search.

Workers who resign may not receive unemployment benefits, depending on the laws of their state. Be sure to have a new job lined up, or some money saved, before you resign.

You probably will receive unemployment benefits if you are laid off. A **layoff** is *a temporary or permanent end to employment ordered by an employer for economic reasons.* Workers may be laid off because the economy is bad and business in general is slow. It could be that their employer—or an entire industry—is doing poorly. A company that lays you off might give you severance pay. If you are a union member, you may also receive income from your union during the layoff. If you are laid off, you may want to learn new job skills that enable you to enter an industry with a more promising future.

At some point in your career, you might be fired. **Firing** is *the permanent dismissal of a worker by an employer.* If your work is poor or your attitude uncooperative, you may be fired.

You may receive severance pay from your employer when you are fired. Unless you are fired for dishonesty or some other gross misconduct, you will probably receive unemployment benefits.

Clarify: Economists divide economic growth into two types. **Extensive growth** occurs when the quantity of factors of production increases (i.e., population growth). **Intensive growth** occurs when the factors of production become more productive (i.e., technological change).

Firing should start you thinking. If you are fired because your work was poor, you need to improve the quality of your work. If you were fired because of an inability to work with others, you need to change your attitude.

Another way of leaving an organization is **retirement**. This is *a worker's decision to leave the work force at the end of his or her career.* While you are many years away from retiring, you can begin planning for it with insurance, investments, and savings. You can also start planning for your emotional well-being by developing interests and hobbies outside your job. Your job is your work; it's not your whole life. Many ambitious workers forget this. When the time comes to retire, they do not know what to do with their leisure time.

YOU INTERACT WITH THE ECONOMY: YOUR PRODUCTIVITY PROMOTES GROWTH

The economy grows when producers use the same resources to produce more goods and services or fewer resources to produce the same goods and services. The key to this growth is **productivity**. This is *a measure of how many goods or services a producer can produce using a given amount of resources.* If productivity goes up, growth occurs.

Explain: Research indicates that the number of individuals covered by company retirement programs is declining. This is due in part to the large number of firms with 10 or fewer employees; retirement programs are prohibitively expensive for small firms. Also, part-time employees are seldom covered by full benefit packages. The disappearance of company retirement programs means increasing reliance on the social security system and on private retirement activities.

Everyone benefits from higher productivity. Consumers are able to choose from more goods and services. Businesses are able to compete better and enjoy higher profits. Workers get the satisfaction of a job well done. They are also likely to receive raises and other rewards, and they are sure to find that their jobs are more secure in a healthy business.

When productivity goes down, everybody loses. Workers find their jobs in danger, as Sheila and her friends learned at the beginning of this chapter. Consumers find that their money buys fewer goods and services. Businesses find it harder to compete, perhaps even to survive. Society loses out because many workers lose their jobs, and because fewer goods and services are available.

The United States Bureau of Labor Statistics measures productivity by seeing approximately how much each worker produces per hour of work. When productivity increases over a number of years, the economy thrives. Over the last twenty-five years, productivity has increased, but not at a uniform rate. Since 1984, productivity has been growing at a slower rate. (Figure 7.2 shows yearly changes in productivity for all workers since 1962.) Some analysts say that workers can help to solve this problem.

What can you, as a worker, do to boost productivity? You can work more efficiently. Don't waste your employer's resources—including the hours of your labor they buy. You can also work more creatively. Find better ways to perform the tasks you are assigned. If those new methods save time and

Average percentage change in the rate of productivity

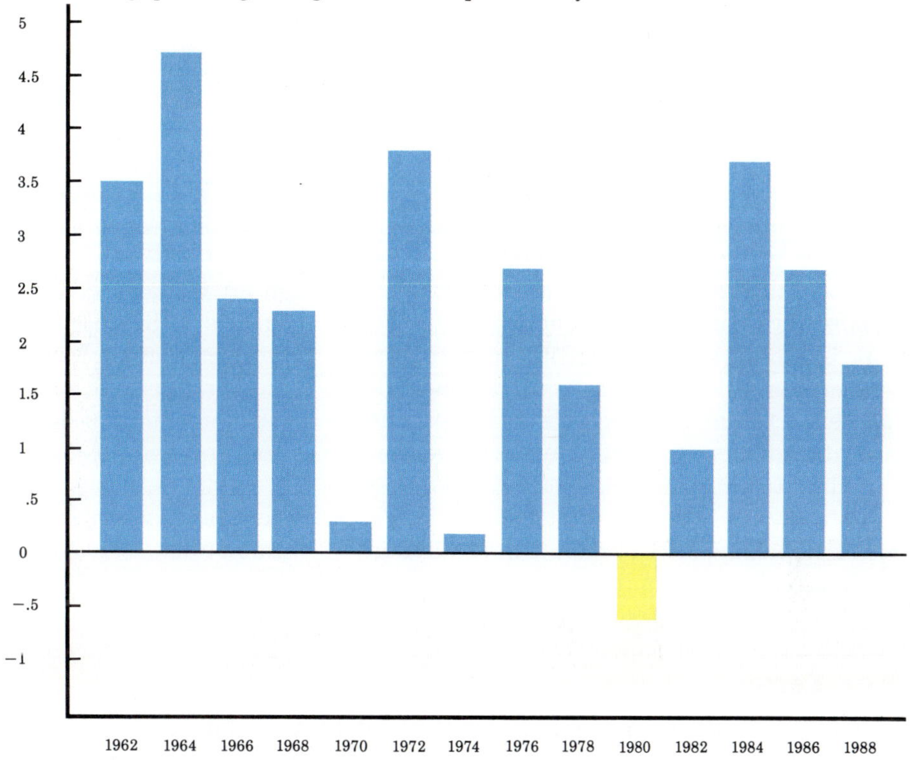

Source: Bureau of Labor Statistics

Figure 7.2 Changes in the Rate of Productivity Since 1962

Summary: The workplace is a complex web of interdependencies. Management will not succeed without the efforts of labor. Labor will not be as successful without new technology. The U.S. economy will not grow without successful and competitive firms. Each worker is an essential part of this process.

Critical Thinking: As the number of low-skilled, higher-paying jobs declines, American workers must become more skilled in order to earn higher incomes. Instead of working on a production line in an auto plant, workers increasingly are operating highly technical equipment (such as robots and computers). What does this say about the crisis in our education system and the large numbers of dropouts? Does this increase the need for an educated work force?

other resources, tell your employer about them. Many organizations pay bonuses to employees who develop such ideas.

Technology can increase your productivity. This does not only mean making new machines to do old tasks. It also means finding new ways to use old machines.

Productivity—especially if based on new technology—has its cost, too. The new equipment costs the business money at first, but this is usually money well spent. By buying more efficient machines, the business saves money in the long run. Some workers believe that technology costs *them*. They see new machines replacing workers. A machine may indeed take over a task once done by a worker. New machines also create jobs for new workers—those who make them, those who use them, and those who fix them. Workers who recognize this fact see new technology not as a threat, but as an opportunity. They adapt to it by learning new skills and finding new ways to use their old skills.

SUMMARY

- Workers must cooperate with others to help achieve the goals of the organization they work in.
- It is management's responsibility to recognize workers' rights. These include the rights to be hired and be paid without discrimination, to earn at least the minimum wage, to be paid extra for overtime, to work in a safe place, and to be paid on time.
- It is workers' responsibility to recognize management's rights. These include the right to expect quality work, reliability, productivity, efficiency, safety, initiative, adaptability, cooperativeness, honesty, and a good attitude.
- Workers may form a union to bargain more effectively with management. Contracts agreed to in collective bargaining state the terms of employment and some of the rights and responsibilities of workers and management.
- When no agreement can be reached, workers or management may ask mediators to help them reach an agreement.
- To try to influence management, unions may go on strike, ask other workers and consumers to boycott the employer, or seek a court injunction. Management can also seek court injunctions, hire nonunion employees, have supervisors do the work, or lock out workers who threaten to strike.
- A worker's status within an organization can change when the worker receives raises, promotions, or transfers. Workers leave organizations by resigning, being laid off or fired, or retiring.

Key Terms

Match each of the following terms with the definition that most suits it.

agency shop	firing	mediator	resign
antidiscrimination laws	grievance procedures	open shop	retirement
arbitrator	injunction	organization	strike
boycott	labor unions	productivity	transfer
closed shop	layoff	promotion	union shop
collective bargaining	managers	raise	work permit
cost-of-living adjustment			

a. a temporary or permanent end to employment ordered by an employer for economic reasons
b. an impartial person who joins labor negotiations to help the two parties reach an agreement
c. a workplace in which new employees must join the union within 30 days of hiring
d. a document that allows a person under the minimum working age in a state to hold a job
e. the people who turn an organization's goals into directions for the workers
f. a worker's decision to leave the work force at the end of his or her career
g. the refusal to do business with an organization or to buy its products or services
h. a group of people working toward a common goal
i. a workplace in which employees are not represented by a union
j. an employer's decision to assign a worker to a job in a different place
k. a measure of how many goods and services a producer can produce using a given amount of resources
l. a workplace in which employers can hire only union members; an illegal practice
m. the permanent dismissal of a worker by an employer

n. laws that forbid employers from refusing to hire workers because of race, age, sex, religion, or other traits
o. an increase in a worker's wages either as a reward for good work or as called for in a contract
p. groups of workers who join together to bargain more effectively
q. to leave a job to work somewhere else
r. an organized stoppage of work by employees
s. an impartial person who examines the proposals of the two parties in a negotiation and makes a decision they must accept
t. steps workers can follow to protest and appeal any employer decision that they feel violates a labor contract
u. a periodic automatic increase in wages that is based on the current rate of inflation
v. an employer's decision to move a worker to a new job with more responsibility as a reward for working well in an old job
w. negotiation over the terms of employment handled by officials of an employer and a labor union
x. a workplace in which new workers are not required to join a union but must pay the union a fee roughly equal to dues
y. a judge's decision ordering a person or an organization to stop an illegal action

Review Questions

1. What are the three requirements of working cooperatively? Give an example of what is meant by one of them.
2. What is a work permit? Who must get one?
3. What rights do workers have regarding their pay?
4. List five qualities that managers have a right to expect of workers. Choose one of these five and explain why it is important.
5. What is a union? Why do workers organize?
6. What is collective bargaining? What conditions of employment are covered in a union contract?
7. What questions should union members ask themselves before deciding to go on strike?
8. When should you ask for a raise? How should you do it?
9. What is the difference between a promotion and a transfer?
10. What is the difference between being laid off and being fired?
11. How does everyone—worker, business, and society—gain when productivity rises?

Projects

1. Innovation often results from businesses spending time and money to research new products and new methods of doing things. Do some research on how businesses do their own research. Write a report outlining how much is being spent on research and development (R&D). Describe any changes in this spending in the past ten years. How does the amount being spent in the United States compare to that spent in other countries?
2. As a class, resolve the problem that opened the chapter. Four students can take the parts of Carla, Dave, Ernie, and Sheila. Other students can take other roles. Assume that all the workers at the plant are meeting after work. Decide what to do.

Earning a Paycheck 8

Introduction: Getting a job is only the first step. The second step is negotiating for the highest wage or salary.

OBJECTIVES

This chapter will help you to:

1. Define the common ways of being paid for work.
2. Describe the major types of fringe benefits.
3. Read and understand a pay stub.
4. Determine whether you need to pay income tax and how and when to calculate your tax.
5. Summarize the benefits governments pay to workers.
6. Explain how taxes affect disposable income.

As Rudolfo was driving home from work, he stopped to pick up his brother Angel. "You wouldn't believe what happened today," he told Angel.

"What?"

"Well," Rudolfo answered, "the clothing store has a policy that after working for one year, salespeople get reviewed."

"So what did they say about you?" Angel asked.

"They were happy with how I worked—customers have complimented me and I get along with the fitters."

"Great," said Angel. "Are they giving you a raise?"

"That's the thing. They made me an offer."

"What is it?" Angel asked.

"I can either take a 10 percent raise in my salary or I can take a cut in my base salary but go on commission," Rudolfo answered. "Then what I earn depends on how much I sell."

"That sounds risky," said Angel. "How much can you count on selling?"

"I know—that's the problem," Rudolfo said. "But with the commission I have no limit to how much I earn—it just depends on how hard I work."

"Well," Angel said as they got home, "do you think you can afford to take a chance?"

CAN RUDOLFO AFFORD to take a chance? What chance is he taking? Rudolfo has to choose between two ways of being paid for his work. To make his decision, he needs to know what he gains by being paid each way—and what he gives up.

EMPLOYEES EARN DIFFERENT KINDS OF INCOME

Emphasize: Workers tend to look at their salary as negotiable and their benefits package as fixed. Employers tend to look at the total value of salary plus benefits. If the cost of a benefit rises drastically, the worker normally does not notice it, but the employer immediately begins looking for ways to reduce this cost.

When Rudolfo goes to work for an employer—or when any of us do—a transaction is taking place. We sell our labor to producers, who use it to produce goods and services for consumers. These producers are our employers. In exchange for our labor, they pay us.

The total amount of money a worker is paid for his or her labor is called **earned income**. Many workers also receive **fringe benefits** in exchange for their labor. These are *insurance, vacation days, sick days, and other ways of paying workers that are not part of earned income.* Another difference between earned income and some fringe benefits is tax. Money income is taxed by the federal government and by many state and local governments. Many fringe benefits are not taxed. Let's look at the different types of money income and fringe benefits.

Workers Are Paid Income in Six Ways

Most workers receive regular payments of money from their employers. In many manufacturing, maintenance, and service jobs, these are wages. A

Activity: Ask your students to list jobs that traditionally pay wages, piecework rate, salary, commission, tips, and a bonus.

Emphasize: Most teens beginning entry-level jobs will be paid a wage. A beginning wage allows them to develop job skills (on-the-job training) and earn a minimum income while doing so.

Discussion: Why would a manufacturer pay assembly-line workers on a piecework basis? What actions are encouraged by the piecework incentive? Which workers would like working on a piecework basis? Which workers would not?

Clarify: Usually salaried workers do not receive extra pay for overtime work; however, sometimes workers receive equivalent time off for overtime work. The overall goal of the salaried worker usually is to get the work done no matter how long it takes to complete it.

wage is *an hourly rate of pay for work.* Workers who are paid wages tend to do a predictable amount of work per hour. Thus an hourly rate makes economic sense. The more hours worked, the more a worker is paid. The hourly rate must at least meet the minimum wage standard set by federal law, except for workers who also receive tips.

Some workers in factory and farm jobs are paid a **piecework rate**. This is *a set rate of pay for each unit of work produced*—per bushel of avocadoes picked, for instance. Income goes up as more work is done. Workers earning piecework rates are also protected by the minimum wage law. They must earn at least the minimum hourly wage and receive the time-and-a-half rate for any hours over forty a week. Workers who earn an hourly wage or work at a piecework rate do not always receive paid vacations or holidays or sick days, however. If they don't work, they aren't paid. Some of these workers do receive paid days off.

A **salary** is *a rate of pay for work that is calculated by week, month, or year.* Of course, a yearly salary of $15,000 doesn't mean that the worker gets only one check in that amount. Employers divide the yearly salary into equal amounts and pay workers every week, every other week, or once or twice a month. Most managers and many office workers are paid salaries, because their duties are very broad and it is hard to predict a certain amount of work they will do each hour or week. Salaried workers usually receive paid vacation, sick days, and holidays. Their salary must equal at least the minimum hourly wage for a normal working week. To get the job done, however, they may need to work many more hours than "normal." Some workers on a salary do not receive extra pay for this overtime. This is especially true of jobs in the middle and upper levels of an organization.

Some salespeople receive a commission, which is income based on the amount of goods they sell.

Focus: Chapter 8 highlights the dilemma faced in deciding between salary and salary plus commission. Salary offers the security of a set income; commission offers the opportunity to earn more (or less if the worker does not produce). Which type of payment do you think the employer would prefer?

Enhancement: Tips are supposed to reward good service. However, if all workers "pool" tips and split them evenly, then individual incentive evaporates since outstanding workers receive a share equal to the worst worker. Similarly, individual incentive is eliminated when a restaurant automatically adds a 15 percent service charge to the customer's bill. This means that the outstanding worker (who might have received 20 percent from the customer) and the worst worker (who might have received no tip) both get a standard amount. Why retain the tipping system if the incentive is eliminated?

Food-service workers, like this waiter, earn much of their income in tips from customers.

Some salespeople are paid a **commission**, *a rate of pay for work that is a percentage of sales made.* Some salespeople earn only a commission. Others earn a base salary to which a smaller commission is added, as Rudolfo will if he chooses this alternative. Either way, a commission can provide a strong motive for these workers to produce more sales.

How can Rudolfo choose between a salary and a salary plus commission? First he must consider how the base salary would meet his needs for steady income. Would he be unable to manage any of his regular expenses? Then he must figure out how much he sells on the average and how much commission he would earn on that amount. He needs to consider how much his weekly sales vary—are some weeks or months very slow? If so, he'll have to be sure to save money to help him through. Rudolfo must recall that each choice has an opportunity cost. Going on commission costs him the security of a set income. Staying on salary costs him the chance of earning according to how hard he works.

Food service workers, taxi drivers, hairdressers, hotel employees, and parking attendants receive much of their income in **tips**. These are *payments, usually voluntary, by customers to service workers.* Tips vary from week to week and from job to job. In some restaurants, all the tip-earners pool their tips and divide them up evenly. Some restaurants automatically add 15 percent to customers' bills to cover tips. Most, however, let customers decide how much to tip.

The final form of money payment is a **bonus**, *an extra payment to a worker as a reward for superior performance by the worker or by the employer.* Not all employers give bonuses. Some give them to all employees at the end of a very good year. Others use them to reward managers for strong performance by their departments or to workers who suggest cost-saving innovations. Some employers pay a bonus to workers who recommend someone who is later hired to fill a job opening.

Discussion: Which forms of payment are **incentive** payments and which are not? Discuss the pros and cons to the worker, employer, and customer of using incentives as part or all of a worker's pay.

Fringe Benefits Reward Performance Less Directly

The income that workers receive as fringe benefits is a less direct payment for their labor. Fringe benefits are still, however, a significant percentage of income. The benefits that large corporations provide can add from 25 to 50 percent to the cost of workers' income.

Fringe benefits serve purposes other than simply increasing compensation. Some, such as paid vacations, improve morale. Others, such as life and health insurance, help guarantee workers' economic security by protecting them from financial hardships. Paying the tuition for classes that workers take encourages them to learn new skills. Profit-sharing plans seek to boost workers' productivity.

A common fringe benefit is vacation with pay, allowing workers a chance to refresh and enjoy themselves.

Note: Chapter 19 examines insurance more closely.

List: Based on class discussion, list potential fringe benefits on the board and discuss which workers would find them most advantageous (i.e., discounts on muffler repair benefits workers with automobiles).

Illustrate: Share the benefit package available to teachers in your district with the students.

Extension: Group policies allow for the spreading of risks. Not everyone stands the same chance of getting sick. By enrolling all the individuals in a company, enough revenue will be raised from everyone (including those who never get sick) to cover the cost of the few who become ill. However, individual policies must cover the costs of individual risks (instead of spreading the risk among a large number of policyholders), thus requiring a higher fee.

Employers provide these benefits because doing so is cheaper than paying workers the extra wages that workers would need to buy the services themselves. A worker might have to pay $600 to buy health insurance, while an employer could provide the same coverage for only $450. The employer can pay less per worker because it buys insurance for many workers at the same time. Employers also provide benefits to compete for workers with other employers. A worker considering two job offers at the same salary might choose the employer who offers an extra week's vacation or more insurance coverage.

What are some typical fringe benefits? You've just read about a few: paid vacations, health insurance, life insurance, tuition reimbursement. Paid holidays and sick days are fringe benefits, too. Some employers allow workers a few paid personal days a year—days the employees can arrange to take off work for such reasons as moving or family emergencies. Some provide day care for children of working parents, or pay part of its cost. Some give employee discounts on their products or offer free samples.

Two fringe benefits offer extra income. A **pension plan** is *a retirement fund for workers created by contributions made by the employer*. Each worker may also choose to pay some income into this fund. A **profit-sharing plan** is *a fund some businesses create by setting aside part of their profits for workers*. Profit-sharing is similar to bonuses, because it is based on company

With the number of two-worker and single-parent families growing, many people predict that providing child-care services will become a more popular fringe benefit.

performance—the more successful the firm, the more is contributed. Unlike bonuses, profit-sharing payments are not received when made. Instead, they go into an investment fund. Each worker receives his or her share only when he or she leaves the company.

Critical Thinking: Both company pension plans and the federal Social Security System are designed to provide retirement funds. How do these two programs differ? Which is better for the individual worker?

Benefit packages vary among employers and from job to job within a company. When they evaluate a job offer, workers should figure in the value of the benefits, along with the wage or salary, determining what it would cost them to buy the benefits themselves. Of course, cost can't be the only standard. Each worker will also decide what benefits are important to him or her. Workers with children might be more interested in life and health insurance or child care. Workers who wish to move up in an organization might prefer to be paid for courses they take.

Some large employers are able to provide benefits to suit workers' varying needs and offer what is called a *cafeteria plan*. In this plan, each worker is able to choose the combination of benefits that he or she wants.

EMPLOYEES RECEIVE THEIR PAY IN DIFFERENT FORMS

Most workers receive their income by check. A check is a convenient way to transport large sums of money. Checks are also safe. A bank will not cash a check for an unknown person unless he or she can show identification, such as a driver's license or major credit card. If a paycheck is lost or stolen, the employer can simply stop payment on the check and issue a new one. Of course, to receive this protection the employee must notify the employer that the check is missing.

Define: In the 1980s the federal government began shifting social service responsibilities from government to the private firm under the description **mandated benefits**. The federal government mandates that all firms over a certain size must provide specific benefits for employees (such as parental leave, plant-closing benefits, or health insurance).

Another advantage is that payment by check leaves a written record. An employer can prove its claims for labor expenses. Workers can document their income.

Some workers are paid in cash. Tips, for example, are usually received in cash on the day customers pay them. Workers are required to report income from tips for tax purposes. A dishonest employer might try to pay workers in cash "under the table." This illegal practice may allow workers to avoid reporting the income and may help the business avoid minimum wage laws. Of course, if the income is reported, cash payments are legal.

Some banks and employers now allow the employer to send workers' regular pay directly to the bank if the worker wishes. Called *direct* or *automatic deposit*, this payment is accomplished by electronic transfer of funds. Both the employer and the worker receive a printed record of the transaction. This method is even safer and more reliable than payment by check. Not all employers offer this service.

Critical Thinking: Should the federal government continue to mandate benefits to be paid by private firms? What are the trade-offs of this course of action?

What do you see when you look at your paycheck? **Gross pay** is *the total amount of income an employer owes a worker for a given period*. The check is made out for less because certain **payroll deductions** have been made. These are *amounts subtracted from gross pay to cover regular payments that are required or voluntary*. The required payments include federal, state, and local income taxes and social security taxes (called FICA). Other deductions

EMPLOYEE NAME		SOCIAL SECURITY NUMBER
ED HO		529-70-7795
EMPLOYEE NUMBER	DEPARTMENT	
17	7	
PAY PERIOD	GROSS WAGES	
Jan. 7- Jan. 20, 1991	336.00	
PAYROLL DEDUCTIONS	AMOUNT	NET WAGES
TYPE		265.58
FEDERAL INCOME TAX	14.20	
FICA TAX	20.32	
STATE INCOME TAX	3.40	
OTHER		
CODE	AMOUNT	
3	2.00	
1	17.50	

CODE
1—Health insurance contribution
2—Savings bond purchase
3—United Way contribution
4—Union dues

Figure 8.1 A Sample Pay Stub

Illustrate: Upon receiving their first paycheck, many teens are taken aback at the difference between their gross pay and their net pay.

may include union dues, payments to charities or pension contributions, or medical insurance premiums. *A worker's take-home pay, found by subtracting deductions from gross pay,* is called **net pay**. Net pay is the actual amount of your check. Gross pay, deductions, and net pay are usually listed on a pay stub that is attached to the paycheck. (See the sample in Figure 8.1.) Keep those pay stubs for your records.

WORKERS PAY INCOME TAXES

Clarify: Although federal income tax is withheld from each pay period, individuals are still required to file an income tax return annually and pay any balance due (or file for any refund owed).

Generally, the biggest deduction from a worker's paycheck is for federal income tax, but there is more to paying federal taxes than just having a sum withheld from your regular paycheck. Wage earners must file a federal **income tax return**. The return is *the form people use to state their income and figure the tax they owe.* Income taxes seem complex, but they needn't be. Let's briefly review who must file, how to file, and how to calculate your taxes. Keep in mind throughout this section that the income limits and form numbers may change. Be sure to keep up-to-date on this information. The basic procedure for filing will probably stay the same, however.

Who Must File

Everyone who earns above a certain income must file a tax return. In 1990, this limit was $5,100 for single persons and $9,200 for married persons who file a joint return. Income means any money received as wages, tips, bonuses, or interest or dividends from savings and investments.

If you earn income in a given year, you receive a statement from the source of the income in the beginning of the following year. Your employer sends you a **W-2 form**, which *lists your gross pay and payroll deductions for the previous year.* (A sample W-2 form appears in Figure 8.2.) Banks that pay interest on savings accounts or corporations that pay dividends send a different form to the persons who earned this income. Copies of all these forms are also sent to the Internal Revenue Service (IRS). Thus, the government has a record of your yearly income.

Note: Employers are required to send out W-2 forms by the end of January. Individuals should make sure that employers have their current address so that these W-2 forms are received and can be attached to the income tax return.

How to File

The IRS has three basic tax forms you can choose from when you file your return. Form 1040EZ can be used only by single taxpayers who meet certain conditions. They must be under 65, cannot be blind, must have earned less than $50,000 in taxable income and less than $400 in interest, received no dividends, and claim only a personal exemption. An **exemption** is *a reduction in taxable income allowed for each taxpayer, for his or her spouse, and for each dependent.* Additional exemptions are also given to people who are over sixty-five or who are blind.

Focus: Increasingly the U.S. government is using social security numbers to track individuals in a variety of activities. Social security numbers are now required for any personal exemption included on tax returns (you, your spouse, and all children). Since banks must submit interest payments by social security number, and employers are required to submit all wages paid by social security number, this number has become a method for tracking personal income and cross-checking taxpayer-reported income.

Single taxpayers who want to claim more than one exemption or married taxpayers can use Form 1040A. The income limit for using this form is also $50,000. There are other restrictions for using this form as well—check with the IRS to see what they are.

With these two forms, you are allowed only a standard deduction for each exemption you claim. Other deductions can be taken, however, if you use Form 1040, called the "long form." For instance, medical costs over a certain amount can lower taxable income. Portions of interest payments on loans are also **tax deductions**. All these deductions are *expenses that reduce the income on which taxes are due.* If the total of all deductions is more than the standard deduction, taxpayers pay lower taxes by itemizing deductions.

Whatever form is used, you must figure total income and subtract deductions. The result is taxable income—the amount that you pay taxes on.

Expansion: The Internal Revenue Service has a variety of materials to assist with teaching about income taxes, such as the videotape series *Understanding Taxes.*

1 Control number	7D1
OMB No. 1545-0008	
2 Employer's name, address, and ZIP code	FIRST BANK 1425 LA COSTA BLVD. SAN BENEDICTO, CA 95001
3 Employer's identification number	08-924-7414
4 Employer's state I.D. number	18-22-119
5 Statutory employee / Deceased / Pension plan / Legal rep. / 942 emp. / Subtotal / Deferred compensation / Void	
6 Allocated tips	
7 Advance EIC payment	
8 Employee's social security number	529-70-7795
9 Federal income tax withheld	$369.20
10 Wages, tips, other compensation	$8,776
11 Social security tax withheld	$528.12
12 Employee's name, address, and ZIP code	ED HO 17109 OCEANVIEW BONITA, CA 95021
13 Social security wages	$8,776
14 Social security tips	--
16	
16a Fringe benefits incl. in Box 10	
17 State income tax	$88.40
18 State wages, tips, etc.	$8,776
19 Name of state	CA
20 Local income tax	--
21 Local wages, tips, etc.	--
22 Name of locality	--

Form **W-2 Wage and Tax Statement 1989**
This information is being furnished to the Internal Revenue Service.
Copy B To be filed with employee's FEDERAL tax return   Dept. of the Treasury—IRS

To find the tax you owe, simply check the tax tables in the back of the instruction book for the form you're using. Then check your W-2 to see how much tax has already been withheld.

Critical Thinking: Many people claim fewer allowances on their W-4 than they are allowed so that they will receive a refund upon filing their annual tax return. In doing so, they are actually giving the federal government a "no-interest loan" during the year. Is there a better way of ensuring that you are not confronted with a large, unexpected payment at tax time?

If the tax you owe is greater than the amount withheld, you need to pay the government the difference. You must send a check or money order payable to the IRS with your completed tax form and a copy of your W-2. If the amount withheld is greater than the tax you actually owe, the government owes you a refund. You'll only receive that refund after you mail in your completed tax return.

The amount of tax withheld depends on how many allowances you claim. You claim these allowances by filling out a **W-4**, *the form a worker uses to instruct an employer how much income tax to withhold.* The more allowances, the less money is withheld each time you are paid. A simple guide is to claim as many allowances on the W-4 as you will claim exemptions when you file your tax return. Then the amount withheld from your pay will roughly equal the tax you will owe for the year. Some taxpayers do otherwise, however. Some people prefer to have more income during the year, so they ask for many allowances. Thus their employers withhold less. When it comes time to file their tax return, these people with probably have to pay. Others claim no allowances, so that more tax is withheld than they will probably owe. They hope to receive a refund when they file their tax return.

Explain: Taxes can influence behavior. If the government wants to encourage a specific behavior (saving, for example), then taxes on this behavior could be decreased or eliminated. If the desire is to discourage behavior (credit use), then tax policy could be designed to accomplish this.

When to File

The deadline for filing the federal income tax return is April 15 of the year after income is earned. There is a penalty fee for filing late unless a taxpayer requests an extension of the deadline. The request must be made using the proper form. The extension is granted automatically. Any tax due must be paid by April 15. If it is not, the government charges a penalty fee and interest. These charges are made even if an extension was granted—the extra time applies to the date of *filing* a return, not the date taxes are due.

If you are to receive a refund, the IRS should pay you within forty-five days of April 15. If you received an extension and filed later than April 15, the refund is due forty-five days after the date you filed.

World Economy: U.S. taxes as a percent of GNP, although they have been rising, continue to be below that of many other developed nations.

How to Get Help

The IRS offers taxpayers two kinds of help. Lower-income, elderly, handicapped, and non-English-speaking taxpayers can get assistance from local offices of the IRS. All taxpayers can receive information on over 140 topics by calling special phone numbers and hearing prerecorded tapes. Post offices, libraries, and banks may have more information on these services.

Taxpayers can also pay to have their taxes prepared by a person or business. If you plan to use such a service, be sure to use someone who knows the tax laws and will fill out your return correctly. Professional tax preparers must sign all returns they prepare. The fee the tax preparer charges can be claimed as an itemized deduction.

Employees must pay taxes on the income they receive.

Research: Ask your students to research state, county, and local tax rates.

Critical Thinking: The federal public debt grew from $541.4 billion in 1975, to $2,600.8 billion in 1988. What causes public debt? An annual deficit can be eliminated by either decreasing spending, increasing revenue, or a combination of both. Ask your students to analyze the costs and benefits of these approaches. Emphasize **who** bears the burden of decreased government programs or increased taxation and analyze the long-term effect on the economy.

Research: Ask your students to investigate the Gramm-Rudman-Hollings deficit reduction law and its effect, if any, on federal budgets.

State and Local Income Taxes

Most states also have income taxes (only seven do not). Rates vary greatly, up to a high of 17 percent. Many large cities have income taxes as well. These tax rates also vary, the average being about 2 percent. Most residents of these cities and states must also file the returns for these taxes by April 15, but there are exceptions. Check with your city and state departments of revenue or taxation for details on who must file, how to file, and when to file. These offices may also be able to help you fill out your return. Professional tax preparers can also complete state and local returns.

GOVERNMENT USES SOME TAXES TO PROVIDE BENEFITS FOR WORKERS

Governments provide services with the money they collect in taxes. Some of these services are direct payments of money to people. Let's look at some of these payments.

Social Security Pays Retired and Disabled Workers

Social security payments are made *to eligible workers (or their families) who have retired, become disabled, or died.* To be able to receive these payments, workers pay a part of their income in social security taxes. The taxes are collected and the benefits paid by the Social Security Administration (SSA). The tax rate and the qualifications for benefits have changed often in recent years, and they are sure to change again. For up-to-date information, contact the local office of the SSA. Not all workers are covered by this system. Many state and local government workers have their own plans. Before 1984, federal government workers did not belong to the system either, but those hired afterward are now included.

Before you start your first job, you must get a social security number. You can apply for this nine-digit number by getting the form shown in Figure 8.3 from a local SSA office or a post office. The number is used by

Research: Ask students to research the history of the Social Security Administration.

Activity: Students can check on their social security account balance by contacting the nearest Social Security Administration office, obtaining the appropriate form, and completing the request. Some businesses offer to check your Social Security balance for you for a fee. This activity shows students that they can do this themselves. There is no need to pay someone else to check the balance for them.

Critical Thinking: Currently, the amount that workers and employers pay into Social Security is in excess of the amounts being paid out. The surplus balance of this fund is being used to offset the federal deficit rather than being "saved" to fund future payments. Ask your students to research this topic and evaluate the costs and benefits of this practice.

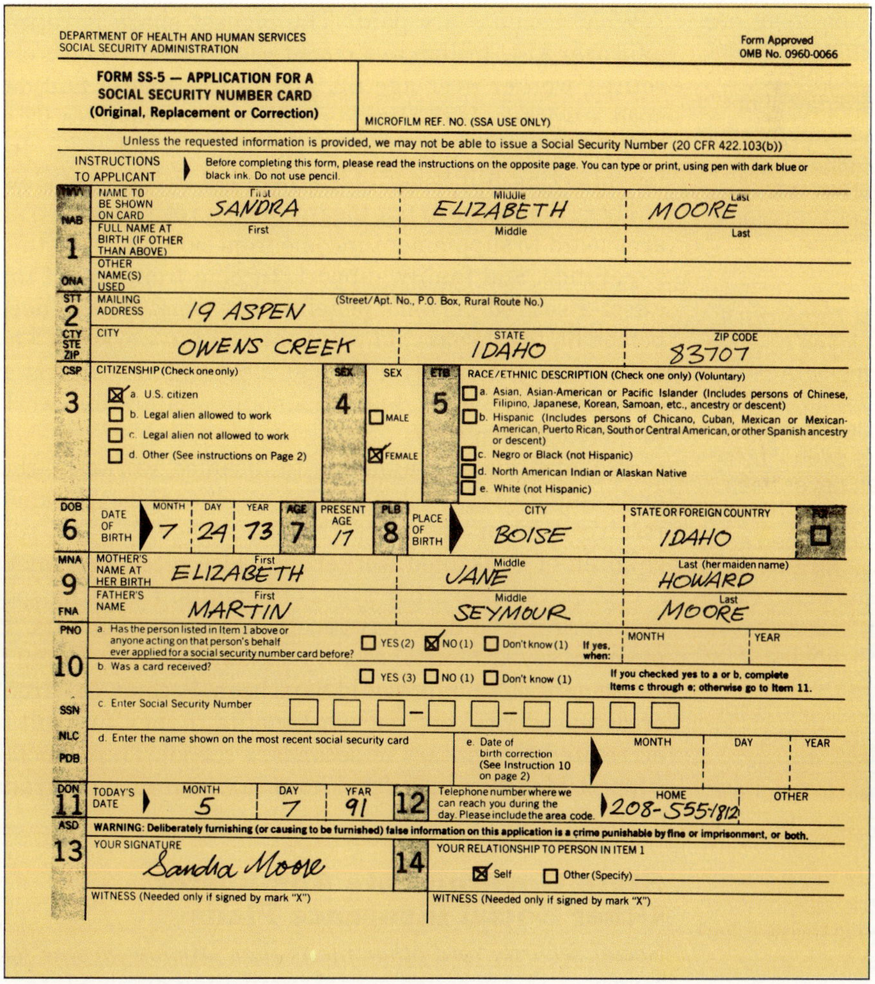

DEPARTMENT OF HEALTH AND HUMAN SERVICES
SOCIAL SECURITY ADMINISTRATION

Form Approved
OMB No. 0960-0066

FORM SS-5 — APPLICATION FOR A SOCIAL SECURITY NUMBER CARD (Original, Replacement or Correction)

MICROFILM REF. NO. (SSA USE ONLY)

Unless the requested information is provided, we may not be able to issue a Social Security Number (20 CFR 422.103(b))

INSTRUCTIONS TO APPLICANT ▶ Before completing this form, please read the instructions on the opposite page. You can type or print, using pen with dark blue or black ink. Do not use pencil.

NAA / NAB 1 — NAME TO BE SHOWN ON CARD: First SANDRA; Middle ELIZABETH; Last MOORE
FULL NAME AT BIRTH (IF OTHER THAN ABOVE): First; Middle; Last
ONA — OTHER NAME(S) USED

STT 2 — MAILING ADDRESS: 19 ASPEN (Street/Apt. No., P.O. Box, Rural Route No.)
CTY STE ZIP — CITY: OWENS CREEK; STATE: IDAHO; ZIP CODE: 83707

CSP 3 — CITIZENSHIP (Check one only): [X] a. U.S. citizen; [ ] b. Legal alien allowed to work; [ ] c. Legal alien not allowed to work; [ ] d. Other (See instructions on Page 2)

SEX 4 — SEX: [ ] MALE; [X] FEMALE

ETB 5 — RACE/ETHNIC DESCRIPTION (Check one only) (Voluntary): [ ] a. Asian, Asian-American or Pacific Islander (Includes persons of Chinese, Filipino, Japanese, Korean, Samoan, etc., ancestry or descent); [ ] b. Hispanic (Includes persons of Chicano, Cuban, Mexican or Mexican-American, Puerto Rican, South or Central American, or other Spanish ancestry or descent); [ ] c. Negro or Black (not Hispanic); [ ] d. North American Indian or Alaskan Native; [ ] e. White (not Hispanic)

DOB 6 — DATE OF BIRTH: MONTH 7; DAY 24; YEAR 73
AGE 7 — PRESENT AGE: 17
PLB 8 — PLACE OF BIRTH: CITY BOISE; STATE OR FOREIGN COUNTRY IDAHO; FCI [ ]

MNA 9 — MOTHER'S NAME AT HER BIRTH: First ELIZABETH; Middle JANE; Last (her maiden name) HOWARD
FNA — FATHER'S NAME: First MARTIN; Middle SEYMOUR; Last MOORE

PNO 10 — a. Has the person listed in Item 1 above or anyone acting on that person's behalf ever applied for a social security number card before? [ ] YES (2) [X] NO (1) [ ] Don't know (1) If yes, when: MONTH; YEAR
b. Was a card received? [ ] YES (3) [ ] NO (1) [ ] Don't know (1) — If you checked yes to a or b, complete items c through e; otherwise go to Item 11.
SSN — c. Enter Social Security Number ☐☐☐-☐☐-☐☐☐☐
NLC / PDB — d. Enter the name shown on the most recent social security card
e. Date of birth correction (See Instruction 10 on page 2) ▶ MONTH; DAY; YEAR

DON 11 — TODAY'S DATE ▶ MONTH 5; DAY 7; YEAR 91
12 — Telephone number where we can reach you during the day. Please include the area code. ▶ HOME 208-555-1812; OTHER

ASD — WARNING: Deliberately furnishing (or causing to be furnished) false information on this application is a crime punishable by fine or imprisonment, or both.

13 — YOUR SIGNATURE: Sandra Moore
14 — YOUR RELATIONSHIP TO PERSON IN ITEM 1: [X] Self [ ] Other (Specify)
WITNESS (Needed only if signed by mark "X")
WITNESS (Needed only if signed by mark "X")

Figure 8.3 The Form Used to Apply for a Social Security Number

Note: It is important that students realize that the amount of Social Security tax they pay is matched by their employer. Thus, the tax is actually double the amount they see on their check stub.

Research: Ask students to research current SSA regulations such as payment level at different retirement ages; tax policy; medicare payment levels (or co-payment levels); eligibility requirements; and regulations regarding other income.

Critical Thinking: If an employee covered under the SSA dies, the surviving spouse can collect survivors' benefits even if he or she has never been paid income. If the survivor *has* earned income in the past, then he or she must choose between survivors' benefits and his or her own SSA benefits. (An individual cannot collect both.) Is this fair? Who does this discriminate in favor of? Who does it discriminate against? Why has there been *no* public clamor for a change in these rules?

the SSA and other government agencies to identify you. It enables them to keep track of the taxes you have paid and the benefits you are eligible for.

When you start to work, your social security tax will be deducted from your pay. The tax is a percentage of all your income from work up to a maximum amount. In 1990 the rate was 7.65 percent of income up to $51,300. Your employer matches this with an equal payment. Self-employed people pay 15.3 percent of their income—equal to both the employee and employer share.

The benefits you will one day receive will be based on your lifetime average of earnings, using a complex formula. Eligibility for benefits is based on the number of *quarters* (three-month periods) you have worked and paid the tax. You can check SSA's records of the quarters you've worked and the amount you've paid by requesting this information with a postcard form SSA provides. It's a good idea to check every three years because SSA's records cannot be changed after that period.

What benefits are paid? The biggest share is retirement benefits: SSA paid over $141 billion in a recent year. These benefits are paid to any eligible retired worker over age 62, and to the spouse and dependent children of such a worker. If the worker retires between ages 62 and 65, the monthly benefit is lower than if he or she had retired at 65. In the future, the age for collecting full benefits is scheduled to increase slowly to 67.

These benefits are not meant to be a retired person's entire income. They are meant to supplement income from savings, investments, insurance, pension funds, and family support. Income from any of these sources does not affect a retired person's benefits, but work income does. In 1990, a retired person 65 to 69 years old who continued to work lost $1 in benefits for every $3 of work income over $9,630 a year. This ratio is expected to stay the same for many years, but the amount of allowable work income is expected to increase each year.

SSA also makes payments to disabled workers—those who are injured and cannot work. Such a worker receives the same amount he or she would receive if he or she were retiring at age 65. The spouse and dependent children of a disabled worker may also receive payments.

SSA pays three other types of benefits. First, the spouse and dependents of a worker who dies may receive survivors' benefits. These may include a payment toward burial costs and monthly checks equal to what the worker's retirement payments would have been. Second, children of retired, disabled, or deceased workers receive benefits if they are full-time students in an accredited elementary or secondary school. Third, social security taxes also support Medicare, a federal hospital insurance program for people who are over 65 or disabled.

State Governments Administer Other Social Insurance Plans

Social security and other plans that provide income for people who can no longer work are called **social insurance** plans. State governments provide several important kinds of social insurance. Chief among these are unemployment compensation and workers' compensation.

Critical Thinking: Some states allow individuals who have voluntarily quit their jobs to collect unemployment benefits. Should these benefits be reserved for those who are involuntarily out of a job because of layoffs or firing?

Unemployment compensation involves *payments to workers who have lost their jobs and are willing but for a time unable to find new ones.* Each state sets a maximum number of weeks a worker can receive benefits. It also sets a minimum number of months a worker must have worked to be able to receive benefits. The benefits are paid from a fund to which all employers in the state contribute. The size of a person's benefits depends on previous income.

Unemployment compensation protects workers. These payments help reduce the shock that a layoff or firing can cause. Workers who quit are not eligible. Workers lose these benefits if they refuse the chance to take a job that is comparable to the job they lost. These payments also protect society. Because unemployed people are receiving some income, they can more easily pay their debts and meet their regular expenses. Thus, demand for goods and services doesn't drop and fewer other workers lose their jobs.

Clarify: When taxes from all sources are included the total incidence appears to be closer to one-third of personal income. This means that you control only two-thirds of the income you earn.

Worker's compensation is another state-run social insurance plan. It provides *payments to cover the medical costs and lost income of a worker who is injured on the job.* Some states have funds to which all employers contribute, as for unemployment compensation. Others require employers to buy insurance. If the time away from work is expected to run at least one year, the worker may also receive disability payments from SSA.

YOU INTERACT WITH THE ECONOMY: YOU USE YOUR DISPOSABLE INCOME

The money you have left after you pay your taxes is your *disposable income.* About how much does the average worker pay in taxes? In 1988, total personal income in the United States was about $4.06 trillion. About 23 percent of that total—$945 billion—was paid in taxes to federal, state, or local governments. In other words, one of every four dollars earned goes to taxes. (Of course, the rate varies from person to person.)

Summary: Workers provide the factor of production called labor. In turn, they are paid in a variety of ways for their labor. A variety of payments are deducted from this gross income, which determines a worker's disposable (or net) income.

After you've paid all your taxes, disposable income is what you have left. It is the money you have to satisfy your wants. The way you use that resource is up to you. Some decisions will be fairly predictable: everybody needs food, clothing, and shelter. Even for these necessities, though, you have a wide range of choices.

Your decisions affect the amount of disposable income you have. You *can* act to influence how much tax you pay. Setting tax rates is a political decision, so your voice and vote count. What career you decide to enter and what job you choose to take affect what your income will be before taxes.

How you use your disposable income has a very direct effect on other parts of the economy. The reason is quite simple. No business succeeds without customers, and all customers are free to choose what businesses they patronize. Therefore, your "dollar vote" determines the success or failure of businesses.

SUMMARY

- Workers are paid by their employers in exchange for their labor. Most income is paid in money. Some payment takes the form of fringe benefits.
- Workers are paid with wages, salaries, commissions, tips, and bonuses.
- Fringe benefits include vacation, life and health insurance, holidays, sick days, employee discounts, pension plans, and profit-sharing plans. They vary from employer to employer.
- Workers can be paid by check or by electronic transfer. Some payments are also made in cash, but those payments must be reported for taxes.
- Workers paid by check or electronic transfer often receive a pay stub or statement that indicates gross pay, payroll deductions (mostly for taxes), and net pay.
- Workers figure federal income taxes by filing a tax return with the Internal Revenue Service. Those who owe less tax than was withheld from their checks will get a refund. Those who owe more than the amount withheld must send the IRS the difference.
- Most state governments and some city governments also tax income.
- Federal and state governments use tax revenues to provide services to the public. Some of these services take the form of payments to protect the security of workers who are retired or temporarily or permanently unable to work. Some payments also go to those workers' dependents.
- The money you have left after you pay your taxes is disposable income. This is the money you can use to satisfy your wants. In deciding how to use it, you affect other areas of the economy.

Key Terms

Match each of the following terms with the definition that most suits it.

bonus	income tax return	salary	unemployment compensation
commission	net pay	social insurance	W-2 form
earned income	payroll deductions	social security	W-4 form
exemption	pension plan	tax deductions	wage
fringe benefits	piecework rate	tips	worker's compensation
gross pay	profit-sharing plan		

a. a form filled out by an employer that lists a worker's gross pay and payroll deductions for the previous year

b. an extra payment to a worker as a reward for superior performance by the worker or by the employer

c. amounts subtracted from gross pay to cover regular payments that are required or voluntary

d. expenses that reduce the income on which taxes are due

e. the total amount of money a worker is paid for his or her labor

f. a rate of pay for work that is calculated by week, month, or year

g. payments by the state government to workers who have lost their jobs and are willing but for a time unable to find new ones

h. a retirement fund for workers created by contributions made by the employer

i. the total amount of income an employer owes a worker for a given period
j. the form a worker uses to instruct an employer how much income tax to withhold
k. an hourly rate of pay for work
l. payments, usually voluntary, by customers to service workers
m. payments by the federal government to eligible workers (or their families) who have retired, become disabled, or died
n. a worker's take-home pay, found by subtracting deductions from gross pay
o. insurance, vacation days, sick days, and other ways of paying workers that are not part of earned income
p. payments by the state government to cover the medical costs and lost income of a worker who is injured on the job
q. a set rate of pay for each unit of work produced
r. a fund some businesses create by setting aside part of their profits for workers
s. a rate of pay for work that is a percentage of sales made
t. the form people use to state their income and figure the tax they owe
u. a reduction in taxable income allowed for each taxpayer, for his or her spouse, and for each dependent
v. social security and other plans that provide income for people who can no longer work

Review Questions

1. What are some of the differences between a wage and a salary?
2. What kind of workers are paid commissions?
3. List five common fringe benefits. Why do employers provide these benefits?
4. What is the relationship of net pay to gross pay?
5. What are some common payroll deductions?
6. Who must file a federal income tax return?
7. How are federal income tax returns filed? What is the deadline for filing? Are there exceptions?
8. When is a refund due a taxpayer? When is a payment due the IRS?
9. Who pays social security taxes? Who collects benefits?
10. How do states pay for unemployment compensation?
11. What is disposable income? What do people use it for?

Projects

1. Talk to some workers whose income varies—food service workers who earn tips or salespeople who earn a commission. Find out how they manage to make plans when their income changes. Ask what they do to earn as much in tips or commissions as they can. Discuss in class these ways of getting paid—do they seem too risky or do most students like the chance to earn more?
2. The federal government allows people to deduct from their taxable income any political campaign contributions they made. Hold a class debate over whether the policy is a good idea.
3. Social security taxes and benefits have become a major political issue in recent years. Research any newspaper or magazine articles on the social security system. You'll find information on the eligibility for benefits, cost-of-living adjustments in benefits, changes in the tax rate and maximum income amount, and the question of future funding of the system. Focus on one of these areas and report to the class.

PART FOUR

Managing Your Resources

Planning to Use Your Resources 9

Overview: We should develop a plan for using our scarce resources in a way that will maximize our satisfaction.

OBJECTIVES

This chapter will help you to:

1. Outline a basic consumer method you can follow to plan your buying.
2. Explain how planning helps you manage your resources.
3. Identify alternatives to buying goods or services.
4. Make a budget for your time.
5. Identify ways to develop your skills.
6. Describe ways to increase your personal energy.
7. Create a budget for your money.
8. Describe how inflation and deflation affect budgets.

Sonya looked across the cafeteria table at George, who was finishing his third cup of coffee.

"What's with all the coffee, George?"

"I've got to do something so I can stay up after work tonight to write that history paper," George answered.

"You were going to do that last weekend!" said Sonya.

"I couldn't. I had to work more hours. After that play we went to and the clothes I bought, I don't have any money left for the Washington trip. Not to mention that camera I want to buy—it's more expensive than I thought it would be. And I've been working for two months already! I've got to start working more hours, or I'll never get the money together."

"Maybe, but if you keep this up, you'll sleep through the whole trip!" said Sonya. "There's another way to make sure you have the money, you know."

"What's that?" asked George.

"Well, you're always buying things! Why don't you stop spending everything you make and put a little money away every week, instead of trying to save it all at once? Then you wouldn't have to overload yourself," Sonya suggested.

"You're right—that would be easier!"

"There's another thing," Sonya said. "Maybe you don't have to buy a camera after all. Couldn't you borrow your sister's for the trip?"

"That would sure help—thanks, Sonya!"

Define: **Consumers** are buyers of goods or services. A business can be a consumer when buying office supplies, equipment, or printing services.

SONYA HAS THE RIGHT IDEA. Unless George works out a plan for managing his resources, he'll waste them. He's spending too much money and he's using all of his time and energy—he's not even getting enough sleep. These personal resources are valuable, and we all need to think before we use them. In this chapter you'll learn how you can plan to get the most out of your resources. First, let's see how planning fits in with other decisions we make.

PEOPLE USE THE BASIC CONSUMER METHOD

Demonstrate: George thinks only of *buying* a camera. Sonya has pointed out an alternative; he may be able to borrow his sister's camera. What might be some other alternatives?

Many of the economic decisions we make involve our consumer role. As we try to satisfy our wants, it's helpful to plan how we'll use our resources. That way we can get the most out of them. Planning, in fact, is the first step of the **basic consumer method**. This is a *seven-step process of planning and carrying out buying decisions:*

Step 1. *Plan* by identifying your wants, seeing what resources you have, and choosing which resources to use to satisfy which wants.

Step 2. *Gather and evaluate information* on which products may satisfy your wants.

Step 3. *Comparison shop* to decide what to buy and where and when to buy it.

Step 4. *Decide whether to use cash, credit, or savings* to pay for what you want.

Step 5. *Decide whether to buy the item* or whether to wait for a better time.

Step 6. *Buy the item*—if that's your decision.

Step 7. *Evaluate the purchase* after using the product for a while.

Note: Note the similarity between the decision-making process and the basic consumer method.

This chapter and the next three will discuss these steps separately, but they are all actually related. For instance, what you decide to buy (Step 3) can determine how you will pay for it (Step 4)—few people have enough cash on hand to by a new car. While comparison shopping you may change your mind about what you want. Suppose George wants a jacket for the trip. While he's looking for the best price, he may realize that an all-weather coat will be more useful than the jacket he meant to buy.

These seven steps are similar to the systematic decision-making method. In fact, the first step follows this method. Planning means defining the problem (by listing your wants), identifying your goals and resources, and choosing which wants you will satisfy and which resources you'll use. Sometimes you decide to use your skills, time, and energy to make something for yourself. Other times you decide to use your money to buy something.

Expand: The principle of **substitution** applies to consumer decisions as well as to producer decisions. Consumers can substitute their money for their time, or vice versa, depending on the opportunity costs of those resources.

PLANNING HELPS US USE RESOURCES EFFECTIVELY

We use our personal resources—time, money, energy, and skills—to satisfy our wants. We may have a limited amount of those resources, but we can use them in a variety of ways. By always choosing to buy goods and services, we ignore many alternatives. If we manage *all* our resources, not just money, we can get the most out of them.

Illustrate: In Chapter 2 Angela is considering changing the oil in her car herself, rather than paying a mechanic to change it. However, maybe George could barter with Angela; he would change her oil if she would loan him her camera.

We Have Alternatives to Buying New Goods and Services

Defining a problem broadly helps us see more alternative solutions. We have six alternatives to buying: we can substitute other resources, make something ourselves, barter, use possessions carefully to make them last, rent, and do without. Suppose you bent the frame of your bicycle in an accident. Because you need your bike to get to school, your first reaction is to buy a new one, but you have alternative ways of solving your problem:

- By *substitution*—you could walk to school, take a bus, or get a ride from a friend.
- By being a *"do-it-yourselfer"*—possibly you could repair your old bike for a lot less than it would cost to buy a new one.
- *By bartering*—you could trade something you have but don't want for someone else's spare bike.

There are three other ways to get what we want without having to buy something new:

Define: **Rent** is a payment made periodically in return for the use of someone else's property. A **lease** is a contractual agreement to pay a specified amount for the use of someone else's property over a specified period of time.

- *Product care and maintenance—the proper use and care of goods to stretch their lives* is **product care and maintenance**. A car that has regular oil changes and tune-ups and is driven safely and carefully will last a long time. Taking care of what we have saves us from needing to buy new things.
- *Renting—paying a fee in return for the temporary use of some good or property* is **renting**. A band might rent a van to transport instruments and equipment to performances.
- *Doing without*—we cannot satisfy all of our many wants. By comparing them, we can see how important they are to us, figure out how many resources we need to satisfy them, and then decide which ones to satisfy and when.

Critical Thinking: We have often been called a "disposable society." What are the costs and benefits of using disposable products versus products with a long life?

Planning Has Many Benefits

George's problem, which opened this chapter, highlights the fact that a lack of planning can make scarcity worse. Even though he's earning money now, George still doesn't have enough to do everything he wants. His time is also limited. He can't work extra hours without taking away from his school work, and the extra work uses a lot of energy, too.

Having products properly cared for and maintained helps them last longer, avoiding the need to buy new ones.

On the other hand, planning can help George manage his resources so he'll achieve his goals.

Planning requires using some time and energy, but it offers many benefits:

Discussion: Ask the class to list their long-range goals. Describe how planning will help them achieve these goals.

- It helps you achieve your goals because it shows you how to reach them.
- It helps you use your resources effectively because you carefully consider alternative uses.
- It helps you live within the limits of your resources because you start with a clear idea of those limits.
- It helps you foresee future needs because you consider your long-range wants.
- It helps you satisfy your most important wants first because you base your choices on how you rank your wants.
- It helps you measure your progress toward reaching your goals because it provides standards for you to meet.
- It helps you avoid costly and wasteful impulse purchases because you carefully weigh your actions first.
- It makes choices easier because you list all your options and identify the opportunity cost—the value of the next most attractive want that you give up when you choose an alternative.

Stress: Time has an opportunity cost that is often overlooked. When individuals consider the cost of a decision, they seldom consider the opportunity costs of their time.

MANAGING YOUR RESOURCES

We can use our limited resources most effectively by managing them. But how do we make a plan? Where do we start? The first resource to manage is the one we are always aware of—time.

Illustrate: Articles on time management usually recommend making a daily "to do" list. This provides the satisfaction of actually crossing off items on your "to do" list once they are completed while allowing you to prioritize the things you must accomplish. Make sure your "to do" list is not so detailed that you are inundated by trivia!

Budgeting Your Time

Time is one thing we spend constantly. We are always using it up, whether wisely or foolishly. We can manage our time to enhance our other resources—skills, energy, and money—or we can fritter it away. Wasting time won't satisfy any wants. We must plan how to use our time.

Start planning by identifying your goals, or what you want to achieve. You have long-term goals and short-term goals. A long-term goal may take a few years, such as finishing school and entering a career. Short-term goals are achieved within days, weeks, or months. Day-to-day time planning mostly focuses on short-term goals, but remember that long-term goals are also affected by short-term choices. For example, the amount of time George spends studying each week affects his grades, the skills he learns, and his chances of getting a good job when he's out of school.

How do you figure out what to do every day? Begin by listing all the things you want to do within a certain time, say a week. Write down everything you want—don't skip over something because you don't think you can do it. Don't forget to leave time for rest and entertainment or school work and obligations to others.

Now figure out how much time you will need to achieve each goal. Remember to make realistic estimates. Consider how quickly you can work, but also allow time for unexpected problems. Next, figure out how much time you have by subtracting the hours you spend sleeping, going to school, and eating meals. What's left is free time, to use as you wish.

Now put your goals in order of importance. You need to choose between conflicting goals, like taking extra courses to graduate early and participating in activities after school, since there isn't enough time to do everything. You'll need to consider time sequence, too. Christmas shopping must be done before Christmas. Term papers must be researched and written before they're due. Here are a few guidelines to help you plan your activities:

- When possible, alternate types of activities so you won't lose interest. Follow a morning of work with an afternoon of relaxing.
- Allow enough time—working too quickly can cause problems that you'll need to take time to solve later.
- Avoid putting things off (which is called *procrastination*)—making up for lost time often takes longer.
- Group similar activities together so you won't duplicate your effort—do all the errands you can in one shopping trip.
- Do unpleasant things first—you won't mind them so much if you get them out of the way.
- Think ahead—anticipate tomorrow's gas needs and stop at a gas station on the way home.
- Be reasonable and don't overload yourself—allow time for fun.

Once you realize how many things you can get done, you won't want to dawdle or procrastinate.

Illustrate: You may want to break down overwhelming activities on your short-term list. If you have to write a term paper break that down into (1) research the term paper; (2) sort and organize references; (3) write first draft of paper; (4) edit; (5) revise and complete paper.

Stress: Intersperse time-consuming activities with those that are quick and easy. People seldom look forward to a time where everything they have to do is a major project.

Expand: Everyone needs time to relax. If your list is all work, you will not refer to it as easily. Take time for yourself.

Expand: If you do not complete everything on your list, evaluate *why* these activities were not done. Did you postpone doing them because you did not allow enough time? Did you put them off because you really did not want to do them?

A good time budget allows enough time to reach all the goals we have set.

Activity: Ask your students to maintain a log for the next week. At the end of the week they should evaluate if they were too detailed or not detailed enough. Use the log as a basis for developing a "to do" list for the next week.

Define: We all have **inherent skills**, skills which already exist within us. Some may inherently be good at working with numbers; others may inherently be good at working with their hands. We can improve inherent skills through practice or learning. Many times, people without a specific inherent skill can learn that skill.

Critical Thinking: The United States has traditionally led the world in worker productivity primarily because of skilled workers. Ask your students to examine the quality of the skills and ability of today's young people (tomorrow's workers) and write a paper contemplating the future productivity of the U.S. work force.

Table 9.1 How George Spent His Time in the Past and His New Time Budget

	Use of Time in Past (in hours)		Time Budget for Future (in hours)
	Week 1	Week 2	Each Week
School	35	35	35
Job	16	22	17
Getting to school and to work	10	10	10
Studying	13	11	15
Eating	14	14	14
Sleeping	51	48	56
Plays/movies	11	13	6
Being with friends/family	11	9	8
Reading	2	0	2
Exercising	2	1	3
Other	3	5	2

George needs a time budget. He wants to work, study, and attend plays with Sonya, without sacrificing his sleep. He must calculate how much time he needs for each and decide which things he wants to do most. George's time budget is shown in Table 9.1. Compare it to how he spent his time during the previous two weeks.

Developing Your Skills

Skills are important because we can use them to acquire and use other resources. **Skills** are *our talents and our ability to develop them.* Decision-making skills help us make plans. Planning skills help us use time, energy, and money. An amazing number of skills—from plumbing to animal training—can be used to earn money. Such skills as cooking help us satisfy our wants.

We all have skills, and our skills may be more valuable than we assume. People with mechanical ability can save money by doing their own household repairs and car maintenance. They can even exchange this work with neighbors for money, for goods, or for services the neighbors can perform.

The wonderful thing about skills is that these resources can increase. There are many ways to learn new skills and to develop existing ones:

- *Schools*—this is the only place where some skills, nursing for example, are taught. It's also the best place to learn most skills, because they are taught thoroughly. High schools, trade schools, technical schools, military schools, correspondence schools, and colleges all offer countless courses in many skills.
- *Family and friends*—everyone starts learning some skills—such as cooking and cleaning, shopping and budgeting—at home. You can learn others from skillful friends.
- *Reading*—"how-to" books or newspaper or magazine articles can teach skills from repairing appliances to bookkeeping.
- *Home computers*—these aids use visual stimulation and easy practice to

help people learn many new skills. Knowing how to use a computer is itself an important skill these days.

Emphasize: We must constantly improve our skills and gain new skills. Unless we continue to improve our skills we will become less productive and less valuable to our employers.

Any skill is increased with practice. Setting aside time to practice your skills can benefit you in the long run. When you can perform a skill well, you like doing it more and derive more satisfaction from it. Once you become good at something, you may be able to earn extra income by selling that skill.

Maintaining Your Personal Energy

Focus: Teenagers seldom think about maintaining personal energy. At this age, they are able to overcome a lack of sleep and a poorly balanced diet fairly rapidly. However, this is the time when their habits become established. So, it is important to spend some time on good eating, sleeping, and lifestyle habits because of the long-term affects.

George thought he was maintaining his energy by downing cups of coffee. Like many people, he thought about energy only when he was out of it. **Personal energy** is *our physical capacity to do things.* Without energy, we'd be unable to do anything to achieve our goals.

Personal energy springs from a well-cared-for mind and body. Maintain your energy by eating well, resting, and getting enough exercise. For too many people, meals are haphazard. French fries here and an ice cream cone there do not make good nutrition. It takes a little thought to plan nutritious meals in advance, but the increased energy is worth it.

You also have to pace yourself by resting and getting enough sleep. Without proper rest, your ability to do your best work suffers. The paper George writes when he's tired won't be as good as one he writes when he's alert.

Illustrate: Point out some bad habits (all nighters, junk food, etc.) and their negative consequences.

Regular exercise can actually increase physical energy by helping the body work more efficiently.

Explain: Spend some time on exercise and the different ways to exercise. It is important to identify the advantages and disadvantages of each form of exercise.

Emphasize: Examine the costs of substance abuse by leading the students in a discussion of these costs.

Explain: A budget is an analysis of your goals and your resources and a way of matching the two. You will not be able to maintain your budget if it is unreasonable or if someone else determines the spending limits. Your budget must reflect you and your desires.

Note: Incorporate your log in your financial budgeting. Again, stress the substitution of time and money.

Like skills and money, personal energy is a resource that can increase. Exercise increases energy by making the body work more efficiently. Don't forget to schedule some time to work out.

In addition to factors that increase energy, there are things to avoid because they decrease energy. Some drugs, like alcohol and narcotics, are recognized as dangerous and their effects can be dramatic. People who think they can use them and still live up to their full potential are kidding themselves. Other substances, like nicotine, caffeine, and some over-the-counter drugs, are known to be harmful but are not taken seriously enough. George, trying to keep himself awake by drinking coffee, is getting stimulation, but he's not producing energy. Look back at Table 9.1. By budgeting his time carefully, George is able to get more sleep and spend more time exercising. As a result, he'll be more alert and do better work.

The best way to keep these energy drains from becoming habits is to develop a positive attitude and work to keep it. Don't ask what you can get away with in terms of drugs and foods. Get the best for yourself—nutritious food and enough exercise will produce more energy.

Budgeting Your Money

If George is really serious about setting money aside from each paycheck, he needs more than good intentions. He needs a budget. A **budget** is *a plan to achieve goals by fitting expenses to income.*

There are three stages of budgeting:

1. Preparing for the budget
2. Making the budget
3. Using the budget

Preparing for the Budget Before he actually makes a budget, George must become aware of his spending patterns. He should keep a record of how he spends his money for two or three budget periods. A budget period should coincide with a person's pay period or bill-paying period. For instance, because George gets paid every week, it's easier for him to think in terms of weekly amounts. George has written down his expenses for the past three weeks (see Table 9.2). Note how much money comes under "unknown." Without a plan, George doesn't know where his money is going.

Setting goals is the first step toward achieving them. Start with **long-term goals**—*goals to achieve in the distant future,* such as buying a car next year or paying for college. Then list **short-term goals,** which include *goals to achieve in the near future.* For instance, George wants to cover his school expenses and go on the class trip. He also needs to consider what other expenses will arise, such as the cost of transportation to his job. While your budget will probably be a short-term plan, like George's, be sure to keep your long-term goals in mind. Money spent this week or this year won't be around next year.

At the beginning, list all your goals and make choices only after considering each one. Also, think about what additional costs each choice might

Emphasize: You are budgeting your actual disposable income (take-home pay). Approximately one-third of your salary is used for taxes or other deductions and is not available for you to spend as you want. This is the point where increased costs of government activities become personally meaningful.

Critical Thinking: Remind students that part of their income is fringe benefits. Provide a sample benefit package and ask students to examine which benefits they would prefer to eliminate and receive cash instead. Examine why they do not have this option.

Explain: Be conservative when developing your base budget. For example, if your students earn between $10 and $20 a week babysitting, they should not build a budget based on $20 per week income. They should estimate an income closer to $10 per week.

Table 9.2 How George Spent His Money Before Making a Budget

	Week 1	Week 2
Weekly Income	**$55.00**	**$70.00**
Transportation	7.50	7.50
Savings for trip	0	10.00
Clothes	0	0
School supplies	4.00	0
Meals	9.00	11.50
Plays/movies	22.00	25.00
Books	3.00	6.00
Unknown	9.50	10.00
Total expenses	55.00	70.00

involve. Even if George borrows a camera to take pictures on the trip, he still has to set aside some money for film and processing.

Making the Budget After listing all the things he wants, George must consider his chances of getting them. This requires estimating, or predicting, his income for the budget period. No one knows for sure what will happen in the future, but since spending goals will be based on this prediction, the estimate must be as accurate as possible. George should count only the income he's sure to receive. It's probably best not to count gifts until they are received—they can be used for savings or for extras like concert tickets and records.

Remember, too, to count only take-home pay, not gross salary. Taxes and other deductions from pay are not available for spending.

Some budgeters have to deal with variable forms of income that cannot be predicted accurately, such as tips or income from services like lawn care or babysitting. These people should base their estimates on past experience, either from the previous year or from the preliminary record-keeping period.

Once income is calculated, consider expenses. Budgeters encounter two types. **Fixed expenses** are *expenses that stay more or less the same over time and that must be met by a certain date,* such as rent or taxes. Fixed expenses can also arise from obligations taken on—for instance, a loan that needs to be repaid. George's fixed costs include transportation to school and work. **Variable expenses** are *expenses that change each month and that we may be able to control.* These include entertainment, food, and travel. George's variable costs include what he spends on clothes, meals, and plays.

A budget should cover essentials first: begin by subtracting fixed expenses. Some of these are regular payments due each week or month. Others, like car insurance or tuition fees, are irregular—they occur once or twice a year. These costs are easier to meet if you set aside a small amount of money every budget period. George follows this principle in saving money for his trip. You can use spending records from the past to estimate these irregular costs for the coming year.

After meeting all fixed expenses, decide how much to save. **Savings** are *money set aside for future use.* Some people save to buy expensive goods, like a television. Some save for the long term to provide for retirement.

Activity: Ask students to list typical fixed and variable expenses for their age group.

Explain: By saving regularly for large, irregular fixed expenses (such as auto insurance) students will not be faced with attempting to pay the entire amount out of one budget period. They will also be able to adjust this amount if the price is increased or if additional expenses occur.

Note: Savings is deducted from income before variable expenses are calculated. This emphasizes the fact that saving for something you want is very important even if it is only a little each month.

Focus: Most of us find our expenses are greater than our income. Therefore, the decision-making process may be helpful in deciding how to reduce expenses. Also, the substitution of alternatives may be helpful (riding the bus instead of driving a car).

Some save just to get into the habit of saving. Savings might also be for emergency expenses. Saving is a good habit, and everyone's budget should provide for some savings, no matter how small the initial amount may be. George plans to set money aside not just for the trip, but also to build a reserve fund.

Next, George deducts his variable expenses—the money he'll use for food and entertainment. Now comes the moment of truth. If the total of expenses and savings equals income, then the budget works. If income is greater than expenses and savings, you can make some pleasant choices—save more, give to charity, spend more on yourself, or perhaps buy a present for someone else.

If your income is less than your expenses and savings, you must balance the budget by cutting expenses. Here are some hints for fixing a lopsided budget:

- Check your math carefully.
- Be sure you made reasonable estimates—remember to base them on spending patterns and goals.
- Don't cut savings without making sure that the new amount will allow you to meet your goals.
- Don't cut an important item just because it's large; if necessary, reduce costs in categories that are less important.
- Look for substitutes that save money, such as walking to school instead of driving.

Budgets often don't work out the first time, and you may need to make adjustments. Table 9.3 compares George's trial budget, on the left, to his

Table 9.3 George's Trial Budget and His Final Budget After Adjustments

Trial Budget			Final Budget (per week)
Week 1	Week 2		
$60	$60	Income	$60
		Fixed Expenses	
7.50	7.50	Transportation	7.50
		Savings	
5	5	Reserve fund	5
10	10	For trip	10
10	10	For clothes	10
		Variable Expenses	
2.50	2.50	School supplies	2
13	13	Meals away from home	10
10	20	Plays/movies	10
6	6	Books	3
5	5	Other	2.50
$69	$79	Total expenses plus savings	$60

Discussion: Use of personal credit is at a all-time high. Ask your students what this indicates about personal budgeting. What will this large amount of debt mean for future budgets?

Note: Budgets are not written in stone. Some months you may have to trade off one budgeted expenditure for another, more important expenditure. You should always examine past budgets to improve future budgets.

Illustration: Some people put their budgets into practice by dividing their income into categories, labeling envelopes with these category names, and keeping transportation money in the transportation envelope, food money in the food envelope, entertainment money in the entertainment envelope, etc.

Critical Thinking: Assist your students in examining the federal budget. Describe the balancing act between reducing expenses and increasing revenue.

This young married couple works out their budget together so that both of them will be more committed to using it.

final budget, on the right. Notice that he made his budget balance by adjusting his variable expenses.

Using the Budget George shouldn't go to all the trouble of analyzing his expenses and income only to stick the budget in a drawer. He must check the budget before he spends any money. He must keep it up to date by keeping records of his spending.

There are lots of ways to do this. George could carry a little book and record cash expenditures as he makes them. He might keep all his records at home and update them each evening. Either way, he must keep records and occasionally compare them to his budget to see whether any category needs adjusting. If he spends less for clothes than he expected, there will be more money for savings or entertainment. If he is late leaving for work one day and has to take a cab, he may have to skip buying a new novel that week, perhaps borrowing it from the library instead.

If emergencies come up, some budget items may need major adjustments. For instance, if you break your glasses, you may have to forgo buying something to pay for a new pair.

Using a budget also means evaluating it. Budgets are based on estimates of income and expenses. At the end of the budget period, check these estimates and if necessary adjust them for the next period. After a few months, patterns may emerge. You may have allotted too little for necessities like food or occasional expenses like car maintenance. If so, change the budget to provide for these things. If you come up with new goals or new sources of income, be sure to change your budget.

Emphasize: A family budget should be drawn up by the entire family. This way, opportunity costs and trade-offs can be discussed before the process is implemented.

Family Budgets George's budget was a personal one. A family also needs to make a budget that accounts for the incomes and expenses of all its members. Making a family budget involves the same steps as making a personal budget, but it is a little more complicated. Because several people are involved, there are more wants and resources to be considered. Also, expenses—like rent, medical care, vacations, insurance, food, and clothes—are larger and involve more responsibility. This responsibility may be shared by all family members who contribute to the budget. To achieve its goals, a family works together as a unit, with members sharing with one another and helping one another. Everyone can work together to make the budget and to make it work.

YOU INTERACT WITH THE ECONOMY: INFLATION AND DEFLATION

Define: Would **cost-push** or **demand-pull inflation** exist if there were not a drastic expansion of the money supply? An expansion of the money supply will increase demand, thus stimulating demand-pull inflation. If costs in some industries are rising, this should mean a reallocation of resources from other purchases in order to pay the increased cost of the higher priced products. Or, it may mean a reduction in demand for the higher-cost products. It is only through expansion in the money supply that we are able to purchase the same quantity of goods and services at higher costs.

Budgets are based on estimates of future income and expenses. Sometimes these estimates are wrong. Getting a raise means income goes up. Higher prices mean expenses go up.

Budgets are based on current prices, but prices change. If one store raises prices on shirts, that change might have a small effect on your clothing bill. If many manufacturers and retailers raise their prices, the effect on your whole budget can be dramatic. *When the general level of prices increases*, it is called **inflation**.

Inflation has the effect of decreasing a consumer's buying power. **Buying power** is *the amount of goods and services a dollar will buy*. If notebooks are $1.29 this year instead of last year's 79 cents, your buying power has decreased.

There is much disagreement over what makes inflation happen, but two causes are often suggested. One is that rising costs push prices up. For instance, the combination of higher energy costs, labor costs, and prices of raw materials helped push up the prices for most products in the 1970s. Another possible cause of inflation is rising demand for products and services. When a lot of money is available, people demand more goods. This increased competition among consumers for the same amount of goods and services pushes prices up. Either way, inflation only exists if most prices are rising—price increases in just one or two items doesn't make inflation.

If people expect inflation to continue, demand will increase—consumers will try to buy what they want now to avoid paying more later. Inflation discourages saving because the dollars that are saved now will be worth less in the future. It encourages people to buy on credit. By buying something now and paying for it later, consumers can pay with dollars that are worth less.

We have experienced inflation generally since 1945 and at higher levels since 1970 (see Figure 9.1). It has been hard to fight inflation, although the

Expansion: One of the major results of inflation is a redistribution of income from people with **fixed** incomes to those with **flexible** incomes. People with fixed incomes have incomes with declining purchasing power. People with flexible incomes benefit because their incomes rise to maintain the same or greater purchasing power. **Savers** are hurt by inflation, because the money they save will be worth less in the future. **Debtors** benefit because they are paying off the loan with cheaper money; **creditors** (lenders) are hurt because they receive cheaper money in return for their loans.

World Economy: Provide examples of **hyperinflation**. In 1985 Bolivia's annual inflation rate was 3,400%. That means that a $20 dinner in 1984 would cost $680 in 1985. In Germany in the 1920s inflation was so high it took a wheelbarrow of Deutsche marks to buy a loaf of bread (in 1922 the German inflation rate was about 5,470% and in 1923 the rate was 1,300,000,000,000%).

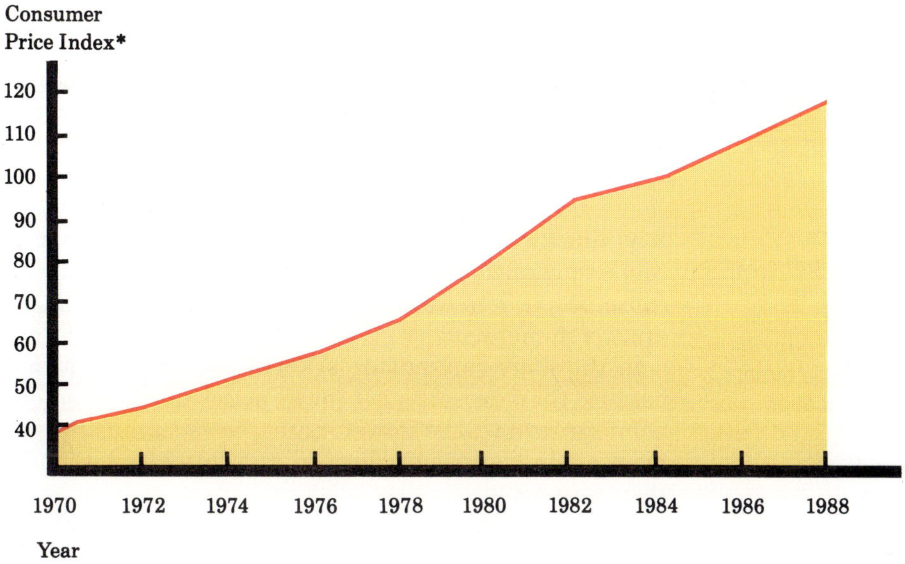

*A consumer price index assigns a value of 100 to a base period (here 1982–1984). This makes it possible to compare costs in different years.

Source: Bureau of Labor Statistics

Figure 9.1 The Rise in Prices since 1967

government has tried many tactics. Among these are raising taxes, slowing the growth of spending, and slowing the growth rate of the money supply. These tactics tend to decrease consumers' demand for goods.

You can reduce the effects of inflation on your budget by shopping carefully. Put off buying until you've checked prices at several stores. Substitute similar items that cost less. Shop at discount stores. Compare prices and watch for sales. Avoid unnecessary high-cost items. Buy foods in season,

Table 9.4 Fifteen Ways to Combat Inflation

1. When price is low, buy in quantity *if* the larger quantity will be used.
2. Use coupons and rebates for products you would normally purchase.
3. Hold down credit purchases; pay within 30-day no-charge period.
4. Buy only the quality needed, such as the grade of food suitable for a certain type of preparation.
5. Don't pay for unnecessary convenience.
6. Don't pay for unnecessary packaging.
7. Think ahead: planning shopping trips saves money; emergencies cost extra.
8. Buy used or irregular goods if they show no damage.
9. Comparison shop for stores and brands.
10. Don't buy expensive frill products.
11. Examine habitual expenses—is a better, cheaper alternative available?
12. Watch energy use for appliances, cars, and housing.
13. Don't waste.
14. Delay purchases on new products or seasonal goods until the price comes down.
15. Avoid impulse buying.

when their prices are lowest. Buy items at traditional sales times. Buy things in quantity when you get a discount for doing so—and if you need the quantity. Table 9.4 summarizes these hints and offers a few more.

Summary: We have limited resources and unlimited wants. Therefore, we must develop and adhere to a plan to spend these resources in order to obtain the maximum satisfaction. These plans can be hindered by economic events such as inflation.

The opposite of inflation is **deflation**, which is *a decrease in the general level of prices.* Deflation increases buying power and encourages people to save. Whether people will spend more or save more depends on how long they expect the deflation to last. If they believe that prices will increase soon, they will buy now. If they expect prices to continue to drop, they will save money now and buy later. Deflation discourages buying on credit because people won't want to repay the money they borrow with dollars that are worth more.

In the short run, businesses will probably produce less during deflation because they expect to get lower prices for their products. As a result, economic growth will be slower. Later, however, businesses will start to produce more again because production costs are also lower. Economic growth will then resume.

In recent years we have had few deflationary periods. Although low prices are good for the consumer, less production leads to slowed economic growth and to unemployment. Therefore, the federal government may spend more to try to boost production.

SUMMARY

- In the consumer role, we manage our resources to satisfy our wants. Consumers follow seven steps: planning, getting information, comparison shopping, determining how to pay for the purchase, deciding if and when to buy, buying, and evaluating the purchase.
- There are many alternatives to buying a good or a service, including substituting less costly items, doing-it-yourself, bartering, product care and maintenance, renting, and doing without.
- Planning helps us to use our resources effectively and to live within our means. It helps us to foresee future needs and satisfy our most important wants. Planning helps us to avoid impulse buying and measure our progress toward achieving overall goals. It makes choices easier by making the opportunity cost clear.
- Time is an important resource because we use it to earn money and develop skills. Planning is the key to efficient use of time, so making a time budget is helpful.
- Skills are a resource that can be increased by going to school, learning from others, reading, and using computers. Practice enhances all skills. With our skills we can satisfy our wants and earn money.
- Without personal energy, we would be unable to do anything. Good nutrition, proper rest, adequate exercise, and avoiding drugs all help us maintain or increase our energy.
- Budgeting our money helps us use it wisely and provide for our future wants. Making a budget involves keeping a spending record, setting goals, estimating income and expenses, tallying savings and expenses, and balancing the budget. Unless we use the budget, we've wasted our time—a budget should be followed.
- When inflation occurs our dollars buy less. When deflation occurs our dollars buy more. To reduce the effects of inflation on our

budgets, we can shop carefully, comparison shop, make cheaper substitutions, eliminate expensive frills, buy foods in season, and watch for sales.

Key Terms

Match each of the following terms with the definition that most suits it.

basic consumer method	fixed expenses	product care and maintenance	short-term goals
budget	inflation	renting	skills
buying power	long-term goals	savings	variable expenses
deflation	personal energy		

a. goals to achieve in the distant future
b. paying a fee in return for the temporary use of some good or property
c. our talents and our ability to develop them
d. a plan to achieve goals by fitting expenses to income
e. expenses that change each month and that we may be able to control
f. a decrease in the general level of prices
g. a seven-step process of planning and carrying out buying decisions
h. goals to achieve in the near future
i. the proper use and care of goods to stretch their lives
j. our physical capacity to do things
k. expenses that stay more or less the same over time and that must be met by a certain date
l. money set aside for future use
m. an increase in the general level of prices
n. the amount of goods or services a dollar will buy

Review Questions

1. What are the steps of the consumer method? How is it like systematic decision making?
2. What are the alternatives to buying? Give an example of three alternatives to buying a desk.
3. Name three benefits of planning. Give one example of how planning can save you time or money.
4. Why should time be budgeted?
5. How can you develop skills? What are skills used for?
6. How can you maintain or increase personal energy?
7. Outline the steps involved in making a budget. After making a budget, what's the most important thing to do?
8. What is the difference between a fixed expense and a variable expense? Define each and give examples.
9. What reasons are there for saving?
10. Define inflation. How does it affect the economy? Name three things consumers can do to fight inflation.

Projects

1. Make a budget for spending your time during the week. Include sleeping, eating, school, studying, relaxation and entertainment, working, and anything else you do. Compare your time budget with George's. How can you use your time better?
2. Suppose you needed to use your skills to supplement your earnings. What are your skills? What possibilities do they offer you for increasing your income or stretching your other resources? Do your friends have any skills that complement yours? Outline

how you could use an existing skill or develop a new one that could expand your resources.

3. Make a budget for a week. Keep a record of all you spend for a week. At the end of the week write down all your goals and estimate your income for the next week. Decide how much you want to save. Estimate costs based on how you spent money the first week. Tally up your projected savings and expenses and subtract them from estimated income. If necessary, make adjustments to make it balance. Now follow your budget as best you can during week two. Evaluate your success. Write a list of suggestions based on what you learned from trying this sample budget.
4. Investigate price increases. Select about fifteen items around the house. Pick some that your family buys frequently, like milk and bread, and some that it buys less often, like TVs. Find out how much your family paid when the item was last purchased, and compare this to the item's present cost, either by checking a store or looking in the newspaper. Group together the items that have increased in price, those that have decreased, and those whose prices have stayed the same. For each item, try to explain why price behaved the way it did. Have there been changes in supply and demand? What were they?
5. Are you getting enough sleep, or are you suffering from sleep deprivation? Here's a surprising fact about sleep: teens need more of it than adults or children. Researchers at the Stanford Research Center suggest that the amount of sleep needed is whatever keeps you awake and alert all day. Go to bed 30 minutes earlier than your usual time for a week. Does this schedule adjustment affect your alertness and physical health? Enter your thoughts in a journal to be shared in class.
6. Discuss items in your family's budget that are affected by inflation. What do you and your family do to combat inflation? Make a list, and then compare it with Table 9.4 on page 153. Share your inflation-fighting suggestions in class.
7. Check to see if your area has a buying cooperative. These are usually large warehouse-type buildings where you can buy groceries and other goods in large quantities. You may have to belong to a particular organization in order to have shopping privileges. Request information from the cooperative to determine if it has membership restrictions. Find out if any students' families belong to the cooperative. What are the advantages and disadvantages of membership? Do you think it would be worthwhile to become a member?

Getting and Using Information 10

Overview: Chapter 10 helps your students expand on and improve the information they have when making decisions.

OBJECTIVES

This chapter will help you to:

1. Evaluate information sources.
2. Identify the forces that influence you to buy.
3. Get information from various sources before you decide to make a purchase.
4. Interpret the appeals and techniques of advertising.
5. Evaluate the costs and benefits of advertising.

Michelle was browsing at a shelf in the library when she turned suddenly and bumped into Ian, knocking his armful of books and magazines onto the floor.

"Watch out!" cried Ian.

"Sorry, Ian! I didn't see you. Let me help you pick them up. Why do you have all these computer books?" Michelle asked.

"My folks want to buy a home computer, and I'm trying to find out which one's the best for us," Ian said.

"No kidding! What's your family going to do with a computer?"

"Well, my parents want to use it for the family budget, and Melissa can use the computer to practice her reading and arithmetic. I'd like to learn something about programming."

"That sounds boring," said Michelle. "Wouldn't you rather play video games?"

"Sure—we want to use it for games too," Ian laughed.

"That's better! So, which one will you buy?"

"I don't know yet—I have to look around and find one that does everything we want and has a good price," answered Ian. "First I'm going to talk to the people in computer stores. And I have to finish looking through these books and magazines. Want to help?"

"No thanks," called Michelle as she walked away. "But I'll come over and play those games when you've got the thing installed!"

Note: Ian will benefit by reading about computers before talking with salespeople. Then he will know what questions to ask and will be in a better position to evaluate the salesperson's response.

BOOKS AREN'T THE ONLY THINGS that will help Ian search for the right home computer for his family. He will also read advertisements, talk to salespeople and other computer owners, and try out some computers himself. All of these sources will give him **information**—*facts about goods and services that can be used to evaluate alternatives.*

In this chapter, you'll learn where to find information, how to evaluate it, and how to tell the difference between information and influences. You'll also learn how to interpret the ads you see and hear every day.

RESOURCE MANAGERS GET AND EVALUATE INFORMATION

Clarify: Time has a cost. Time spent researching computers (a purchase with a high price) is more worthwhile than time spent researching salt (a purchase with a very low price).

Ian is managing his resources. He is using his time and energy to get information about home computers. He'll then use his time and skill to evaluate this information and recommend which brand to buy. This choice will help his family use another resource—money. By doing this, Ian is building another resource—skill at getting and using information.

Information helps us to make good decisions. Imagine what might happen if Ian's family simply buys the first computer that looks good to them. Once

Note: Ian's decision making is aided by first analyzing his uses for the purchase. Computers are an excellent example since some types are better for business applications (budgeting) while others are better for games.

Note: Your students will find that the decision-making process tends to be similar in all situations.

World Economy: In most command economies, gaining and using information is not as important as it is in the United States. In fact, in the U.S.S.R. in 1990 there was virtually no choice (other than the black market) for most goods and services. People had to stand in line and then purchase whatever was available even if, in the case of shoes, the size was wrong. They then had to barter using the wrong-size shoes to trade for something else they wanted.

Comparison shopping and information gathering often overlap—newspaper ads tell where to find good prices.

they get it home, they may find that it's great for games but not for budgets. Maybe they would end up with a costly, complex machine with lots of features they don't really need—they'd be better off with something simpler at half the price.

Information is the resource manager's most valuable tool. Although getting information is a separate step in the basic consumer method, it overlaps with the other steps:

- To plan a budget we need information about the prices of what we might buy.
- When comparison shopping, we get information about products, stores, and prices.
- To determine how to pay for a purchase, we need information about cash, credit, and savings.

Resource Managers Evaluate Information

Simply getting information isn't enough, though. We must evaluate information to be able to use it. We must see whether the source of the information is reliable and objective and whether the information itself is complete and relevant to our wants.

Note: The completeness and relevancy of information is only important if the shopper has identified his or her goals and needs.

Discussion: Invite students to give examples of recent purchases they have made and the information they used in making these purchases.

Clarify: Do not discount the value of talking with a user of a product. Although his or her experience may be limited to one product, it is valuable to your analysis (especially if the experience is negative).

Illustrate: There is widespread controversy over the lack of objectivity when specific airlines sell reservations services to travel agents. Airlines providing the service tend to list their flights and prices more prominently than flights of other airlines. A travel agent using reservation service A will more often book flights on airline A. This may work to the disadvantage of the individual flyer.

First, consider whether the source of information is *reliable*. Suppose you want to buy a guitar. Your friend may recommend the brand he uses, but he only knows about that brand. He may mean well, but he really isn't helping much. You need a more reliable source, like a guitar teacher or a guitar handbook.

The source of information should also be *objective*. A music store owner may recommend the SuperSound guitar over the Fine Tone. That could be because she sells the SuperSound and not the Fine Tone, or because she makes more profit on the SuperSound. Consider whether your source—who may be knowledgeable—has a special interest in recommending one product over another.

Evaluate the information itself, too. Is it *complete?* Has the product been compared to other brands? Does the comparison show the weaknesses as well as the strengths of each brand? Does the information include all the costs of owning the product? For instance, it would be foolish to buy a car without considering how much gas it uses.

Finally, make sure the information is *relevant* to your wants. Don't be sidetracked by unimportant advertising claims like whether a movie star likes one brand of clothes. Find out if *you* like it. Also, look to see if the information is appropriate for your use of the product. Ian may learn that one computer is great for business uses, but since he's not in business, this point means little to him.

Evaluate the information that you get from a salesperson for objectivity.

Distinguish between Influences and Information

Activity: Bring print ads to class, divide the class up into teams, and ask each team to analyze an ad: (1) What information is presented in the ad? (2) How does the ad attempt to influence you to buy the product or service? and (3) What emotion does the ad appeal to?

Information brings us closer to deciding which product to buy. It isn't the only thing that affects our choice—we are also swayed by our feelings and by outside pressures. Ian may be drawn to one computer because his friend has it or because of a promotional display. These things could affect his choice without adding to his knowledge about computers. We are all subject to various **influences,** or *forces inside and outside us that affect how we think and act.*

Influences are not the same as information, even though they often come in the same package. Manufacturers and sellers are seldom objective when describing their own products, but the pamphlets they print can still be informative. For example, a computer maker may publish booklets that not only praise its computers, but also describe their uses and explain computer terms. The smart consumer separates the facts from the promotion. If we identify and examine the things that influence us, we can keep them from swaying us too much.

INFLUENCES AFFECT OUR BUYING DECISIONS

Expansion: The library will have resources on values clarification. Have your students begin clarifying their values. Point out that their values influence every decision they will make. Help them identify the consequences of their values without being critical.

Some influences are personal—they come from our own circumstances and desires. Others are external. These are pressures we feel from other people or from our society.

Personal Influences

Values—beliefs about what is important in our lives—shape wants. Someone who values clothes will spend more on his or her wardrobe than someone who doesn't. Someone who values reading will buy books. By being aware of our own values, each of us can make satisfying decisions.

Illustrate: Develop an example of a **life cycle**. During an individual's life cycle, he or she will go through a series of stages (infant, childhood, teenager, young adult, beginning family, mature family, middle-aged, and aged). Discuss these stages.

Income also influences wants. As people earn more money, they may save or invest more, buy a more expensive car, or take a vacation. A larger income lets them satisfy more wants, but the more resources someone has, the more important it is to manage them wisely. To say "I'm earning more money now, so I might as well spend it" ignores the fact that responsibilities increase as we get older.

As family status changes, wants change. For instance, someone starting to live away from home may need to buy furniture and pots and pans. Habits create patterns of living. Not all habits need to be broken, but remember that they are strong influences. It's useful to question habits from time to time.

The desire to impress others is also a strong influence. People are often tempted to buy things that they feel will make them accepted or admired.

External Influences

Economic conditions have a direct influence on our wants. When the economy is performing poorly, people spend less. They want to save and hold on

Explain: If the public expects the economy to grow, people will not be as concerned about protecting themselves. If the public expects an economic slowdown, people will take measures to protect their lifestyle.

Critical Thinking: Invite your students to examine the influence of peers. Why is peer influence so strong at this age?

Discuss: Lead a class discussion on different cultures and their lifestyles. Include the role of the family, attitudes toward education, etc.

Activity: List today's teen fashion favorites. Encourage students to identify what influences these fashion trends (if styles from the 1950s or sports team uniforms are popular), and examine trends five to 10 years ago.

The ethnic group we belong to can influence many of our values, interests, and wants.

to what they have. When the economy is growing, there are more opportunities to earn money and more hope for the future. People are more willing to spend their money.

Culture is another important influence. Customs, traditions, and social values surround us. Thanksgiving is celebrated nationwide every year with feasts and family reunions, and the customs of other groups reflect special values. Different ethnic groups, for example, enjoy different kinds of food or clothes.

Fashion reflects tastes that change over time. Everything from hairstyles to houses is subject to fashion. The desire to be in style influences our decisions. Have you ever bought a sweater because it was in style—or returned one because it wasn't?

Our family influences us in ways we may not realize. If parents avoid one model of a refrigerator, their children may follow their example later on.

Another external influence is friends. **Peer pressure** is *the influence created by our desire to be accepted by people our own age.* It is hard to resist. We find it easier to choose clothes, activities, and views that our friends favor. Remember, though, that doing so isn't always satisfying. Someone who joins her friends every afternoon at the video game arcade may not really be enjoying herself. She might prefer to spend her time swimming but not want the group to think she's different.

Another influence is **sales pressure,** which is *the use of tactics by salespeople to persuade consumers to buy*. Salespeople can be quite helpful, but sometimes they try to pressure us to buy their product. Look out for these signs of sales pressure:

Role-play: Have your students role-play a situation with a high-pressure salesperson. One student can play the salesperson; another student can play the role of the customer. Invite the class to critique the customer's response and suggest improvements.

- The salesperson insists that you buy now.
- Your conversation with one salesperson is joined by a second.
- The salesperson hints that someone else is going to buy the item if you don't.
- The salesperson flatters you.
- The salesperson tries to appeal to your desire to impress others.

The best way to resist these tactics is to insist that you need time to consider your decision. If the pressure continues, report the salesperson to his or her manager. If the manager doesn't respond satisfactorily, send your complaint higher up in the organization, to the Better Business Bureau, or to the local, state, or federal government.

WE GET INFORMATION FROM FOUR SOURCES

We get information from people we know, businesses, organizations that test and rate products, and the government. Wherever we get it, we should make sure that the information—and the source—is reliable, objective, complete, and relevant.

Extension: New labeling laws are being considered which would require additional information. Check with the Food and Drug Administration regarding the latest in labeling requirements.

Personal Sources

We often start getting information from family and friends who have used a product or service. These people are useful because they may know and understand our preferences, and they can answer our questions and explain what they mean.

The search for information must go beyond friends and family, however. Their knowledge may be limited, or they may have long-standing buying habits and prejudices. Sometimes people are not willing to admit that they made a poor choice. A cousin may believe that his or her stereo was a good deal, but perhaps it wasn't. Check it out for yourself.

Consumers Use Business Sources

Business provides a great deal of information that can be helpful.

- *Labels* contain many useful facts. For instance, food labels list the product's name, its weight, the ingredients (in order of weight), and the nutrients it provides. Food labels also include the maker's name and address. Other goods, from clothing to new cars, also have labels that inform us.
- *Promises by manufacturers or sellers that their goods meet certain standards* are called **warranties.** They promise to repair or replace all or part of an item at no charge if something goes wrong with the product within a certain period of time.

Research: What is a trade association? How do trade associations represent competing firms within an industry?

Extension: Invite a representative of the local Better Business Bureau to class to discuss the organization and its activities.

Activity: Develop a matrix with the business sources given in the text down the left side. Across the top, arrange the qualities on which these sources could be evaluated (product knowledge, bias, pressure, accessibility, etc.). Lead students through a discussion evaluating all these business sources of information.

- *Advertisements* announce new products and tell us where to get goods, how to use them, and how much they cost. Ads are an important source of information, but one that we must use carefully. Later in this chapter we'll focus on how to separate an ad's information from its influence.
- Although *salespeople* may pressure us, they can also give us helpful facts, especially if we do product research beforehand. The salespeople who work in stores that sell only one kind of product (cameras, for example) often are quite knowledgeable about those goods.
- Manufacturers and sellers print *information booklets* for consumers. They can be helpful—but remember that they may not be objective. Manufacturers often supply use and care manuals with their products.
- *Groups of people or businesses who join together to promote their common interests* are called **trade and professional associations.** They may supply materials describing products or promoting one type of product over another. For instance, the American Wool Council may have pamphlets explaining why it thinks wool is better than other fibers. Trade associations usually do not recommend specific brands since competing makers may belong to the same group. However, many have offices that give general product information and that list local sellers. These offices are listed in the *National Trade and Professional Associations of the United States,* which may be found at the library.
- The businesses in many communities have joined to promote ethical practices in advertising and selling. The groups they form are called the **Better Business Bureaus** (BBBs). These are *nonprofit corporations that protect businesses and consumers by helping businesses to regulate themselves.* The BBBs do not compare products or give price information. They can tell you if any complaints have been made against a business, and how they were handled. There are BBBs in every state except Montana, North Dakota, South Dakota, West Virginia, and Wyoming.
- *Underwriters' Laboratories* (UL) is a group that tests electrical products for safety. It is wise to buy only products that have the UL seal of approval (see the sample in Figure 10.1).

Figure 10.1 The Underwriters' Laboratories Seal of Approval

Activity: Bring to class several consumer-help columns from the local paper. Ask students to review these columns in terms of: (1) the audience the columns appeal to; (2) does the column take current conditions of the economy into consideration? (3) biases of the column; (4) consumer tips provided; and (5) does the column view the consumer, business, labor, or government as "good guys" or "bad guys"?

- The mass media give a great deal of information. Newspapers print columns with hints about good buys, do-it-yourself projects, discount stores, and recipes that save money. News items tell us about consumer laws and other news, as do radio and TV news shows and other programs. Some magazines, like *Changing Times* and *Money,* deal only with consumer topics. Many others, like *Better Homes and Gardens* and *Good Housekeeping,* also give useful information. Some special interest magazines study and rate competing products. For instance, Ian can read about different brands in computer magazines. He can also refer to reports by organizations that test products.

Organizations That Test and Rate Products

Research groups have been organized to test products available to buyers. These organizations usually decide what characteristics are important to the product and test competing brands for their performance. They are not concerned with how people like a product, but only with whether the product does what it is supposed to do. Goods and services like cars and appliances, clothes, packaged foods, and entertainment and hobby goods are tested. These groups only test national brands, ignoring local or generic products. Some items are tested often. Cars, for example, are tested every year. Prices are also published.

Clarify: It is important that students note the rating system and attempt to identify the biases in testing organization reports. *Consumer Reports* published an evaluation of coffee based on the tasting results from a panel of "coffee experts." Without duplicating the test, it is difficult to evaluate how closely the "experts" tastes are to yours.

There are three major groups of this kind, each of which publishes a magazine that gives the test results:

- Consumers' Research publishes *Consumers' Research* magazine.
- Consumers Union publishes *Consumer Reports* and an annual *Buying Guide.*

The ratings vary from group to group, but each publication explains its rating system.

Remember that you can't rely only on these groups for information. They do not test all of the competing brands on the market. You may be interested in one that they don't test. More important, these groups test according to their own standards, not yours. Base your decision on your wants, using information from these tests only as a guide.

Governments Provide Information

Critical Thinking: Can information from the government be biased?

State and federal agencies and some local governments issue information for the public. The units of the federal government that do so are listed in Table 10.1.

State agencies that offer information include those that oversee banking, utilities, and insurance, consumer affairs divisions, and the attorney generals' offices.

Government information is not always related to specific products. Nevertheless, it can be valuable. The best way to get information from federal

Table 10.1 Units of the Federal Government That Provide Consumer Information

Specific offices or divisions to contact are in parentheses.

Cabinet Departments

Agriculture (Agricultural Marketing Service; Animal and Plant Health Inspection Service; Extension Service; Food and Nutrition Service; Food Safety and Quality Service; Office of Information)
Commerce (National Bureau of Standards; National Marine Fisheries Service; Office of Consumer Affairs; Patent and Trademark Office)
Health and Human Services (Food and Drug Administration; Office of Consumer Affairs; Public Health Service; Social Security Administration)
Housing and Urban Development (Fair Housing and Equal Opportunity Division; Federal Housing Administration)
Interior (Fish and Wildlife Services; National Park Service)
Justice (Citizen Complaint Center)
Labor (Occupational Safety and Health Administration; Office of Information, Publications, and Reports)
Transportation (Federal Aviation Administration; National Highway Traffic Safety Administration; Office of Information)

Noncabinet Offices

Commodity Futures Trading Commission (Office of Public Information)
Consumer Product Safety Commission (Office of the Secretary)
Environmental Protection Agency (Office of Public Affairs; Public Inquiry Center)
Equal Employment Opportunity Commission (Office of Public Affairs)
Federal Communications Commission (Office of Consumer Assistance and Small Business Division)
Federal Deposit Insurance Corporation (Office of Consumer Programs)
Federal Reserve System (Office of Consumer Affairs; Office of Publications)
Federal Trade Commission (Bureau of Consumer Protection; Consumer Inquiries; Office of Public Affairs)
General Services Administration (Consumer Information Center)
Interstate Commerce Commission (Office of Consumer Protection; Ombudsman's Office)
National Credit Union Administration (Assistant Director for Consumer Affairs)
National Transportation Safety Board (Public Inquiries Section)
Nuclear Regulatory Commission (Consumer Affairs Officer, Office of Public Affairs)
Pension Benefit Guarantee Corporation
United States Postal Service (Consumer Advocate, Office of Consumer Affairs)
Securities and Exchange Commission (Office of Consumer Affairs)
Small Business Administration (Office of Public Communications)

Critical Thinking: Encourage students to consider the consequences of a fourth, unelected arm of government. See Table 10.1.

sources is to write the main office, which is usually in Washington, D.C. Some have toll-free numbers that you can call to ask questions. Some agencies also have local, state, or regional offices that you can also call or visit. The *U.S. Government Manual,* which you can find in your library, lists every government department and agency and gives the addresses and phone numbers you can use.

ADVERTISING IS A SOURCE OF INFLUENCE AND INFORMATION

Advertising is *a message meant to create interest in a product or service and to persuade consumers to buy it.* American businesses spent over $60 billion in a recent year to advertise their products. Figure 10.2 shows the five product types that spend the most on ads in two popular media. Wherever ads appear—on billboards, in print, on radio, or on TV—they use similar methods.

Note: Advertising and promotional spending in the United States in 1987 was estimated to be over $100 billion.

Demonstrate: Display a variety of print ads and assist the students in analyzing the type and the amount of information given in each ad.

Critical Thinking: Television advertising for cigarettes and alcohol has been banned for some time. Did this lower the price of these products? Did it decrease demand for these products?

Wise consumers compare prices by checking advertisements for different stores. Many newspapers carry advertising supplements. Stores even send advertisements to consumers' homes through the mail.

Advertising Contains Information

Ads are probably the biggest source of information on new products and services. We would never hear of many goods if they weren't advertised. Ads also give price information by telling us of sales, specials, and rebates. We can compare prices by checking the ads for different stores. Ads also give performance information, like a car's gas mileage. Other features of products are explained and illustrated in ads, too. Ian first learned about the variety of computers available, their prices, and where to buy them from newspaper ads.

Advertisers Try to Influence Consumers

While ads give useful information, we must get that information by seeing through their attempts to influence us. Advertisers appeal to us in different ways. Let's compare these appeals by seeing how each would be used to sell the Panther XL, a fictional new sports car.

- *A message that aims at consumers' practical needs in a logical way* is a **rational appeal.** The Panther ad would describe how the car combines high gas mileage and engine power, or the ad might proclaim the car's low price or the dealer's easy financing terms.

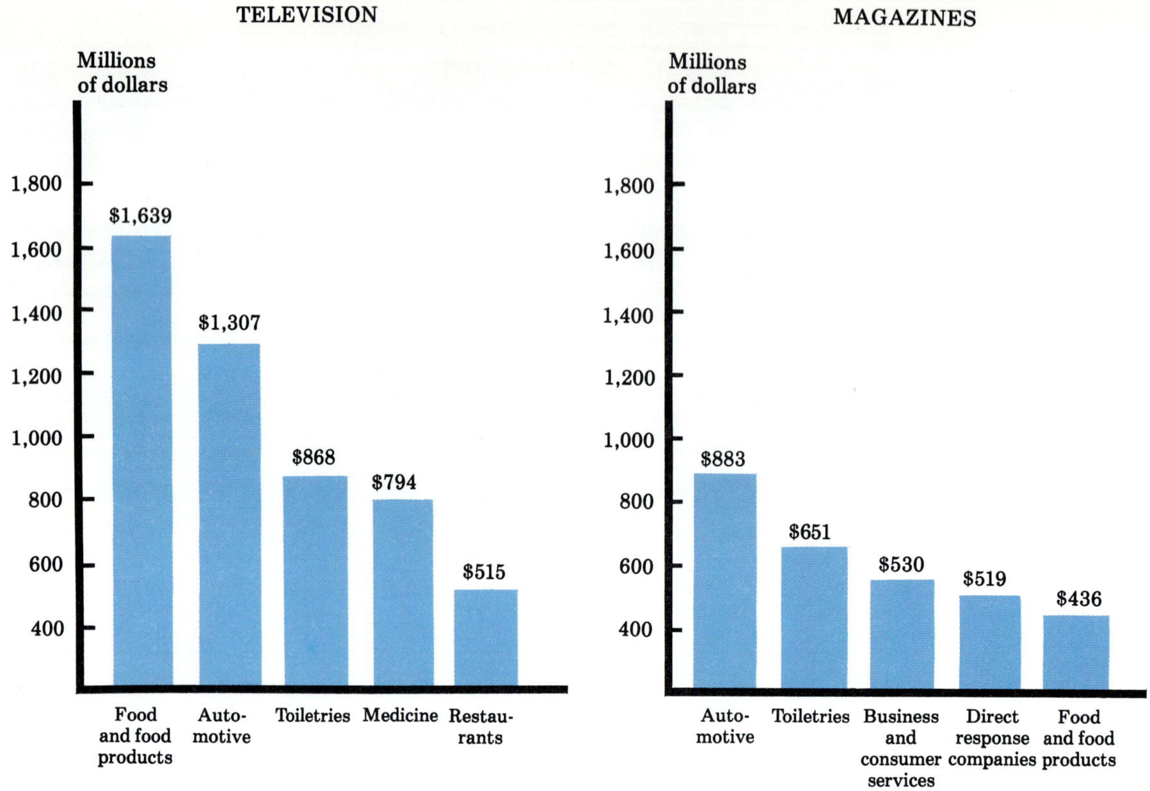

Figure 10.2 The Top Five Product Types That Advertise in Different Media

Activity: Ask students to evaluate the appeals used in TV commercials, and discuss in class when each of these appeals would be most successful and when they would not.

Critical Thinking: Since the 1960s advertising has been criticized for selling products using females as sex objects. Has this practice declined or stopped? Why or why not? Are males ever used as sex objects in an ad?

- *Ads aimed at consumers' psychological needs and desires* are **emotional appeals.** These appeals relate a product to love, friendship, or success. A Panther ad with this appeal might portray how a timid person turns into the most popular person in town by buying this flashy car.
- Most ads use *positive appeals*—they contain all the good news about a product and none of the bad. Sometimes, though, an advertiser uses a *negative appeal,* discouraging our business to grab attention. Above a picture of the Panther, a headline might boldly state, "The Panther XL is not for you." Startled by this admission, you read on—only to discover that it isn't for you if you're dull and cheap.
- *Humor* is a powerful way advertisers can get us to remember their products. A Panther ad might poke fun at less sporty cars by showing them sputter and stall while the Panther glides along the highway easily.
- *Sex appeal* is used to sell a tremendous variety of products. A group of admiring men might surround a smiling woman who owns the Panther. The advertiser is assuring us that we, too, can have romantic success by buying this car.
- *Fear appeal* is effective when the ad is directed at a fear already present in our minds. A Panther ad may show the worried owner of another car stalled on the side of the highway at night, to play on our fear of cars that break down.

Of course, these appeals are often combined in one ad. Most ads contain some rational appeal, and humor and negative appeals are often used together. Fear and sex appeals are types of emotional appeals. By seeing through what the ad says, we can understand how the seller is trying to influence us. If we screen out the emotional appeals, we can get more information from the ad.

To make these appeals work, advertisers use different *techniques*—the way the appeal is presented. Recognizing these can help us use ads instead of being used by them. Let's see how each technique would be used to sell the Panther XL.

- *Someone proclaims his or her satisfaction with the product* in a **testimonial.** A Panther ad might have five different owners praising the car for its ride and sleek look. A variation is the *endorsement*—a testimonial made by a celebrity. A famous race car driver, for instance, might declare his or her delight with the Panther's road handling.
- *Problem-solving* ads often present imaginary situations of daily life. Poor Charley can't get a date until he buys the Panther XL. Then he spends all day answering the phone and all night taking out attractive women.
- The *demonstration* ad shows us how the product works. We may see how the Panther hugs the road on turns or watch it accelerate from zero to 60 in 2.7 seconds.
- The *scientific test* presents us with the favorable results of "objective" tests. We're told that an independent testing lab examined the Panther and rated it excellent or very good on ten tests.
- In a *product comparison,* the Panther is compared in some way to other cars. Competing brands may not actually be named, but sometimes they are. Whether or not they're identified, the advertised brand is always the winner.
- *Life-style* ads associate the product with glamour or excitement or success. We may see an expensively dressed couple drive their Panther up to the door of a mansion.
- The *bandwagon* approach tries to attract new buyers by describing a product's popularity. The ad may emphasize the awards the Panther has won or proclaim it the top selling sports car.

Table 10.2 lists some words that are often found in ads and explains what they mean. Sometimes advertisers use these words in a misleading way. If they do, consumers can do something about unfair or deceptive ads.

Advertising Is Regulated

Media, industry, and government have made efforts to make sure that advertising is used fairly. Radio, TV, and print media may not allow certain presentations that do not meet their standards. These standards are set by groups like the Direct Marketing Association, Outdoor Advertising Association of America, and the American Association of Advertising Agencies. Ad agencies, through the American Advertising Federation and the American

Activity: While evaluating TV commercials, students should also identify the techniques being used.

Research: Have students contact the media and obtain copies of advertising standards. You may want to invite a representative from the media or advertising agency to speak to the class.

Activity: Students will develop their own advertising campaign. Divide the class into teams of three to five students and assign each team a product, activity, or cause for which they develop an advertising campaign. Some teams will adhere to industry standards; some teams will be free from any standards in their campaign. Encourage each team to develop a print ad and a TV or radio spot. Once the campaigns are completed, the teams will present them to the class (giving no indication to the class as to whether the team was required to adhere to standards). The rest of the class will decide if standards were adhered to, and to critique the campaigns.

Table 10.2 Words to Look for in Advertising

Word	Explanation
Clearance	This should mean that the seller has reduced the usual price in order to sell its stock of the product.
Comparable value *or* compare at	The advertiser implies that another business or product is sold at a higher price. Ask yourself, how comparable are the two products?
Formerly sold at	The item was sold at the stated price in the past and is being offered for less now. Ask yourself, how long ago was the higher price charged? Are other stores selling it for even less?
Introductory offer	This should mean that a new product is temporarily being sold at a lower price than it will in the future.
Manufacturer's list price *or* suggested retail price	The advertiser states the price that the maker *suggests*, but often all sellers offer the product for less. Ask yourself, does anyone sell it for list price? Is a larger discount available elsewhere?
Regularly	The "regular" price should be the price the seller charged immediately before offering the sale.
Special	This refers to a temporary price reduction that is limited in some way, often in the number of units of the product that will be sold at this price.
Up to ___% off	Only some items will have the maximum price cut — others will be reduced less.

Demonstrate: Obtain information from the local Better Business Bureau regarding the National Advertisers Division and the National Advertising Review Board.

Critical Thinking: Why would an industry voluntarily set standards for itself? Why would firms within an industry voluntarily respond to complaints from organizations such as the Better Business Bureau?

Research: Students will investigate the Federal Trade Commission to determine its level of activity, program emphases, and examples of recent regulatory activity. Compare this to the activities of the Better Business Bureau and other industry organizations.

Discussion: Ask students if they have run into "bait and switch" sales tactics. Discuss the difference between "bait and switch" and merely pointing out the difference in quality between two different items.

Association of Advertising, also work to keep the messages they create fair and honest.

Industry regulates itself through two groups that are part of the council of Better Business Bureaus. The National Advertisers Division (NAD) hears complaints made by consumers and businesses about national ads. The NAD tries to persuade the business to stop using an ad that it decides is misleading. If it can't convince the business, it sends the complaint to another part of the BBB, the National Advertising Review Board (NARB). This group appoints a five-person panel to hear the case. Most advertisers go along with the panel's finding. If the NARB suggests it, they stop using the ad.

The **Federal Trade Commission** (FTC) is *the federal agency that, among other tasks, protects consumers from ads that are unfair or deceptive.* Complaints are filed either by businesses, consumers, government officials, or trade groups. The FTC gathers evidence about the ad and decides whether to drop the case or issue a complaint. If it finds an ad unfair, the FTC can fine the advertiser, order the ad to be stopped, or order a corrective ad to be placed.

The power of the agency is fairly broad, because the definitions of *unfair* and *deceptive* are vague. Still, there is one type of ad that the FTC clearly finds illegal. **Bait-and-switch advertising** occurs when *a store advertises a low price on one item to lure shoppers in, only to talk them into buying a* *more costly item.* If a salesperson refuses to show you the low-priced good or downgrades its quality while praising the more expensive product, or says the advertised item has been sold out, bait and switch may be involved. Report this practice to the state attorney general or to the Federal Trade Commission.

Explain: A goal of advertising is to persuade consumers that they have a need and that a particular product or service will satisfy this need.

Other government agencies regulate ads for particular kinds of goods and services. The Food and Drug Administration, for instance, oversees ads for prescription drugs.

YOU INTERACT WITH THE ECONOMY: THE COSTS AND BENEFITS OF ADVERTISING

Illustrate: If advertising were all-powerful in persuading consumers to buy products they do not want, how do you explain the Edsel, Maxwell House coffee in the filter packs, Betamax, and Stouffer's Freshness foods?

Advertising is controversial. Some people hate it, and others enjoy it. Most simply learn to live with it. John Kenneth Galbraith, a noted economist, has leveled the strongest charge against advertising. He claims that ads take away the consumer's power in the marketplace. Instead of responding to consumers by making what they want, he argues, producers use ads to create consumer wants. In this view, buyers are manipulated by producers to prefer one fast-food hamburger over another. People who defend advertising deny this charge. They point out that beyond our need for food, clothing, and shelter, our wants vary. If some of us are persuaded to try one hamburger and others another, what's the problem? No ad forces a consumer to buy, defenders say—especially if the product doesn't satisfy buyers the first time they try it.

Critical Thinking: The Public Broadcasting System is publicly supported and is not supposed to carry advertising. Does this mean that no firms are advertised on PBS stations?

Critics claim that spending more than $118 billion each year on advertising is wasteful. After two competing companies run ads for their products, people will buy about the same amount of each brand that they would have in the first place, they say. Why bother spending the money? Defenders answer that the ads contain information about each brand. Only by having that information can consumers make satisfying decisions.

Another charge is that ads limit competition. With more money to spend on ads, critics say, larger companies can keep smaller ones out of the market. Defenders respond that ads work to promote competition. By giving smaller producers a chance to reach the public, ads help prevent large businesses from controlling a market.

Note: An increasingly used form of advertising is product placement in movies. The best known example is the use of Reeses Pieces in the film *ET.* Ask students to look for product placement in the next movie they see.

Some people also charge that ads increase prices. The high cost of commercials and colorful print ads drives up the prices of the goods they promote, but defenders reply that ads actually reduce prices. By creating huge national markets for a product, ads allow producers to make more goods at a lower cost. This saving results in lower prices.

The most popular argument against ads is that they're bothersome. People can't enjoy radio music, a TV show, or a magazine article without being interrupted by the ads. As advertisers are quick to point out, the money spent on ads pays for the music, TV shows, and magazines people enjoy. With no ads, there would probably be no entertainment.

SUMMARY

- Resource managers gather information to decide how best to use personal resources.
- We evaluate sources of information to be sure they are reliable and objective. We evaluate the information itself to be sure it is complete and relevant.
- Information can be used to evaluate our alternatives. Influences are the personal and external forces that affect our decisions.
- Personal influences include our values, income, family status, age, habits, and desire to be accepted. External influences include the economy, culture, fashion, our family, peer pressure, pressure from salespeople, and advertising.
- Consumers can get information from family and friends, business sources, and the government. Three organizations test products and rate their performance.
- Advertising is both an influence and a source of information. Ads try to influence us through rational, emotional, positive or negative, humorous, or fear appeals.
- Advertising techniques include testimonials, problem-solving, demonstration, scientific tests, product comparisons, life-styles, and the bandwagon.
- Advertising is regulated by the media and by the advertising business itself. The National Advertisers Division of the Council of BBBs and the National Advertising Review Board try to protect consumers and businesses from unfair ads.
- The government also regulates advertising. The Federal Trade Commission has broad powers over advertising and takes action against unfair or deceptive ads.
- Advertising has critics and supporters. Critics say ads reduce the consumer's power, create waste, lower competition, raise prices, and interrupt our enjoyment of entertainment. Supporters say ads can't make people buy things they don't want, and that they provide information, promote competition, help lower prices, and pay for our entertainment.

Key Terms

Match each of the following terms with the definition that most suits it.

advertising
bait-and-switch advertising
Better Business Bureaus
emotional appeal
Federal Trade Commission
influences
information
peer pressure
rational appeal
sales pressure
testimonial
trade and professional associations
warranties

a. an advertising message that aims at consumers' practical needs in a logical way
b. an advertising technique in which someone proclaims his or her satisfaction with a product
c. forces inside and outside us that affect how we think and act
d. an advertising message that aims at consumers' psychological needs and desires
e. the influence created by our desire to be accepted by people our own age
f. a message meant to create interest in a product or service and to persuade consumers to buy it
g. the use of tactics by salespeople to persuade consumers to buy
h. facts about goods and services that can be used to evaluate alternatives
i. promises by manufacturers or sellers that their goods meet certain standards
j. groups of people or businesses who join together to promote common interests

k. nonprofit corporations that protect businesses and consumers by helping businesses to regulate themselves
l. the agency of the federal government that, among other tasks, protects consumers from ads that are unfair or deceptive
m. an illegal practice in which a store advertises a low price on one item to lure shoppers in, only to talk them into buying a more expensive item

Review Questions

1. What four sources can you get information from? How can you evaluate it?
2. What is the difference between information and influences? Give examples of each.
3. List five business sources of information for consumers.
4. What organizations test and rate products? What two cautions should you remember in using their ratings?
5. Name three federal government agencies that provide information for consumers.
6. Is advertising an influence or an information source? How can we use ads?
7. Name and describe three advertising appeals.
8. Name and describe three advertising techniques.
9. Who regulates advertising?
10. What are the arguments for and against advertising?

Projects

1. Investigate what factors influence you to buy. List all the purchases you've made in the last week. Use the lists of personal and external influences in the text to identify why you bought what you did. Why did you buy ice cream instead of yogurt or go to one movie instead of another? Now, list what sources of information you used. Compare your lists with those of classmates. Make a chart showing what factors influence you for particular types of purchases (food or entertainment, for instance).
2. Pick a product that you or your family is about to purchase. Gather all the information you can about competing brands and decide which one is best for your needs. Now go to the library and look up the product in *Consumers' Research* or a *Consumer Reports* publication. Is your evaluation of the product similar to theirs? Would you choose a different product brand based on their information? Explain your choice to the class.
3. Set up your own product test. Discuss the criteria, the number of samples you will use, and how you will conduct the test. Report your test findings to the class.
4. Sample three advertisements from print, three from radio, and three from TV. Describe them briefly. Identify the appeals and techniques of each. Evaluate them for fairness and honesty. How much information do they contain, and how much influence? Tell the class what you've found.
5. Make up an imaginary product or service, complete with name, price, and features. Decide what kind of person you want to sell it to. Create at least two ads for it, using different appeals and techniques.

Comparison Shopping 11

Overview: Chapter 11 examines the final step of the purchasing process — that of actually deciding what to buy, and where and when to buy it.

OBJECTIVES

This chapter will help you to:

1. Compare competing goods and services.
2. Locate and evaluate alternative sellers of a good or service.
3. Calculate the best time to buy a good or service.
4. Explain how consumer choices determine the success or failure of suppliers and products.

Michelle met Ian after school. "Hi, Ian. Have you finished your research on home computers yet? Which one are you going to buy?"

"Not so fast, Michelle," Ian said. "It isn't just my decision, you know—the whole family is in on it."

"OK, but what have you found out?"

"The way I figured it," Ian said, "I had to answer four questions: which computer should we buy? what store should we buy it from? should we buy it now or later? and how shall we pay for it?"

"All right, all right—what are the answers?" Michelle asked impatiently.

Ian opened his notebook and glanced at what he'd written. "First, which computer. I skipped the ones that weren't right for us—business computers, machines good only for games, and the expensive ones. It came down to Super Comp and the M-120. I picked Super Comp. It has more memory and a color monitor, and it includes a few programs for not much more money. A color monitor is extra for the M-120 and it doesn't include programs. And Super Comp's instructions are easier to follow."

"Where are you going to get it?" Michelle asked.

"Watson's Computers. No other store has lower prices, and the people there really know the products. I spent hours there trying out different computers and asking the people questions, and they always helped."

"And when are you going to get it?"

"Well," Ian said. "I did some reading to see if anyone expects new models to come out this year that will offer more features for less money. But they don't. So I'm going to tell the family tonight that the best time to buy is—right now!"

Discussion: Ask students to name possible purchases for their age group. Analyze whether or not it is feasible to comparison shop for these items.

Explain: If the costs of comparison shopping are low or the benefits high, then comparison shopping will be beneficial.

BEFORE MAKING A PURCHASE consumers make many decisions. When they make their budgets, they decide roughly how much they're willing to spend. They then decide four things: what to buy, where to buy, when to buy, and how to pay for it. In this chapter, you'll learn about the first three decisions. You'll learn about the fourth in the next.

To decide what, where, and when to buy, we **comparison shop.** We *examine the price and quality of competing goods and services to find the best buy*. Shopping helps us evaluate competing products. It helps us check the prices, quality, and services that competing sellers offer. In comparison shopping we also consider whether the price will go up or down in the future. We can also shop carefully for the best way to pay for a purchase. In other words, shopping helps us use our resources more efficiently.

We don't always comparison shop. First, we don't always have alternative sources to compare. Some utilities and government services come only from one supplier—only one electric company operates in an area. Second, comparison shopping isn't always worth the time. If the battery in your portable radio goes out, you won't spend time comparing the prices of batteries at many different stores. You'll buy a new battery at a store you think has reasonable prices. If the battery on your car goes out, though, you'll spend more time looking for a replacement. Why? A car battery is much more expensive than a radio battery, and competing brands perform differently and offer different warranties. Generally, we comparison shop when we want to buy something so expensive or complex that we want to be sure we get the good or service that's best for us and when we feel it's worth the cost of time to shop.

Discussion: Ask students to provide examples of comparison shopping they have conducted recently.

We could probably benefit from comparison shopping more often. Don't assume that some items are too inexpensive to be worth shopping for. Magazines are often cheaper by subscription than they are bought at the newsstand. Saving 50¢ an issue on a weekly magazine adds up. Also, many consumers compare the costs and services of the many companies that now sell long-distance telephone service.

SHOPPING FOR A GOOD OR SERVICE

With the thousands of goods and services people buy, it would seem impossible to give general rules about how to shop, but it isn't. We can use certain standards to compare any product, no matter what it is. On the next few pages, we'll list and describe these factors, but we have three cautions to keep in mind on how to use these shopper's guides.

Emphasize: Trade-offs are an important factor in purchase decisions because you seldom will be able to satisfy all the criteria important to you.

First, remember to adapt these lists according to your own wants. You're buying to satisfy yourself (or, like Ian, you and your family). Rank these standards according to how important they are to you.

Second, keep in mind that some of the standards listed here may be important in shopping for one product or service, but not for another. In shopping for a home computer, Ian had to think about accessories because the basic unit cannot be used alone. In shopping for a shirt, though, you're looking for something that's ready to use.

Emphasize: By developing a decision-making matrix listing the alternatives down the left, and the standards used to evaluate the alternatives across the top, you easily will be able to compare alternatives and come to a decision.

Third, and most important, remember that in comparing different products and services, you make trade-offs. A low-priced item may not last long. A custom-made one may cost more. The question you must ask is how much quality you can get for the price you're willing to pay.

How to Compare Goods

Consumers compare competing products by looking at ten standards.

Clarify: When asking questions about suitability, keep all factors regarding obtaining information in mind.

- Most people start by looking at a product's *price*. While price is important, it isn't the only thing to consider. Find out what you are getting—or giving up—for that price.
- The *intended use* of the product determines what qualities you'll need in it. Ian knew his family wanted a home computer for games, budgeting, and learning. He could eliminate business computers or machines that only play games because they weren't suitable. To decide whether a product is suitable, ask a few questions: Is this the size, shape, and color you want? Is it well made? Do you need special instructions or knowledge to use the product? Are the instructions included? Are they clear? Is the

product ready to use? Does it go with anything you already own that you'll be using it with?

- Consider what *accessories* you already have or must buy to be able to use the product. Does one brand include more than another? Ian used this important factor in choosing one computer over another. Another question is whether you need all the accessories that are included—some options add greatly to the price of a new car.
- Look at the product's *performance*. How well does the product do what it is supposed to do? Is one computer's memory larger than another's? Will a raincoat really keep you dry?
- Consider the *product's life*. How long will you be able to use it? How long do you *want* to be able to use it? Does one brand last longer than another?
- Check the *care* required by the product. The difference between polyester slacks and wool slacks isn't just wool's higher price and longer wear. Polyester can be washed; wool must be dry-cleaned.
- Look at how *safe* the good is. Appliances and cars should at least meet minimum standards for safety set by the government. Safety is also important with such products as children's toys.
- Another characteristic to check is *consumer protection*. Many products offer **warranties,** which are *promises by manufacturers or sellers that their goods meet certain standards*. Compare the warranties that come with different brands—stores are required by law to allow you to read warranties for products costing more than $15.
- The *services* offered with a product vary by store and even by manufacturer. For instance, Ian found that some computer makers had toll-free telephone numbers that owners could use to call for help. Check to see if the maker has authorized service centers near where you live and if replacement parts are easy to get.
- The last feature we check is a product's *reputation*. Has the manufacturer been around for a long time? Does it make quality products? Of course, you shouldn't buy only products that have been on the market for a long time. Sometimes new companies make products with better quality or sell them at a lower price. Still, find out what you can about the new maker's reputation, too.

Illustration: If Ian already had a monitor, he would benefit by buying a computer that was available in components rather than in a self-contained unit. If he does not have a monitor, then the price of this component must be added in when comparing to the price of a self-contained unit.

Note: How do you judge a product's performance? One way is to purchase a periodical that specializes in the product you are considering (*Road and Track, PC Magazine,* or *Consumer Reports,* for example) and use their ratings. Make sure that their evaluation criteria correspond to yours.

Table 11.1 shows how to use these standards to compare brands when you shop for two common items—a television and shoes.

How to Compare Services

People buy many services, from restaurant food to entertainment, health care to car repair. In comparing services, we use six standards.

- Again, *price* is the first point most consumers look at, but it shouldn't be the only one. In buying services, as in buying goods, find out exactly what you're getting for your money.
- Probably the most important point is to identify *what you want performed*. Many services are custom made to fit the purchaser's desires. In that case, you must say what you want. To do so, buyers and sellers sometimes create an agreement detailing what should be done. Borrowers and lenders sign credit contracts, for instance. Other times the agreement is less

Discussion: How important is service? That depends on whether or not you can perform some of the service. If you enjoy and are good at working on a automobile, then service is less important. If you have never used a microcomputer, then it may be very important to have someone who can answer questions while you are learning.

Table 11.1 Using Ten Standards to Compare Two Types of Goods

Standard	Television	Shoes
Price	Compare prices of competing brands; compare credit cost.	Compare prices of competing brands.
Intended use	What type of TV do you want: color or black and white? console or portable? large or small screen?	What type do you want: dress or casual? winter? special use (running, hiking)?
Accessories	Do you want model to connect to video recorder or cable? Do you want remote control? Is table included for portable?	How well do shoes match wardrobe?
Performance	What is the quality of picture and sound?	How well do shoes fit?
Product life	If short-term need, may be worthwhile to lease. If long-term need, how well made is the set?	How well are shoes made? Will they hold up to probable frequency of wear?
Care	What is probable frequency of servicing?	Any special care instructions?
Safety	Is model approved by Underwriters' Laboratories?	Doesn't apply.
Consumer protection	What warranties are offered? What do they cover? Is an authorized service center nearby?	What warranties are offered?
Seller services	Are service contracts offered? How much do they cost? Will the seller deliver?	Doesn't apply.
Maker reputation	What is maker's history of quality work?	What is maker's history of quality work?

Critical Thinking: Some service providers will ask for partial payment "up front." There are two reasons for this: (1) to purchase supplies; and (2) to better insure that you will pay for the service. This request is valid in that if you do not pay for a completed service, there is no way to reclaim the service and resell it. However, never pay the entire amount before the service is provided; that would leave you without any protection.

formal—a person tells a hair stylist "half an inch off the sides, a little more off the top."

- Naturally, you have to compare *how well the service is performed.* Was it a good haircut, or a bad one? If you haven't bought the service from this seller before, you can ask others who have, perhaps getting their names from the company that provides the service.
- Find out *how long the service will last.* One paint job may last longer than another if the painter uses higher quality paint. Obviously, this won't apply to some services.
- *Consumer protection* is important when buying some services. Careful consumers get written contracts for complicated services like home improvements.
- Finally, check the *reputation* of the firm providing the service. Does one airline frequently lose baggage? Are one company's buses often late? You can get this information from other consumers or from books and magazines, but remember to evaluate the information you get.

Table 11.2 shows how to use these six standards to compare different suppliers of two common services—auto insurance and music lessons.

SHOPPING AT DIFFERENT SELLERS

Where we buy is as important as what we buy. Every product or service we want is sold by many businesses, and it's worthwhile to shop carefully to find the right one to buy from. We buy many things in stores, but we also

Table 11.2 Using Six Standards to Compare Two Types of Services

Factor	Auto Insurance	Music Lessons
Price	Compare rates and coverages.	Compare fees for lessons and any extra charges.
What you want performed	Find out what coverage is required by your state and decide if you want more.	What instrument do you want to learn to play? What level of skill do you want to attain?
How well the service is performed	What is the company's record for settling claims? How helpful is the agent or company representative?	What is the training and background of the instructor? Are lessons individual or group?
How long the service will last	Doesn't apply—insurers sell policies for the same length of time.	How long are the lessons?
Consumer protection	Check your state insurance laws.	Are there refunds for cancelled classes?
Supplier reputation	Talk to others who have insured through the company or agent.	Talk to others who have taken lessons.

buy from businesses that aren't stores. Therefore, in this section we're going to refer to all these alternatives not as *stores,* but as *sellers*.

Note: Some of the qualities we look for in a seller determine some of the responsibilities of the workers. A reputation for honesty and reliability reflects not only the attitude of the owner, but the attitudes of the workers as well.

How to Locate and Evaluate Alternative Sellers

Looking for alternatives is an important part of decision making. The more options we have to choose from, the more likely we are to find one that is satisfying. How do we locate alternative sellers? First, we use our past experience. We can also turn to other sources of information—our family and friends, the Yellow Pages, ads in newspapers and magazines, local trade, professional, or business organizations, and all levels of government.

What do we look for in a seller? Obviously, the first thing is that the seller provides the good or service we want! There are other features we expect, as well. Consumers want sellers of goods and services to meet seven standards:

Expansion: Some businesses do not accept credit cards because of the additional expense. Sometimes it is to avoid taxes. Cash is harder to trace.

- *Competitive prices*
- A *selection* of goods or services from which to choose
- *Quality* goods or services
- *Convenience* in location and hours or in the method used to provide goods or services
- Acceptance of *different methods of payment*—checks as well as cash, or more than one kind of credit card
- *Courteous and helpful* salespeople
- A *reputation* for honesty and reliability

Discussion: People generally will not drive all over town in order to comparison shop for an auto. However, if several dealerships are congregated in one area, people will visit several dealers before making a choice.

In the next section, we will describe some of the different types of businesses that sell goods. The businesses that sell services cannot be grouped into types the way sellers of goods can, but we can still shop among suppliers of services by using the list above.

Comparing Different Sellers of Goods

Department stores are *large retail businesses that sell a wide variety of products in one store*. These stores sell clothing and accessories, housewares,

Many consumers choose to buy fresh produce from sellers other than supermarkets.

List: During class discussion, list the stores in your area which fit into each category.

Discussion: The quality of items differs among retailers. You would expect a different mix of items and differing quality between K-Mart, Sears, and Neiman-Marcus. In urban areas you may find a difference among stores of the same chain because a local store will stock items demanded by local customers.

gifts, appliances, and home furnishings. Department stores often have a variety of similar products in different price ranges. Many issue their own credit cards, and some accept bank credit cards as well. Most accept personal checks. Other department store services include sales assistance, delivery and installation, gift wrapping, the return of unsatisfactory items, and theater ticket sales.

Discount department stores are *retail businesses that sell a variety of products but at lower prices than department stores.* These stores keep their operating costs low by spending less on displays, facilities, and extra services. As a result, they can charge less than department stores. Most discount stores accept bank credit cards, and some issue their own credit cards. Most accept personal checks. Beyond that, they generally provide fewer services than department stores.

Supermarkets are *large self-service stores that carry a wide variety of products, but primarily food.* They sell food, cleaning, and paper products in national brands and generic packages. Some supermarkets sell products like housewares, toiletries, toys, books and magazines, medicines, and flowers. Although they are largely self-service, many supermarkets have workers staffing their meat, deli, pharmacy, and bakery sections. Most supermarkets accept customers' checks.

Discount supermarkets are *large self-service food stores that have lower prices than regular supermarkets but fewer services.* They may be called

Illustrate: Why would you shop at a higher-priced convenience store? Primarily because of the convenience, accessibility, and speed. If all you want to buy is a quart of milk, it is much faster and easier to shop at the convenience store than it is at the full-service grocery.

Note: Factory outlets have had mixed success depending on the area of the country.

Critical Thinking: Will prices in a specialty store be higher than prices in department stores?

Two things shoppers desire are a range of products and a range of prices.

warehouse stores or *no-frills supermarkets*. These stores often have less variety than supermarkets and may not have specialty sections like delis and bakeries. They may not accept checks, taking cash only. Some even require shoppers to bring their own shopping bags.

Convenience stores are *small food retailers that have long hours and neighborhood locations*. They sell staples like milk and bread, convenience foods, cleaning products, over-the-counter drugs, and newspapers and magazines. They generally have a limited selection and somewhat higher prices than larger stores. Their major selling feature is in their name—*convenience*. They are often open twenty-four hours a day.

Specialty stores are *retail businesses that carry a wide selection of a few related products*. Examples include clothing, toy, camera, appliance, produce, record, craft, and auto parts stores. While they may sell products in a limited category, they generally offer a wider selection of these items than a department store does. Many accept personal checks and credit cards, but it depends on the type of store—a local butcher probably won't take a credit card. One advantage of specialty stores is that salespeople may know more about what they sell than some salespeople in a larger store would.

Factory outlets are *stores that sell specialized products at discount prices*. Some are located near the factories that make the products. Others are clustered together in malls or shopping centers and carry goods from several makers. Outlets generally sell discontinued products (items that producers aren't making any more), seconds (goods that don't quite measure up to the maker's quality standards), or simply surplus goods. Outlets provide few services, though they may take credit cards and checks. They usually have little sales help and may not allow returns.

Extension: The biggest breakthrough in competition occurred with the first Sears-Roebuck catalog. Before that, the only store available (without traveling for days to another town) was the local general store. However, the selection was limited, and since there was a monopoly, the price was high. With the publication of the catalog, people now had another place to shop, with a much larger selection. They also had a way to compare prices; thus, even the prices at the local general store decreased because of the competition.

Consumers can also buy goods outside of stores. **Catalog selling** is *offering a variety of products for sale through catalogs mailed to consumers' homes.* Shoppers choose what they want from the catalog and then mail or call in their orders. Customers can pay by check, money order, credit card, or cash—though mailing cash is unwise. Some catalogs are mailed by department stores; others are issued by companies that sell only in this way. Catalog selling saves consumers time, money, and energy, but it has three disadvantages. First, buyers cannot inspect the item before buying. If the item is fully described and illustrated, however, shoppers know what they're getting. Second, while catalog shopping saves the buyer the cost of traveling to stores, he or she must pay shipping charges. Third, consumers who buy through catalogs have to wait a few weeks to receive their merchandise.

Mail-order clubs are *sellers that offer specialized products to members through the mail.* They sell such things as books, tapes, and specialty foods. Some make attractive introductory offers—say four tapes for $1—to persuade consumers to join. They may also require members to buy a specific number of additional goods within a certain time. Although mail-order clubs often sell items for less than a store would, someone who buys unwanted goods in order to meet membership requirements is hardly saving money. Many clubs allow members to cancel membership at any time once the required purchases are made.

Consumers have rights when they order goods by mail. They must receive the ordered merchandise by the date the seller promised it. If no date is promised, they must receive it 30 days after the order was placed. If these dates are not met, the buyer can cancel the sale and get a refund.

Critical Thinking: Why are more and more consumers turning to catalog shopping?

Direct selling is *a method of offering goods for sale to consumers in their homes.* Some businesses hire salespeople to sell to individuals. Others arrange product parties in one consumer's home to offer goods to a few people at a time. Plastic containers, cosmetics, clothing, and jewelry are all sold by direct selling. Some direct sellers hire consumers to do the selling. These salespeople earn cash, discounts, or free products according to how much they sell. Direct selling can save consumers time and money. Some people, however, feel added pressure to buy when confronted in their homes by a salesperson. For this reason, the law allows consumers three days to cancel any purchase made in their home if the price is over $25.

Note: One reason mail-order clubs are financially successful is that many members forget to return the card declining to purchase for any given month. Since members must expend effort not to buy, they forget and end up buying more than if they had to expend effort in order to purchase.

Some goods can be purchased from **vending machines**—the familiar *coin-operated machines that sell products from apples to soft drinks.* Often set up in schools, offices, and public buildings, these machines offer convenience. Most have little variety, however, and prices are usually higher than those for the same goods outside the machines.

Consumers can also buy from other consumers. **Flea markets** are *gathering places where consumers sell used merchandise to other consumers.*

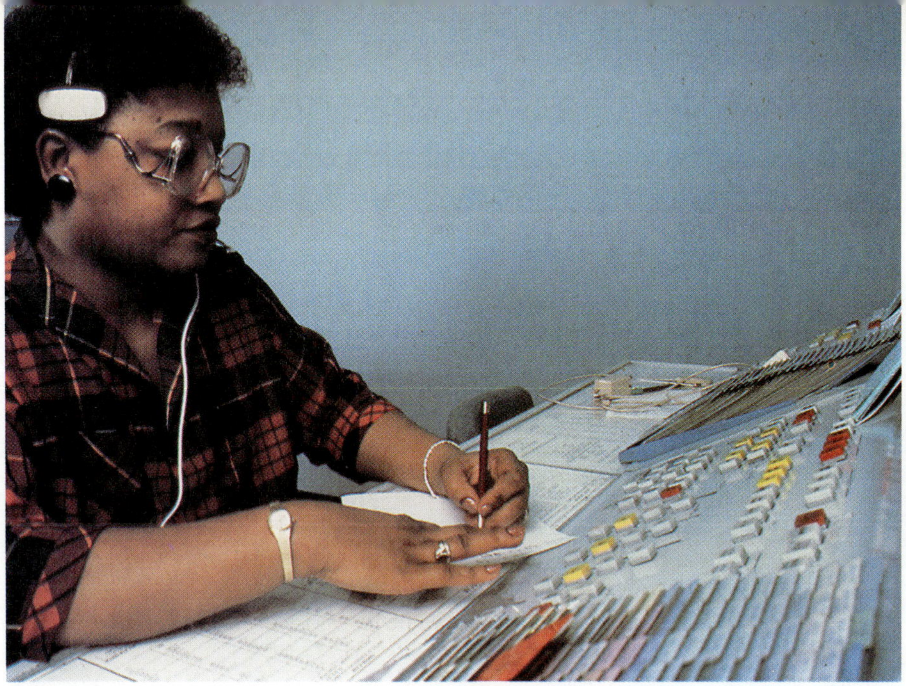

Telemarketing is another way of offering goods and services to consumers. Telemarketers try to sell their products by calling consumers on the phone.

Garage sales and *yard sales* are similar, but there is usually only one seller, and the selling is done in that person's home. Consumers who wish to sell something often advertise in local newspapers or in magazines. These sources may offer lower prices, but no guarantees to shoppers on selection, quality, or performance of the goods sold.

At **auctions,** *property or merchandise is bought by the highest bidder.* Consumers who go to auctions are wise to find out what an item is worth before bidding on it. Sometimes, in the excitement of bidding, people forget themselves and end up paying a lot of money for something of little value. Examine the goods before the auction if possible.

Some people shop at home by computer, although this technique is not yet widespread. It is hard to tell how much computer shopping we will be able to do in the future, or whether the method will be widely available, but some people see it as an area with great potential. Computer shopping has the same advantages as catalog shopping—it saves time, money, and energy. It also has similar disadvantages—the buyer cannot inspect the goods, must pay for shipping, and must wait for delivery. Still, if enough businesses get involved, computer shoppers will be able to compare a variety of products with ease.

Table 11.3 compares the advantages and disadvantages of all these different sellers.

Table 11.3 Advantages and Disadvantages of Different Sellers of Goods

Type of Seller	Advantages	Disadvantages
(1) Department store	Variety of products, prices, services, and payment methods.	Higher prices than (2); service in (6) may be better.
(2) Discount department store	Lower prices than (1); variety of payment methods.	Fewer services and less selection than (1).
(3) Supermarket	Variety of food and other products, brands, and payment methods.	Higher prices than (4); service in (6) may be better.
(4) Discount supermarket	Lower prices than (3); variety of packaged foods.	Less selection and fewer services than (3).
(5) Convenience store	Convenient location and hours.	Somewhat higher prices than (3) or (4); little variety.
(6) Specialty store	Variety of related goods; possibly knowledgeable salespeople.	Possibly not as many services as (1) or (3).
(7) Factory outlet	Low prices for related goods.	Few services; not all goods sold this way.
(8) Catalog selling	Saves time and energy; prices lower than in stores (shipping charge added).	Inability to inspect goods; wait for delivery.
(9) Mail-order clubs	Money-saving introductory offers; prices lower than in stores (shipping charge added).	Possibly required to buy more goods; wait for delivery.
(10) Direct selling	Convenient, possibly lower prices.	Possible pressure to make purchase.
(11) Vending machines	Convenient.	Limited variety; higher prices.
(12) Other consumers	Often lower prices.	Generally used goods; no guarantee on quality.
(13) Auction	Can purchase rare or unusual goods.	Bidding may send price high.
(14) Computer shopping	Saves time and energy; possibly wide selection in future; prices lower than in stores (shipping charge added).	Not yet widespread; inability to inspect goods; wait for delivery.

SHOPPING FOR A GOOD PRICE

Smart consumers know that prices don't always stay the same. By watching and planning carefully, they buy when prices are lower than normal. In that way, they manage their money to get the most out of it.

Illustrate: The best time to buy holiday wrapping paper, ribbons, and ornaments is December 26. Because the demand for these accessories is seasonal, the demand falls when the season is over. This is accompanied by a decrease in price.

Consumers Take Advantage of Price Changes

Knowing what makes prices change helps consumers time purchases wisely. Prices go up or down when changes occur in five factors: demand, supplier's cost, competition, technology, and government regulation.

Consumer demand is the quantity of a good or service that consumers want to buy. If demand goes up, price can go up. Because many football fans want to see a Super Bowl game, ticket prices are higher than for regular-season games. If fewer people want a good or service, suppliers may need to lower the price. An unpopular movie is pulled from the more expensive, first-run theaters quickly and begins to play in the discount houses.

Rises in producers' costs can send prices higher. A few years ago, frost destroyed the coffee crop in Brazil, where much of the coffee we buy comes from. Forced to pay more for coffee beans, sellers charged consumers more for coffee. How high prices can rise, though, is limited by how much consumers are willing to spend. When coffee prices rose too high, many people bought tea and other substitutes instead of coffee.

Expansion: An interesting result of the high coffee prices is the long-term shift in consumer demand. Consumer demand for coffee never rose back to pre-freeze levels. Presumably, many consumers who substituted tea, cola, water, etc. remained with those products once the price of coffee dropped.

Another influence on price is competition. The greater the number of producers that offer a good or service, the lower its price will usually be. An example of this principle is videocassette recorders (VCRs). The first models, introduced in 1975, sold for about $2,000. Five years later, when more companies were making VCRs, the average price was around $1,000. As VCRs became cheaper and easier to produce, the price dropped. By 1990, the average cost of a VCR was $200. In addition, as production techniques improved and prices fell, quality improved.

As the VCR example shows, technological changes can bring prices down, too. At the beginning of the chapter, Ian checked to see if newer computers were expected to come out soon. He knew that improved machines would drive prices down.

Government regulations have an impact on prices. A federal agency in the early 1980s reduced its control of passenger air fares. The result was lower prices on long flights. Airlines began competing for more passengers by offering their long trips for less. Sometimes new regulations drive prices up because they increase producers' costs.

Illustration: Another example of the effects of competition on price is the voluntary trade limitation of Japanese autos. Not only are the Japanese now sending only their higher-priced autos, but U.S. automakers have less incentive to improve their productivity and decrease prices. Thus, the price of all autos is increased by this limitation on imports.

Knowing Good Times to Buy

How can we take advantage of price changes? First, watch the news for changes in the five factors discussed above. Second, follow a few simple rules:

- Take advantage of sales
- If possible, buy goods according to their season
- Watch for rebates
- Compare brands

When sellers want to increase demand—or reduce supply—they offer sales. In **promotional sales,** *sellers offer lower prices to stimulate demand.* A maker may offer a two-for-one promotional sale to introduce a new toothpaste. A store with few customers may reduce prices to attract more. In **clearance sales,** *sellers offer low prices to unload unwanted supply.* Clearance sales help stores get rid of out-of-season items before the new shipments arrive.

Note: The way to increase the quantity demanded is to reduce the price. Likewise, the way to reduce the quantity demanded is to increase the price. This is the allocative function of price.

Use sales to stock up on items you need. For instance, many shoppers buy all their paper or canned products in quantity when they're on sale. Table 11.4 lists the months that many items are commonly on sale.

Still, consumers need to use sales carefully. Follow these three hints:

- Never buy something just because it's on sale. It's no saving to spend money on something you won't use.
- Limit your purchases to sale items. Sometimes stores reduce prices drastically on one item, but not on others. The sale goods are called **loss leaders,** because they are *items sold at or below cost to attract customers into a store so they will buy other goods not on sale.*

Table 11.4 **Months That Items Are Typically on Sale**

Month	Products
January	Appliances, dishes, houseware, linen, stereos
February	Bedding, dishes, houseware, toys
March	Skates, ski equipment, winter coats
April	Coats, dresses, infants' clothes, men's suits
May	Blankets, linen, televisions, tires, towels
June	Building materials, dresses, televisions
July	Appliances, children's clothing, radios and stereos, refrigerators and freezers
August	Air conditioners and fans, bedding, gardening supplies, men's clothing, school clothing and supplies, tires
September	Batteries and mufflers, dishes, gardening equipment, houseware, new cars
October	Bicycles, glassware, school clothing and supplies
November	Children's clothing, dresses, men's suits, ranges
December	Blankets, shoes

Discussion: What is the difference between rebates and coupons? Why would manufacturers offer rebates instead of dropping the price?

Critical Thinking: Why would a manufacturer produce goods under another company's name? (For example, the Ford Probe is made by Mazda; Dodge Stealth is made by Mitsubishi.)

Activity: Perform a peanut butter taste test using a brand name, a store brand, and a generic. Allow students to evaluate the differences for themselves.

Activity: Using supply-and-demand graphs, illustrate why produce is more expensive out of season or at the beginning of the season. Why is produce cheaper at season's peak?

- Be sure that a sale is a sale. Sellers may misuse the terms *suggested list price* and *sale price.* The **suggested list price** is *the price a maker recommends that sellers use for its products.* In many cases, though, no one sells the product at that price. What one store calls a *sale price* may just be the going rate for that product at most stores.

You can save money by taking advantage of seasonal changes in supply and demand. There are better and worse times to buy most goods and services. Decreased demand lowers prices for such things as swim suits in late August and greeting cards after holidays like Christmas and Chanukah. Fresh fruits and vegetables cost more out of season, when they must be imported, and at the beginning of a local growing season, when people are eager to taste the new crop. Waiting to buy until the season's peak holds down food costs.

You can also save money by taking advantage of a **rebate.** This is *the refund of part of a product's purchase price given by producers to increase demand.* Rebates can save money, but be sure the product is a good buy. Analyze why the rebate is being offered. Is the product being replaced by an updated model? Are sales low because the product is not as good as its competitors? Saving money on a poor product is no bargain. If you do buy a rebated item, be sure to get the terms clearly spelled out. Ask for the form you need to return to collect your refund.

The fourth way to save money is to compare brands. A **brand** is *the name or trademark that identifies a product.* Some branded products are sold nationally; others carry the names of regional or local stores. While national brands are well known, their prices include high advertising and packaging costs. Store or house brands generally equal national brands in quality, but are cheaper because of lower costs. Priced even less are **generic** or **unbranded products.** These are *goods that are identified only by the contents of a package, not by the store's or manufacturer's name.* For example, a generic product would be labeled simply *peanut butter* instead of having a

Discussion: Encourage students to give examples of how firms respond to customer demands.

Critical Thinking: When U.S. auto sales declined, auto companies and their unions called for increased protection from imports. Analyze the consequences of this action.

Note: Competition is the best consumer protection. Competition ensures the lowest price, the greatest quantity, and the largest selection.

A wide range of foodstuff is sold in no-brand generic packages, which offer quality similar to brand-name products for less money.

national name like *The Nuttiest* or a store name like *Cheap Food*. Packaged foods, drugs, paper products, and cleaning supplies are all sold as generic products.

YOU INTERACT WITH THE ECONOMY: CONSUMER CHOICES DETERMINE BUSINESS SUCCESS

Consumers' choices are important to businesses. They mean success or failure for a product or a company.

The history of the American automobile industry shows consumers' power. After United States automakers dominated the market for years, their sales began to fall. Consumers began rejecting standard-sized American-made cars in favor of smaller, gas-saving imports. Also damaging to American automakers was the reputation foreign cars had for better quality. When sales of American cars slumped, the automakers lost profits. They were forced to change production plans, spend money revamping their factories, and compete harder.

Businesses adapt to consumer demand all the time. Fast-food chains responded when consumers got tired of their limited menus. They added breakfasts, new sandwiches, and salad bars. To meet the growing market of health and fitness enthusiasts, stores began stocking more exercise clothing, vitamins, and health foods. Businesses also react to consumer disapproval. Think of how many TV shows are cancelled because not enough people watch them. Also, if consumers aren't buying goods because prices are too high, watch those prices drop.

Summary: To make a final product decision that will maximize our satisfaction, consumers must carefully consider which product to buy, where to buy, and when to buy.

Manufacturers, service firms, and sellers spend millions of dollars each year on market research. They try to find out what is popular and why, which new products and services will sell and which won't. If consumers didn't have the freedom to choose, this research wouldn't be needed. Because success depends on making consumers happy, businesses try to supply what they want.

Critical Thinking: Can producers in a competitive market ignore consumer desires?

Remember that businesses exist to make money. Their aim is to produce and distribute products and services that sell. Consumers can let them know what they want. Comparison shop for the best products and return those that are unsatisfactory, or never buy them again. Tell other consumers about firms that sell quality goods and those that offer poor service. Consumers have power, but it means nothing until they use it. Don't take your consumer decisions lightly—businesses don't!

World Economy: Consumers in command economies have much less choice regarding products and where to obtain them.

SUMMARY

- Comparison shopping helps consumers decide what, where, and when to buy and how to pay for the purchase.
- Consumers compare goods by considering price, intended use, accessories, performance, product life, care, safety, consumer protection, services included, and the maker's reputation.
- Consumers compare services by considering price, the service to be performed, how well it is performed, how long it will last, consumer protection, and the reputation of the provider.
- Consumers locate sellers by using past experience and talking to friends and family. They can also search advertisements, check the Yellow Pages, and ask trade, professional, and business groups and government agencies.
- In evaluating a seller of goods, consumers check for competitive prices, selection, quality of goods, convenience, methods of payment, courteous and helpful salespeople, and the seller's reputation.
- Consumers have a choice of buying goods at a variety of stores and through catalogs, mail-order clubs, direct selling, vending machines, auctions, and garage sales.
- Prices change. Consumers determine when to buy by watching demand, suppliers' costs, competition, technological developments, and government regulations.
- Consumers take advantage of price by taking advantage of sales, buying goods according to their season, using rebates, and comparing brands.
- Consumers' buying decisions cause the success or failure of businesses. Businesses care what consumers want because they won't make a profit unless they provide goods and services that consumers will buy.

Key Terms

Match each of the following terms with the definition that most suits it.

auction
brand
catalog selling
clearance sale
comparison shopping
convenience stores
department stores
direct selling
discount department stores
discount supermarkets
factory outlets
flea market
generic or unbranded products
loss leaders
mail-order clubs
promotional sale
rebate
supermarkets
specialty stores
suggested list price
vending machines
warranties

a. large retail businesses that sell a wide variety of products in one store
b. large self-service stores that carry a wide variety of products, but primarily food
c. retail businesses that carry a wide selection of a few related products
d. retail businesses that sell a variety of products but at lower prices than department stores
e. stores that sell specialized products at discount prices
f. a method of offering a variety of products for sale through catalogs mailed to consumers' homes
g. large self-service food stores that have lower prices than regular supermarkets but fewer services
h. examining the price and quality of competing goods and services to find the best buy
i. a method of offering goods for sale to consumers in their homes
j. coin-operated machines that sell products from apples to soft drinks
k. small food retailers that have long hours and neighborhood locations
l. items sold at or below cost to attract consumers into a store so they will buy other goods not on sale
m. a situation in which sellers offer lower prices to stimulate demand
n. the price a manufacturer recommends that retailers use for its products
o. promises by manufacturers or sellers that their goods meet certain standards
p. a gathering place where consumers sell used merchandise to other consumers
q. a situation in which sellers offer lower prices to unload unwanted supply
r. goods that are identified only by the contents of the package, not by the store's or manufacturer's name
s. the refund of part of a product's purchase price given by producers to increase demand
t. the name or trademark that identifies a product
u. a selling method in which merchandise is bought by the highest bidder
v. sellers who offer specialized products to members through the mail

Review Questions

1. Which four decisions does comparison shopping help us make?
2. What are some reasons for not comparison shopping? Are consumers always right in not comparison shopping?
3. What standards do consumers use to compare goods? How important is price?
4. What standards do consumers use to compare services? How important is price?

5. How can consumers locate alternative sellers of goods and services?
6. What factors do consumers use to compare competing sellers of goods and services?
7. Name four types of stores where consumers can shop. What distinguishes each one?
8. Name three ways to buy goods outside a store. What makes each one different?
9. What five factors make prices change? How can consumers use them?
10. Describe the two types of sales. Are what sellers call *sales* always good buys for consumers?
11. Compare the three types of brands.
12. How do consumer choices affect businesses? Do businesses care what consumers think?

Projects

1. Pick a good or service you'd like to buy. Make a chart to help you evaluate three competing products or providers of that service according to the standards given in the text. Are there any other things you'd want to look for? Add them to the chart. Rate each product as excellent, average, or poor according to each standard. Which one would you buy? Report to the class.
2. Select a product you are interested in buying (perhaps the product you evaluated in project 1). Identify at least three sellers you could buy it from. Make sure each one is a different type (that is, don't pick two department stores or two supermarkets) and try to choose at least one seller that isn't a store. Where would you buy the item and why?
3. Choose a sale item advertised in your local paper. Compare the sale price to the regular price for the same item in other stores and to the price at discount stores. See if the sale is really a sale.
4. Do a competitive brand test. Choose a supermarket product you use often. Buy at least three different versions—a national brand, a store brand, and (if possible) a generic good. (Include store brands from different stores if you can.) Note the differences in performance or taste, if any.
5. There is a new twist in the telemarketing business – you pay for the sales pitch as well as the telephone call! You can use a 900 number to order products, vote in an opinion poll, or talk with other teens on a "talk-line." The 900 number can be a great way to get information or to do business if you know exactly what you are getting and how much it will cost you. However, the Federal Trade Commission (FTC) is checking into complaints that some consumers have been charged very high prices for the 900-number service or have not received the goods advertised. Contact the FTC, 6th and Pennsylvania Avenue, N.W., Washington, DC 20580, and the National Consumers League, 815 15th Street, N.W., Suite 516, Washington, DC 20005 for printed information about 900 numbers. Prepare a report to be presented in class on the abuse of 900 numbers and what the consumer needs to watch out for.

Saving, Spending, or Borrowing Money 12

OBJECTIVES

This chapter will help you to:

Overview: Chapter 12 helps students examine how they may pay for the goods and services they desire.

1. Determine whether to use cash, credit, or savings to pay for a purchase.
2. Explain why financial institutions offer and charge interest.
3. Compare interest rates of different savings accounts and credit agreements.
4. Operate a checking account.
5. Describe methods of electronic banking and what rights consumers have when using these methods.

Ian met with his family to present the results of his research into home computers. He recommended that they buy the Super Comp at Watson's Computers.

"It's $1,800—that's $200 less than the limit we set," Ian exclaimed. "I think we should get it now!"

"Slow down," Mrs. Conyers said. "There's another question we have to settle first."

"That's right," his father said. "We have to find the best way to pay for it. How much have we saved for the computer so far?"

"$300," Mrs. Conyers answered. "It would probably take us a year to save the rest."

"But that's no good," said Ian. "We couldn't use it in the meantime."

"Well, does the store offer credit terms?" Mr. Conyers asked Ian.

"I think so," he answered. "But I'm not sure. I'll check!"

"Why don't you?" Mrs. Conyers said. "Find out what the interest rate would be and how many payments would be involved. Base your questions on a down payment of $300. Then we'll decide whether it's worth it to borrow the money." As she finished, Ian was putting his coat on and heading out the door.

Explain: If you borrow money from someone else, you pay interest. If you loan money to someone else, you receive interest.

IN THE LAST CHAPTER you saw how consumers answer three questions: what, where, and when to buy. In this chapter you'll learn how consumers answer another question before they make a purchase—how to pay for it. In making this decision, consumers use their skill at comparison shopping.

CONSUMERS DECIDE HOW TO PAY FOR PURCHASES

Discussion: Ask your students to analyze other sources of money that could be used instead of credit in case of an emergency.

Consumers choose to pay for their purchases in one of three ways: using cash or cash substitutes, buying on credit, or saving and buying later. By using cash, you buy now and pay now. You hand over $100 and walk home with a small stereo. By using credit, you borrow money from a bank or store to buy now and pay the money back later. You sign a credit agreement, walk home with the small stereo, and over six months make payments to the business totaling $110. By using savings, you are, in effect, paying now and buying later. You set aside $10 a week—reserving the money rather than spending it. When you've collected the $100, you buy the stereo.

Each method has advantages and disadvantages. To choose a method, consumers evaluate their alternatives using seven factors:

Critical Thinking: What happens to the economy when credit use drops, and people concentrate on paying off all the debt they have accumulated?

- The *immediacy* of the need to buy. In an emergency, for example, there's no time to save. If a car breaks down, credit may help you meet a large repair bill.
- The *price* of the item. Few people can buy a costly item like a new car without credit.
- The *frequency* with which you make the same purchase. You can save for expenses that come up regularly but infrequently, like club dues, but you'll probably use current income to cover frequent costs like food.

Clarify: In the photograph, the business has agreed to discount purchases for the use of cash (or it could have raised prices for the use of credit). This evolves from the fact that firms which accept credit cards must pay the credit card company a percentage of the sales for the use of these cards. This payment is in addition to the interest rate paid by consumers for the use of the card.

Critical Thinking: The text suggests that consumers "expand their buying power by using credit." What does this mean? Is the reference to current buying power or future buying power?

Discussion: If the use of credit raises the costs of the seller as well as the costs of the buyer, why do firms continue to encourage the use of credit?

The method of paying for a purchase may affect the price of a good or service.

- The *availability* of the method. Does the business you want to buy from offer credit or take checks? If not, you'll need to use another method—or buy from another business.
- The *convenience* of the method. It may be easier to charge a purchase than to write a check, or safer to carry traveler's checks than cash on a trip.
- The *cost* of the method. You may feel that the interest charged for borrowing money is too expensive. Fees may make certified checks, money orders, or traveler's checks unattractive, too.
- The *opportunity cost* of the method. Any method of paying for a purchase has a cost—you must give up something else you want to use the method you choose. If you buy with cash, you give up the chance to expand your buying power by using credit. By saving for a purchase, you give up the chance to enjoy the purchase sooner. By using credit, you may give up the chance to buy something else you want—since credit sometimes adds to the cost of a purchase, you'll have less money to make other purchases.

SAVING AND BORROWING BOTH INVOLVE INTEREST

Saving and borrowing are two sides of the same coin. Someone who has a savings account receives money (interest) from the financial institution that uses the money in the account. Someone who borrows pays money (interest) to use the lender's money.

Clarify: Financial institutions are profit-making firms that provide financial services. Their income comes from the interest charged. All expenses must be paid out of this income (including explicit costs, implicit costs, and a normal profit).

Consumers Earn and Pay Interest

Lenders provide financial services for profit. They get income from borrowers who pay **interest,** which is *a fee for the use of money.* A person who borrows $100 might pay back $110. The $10 is interest. The lender uses part of the interest to cover costs like paying employees or buying office supplies. It keeps the rest as profit.

Many lenders are also savings institutions. People deposit their money, and the institution pays them interest for the right to use it. Someone who deposits $100 may, after a year, have $106. Lending interest rates (the rates paid by borrowers) are higher than savings interest rates (the rates paid to depositors). This is because these institutions must take in more money than they pay out if they are to make a profit.

Extension: Interest rates differ, with the range usually from 7% to 18%. The difference depends on: (1) the amount of risk undertaken through the loan; (2) the length of time, or maturity, of the loan; (3) the size of the loan; (4) the taxability of the loan at the federal, state, and local levels; and (5) market imperfections such as a banking monopoly.

The amount of money saved or borrowed, to which interest is added, is called the **principal.** In the above examples the principal is the $100 borrowed or saved. Interest is expressed as the percentage of the principal that is paid over a certain period of time. The institution would say, "The interest we pay is 6.7 percent per year," or "The interest you pay is 1.5 percent per month."

Calculating Interest on Savings

To find out how much money savings will earn, multiply the principal (the deposit) by the interest rate and by the length of time the money is in the account. Let's see how much a savings account of $100 would earn in a year at 6 percent interest per year:

Principal		Rate		Time		Simple interest
$100.00	×	.06	×	1 year	=	$6.00

Activity: Ask students to survey interest rates for borrowing and saving in your area. Investigate the rates offered by banks, savings and loans, private loan companies, and credit bureaus.

If the $100 was in the savings account for only six months, it would earn less:

Principal		Rate		Time		Simple interest
$100.00	×	.06	×	.5 year	=	$3.00

Financial institutions usually compound the interest on savings accounts. **Compound interest** means *interest is added to the principal as it is earned so that it, too, earns interest.* As a result, the account grows larger each time interest is added.

The more often interest is compounded, the more money is earned. For example, $200 saved at 6 percent and compounded once a year earns $12.00 a year. If the interest is compounded *semiannually,* or twice a year, the account earns more:

Principal		Rate		Time		Interest
$200	×	.06	×	.5 year	=	$ 6.00
$206	×	.06	×	.5 year	=	6.18
Total interest earned in 1 year					=	$12.18

Note: Interest is usually expressed as an annual percentage. A 5% interest rate would pay a return of 5% per year.

Institutions may compound interest quarterly (every three months), monthly, weekly, or even daily.

To choose a savings institution, shop for the highest interest rate. It can be hard to compare saving plans, though. First, the interest rate may vary from one institution to another. Second, the period for compounding may vary. Third, institutions even differ on the date they start paying interest. Some pay interest only on money in the account for the entire compounding period. Others pay interest on the amount in the account on a certain date. Consumers earn the most when interest is paid from the day of deposit to the day of withdrawal.

Extension: It is recommended that consumers should "shop for the highest interest rate." Financial institutions and the protection of depositors' money is discussed in Chapter 16.

To be able to compare interest rates, use the **effective annual yield.** That is *the actual yearly interest rate for savings, found by dividing one year's interest by the principal.* Follow two steps to find this figure:

1. Find the actual dollar amount of interest received after one year. In the examples above, $200 saved at 6 percent interest compounded semiannually earned $12.18 after one year. Compounded annually, it earned $12.00.
2. Divide the interest by the principal to find the effective annual yield:

Interest		Principal		Effective annual yield
$12.18	÷	$200	=	6.09%
$12.00	÷	$200	=	6.00%

Critical Thinking: Assume you were a financial institution. Would you maintain your profitability if you paid a higher rate of interest for savings accounts than you charged for loans? Why or why not?

As you can see, when interest is compounded twice a year, more money is earned on the same amount of principal. You can use this formula to compare any savings accounts, no matter what the interest rate or compounding period.

Calculating Interest on Borrowing

Discussion: If the interest rate for a loan is a fee for the use of money, why do some banks add other lenders' fees to the amount of the loan? Why aren't these fees included in the interest rate?

Borrowers pay interest to the financial institution, rather than the other way around. The cost of borrowing money may not only be interest, however. Some lenders charge other fees. The **finance charge** is *the total dollar amount a borrower must pay, which includes interest plus any other lender fees, such as service charges or insurance.* Service charges are fees lenders charge to cover their costs. For example, the lender may charge $1 a month to record the monthly payment. Credit insurance can be bought for protection in case the borrower can't finish repaying a loan. If you become disabled and can't work, for instance, the lender will use the credit insurance to cover some or all of the remaining payments. Some lenders require borrowers to buy credit insurance. Others let the borrower choose.

The Cost of an Installment Loan A common type of consumer credit is called **closed-end credit,** or an *installment loan*. In this type, *a fixed amount* *is borrowed at a fixed charge for a fixed period and repaid in fixed payments.* At the time of purchase, the borrower often pays part of the item's price, which is called a *down payment.*

Emphasize: Distribute an APR statement to the class for review. The requirement of an Annual Percentage Rate statement is only beneficial if the consumer realizes what it is and uses it in comparison shopping for credit.

Let's see how this works by examining the credit plans Ian found for buying the home computer. Recall that the computer cost $1,800. In Plan A, Ian's family could pay a $300 down payment, then make 24 monthly payments of $75. This means they would pay a total of $2,100—$1,800 for the computer and $300 in finance charges. In Plan B, they could put $300 down and pay $55 a month for 36 months, which includes a $480 finance charge.

How can Ian compare these plans to find the best credit terms? Because they cover different lengths of time, the only way to compare the two plans is to express them in terms of the same period of time. The **annual percentage rate (APR)** does just that. The APR is *the yearly cost of a loan, expressed as a percentage of the principal.* It translates the finance charge into the interest rate for one year.

Discussion: When would consumers most likely use closed-end credit versus open-end credit?

Under the Truth-in-Lending Law, lenders *must* tell a borrower the APR and finance charge before signing a credit agreement. Ian found that Plan A has an APR of 19.20 percent. Plan B's APR is 20.93 percent. The second plan's APR is higher because a bigger part of each monthly payment goes to pay off the finance charge and less is used to pay off the principal. In both plans, the principal is being paid back gradually, but in Plan A it is paid back faster. Ian's family sees that Plan A is better—because the APR is lower, the finance charge forms less of their payments. Of course, that plan is only desirable if they can afford the higher monthly payments.

Activity: Review the methods of figuring credit balances. Be sure students understand which method is most beneficial to the creditor and which is most favorable to the borrower. Examine a credit contract so that students will be able to identify the method being used.

The Cost of Open-End Credit Many people make purchases using store charges and credit cards. With installment loans, like those Ian looked at, one sum is borrowed at the beginning and repaid in equal payments. Credit cards and store charges, which are called **open-end credit,** are different. *The amount a borrower owes increases each time a purchase is made and decreases each time a payment is made.* Suppose the lender bills you every month. If you make a $100 purchase and a $25 payment, what amount does the lender use to calculate the interest you owe?

The lender can choose one of three ways to figure out the balance. With the **adjusted balance method,** *the lender subtracts any payments made during the billing period to find the principal.* After a $100 charge and a $25 payment, the adjusted balance is $75.

Explain: Credit is not considered a part of the money supply because credit is a loan. The credit user is borrowing someone else's money for a period of time and agreeing to pay that money (plus specified interest) back at specified intervals.

In the **previous balance method,** *payments made during the billing period are not deducted.* You pay interest on the last billing period's balance, whether you made a payment or not. Calculated this way, the balance in the example would be $100.

In the **average daily balance method,** *the lender adds the balances for each day in the billing period and divides the total by the number of days in the period to find the principal.* Suppose the billing period begins on March 1 and ends on March 30. You begin the month with a $0 balance. On March 5 you charge $100 worth of goods. On March 22 you pay $25. The balance is calculated like this:

Emphasize: The most beneficial thing that can be taught to students is how to help themselves. Research shows that the general public does not understand the APR or the method of figuring the balance and therefore does not use this information. Help students understand why this information is on the credit contract, what it means, and how they can use it to make the best decision.

Time period	Number of days		Balance each day		Total
March 1–4	4	×	$ 0	=	$ 0
March 5–21	17	×	100	=	1,700
March 22–31	10	×	75	=	750
Total balance				=	$2,450

Total balance		Days in billing cycle		Average daily balance
$2,450	÷	31	=	$79.03

The method used for calculating the balance makes a difference in how much interest is charged. This is true even if the interest rate is the same:

	Adjusted balance	Average daily balance	Previous balance
Monthly interest rate	1.5%	1.5%	1.5%
Balance	$75	$79.03	$100
Interest	$1.13	$1.47	$1.50

Lenders can choose any one of these methods to calculate the balance, but they are required by law to explain which method they use. This information often appears in the credit agreement or on the backs of the bills they send to their customers.

CONSUMERS USE CASH OR CASH SUBSTITUTES

Review: The transactions we are examining are examples of **voluntary exchange**. This chapter introduces different mediums that can be used in this exchange—cash and cash substitutes.

Extension: The definition of the U.S. money supply is **M1.** M1 is composed of cash and checkable deposits.

Using cash—paper money and coins—to make purchases is simple and direct, but we can't carry all of our cash with us. We often use cash substitutes for safety and convenience, for better record-keeping, or for meeting a seller's payment requirements.

Consumers Choose from Five Alternatives to Cash

There are five substitutes for cash: personal checks, certified checks, cashier's checks, money orders, and traveler's checks. Let's see how each is used.

- **Personal checks** are *written orders drawn on an account in a financial institution to pay cash on demand.* Checks are safer to carry or mail than cash, and they provide proof of purchase. Store clerks often ask for some identification before accepting a check. As the *drawer,* you write a check to a person or business for any amount up to the total in your account. The recipient of the check, called the *payee,* collects the money from your financial institution (called the *drawee*), which then deducts the amount of the check from your account. We'll discuss how to operate a checking account later in the chapter.
- **Certified checks** are *personal checks that the drawee guarantees an account has enough money to cover.* The drawer makes the check out for an exact amount and gives it to the drawee. For a fee, the drawee then holds aside money from the checking account. This guarantees—or certifies—to the payee that funds exist to cover the check. These checks are some-

Discussion: Discuss the five cash substitutes and determine when each of these substitutes would most likely be used.

Extension: Money is an integral part of the economic system. When functioning properly, the monetary system encourages full production as well as full employment. When malfunctioning, the monetary system can contribute to fluctuations in output, prices, and employment.

Definition: In discussing the definition of money consider the functions of money: (1) a medium of exchange; (2) a measure of value; and (3) a store of value. Anything that performs these functions can be money.

World Economy: Through time, a variety of cash substitutes have been used throughout the world. Ask students to research what has been used as money in the past and what constitutes money in other countries today.

Checks are safer to carry than cash, but merchants often require identification before they will accept a check.

times required by a payee who wants to be certain that a check will be cashed.

- **Cashier's checks** are *checks drawn on a financial institution's own funds.* Cashier's checks are like certified checks except that they can be bought by anyone, even people who don't have an account with the drawee. Someone who buys a cashier's check pays the full amount plus a fee.
- **Money orders** are *cash substitutes that can be bought from financial institutions, the post office, or other sources.* You pay the issuer the amount of the money order plus a fee and receive a money order and a receipt. You fill in the name and address of the payee. Money orders are a safe way to pay by mail. If the money order is lost or stolen, you can use the receipt to claim a refund.
- **Traveler's checks** are *checks for fixed amounts that are protected by the issuer against loss or theft.* You sign each traveler's check when you buy it and then again when you cash it—that way the payee can verify the signature. Traveler's checks come in fixed amounts ($20, $50, $100), and $500), but if a purchase costs less than the amount of the check most businesses give cash as change. If a traveler's check is lost or stolen, you

can get a refund by telling the issuing company the number of the missing check.

Explain: Checks are merely a way of transferring ownership of deposits in financial institutions. Since these deposits generally can be converted into currency upon demand, they are correctly considered a part of the money supply.

How Checking Accounts Work

Consumers can choose from different types of checking accounts. **Regular checking accounts** are *demand deposit accounts offered by financial institutions*. Some charge fees, which are figured in two ways. A fee may be charged if the balance in the account falls below a certain minimum. This type of account is free if the balance stays above the minimum. Fees may also be based on the number of deposits made and checks written during a month. This type of account is less costly for people who write few checks.

With an **interest-bearing checking account,** *the institution pays interest on the balance*. These accounts are sometimes called *NOW accounts* (short for *n*egotiable *o*rder of *w*ithdrawal). Sometimes fees are charged. If you're considering a NOW account, estimate whether the interest you'll earn will be more than the fee you'll pay. If it is less, see if you can earn more interest by putting your money in a different kind of account. *SuperNow accounts* pay higher interest, but also require a higher minimum balance.

Note: Deregulation of the financial system in the 1970s allowed the creation of a variety of checkable deposits. Prior to that, only commercial banks provided checkable deposits.

Operating a Checking Account You open a checking account by depositing money and filling out a signature card. This card lets the institution verify your signature on checks. You put money in your account by filling out a deposit slip with your name, account number, the date, and the amount deposited.

Any check you deposit or cash must be endorsed. An **endorsement** is *the payee's signature on the back of the check*. While a check is *payable* to the payee, the money cannot be *paid* until he or she endorses it. The payee must sign the check using the same name or title that appears on the check's front. For example, if a check is made out to "Davey Jones," Mr. Jones must sign his name that way on the back. If his name is misspelled on the payee line, he must sign it that way and then sign again with the correct spelling.

Emphasize: Warn students about the hazards of a blank endorsement. No one ever intends to lose anything, but losing a check, already endorsed with a blank endorsement, may lead to serious losses.

There are three ways to endorse a check. A *blank endorsement* is simply the payee's signature—the name "Davey Jones." With a blank endorsement, the check is payable to whoever possesses it, even if it's found or stolen. Thus, it isn't safe to endorse a check this way until you are in the bank. A *special endorsement* avoids this risk by making a check payable to a specific person—for instance, "Pay to the order of Sally Hutchinson, Davey Jones." Only Sally Hutchinson can cash or deposit this check now. Payees can also limit the use of a check by writing a *restrictive endorsement,* such as "Pay to Sally Hutchinson only." As Figure 12.1 shows, a restrictive endorsement that says "For deposit only" should also include the number of the account. Checks must be signed where indicated to comply with federal regulations.

Note: The federal government has encouraged faster transfer of funds on checks cashed in the same town. To obtain this rapid transfer of funds (to avoid a 7- to 10-day waiting period), the checks must be endorsed in a specific manner.

When you make a deposit be sure to enter it in the **check register,** *the record book for a checking account*. Remember to add it to the balance in your account. Figure 12.2 shows a page from a check register with a deposit properly recorded.

Figure 12.1 The Three Types of Endorsements

Activity: Ask your local bank for a teaching packet on checks, making sure that you have sample checks, check registers, and deposit slips. Make out a list of transactions for the students to practice writing checks. Emphasize recording numbers clearly and correctly.

You write a check to withdraw money from your account. Always write checks carefully and use nonerasable ink: checks written in pencil can be altered. A correctly written check is shown in Figure 12.3. To write a check properly, follow these steps:

1. Number the check, unless it has a printed number.
2. Fill in the date—don't use some date in the future.
3. Write the payee's name and draw a horizontal line to the end of the blank to protect you from someone altering the check. Write *cash* or your own name if you want to withdraw cash from your account.
4. Write the amount of money in numerals as close to the dollar sign as possible.
5. Write the amount of money in words as far to the left as possible. Use *and* to join dollars and cents and write cents as a fraction. Then draw a line to the end of the blank.

ITEM NO.	DATE	DESCRIPTION OF TRANSACTION	AMOUNT OF PAYMENT		AMOUNT OF DEPOSIT		BALANCE FORWARD	
							477	79
107	3/23	TO Mutual Casualty Co.					128	00
		FOR auto insurance	128	00			349	79
108	3/23	TO Cheap Food					23	75
		FOR groceries	23	75			326	04
—	3/25	TO Deposit					117	52
		FOR Paycheck			117	52	443	56
—	3/30	TO Withdrawal					50	00
		FOR Cash from auto teller	50	00			393	56
109	3/30	TO Public Utilities					34	62
		FOR February elec. bill	34	62			358	94

Figure 12.2 A Sample Page from a Check Register

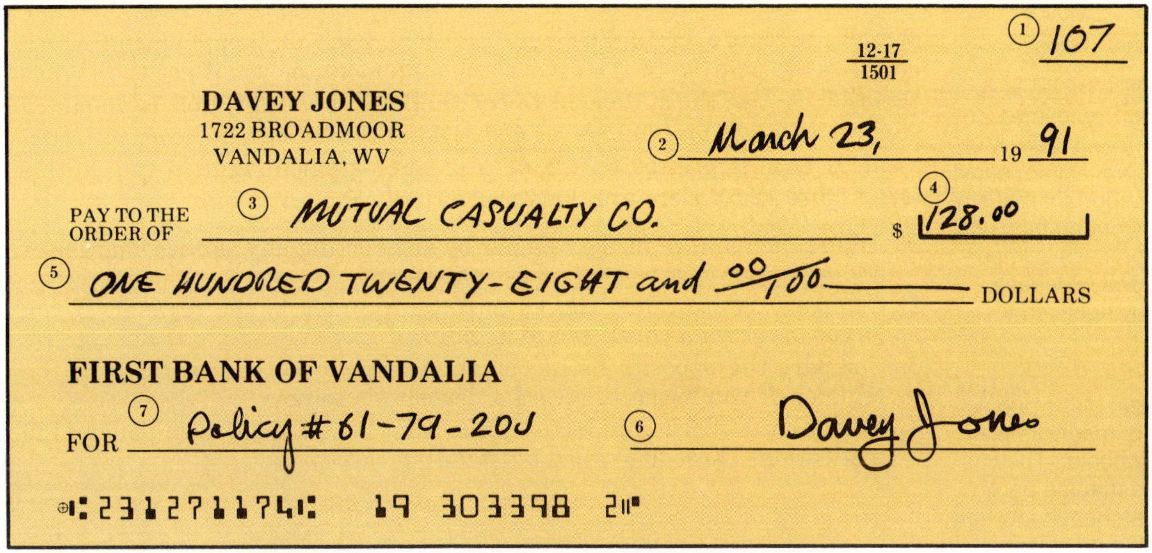

Figure 12.3 A Check That Is Written Correctly

Discussion: Invite a banker to speak to the class regarding the rights and responsibilities of checking-account owners.

Focus: "But I can't be out of money, I still have checks left." This obviously is incorrect, however, too many people rely upon luck and the bank to make sure that they remain solvent. Provide opportunities for your students to practice making out checks, recording those checks in the check register, and reconciling the bank statement.

Discussion: The ability to stop-payment on a check is valuable. When might this procedure be used?

6. Sign the check the same way you signed the signature card. A check is valid only if signed. Never sign a blank check or one made out to *cash* until you're in the bank. If you lose it, someone else could collect the money.
7. Fill in the "memo" blank, if you wish, noting what you wrote the check for.

Remember to record the check in your check register and subtract the amount from the balance. Look back at Figure 12.2 to see how to do this.

Write checks carefully; altered checks may not be accepted. You can make an incorrect check invalid by writing *void* in large letters across the check. Then write a new one. If an uncashed check is lost or stolen, tell the financial institution immediately to stop payment. A **stop-payment order** is *an instruction for a checking account owner to have the financial institution refuse to pay a check.* You must give the institution the check's number, date, amount, and payee. You may also have to pay a fee.

Sometimes people forget to enter a check in the register and deduct the amount from their balance. The next check they write could then result in an **overdraft,** *a check written for more money than an account contains*—or a "bounced" check. Some financial institutions pay overdrafts up to a certain amount. If you don't have this protection, the payee won't receive the money. The institution will notify you and charge a fee. Usually it also returns the check to the payee. You must then deposit enough money to cover the amount of the check—and the fee—and write a new check.

Using Statements At the end of a given period of time, usually on the same date each month, the institution sends depositors a **bank statement.** This is *the institution's record of all deposits and withdrawals made during the period in an account and the balance as of the statement's date.* (See the sample in Figure 12.4.) You'll also receive a list or tape showing which checks were paid up to the date of the statement, or you'll get the checks themselves. Use the statement to **reconcile an account,** that is, *to match your own records and figures for a checking account with those on the statement.* A form is printed on the back of the statement to help you do this (see Figure 12.5). Here are the steps:

Note: Sometimes reconciling a bank statement is not easy! It is important that students understand why this process is important and why each step is necessary.

1. Adjust the balance in the register by subtracting any service charges or adding any interest listed on the statement.
2. Compare the cancelled checks to those recorded in the register. If you forgot to record a check, write it in now.
3. Compare the deposits listed on the statement to those entered in the register. If you forgot to record a deposit, do so now.
4. Total all the checks you have written that have not yet been paid by the institution. These are called *outstanding checks.*

Focus: Many people do not reconcile their checkbooks. They assume that the bank will let them know how much money is in their account. Banks do make mistakes. Therefore, it is up to you to make sure that your account balance is correct.

Discussion: Why would you have outstanding checks? How long should you wait to contact the individual or firm to verify that they received the check?

FIRST BANK OF VANDALIA
12 Main Street
VANDALIA, WV

PERIOD ENDING 04/08/91
DATE OF LAST STATEMENT 03/08/91
ACCOUNT 19-303398

DAVEY JONES
1722 BROADMOOR
VANDALIA, WEST VIRGINIA

DATE	ITEM	CHECK AMOUNT	DEPOSIT AMOUNT	BALANCE
	OPENING BALANCE			347.26
03/08	CHECK #102	17.04		330.22
	CHECK #104	36.34		293.88
03/08	ATM WITHDRAWAL	50.00		243.88
03/11	DEPOSIT		117.52	361.40
03/13	CHECK #106	10.00		351.40
03/17	CHECK #103	18.12		333.28
03/21	CHECK #105	15.25		318.03
03/25	DEPOSIT		117.52	435.55
03/29	CHECK #108	23.75		411.80
03/30	ATM WITHDRAWAL	50.00		361.80
04/02	CHECK #107	128.00		233.80
04/05	CHECK #109	34.62		199.18
04/08	SERVICE CHARGE	5.00		194.18

SUMMARY

PREVIOUS BALANCE	TOTAL DEPOSITS	TOTAL CHECKS	NO. OF CHECKS	NO. ATM TRANS.	NO. OF DEPOSITS	SERVICE CHARGE	NEW BALANCE
347.26	235.04	383.12	8	2	2	5.00	194.18

Figure 12.4 A Sample Bank Statement

Explain: Hints for checking an out-of-balance reconciliation: (1) when reviewing checks and deposits, place a checkmark beside each entry as it is noted; (2) if the difference is divisible by 9, you may have transposed numbers (written 45 instead of 54); or (3) divide the difference by 2, maybe a check was added to the balance (instead of subtracting) thus the net effect would be double.

FIRST BANK OF VANDALIA

To reconcile your checking account:

1. Adjust the balance in your check register by subtracting services charges, if any, or by adding interest, if any.
2. Put the cancelled checks in order and check them off in your register.
3. Check off all deposits listed on the front of this statement.
4. List to the right all checks that you have written that are not returned with this statement.
5. Add the deposits you have made that are not included on the statement.

OUTSTANDING CHECKS

NUMBER	AMOUNT
110	32.19
111	16.20
112	24.93
ATM	50.00
113	20.00
TOTAL	143.32

Write the balance in your register here.	168.38
6. Add the total of outstanding checks.	143.32
	311.70
7. Subtract the total of outstanding deposits.	117.52
New balance—this total should match the balance on the reverse side of this statement.	194.18

Figure 12.5 A Sample Bank Statement

Extension: The most reluctant ATM users are individuals over 60 years old. They claim they feel more comfortable with human contact during the transaction. However, the opposite reaction is indicated by those under 30. They prefer the ATM. Could this be because of the differing opportunity cost of time?

5. Total all the deposits you've made that aren't included on the statement, called *outstanding deposits*.
6. Add the total of outstanding checks to the balance in your register.
7. Subtract the total of outstanding deposits.

This final figure should be the same as the balance on the statement. If not, follow these steps:

- Check to see that you did step 1.
- Check to see that you accounted for all checks and deposits.
- Check the math in your register.
- Check the math in doing the reconciliation.

If you can't find the error, tell your financial institution. The mistake may be theirs.

YOU INTERACT WITH THE ECONOMY: CONSUMERS AND ELECTRONIC BANKING

Expand: Electronic funds transfer is one means for reducing paperwork. The major constraint on the use of EFT is public acceptance.

Fast new methods of handling money let us pay bills or make deposits by pressing buttons or picking up the telephone. This is called *electronic fund transfer (EFT)*. First we'll discuss the different kinds of EFTs; then we'll explain your rights in using them.

- To use some types of EFTs, you must get a plastic card and a personal identification number (PIN) from your financial institution. The card and the PIN allow you to use an **automated teller machine (ATM)**, *a com-*

puter-run unit that takes deposits, gives cash, transfers funds, and gives account information. These machines are often found outside financial institutions or in their lobbies, in shopping centers, offices, or apartment buildings. They provide service twenty-four hours a day.

- Consumers use debit cards to make *point-of-sale transfers.* **Debit cards** are *plastic cards that enable consumers to pay instantly for purchases.* They look like credit cards, but work differently. Credit cards delay payment for a purchase until a bill is received. Debit cards deduct the payment immediately from the user's account. Debit cards are easier to use than checks because no other identification is needed, but you can't stop payment on a debit card transaction. Because the purchase is paid for instantly, be sure your account has enough money.
- Many financial institutions offer the *direct deposit* of paychecks and social security checks. Rather than giving you a check, your employer sends the funds directly to your account. You receive a statement to confirm that the money was deposited. You can also pay bills this way. Each month, for example, the institution can take money out of your account and send it to the electric company.
- Many institutions offer *telephone transfers.* By simply pushing the buttons on a phone, you can transfer money between accounts. You can also use this system to pay bills.
- Home computer banking lets consumers use their own computers to pay bills, transfer funds, or get account information. This will become more widespread with the continued growth of home computer ownership.

Discuss: The enormous growth in financial transactions during the 1960s and 1970s dictated that a way be found to decrease the costs of these activities. ATMs were designed to accomplish this. On the other hand, banks still have to have tellers; acceptance of the other electronic transfers of funds has been spotty. Have EFTs increased the productivity of your bank or merely increased the cost to the bank while increasing services to the customer?

Critical Thinking: Ask your students to analyze the possible use of debit cards. Consider the advantages and disadvantages of "float" (the length of time between making the purchase by check and the check actually being charged to the account) to both the consumer and the bank. The seller should be interested in knowing that the money has been transferred out of the customer's account at the point of purchase because of the decreased risk of insufficient funds.

Automated teller machines make it possible for people to get cash and make transactions twenty-four hours a day.

Summary: Chapter 12 reviews various methods of paying for purchases.

Note: Your PIN is your primary protection in the use of EFTs. Do not write your PIN on the envelope of your card; if it is handy for you, it will be even handier for a thief. In fact, do not note your PIN any place it may be recognized as a PIN (such as your address book, etc.). Do not tell anyone else your PIN, or allow anyone else to see the number when using it. Avoid picking a PIN that would be obvious (such as part of your phone number).

Activity: Encourage students to survey individuals of various ages regarding their use of EFT. Discuss the survey results in class.

Emphasize: Although consumers may have rights regarding EFTs, these rights are limited unless consumers fulfill their responsibilities. Make sure students understand that their legal protection is limited unless they make proper notification.

Many financial institutions offer customers the chance to pay their bills simply by pushing the buttons on their phone.

Here are a few hints on using EFTs safely:

- Never lend your card or reveal your PIN to anyone. If you forget your PIN, the institution will give it to you if you show proper identification. Don't use a familiar number that would be too easy for someone to guess.
- Use the ATM carefully and don't leave it until the transaction is completed. If you have trouble, use the customer service telephone nearby to get help. Don't let anyone else see your number or the transaction you're making.
- Tell the institution immediately if a machine is not working properly.
- Keep the record of the transaction that the machine gives you. Enter all transactions in your check register.
- Tell the institution as soon as possible of any errors on a statement.

What if an EFT card is stolen? What if the computer fails to record a deposit? The Electronic Fund Transfer Act of 1978 protects consumers from some potential problems. Remember that your rights are based on you telling your financial institution of any error. Failing to do so means less protection.

Under this law, your liability for a lost or stolen ATM card is $50 if you tell the institution within two business days of discovering the loss. Failing to say anything within two working days raises your liability to $500. Similar rules apply to errors on a statement. You must tell the institution within

60 days of the statement date or liability goes up, but try to tell the institution sooner.

You may have *no* protection for lost or stolen debit cards. Any amount taken from your account may be gone for good.

SUMMARY

- There are three methods of paying for purchases: using cash or cash substitutes like checks (buy now, pay now); using credit (buy now, pay later); or saving (put money aside now, buy later).
- To choose a method, consumers consider the immediacy of their need for the purchase, the price of the item, the frequency with which they make the purchase, and the method's availability, convenience, dollar cost, and opportunity cost.
- Financial institutions pay savers interest for the use of their money. Borrowers pay interest to lenders for the use of their money. The interest on borrowing is higher than the interest on savings because lenders must cover their costs and wish to earn profits.
- Most savings institutions offer compound interest—depositors earn interest on their interest. The more often interest is compounded, the more money a saver earns.
- Compare interest rates on savings by calculating the effective annual yield, which is the yearly interest in dollars divided by the principal.
- Compare finance charges on loans by using the annual percentage rate (APR), which expresses finance charges in terms of the interest rate for one year. The lower the APR, the less costly the loan. The law requires lenders to state all finance charges and the APR in loan and credit agreements.
- Lenders can figure the balance for open credit—like store charges—in three ways. The adjusted balance method is least costly for consumers, the previous balance method most. The average daily balance method, which lies between the other two in cost to consumers, is probably used most frequently.
- Consumers can choose to use cash or one of five cash substitutes: personal checks, certified checks, cashier's checks, money orders, and traveler's checks. They compare the fees and convenience of these methods.
- Some checking accounts pay interest; some, whether they pay interest or not, charge fees. Checks must be carefully written, recorded, and endorsed. Bank statements should be reconciled promptly.
- Financial institutions offer many methods of electronic funds transfer, including automatic teller machines, debit cards, preauthorized payments, telephone transfers, and banking by home computer. Electronic services are convenient but may also cost money. Federal law protects consumers from loss due to errors as long as they notify the institution promptly.

Key Terms

Match each of the following terms with the definition that most suits it.

adjusted balance method	certified check	interest-bearing checking account	reconcile an account
annual percentage rate	check register	money order	regular checking accounts
automatic teller machine	closed-end credit	open-end credit	stop-payment order
average daily balance method	compound interest	overdraft	traveler's checks
bank statement	debit card	personal check	
cashier's check	effective annual yield	previous balance method	
	endorsement	principal	
	finance charge		
	interest		

a. a written order drawn on an account in a financial institution to pay cash on demand

b. a fee for the use of money

c. the amount of money saved or borrowed, to which interest is added

d. a method of computing savings interest in which interest is added to the principal as it is earned, so that it, too, earns interest

e. the total dollar amount a borrower must pay, which includes interest plus any other lender fees, such as service charges or insurance

f. a personal check that the drawee guarantees the account has enough money to cover

g. a way of finding the principal by subtracting any payments made during the billing period

h. checks for fixed amounts that are protected by the issuer against loss or theft

i. a way of finding the principal by adding the balances for each day of the billing period and dividing the total by the number of days in the period

j. the payee's signature on the back of a check

k. a check drawn on a financial institution's own funds

l. the record book for a checking account

m. the yearly cost of a loan, expressed as a percentage of the principal

n. a demand deposit account on which the institution pays interest on the balance

o. a way of finding the principal in which payments made during the billing period are not deducted

p. a cash substitute that can be bought from financial institutions, the post office, or other sources

q. demand deposit accounts offered by a financial institution

r. an instruction from a checking account owner to have the financial institution refuse to pay a check

s. a computer-run unit that takes deposits, gives cash, transfers funds, and gives account information

t. a check written for more money than an account contains

u. the financial institution's record of all deposits and withdrawals made during a period in an account and the balance as of the statement's date

v. to match one's own records and figures for a checking account with those on the bank statement

w. a plastic card that enables consumers to pay instantly for purchases

x. the actual yearly interest rate for savings, found by dividing one year's interest by the principal

y. a type of credit in which a fixed amount is borrowed at a fixed charge for a fixed period and repaid in fixed payments

z. a type of credit in which the amount a borrower owes increases each time a purchase is made and decreases each time a payment is made

Review Questions

1. What three alternatives do consumers have for paying for purchases?
2. What are the seven factors consumers use to evaluate buying methods?
3. How do we calculate interest? What is compounding? Which method of compounding is best for the consumer?
4. How is the effective annual yield calculated? Why calculate it?
5. What are finance charges?
6. How can you compare the terms offered by different lenders?
7. What are the three ways that balances can be calculated on open-end credit?
8. Name two substitutes for cash.
9. How does a check work? What is a stop-payment order?
10. What are check registers and bank statements? Why reconcile a checking account?
11. What rights do consumers have in using electronic fund transfers?

Projects

1. Choose two items to buy, one priced under $10 and one under $300. Each student should evaluate the available purchase methods for each item according to the seven factors given in the text. Choose a method for each purchase and explain your choice.
2. Go to at least three financial institutions and find out how much interest each pays on a savings account, when the interest is compounded, and when the principal begins to collect interest. Ask an employee at each institution how much interest you would earn in the year on $100 deposited on the first business day of January. Calculate the annual effective yield for each institution. Which is highest? Why do you think it's highest?
3. Get a description of two or three local department store credit terms. Check their interest terms and see which method of calculating principal they use. Don't forget to look for annual percentage rates. Find out if interest rates are the same on both large and small balances. On the basis of your findings, where would you prefer to charge merchandise? Relate your findings to your class.
4. Ask two or three financial institutions for information on their automatic teller machines. Compare the advantages and disadvantages of each. Are the locations convenient? Which one offers the most services? Do all the machines have customer assistance telephones nearby? Are there any charges for using these services? Based on all these factors, which financial institution's machines would you prefer to use? Compare your choice with your classmates'.

Consumer Rights and Responsibilities 13

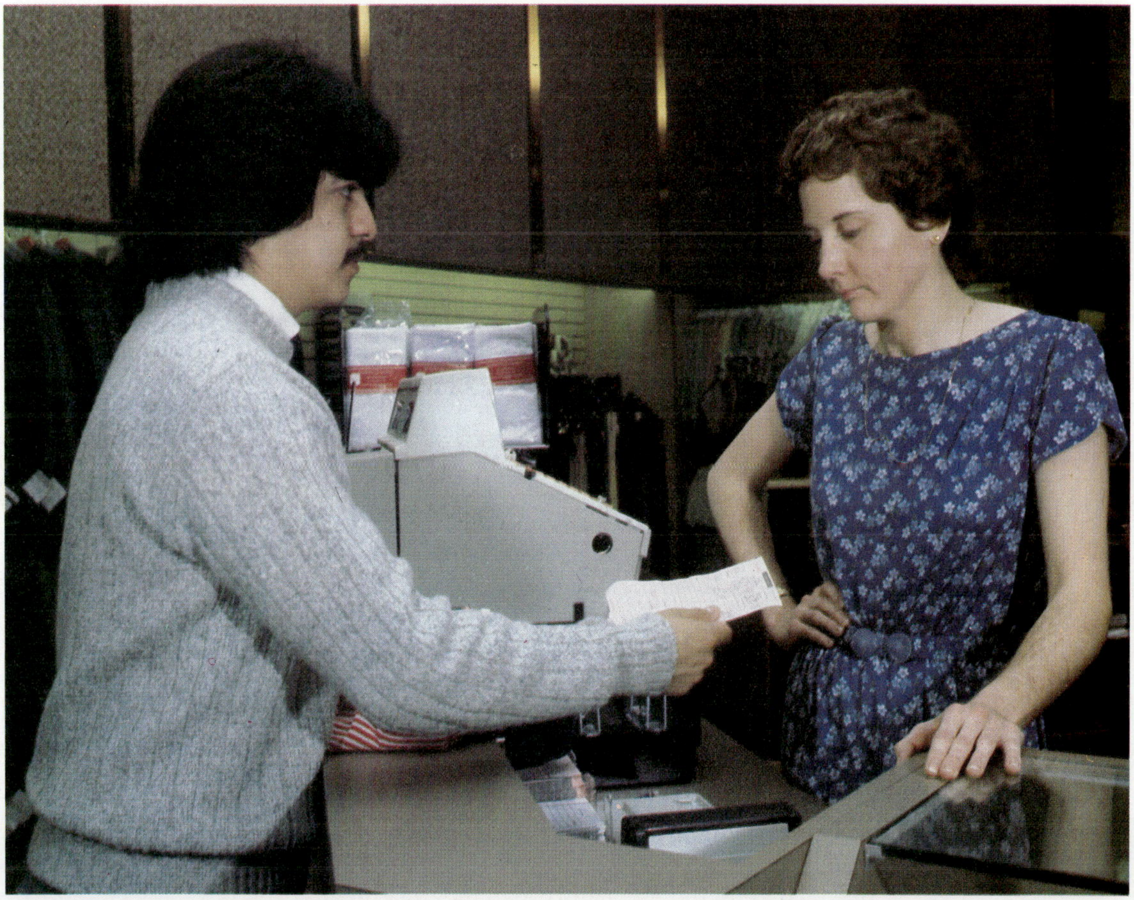

Overview: As participants in the economy, consumers must know and protect their rights, as well as understand and fulfill their responsibilities.

OBJECTIVES

This chapter will help you to:

1. Explain why consumer purchases are contracts.
2. Interpret warranties.
3. Communicate effectively when you think your consumer rights are being violated.
4. Describe the benefits of protecting your rights.

John was waiting for Maria outside the movie theater. She didn't look very happy as she walked up to the ticket booth.

"Sorry I'm so late," Maria said. "Boy, am I mad!"

"What's the matter?" asked John.

Maria answered, "I bought an inexpensive stereo system from Sound Systems, but the thing didn't work."

"So you took it back?" John asked.

"I sure did," said Maria. "I explained the whole thing to the sales clerk and the store gave me a new one."

"So it's all settled, right?" asked John.

"Wrong!" she answered. "That was yesterday! The new one doesn't work either. I spent two hours setting up the stereo. I put all the components together and tried to adjust the antenna. That's why I'm late."

"That's OK," said John. "We can see the next showing of the movie. But what are you going to do now? Go back to Sound Systems?"

"I don't know," Maria said. "They'll probably just give me another stereo that doesn't work. After two tries, I don't think this brand is any good. I want my money back so I can buy another brand. But not from *that* store! I'll never shop *there* again!"

"Why don't you write to the maker of the stereo? Maybe they'd return your money," John suggested.

"I don't want to waste my time on maybes," said Maria. "I want results."

John tried again. "Sound Systems might take your stereo as a trade-in for another brand."

"But I *told* you—I don't want anything from them!" Maria said.

"I'm sorry," said John, starting to laugh. "But if you don't do anything, you're stuck with a stereo that doesn't work."

Discussion: Ask your students if they have ever been dissatisfied with a purchase. Help them identify the problem, the result they expected, and whether or not the result they wanted was justified.

MARIA'S PROBLEM is one most consumers face at one time or another. How do we communicate our consumer problems? How do we protect our rights? Because knowing our rights also means knowing the law, this chapter first explains the legal principles behind consumer transactions. Then you'll learn what to do when things go wrong. Finally, you'll see how, by protecting your own rights, you are helping other consumers.

CONSUMER TRANSACTIONS ARE CONTRACTS

When consumers and producers exchange money for goods and services, they are making a transaction. Transactions are **contracts,** which means that they are *agreements that can be enforced by the legal system.* When we hear the word *contract,* we often picture a lengthy, complex legal document.

Contracts can be very simple, though, and some contracts don't even need to be written. If all the requirements are met, buying an old television from a neighbor is a contract. Let's see what those requirements are.

Clarify: The requirements for a legal contract are the same whether you are purchasing or selling an item or negotiating for a job. This means both parties can be active in attempting to revise the terms of the contract. In fact, voluntary exchange will not take place unless both sides agree to the contract. This does not mean that either side will be completely satisfied. If contractual terms are negotiated, that means both sides agreed to give up something in order to arrive at a compromise. There are some purchases that we expect to negotiate for. No one expects to walk in and buy an automobile for the sticker price, for example.

Contracts Have Certain Requirements

For a contract to exist, four requirements must be met. If all four are not met, there may be an agreement, but it isn't a contract. If all four *are* met, the agreement is enforceable by law. This means that if one person fails to do what he or she agreed to do, the other can ask the courts for help. (Those who agree to a contract are called *parties.*) The four requirements of a contract are:

1. Both parties agree to the terms
2. Both parties give consideration
3. Both parties are competent
4. The agreement has a legal purpose

In some cases, the agreement must also be in writing.

Let's look at each requirement in detail by examining the agreement between Maria and Sound Systems, where she bought her stereo.

Both Parties Must Agree to the Terms A contract begins when one party makes an offer to the other. An **offer** is *the promise to do something in exchange for something another party agrees to do.* Saying "Would you like to buy my car?" is not making an offer; it is asking a question. Saying "I'll sell you my car for $500" is making an offer. To be valid, an offer must be intended, it must be clearly communicated, and it must be definite.

Maria went to Sound Systems looking for a stereo for less than $150. The salesperson pointed out one model and said, "We'll sell you that one for $100." The salesperson made an offer. The offer was intended—the salesperson meant it. It was clearly communicated—Maria understood what the salesperson meant. It was definite—it named a specific stereo and a specific price.

Research: There are many reference books on negotiation. As a research project, students can study negotiation techniques and report their findings to the class.

Maria then accepted the offer by saying, "I'll take it." **Acceptance** is *one party's agreement to accept the other party's offer in exchange for a promise to do something.* To be legally binding, this acceptance must be voluntary. This means the person cannot be forced into accepting the offer.

There are three alternatives to accepting an offer. First, Maria could have turned the offer down. Second, she could have made a *counteroffer*—saying, for instance, "I'll buy it for $95." Then, the salesperson would have to decide whether to accept or reject the counteroffer. Third, she could have given a *qualified* acceptance. For example, Maria might have said, "I'll take it for $100 if you throw in the headphones."

Both Parties Must Give Consideration A contract is an agreement in which both parties give consideration. **Consideration** is *something of value each party to a contract gives up in order to receive the benefit he or she wants.* The law assumes that no one would give up something without getting something else in return.

Illustrate: In most states, if an individual gives someone an automobile, the recipient must pay consideration. That is why many people say they paid $1 for an auto that a family member gave them. It fulfills the requirement for a contract, but it is not onerous.

Discuss: Laws that protect minors by allowing them to void contracts may have unforeseen consequences. It may be more difficult for a minor to sign a contract or to purchase an item requiring a contract. It may even be impossible for a minor to obtain credit. The difficulty stems from the law stating that minors, in some cases, may not be bound by the contract. This means that the sale has additional risks the seller may not be willing to take.

Emphasize: A contract that involves an illegal purpose cannot be enforced.

Critical Thinking: Why do specific types of transactions require the contract to be in writing?

The consideration—what is given up—will vary from contract to contract. It could be an object, like a car. It could be money. A person could give up an opportunity to do something he or she would otherwise be free to do. In exchange for $100, you may promise your parents not to eat ice cream for a year. That counts as consideration—you're giving up your right to eat ice cream.

Maria's purchase met this requirement. Sound Systems gave her a stereo; she gave the store $100.

Both Parties Must Be Competent Being **competent** means that each party is *capable of bargaining effectively with others*. Certain groups of people are defined as less able to bargain equally with other people and thus require legal protection. Insane, drunk, and senile people have this protection. So do **minors**—*people who have not yet reached the age of majority*. That age is eighteen in some states and twenty-one in others.

Minors have the right to declare their contracts void, or no longer valid. This is an option, not a requirement. Once it is exercised, though, both parties must return the consideration they received. A minor who voids a contract must void the whole thing. He or she cannot void an undesirable part of the contract and keep the rest.

A minor's right to void a contract is limited. First, contracts concerning food, clothing, shelter, and medical care may not be voided by a minor who is living on his or her own, outside the responsibility of parents. This person is called an *emancipated* minor. If a minor does live in his or her parents' home, these parents may be held responsible for the contract. Second, minors lose the right to void a contract if they have lied about their age.

Because Maria is eighteen, the age of majority in her state, her agreement with Sound Systems meets this third requirement.

Both Parties Must Have a Legal Purpose A contract must have a legal purpose. An agreement about gambling or another criminal activity is not a contract because it has an illegal purpose. The agreement between Sound Systems and Maria was legal.

Some Types of Contracts Must Be in Writing Some contracts have another requirement—they must be in writing. State laws vary, but four types of contracts generally must be written:

1. Contracts for the purchase or sale of real estate
2. Contracts for the sale of goods for more than $500
3. Contracts that will not be carried out until a year or more after they are made
4. Contracts to pay someone else's debt

Because it didn't fall into one of these categories, the sale of the stereo did not have to be written.

Of course, any contract can be put in writing if both parties desire it. A sample contract is shown in Figure 13.1. As you can see, the written contract does not have to be long. It need only contain what is being offered and accepted, the names of the parties involved, the price and the terms agreed

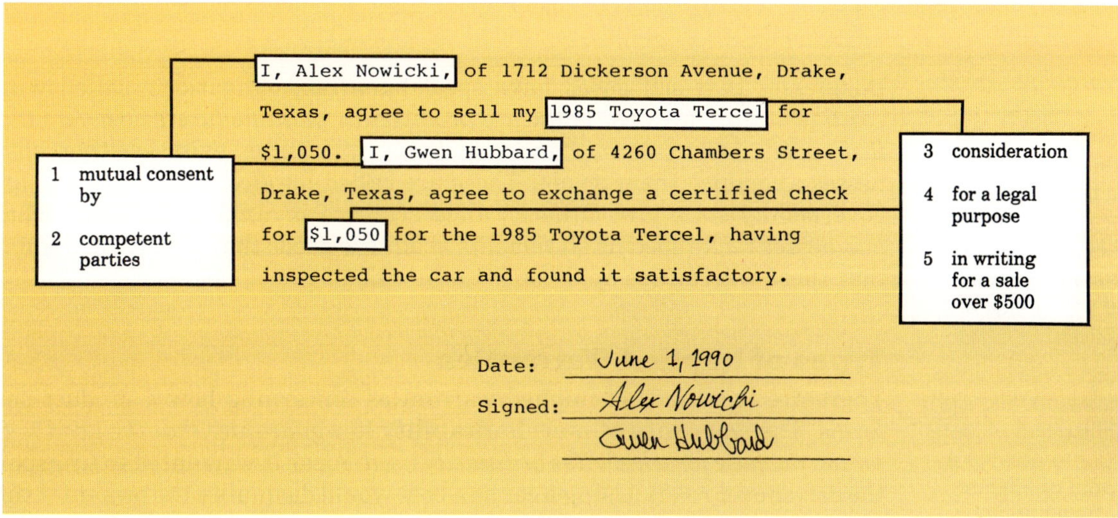

Critical Thinking: Contracts mean that there is a legal means of redress. If a consumer is not satisfied that the seller met all the terms of the contract, the issue can be taken to the courts to obtain a judgment. If consumers are already protected through this means, why is there a need for additional protection through regulatory agencies?

Review: One of the most important functions of government is the enforcement of contracts. As you have pointed out, contracts detail the conditions of transactions. The enforcement of these conditions is essential for the satisfactory completion of these transactions.

to, and the intent of the parties. To make sure that all of this information is included, check all contracts for the following points:

- Names and addresses of both parties
- Dates of the agreement, deliveries, payments, and the end of the contract
- Purpose of the contract
- Description of the goods, services, or consideration involved
- Dollar amount of the price
- (For credit contracts) dollar amounts of all finance charges, down payment, and each payment, and the annual percentage rate
- Penalties for failure of each party to do as promised
- Specific rights and obligations of both parties

What Contract Law Means for Consumers

Both parties to a contract agree to do something. *When either party fails to do what was promised,* he or she has committed a **breach of contract.** This can result in extra expense or harm to the other party, but this person has a recourse. Because a contract is legally enforceable, the injured party can **sue,** which means *to ask a court to settle a dispute.*

Look again at the contract in Figure 13.1. Suppose Alex refused to deliver the car or says he decided not to. If so, Gwen has three choices. First, she could cancel the contract—this means accepting Alex's breach, forgetting about his car, and looking for another one elsewhere. Second, she could sue Alex and ask the court to force him to turn over the car he promised to deliver. Third, if she has already paid for the car, Gwen can sue Alex to get her money back.

Can Maria sue about her stereo? Perhaps. Before we answer this question, though, we need to learn more about contracts for the sale of goods.

SELLERS OFFER WARRANTIES ON THE GOODS THEY SELL

Research: Assign students to research your state laws regarding implied warranties. What specific coverage is granted by law? How does the consumer proceed if these warranties are not fulfilled?

Businesses that sell goods have special contract obligations, called **warranties** or **guarantees.** These are *promises by manufacturers or sellers that their goods meet certain standards.* Some warranties exist whether businesses announce them or not. These are called *implied warranties* and are governed by state law. Others, called *express warranties,* arise only when businesses make specific statements about the goods they sell. Keep in mind that these warranties apply only to the sale of goods, not services.

Types of Implied Warranties

Discussion: Highlight the difficulties of identifying and proving a warranty of fitness. First, how can you prove that the seller knew your needs? Second, did the seller recommend several different models, not just the one you bought? Third, are you partially at fault when you rely completely on the seller's judgment? How do you differentiate between puffing and judgment unless you are also informed? The example of Maria's purchase is clear cut, but most purchase decisions are not.

There are two kinds of implied warranties concerning how a product performs. The **warranty of merchantability** is *a guarantee that the good is fit for the purpose for which it is ordinarily used.* A car is warranted to transport the driver over roads. Using a car as a boat would disqualify the owner for this protection.

The other type, the **warranty of fitness,** is *a guarantee that protects a buyer who relies on the seller's judgment when making a purchase.* For this warranty to exist, three requirements must be met. First, the seller must know the needs of the buyer. Second, the seller must supply or recommend the particular good. Third, the buyer must have relied on the seller's judgment. Suppose Maria had told the salesperson she wanted a stereo system that received signals from a specific radio station. Suppose the seller recommended the "Super Stereo" and Maria bought it. This warranty would be breached if the stereo did not receive the signals.

There are two exceptions to the implied warranties. First, they apply only to purchases from *merchants*—businesspeople who are engaged in their regular business when making the sale. Buying something from a neighbor at a yard sale would not qualify. Second, goods that are bought "as is" do not qualify for these warranties. If a good bought "as is" is defective, the buyer has no protection.

Express warranties are created when sellers make direct statements about what they sell. Express warranties can be made by the manufacturer of a good or by the retailer who sells it. Sellers create these warranties in one of three ways:

Note: An express warranty is easier to prove; however, even express warranties can be contested. Your best protection is still a reputable dealer whose primary concern is continued customer satisfaction.

- The buyer and seller agree on the appearance and performance of a sample. The good that the seller later delivered must look and work just like the sample.
- The buyer and seller agree on a detailed description of the good. Any units that are sold must match the description. For instance, goods bought through a catalog must match the catalog description.
- The seller makes a promise about the appearance and performance of the good. The word *warranty* or *guarantee* need not be used for this kind of warranty to exist. (This is how most warranties are created.)

Not everything a salesperson says to persuade us to buy a product creates

Consumers must be careful to inspect goods sold in a flea market because no express warranties are given.

Note: The Magnuson-Moss Warranty Act states that the warranty is available for your inspection. It does not state that each buyer should receive a copy of the warranty.

a warranty. The law sees some statements as **puffing.** This refers to *exaggerated claims of a product's superiority that are clearly based on the seller's opinion.* Such statements as "This is the best you'll ever see!" or "It's a real bargain!" are puffing. They do not create a warranty.

How to Use Written Warranties

Illustration: Bring to class examples of different types of warranties. Encourage the students to carefully study these examples and identify what is guaranteed and what is not.

Since verbal promises are hard to prove, it is better to have express warranties in writing. The Magnuson-Moss Warranty Act deals with written warranties on goods selling for more than $15. The act specifies that these warranties must be available for consumers to inspect. The act also divides written warranties into two categories.

Warranties may be full or limited. A **full warranty** is *a business's written guarantee to fix or replace a faulty product free within a reasonable time after being told of a problem.* The maker also promises to pay for the removal or reinstallation of the product if needed. Full warranties cannot require the buyer to do anything unreasonable, such as ship a heavy piece of equipment somewhere. Full warranties also apply to anyone who owns the product during the term of the warranty. If the product can't be fixed, the buyer can

Discussion: Many limited warranties require that the product be taken to an authorized service center for repair. They include a listing of service centers or a phone number to call to find out about the nearest center. This may be because the producer wants to make sure that the product has specialized care; it may be because the producer has negotiated a special price with this repair shop; it may simply be that the seller is not interested in making it convenient for you to take advantage of the warranty. As long as this restriction is written in the limited warranty, you must abide by it in order to collect.

Illustration: On a car, you will often find that different parts have different warranties. For example, the tires or the battery will usually have a different warranty supplied by the manufacturers.

Activity: Ask students to bring examples of warranties on products they have purchased.

The law requires sellers to allow shoppers to read a product's warranty before making a purchase.

choose to receive a replacement or a refund. Full warranties can be limited in time, but the time limit must be clearly stated. A full warranty may cover only part of a product.

Any written warranty that is not full is a **limited warranty,** and the written warranty must call it that. Examples are warranties that cover only parts but not labor, those that cover only the first purchaser and not subsequent owners, and those that require the buyer to pay the cost of shipping the product for servicing. There are many other types of limited warranties.

The Magnuson-Moss Warranty Act also requires that written warranties describe the actions buyers must take in order to qualify for coverage. Sometimes, when they try to fix a product themselves, consumers put an end to their warranty protection. Written warranties must also state what the manufacturer or seller will do to remedy a problem. Finally, the warranty must say whether all parts are covered and whether labor costs are also included in the protection.

Take advantage of your right to read warranties before you buy and look for the following things:

1. What is the period of the warranty? Are different parts covered for different lengths of time?
2. Is the warranty full or limited?
3. Does it cover only the first buyer?

4. What is covered—all parts, some parts, parts only, or parts and labor?
5. Who will do repairs—the merchant, the manufacturer, or someone at an authorized service center?
6. Who pays mailing costs?
7. Are any actions by the buyer prohibited?
8. Must the buyer send in an ownership card to register the good's serial number?

Discuss: Often the problem with a new purchase is simply that it is not plugged in, the batteries have not been inserted correctly, or that it has been assembled wrong. How can you make sure that this is not the problem?

Maria checked in the carton of her stereo for a written warranty from the manufacturer, but she didn't find one. Still, her purchase *is* covered by the implied warranty of merchantability. If it does not work as it should, she has the right to have the stereo repaired or replaced. In order to get satisfaction, Maria needs to act—she must communicate her problem to the seller or maker of the stereo.

CONSUMERS CAN COMMUNICATE THEIR PROBLEMS

To resolve a problem to your satisfaction, remember a few points:

1. Most problems can be avoided by reading the directions and by using and maintaining a product properly.
2. If there is a problem, ask yourself whether it is the seller's fault. Did a

Illustration: If Maria can prove that she specifically asked for a stereo that received a given station without any interference, then she has a good case for a refund. To a large extent, Maria's protection depends on how well she expressed her needs and how reputable the dealer is.

Note: Unless the seller has stipulated that full refunds are available, Maria may not be able to insist on a refund. In fact, many times sellers have signs saying that they will only grant an exchange or a credit toward another item.

The owner of a product may be responsible for meeting regular service dates in order to qualify for warranty protection.

Focus: Ask students to think back to any problems they have had with products. Did they work through these steps in order to resolve their problems?

sweater shrink because it was washed improperly? See if information in the product's use and care manual can help you solve the problem.

3. Be calm and stay in control. Describe the problem carefully and clearly and state what you expect. Listen to what the merchant or manufacturer has to say about the problem.
4. Be courteous. Politeness often gets good results.
5. Be reasonable. Avoiding outrageous demands helps solve problems.
6. Be thorough. Provide all necessary information and remember to keep copies for yourself. Keep the box the item came in, as well as sales slips and charge slips, warranties, and service records.
7. Don't give in until the problem has been resolved satisfactorily.

How to Solve Consumer Problems

Discuss: Discuss the process for voicing complaints. First, talk with the salesperson you originally dealt with; if you do not receive satisfaction, ask to talk with the manager (or the salesperson's supervisor); if you are still not satisfied, continue working up the chain of command.

A problem that involves the terms of a written warranty should be handled by following the procedures described on the warranty. It may take time, but the damaged good will usually be fixed or replaced.

For other consumer complaints—like Maria's, which involves an implied warranty—the first step is to return to where you purchased the good. Ask to talk to a salesperson or, in a large store, to the customer service department.

If this step doesn't lead to a solution, ask to speak to the manager or the salesperson's supervisor. Another option is to write to the store's owner.

If the problem still isn't solved, write to the head of the manufacturing or selling firm. Briefly, clearly, and calmly, describe your complaint and request a solution. Figure 13.2 shows a sample complaint letter.

Explain: Table 13.1 on page 220 lists agencies where you can refer your complaint. One of the functions of the Better Business Bureau is complaint resolution. In addition, many industries have a conflict-resolution process. If all else fails, contact a local consumer protection office or the consumer representative at a local TV or radio station or newspaper.

If this doesn't work, you can appeal for outside help from a third party, such as the Better Business Bureau. You could also turn to the local Chamber of Commerce, which is an organization of businesspeople in your community. You could write to a trade or professional association or to a **consumer action panel.** This is *a group formed by manufacturers in some industries to handle consumer problems.* Table 13.1 lists some of these organizations. You might also ask for help from government consumer aid agencies or from elected officials or state licensing boards. Some local newspapers and radio and TV stations have consumer action groups that help solve problems. These groups usually get involved only when the buyer has tried to solve the problem personally. When you contact any of these groups, explain your problem clearly and calmly. Send copies of the letters to the heads of the manufacturing company or store.

Several sources list the names, addresses, and consumer offices of businesses. Local addresses can be found in the Yellow Pages. National businesses are listed in reference books like Standard & Poor's annual directories of corporations, *Consumer Complaint Guide, Help: The Indispensable Almanac of Consumer Information*, and *Everybody's Money Complaint Directory*. The *Directory of National Trade and Professional Associations* gives addresses for those groups. The federal government's *Consumer's Resource Handbook* also lists many firms' consumer affairs offices and prints the

Review: Remember, if you have entered into a legal contract the court system is always a means of redress.

Discuss: Invite a representative of the Better Business Bureau to class to discuss their arbitration program.

Expansion: For decades, attorneys argued that it was unprofessional to advertise. Because of this, consumers had limited access to information about which attorneys specialized in what areas. Finally, in the 1980s two breakthroughs occurred. The American Bar Association agreed that it was feasible for attorneys to advertise their specialty, and less-expensive legal assistance became available through an entrepreneurial legal service.

1611 Cashtown Road
Cooper, WY 82631
April 29, 1991

Duane Kellogg
Circulation Editor
Rock On Magazine
19211 Canyon Boulevard
Los Angeles, CA 95001

Dear Mr. Kellogg:

On December 17, 1990, I wrote to inform you of a change of address, beginning February of this year. I received the February issue of Rock On at my old address, but have not yet received the March, April, and May issues.

Please correct your records to show my new address, which appears above. And please send me the back issues of the magazines or extend my subscription for three months.

Thank you very much for your cooperation. I look forward to receiving my new issues soon.

Sincerely,

Jill Bendix

Jill Bendix

My old address:
3221 Birch Way
Argyle, ND 62713

Figure 13.2 A Sample Complaint Letter

names and addresses of all federal and state government departments that help consumers.

Sometimes a group like the Better Business Bureau or the Chamber of Commerce will settle a consumer problem by offering to arbitrate a solution. In that case, an impartial person hears both sides of the dispute and decides on a solution. Both parties agree to follow the arbitrator's decision.

Sometimes, even after all of this work, there is still a problem. If so, the next step is to go to court.

Define: **Arbitration** is the selection of an individual, agreed to by both sides, to hear and to decide the settlement of a suit. Usually both parties agree in advance to abide by the arbitrator's decision.

Consumers May Take Legal Action

Consumers can take their problems to court in two ways. The more complex and costly way is to hire a lawyer and sue. To find a lawyer, look in the Yellow Pages or ask for names from the local bar association, which is the professional group for lawyers. People whose income is less than a certain limit may be eligible for help from a **legal aid society.** This is *an organization paid for by the government to offer legal help free or for a small fee.* The income limit varies from state to state.

Ask the lawyer about the likelihood of winning a suit and about how much the legal services will cost. Some suits are settled out of court, without a

Table 13.1 Industry and Trade Associations That Consumers Can Write to for Help

American Apparel Manufacturer's Association	Jewelers Vigilance Committee
American Association of Advertising Agencies	Magazine Publishers of America
American Association of Meat Processors	Manufactured Housing Institute
American Automobile Association (has AUTOCAP, a consumer action panel)	Motion Picture Association of America
American Collectors Association	National Association of Personnel Consultants
American Hotel and Motel Association	National Association of Realtors
American Movers Conference	National Association of Securities Dealers
American Society of Travel Agents	National Association of Television and Electronic Servicers of America
American Textile Manufacturers Institute, Inc.	National Automobile Dealers Association
Association of Home Appliance Manufacturers (has MACAP, a consumer action panel)	National Home Study Council
Carpet and Rug Institute	National Roofing Contractors Association
Direct Marketing Association	National Solar Heating and Cooling Information Center
Direct Selling Association	National Tire Dealers and Retreaders Association
Electronic Industries Association	
Indian Arts and Crafts Association	

Research: Have students research the procedures for filing in a small-claims court; or, have someone from the judicial system speak to the class about this process.

Note: Consumers play an integral role in our economy through their **economic vote**. By purchasing a product, consumers are "voting" for that product.

trial, when both sides agree to a solution. Otherwise, the suit is settled after a trial by a judge or jury.

There is another option for problems that involve small amounts of money. Most states have a **small claims court,** *an informally run court created to handle legal disputes over small sums of money.* People present their own case in this court without a lawyer. The size of claims handled in small claims courts varies, but ranges from a low of $100 to a high of $3000. The cost of suing in small claims court is small, and the suit can be settled fairly quickly. One drawback to small claims court, however, is that consumers who win aren't always sure that the firm that loses will pay them. Because the court is informal and involves small sums, its decisions are often not enforced.

All states have some court procedures for small claims. Most have a small claims court system separate from other courts, except Arizona, Delaware, Louisiana, Mississippi, South Carolina, Tennessee, Virginia, and West Virginia. In Arkansas, Georgia, Kansas, Montana, and New Mexico, there are small claims systems only in certain large cities.

YOU INTERACT WITH THE ECONOMY: CONSUMER RIGHTS AND RESPONSIBILITIES

In 1962, President John Kennedy stated the four basic rights of consumers:

1. The right to safety—meaning the right to purchase products that are not harmful.
2. The right to choose—meaning the right to select from competing products at competitive prices.
3. The right to be informed—meaning the right to accurate information.
4. The right to be heard—meaning the right to have channels for communicating problems.

Focus: Although it is important to stress the rights of consumers, it is just as important to stress the related responsibilities. By doing so, we can help our students control their own actions and take charge of their own lives.

Define: A **market economy** is an economy where the private decisions of consumers, resource suppliers, and business firms determine how resources are allocated to produce goods and services. A **command economy** is one where the factors of production are publicly owned and economic decisions are made by the central authority.

Activity: Locate a local consumer affairs representative. Interview this individual regarding the office's orientation, activities, and goals.

If all other methods of resolving a problem fail, a consumer may be able to sue, asking a court to settle the dispute.

In the 1970s, President Gerald Ford added another:

5. The right to consumer education—meaning the right to learn about the marketplace and the consumer's and producer's positions in it.

President Carter added one more consumer right:

6. The right to redress—meaning the right to have a wrong corrected.

Consumers also have more general rights that extend to all actions they engage in. The federal government, for instance, guarantees freedom from discrimination on the basis of race, sex, religion, or national origin. Rights give rise to **responsibilities**—*our duty to act in our best interest and that of other members of our society.* We must use our rights if we want to keep them. We must protect our rights to protect ourselves and others.

Our right to safety makes us responsible for using products safely. Acting safely includes wearing seat belts and driving carefully, using products according to directions, and keeping dangerous products away from children. It also includes responding promptly to product recalls. A **recall** occurs when *a manufacturer discovers, or is made aware of, a flaw in its product and calls back all units that have been sold to fix them.*

Our right to choose makes us responsible for making intelligent choices. We can choose safe products when safety is important, as with toys and

Activity: Survey local stores to determine their policy on shoplifting. Do they prosecute every time? What alternate procedures do they use? Is shoplifting a serious problem in their store?

Emphasize: Our results will always be better when we use a businesslike attitude and provide relevant documentation.

machines, and avoid dishonest businesses or poor quality products. We should also accept our obligation to pay for what we choose.

Our right to be informed makes us responsible for getting information and using it. We can make an effort to get credit information, to be aware of illegal business practices, and to understand and be careful with contracts.

Our right to be heard makes us responsible for complaining when necessary. We can notify businesses or the government when our rights are abused. We can use outside help—like the Better Business Bureaus—when necessary. We can support our complaints with documents, such as receipts, warranties, and copies of letters.

Our right to consumer education makes us responsible for using what we have learned. We should also remember to continue that education by keeping up with changes in laws and regulations and with business practices.

Our right to redress makes us responsible for protecting our interests and for preventing similar offenses from occurring.

Responsible consumers act honestly. **Shoplifting**—*taking goods from stores without paying for them*—is a crime punishable by law. A shoplifter runs the risk of being captured, prosecuted, and punished. Shoplifting also hurts other consumers. To cover the cost of stolen goods and antitheft devices, stores must raise their prices.

Some dishonest people switch price tags on items so that they pay less than the item really costs. This—like shoplifting—hurts other consumers.

Employers expect their workers—especially those who handle money—to be honest and reliable.

Summary: In a market system, consumers and producers interact using a variety of means, some of which involve legal contracts. Consumers have rights as well as responsibilities in this interaction.

Discussion: Worker crime is a widespread problem. These crimes range from stealing notepads or paper clips to stealing millions of dollars. The crimes are difficult to prove and hard to monitor. Prosecution is variable.

Some people also commit **worker crime** by *stealing supplies or products from employers or falsifying time or work records*. These actions harm others by driving up the costs of running a business. Business owners must then increase prices. Worker crime is illegal. The person who commits it may be prosecuted and punished. At the very least, the employee risks being fired.

By acting responsibly, people help create a smoothly operating economy, one that produces sound products that consumers want. Refusing to buy harmful products and complaining about defective ones can lead producers to make better products. Acting honestly in the marketplace—not shoplifting, for instance—avoids making other consumers pay more. Keep in mind that your actions affect others—and theirs affect you.

One way of considering others is to exercise your right to communicate your problems. Many groups offer consumer protection, but the best protection is consumers themselves.

SUMMARY

- Consumer transactions are contracts if they meet four requirements: (1) both parties agree to the terms, (2) both parties give consideration, (3) both parties are competent, and (4) the agreement has a legal purpose. In some cases, the agreement must also be in writing.
- If one party to a contract fails to do as promised, there is a breach of contract, and the other party can cancel it, sue to require that the first party perform as agreed, or sue for damages.
- Sellers give warranties on the goods they sell. The warranty of title guarantees that the buyer has clear title to the item purchased. The implied warranties of merchantability and of fitness arise only in purchases from merchants and cover the performance of a product. An item bought "as is" isn't covered by these warranties.
- Express warranties arise when sellers make direct statements about the quality of their goods. Warranties must be written for a good costing more than $15 and must be available for inspection by consumers before purchasing.
- Consumers have many channels for communicating their problems. In using them, be calm, courteous, reasonable, and thorough. If a problem isn't solved, a consumer can sue. Suits over small sums of money can be handled in small claims court.
- Consumers have the right to safety, to choose, to be informed, to be heard, to have consumer education, and to redress. Those rights create the need to act responsibly, which includes being honest and protecting those rights.

Key Terms

Match each of the following terms with the definition that most suits it.

acceptance	contract	puffing	warranties or guarantees
breach of contract	full warranty	recall	warranty of fitness
competent	legal aid society	responsibility	warranty of merchantability
consideration	limited warranty	shoplifting	worker crime
consumer action panel	minor	small claims court	
	offer	sue	

a. a guarantee that protects a buyer who relies on the seller's judgment when making a purchase
b. an informally run court created to handle legal disputes over small sums of money
c. the promise one party makes to do something in exchange for something another party agrees to do; a requirement of a contract
d. promises by manufacturers or sellers that their goods meet certain standards
e. exaggerated claims of a product's superiority that are clearly based on the seller's opinion
f. one party's agreement to accept the other party's offer in exchange for a promise to do something; a requirement of a contract
g. a guarantee that the good is fit for the purpose for which it is ordinarily used
h. the crime of taking goods from stores without paying for them
i. capable of bargaining effectively with others; a requirement of a contract
j. an organization paid for by the government to offer legal help free or for a small fee
k. something of value each party to a contract gives up in order to receive the benefit he or she wants
l. the failure of either party to do what was promised in a contract
m. the crime of stealing supplies or products from employers or falsifying time or work records
n. an agreement that can be enforced by the legal system
o. a business's written guarantee to fix or replace a faulty product free within a reasonable time after being told of a problem
p. a group formed by manufacturers in some industries to handle consumer problems
q. a person who has not yet reached the age of majority
r. any written warranty that is not full
s. our duty to act in our best interest and that of other members of our society
t. a situation in which a manufacturer discovers or is made aware of a flaw in its product and calls back all units that have been sold to fix them
u. to ask a court to settle a dispute

Review Questions

1. What are the rights of minors who enter into contracts? What limits are there on those rights?
2. What contracts must be written? Give an example of each type.
3. What can someone do if another party to a contract has not acted as promised?
4. What warranties do not apply to an "as is" sale?

5. What information must written warranties include? How can consumers obtain this information?
6. What steps should a consumer take to complain about a faulty product?
7. What are the benefits of taking a case to small claims court?
8. What crimes do people commit against businesses? What are their results?
9. How are consumer responsibilities related to consumer rights?

Projects

1. Select a consumer good that you are thinking about buying or something you would like to buy. Find three or four competing brands in different price ranges. What warranty terms do they offer? Do these terms differ for different prices? Are the warranty terms understandable? Identify any terms that are hard to understand and get them explained.
2. You recently saw a commercial on television for a set of two compact discs called *Sounds from Motown.* You ordered the discs from CD Clearinghouse, Box 1999, Music City, Tennessee, and paid $14.98. The commercial offered a "money back guarantee." When the package arrived, you were angered to see that the two discs were three-inch discs rather than five-inch discs. Write a letter to the CD Clearinghouse asking for your money back.
3. Find out about your state's small claims court. What are the dollar limits on claims? What are the procedures of the court? How much does it cost to sue someone in the court? Write a description of how to bring a case to the court.
4. Find out what consumer assistance there is in your area and make a "Help for Consumers" handbook. First, identify what consumer education classes are offered in your school system. Then locate any government, nonprofit, business, trade, or professional groups that help consumers solve problems. Write down the group's name, address, and telephone number and the name of a person to contact. Be sure to include information on what types of problems the group solves and how they solve them—how long does it take, and what must the consumer be prepared to do?
5. Arrange with your teacher to invite loss-prevention personnel from a local department store to discuss how the store prevents shoplifting. What new technology is used to prevent shoplifting? How do loss-prevention personnel approach a shoplifter? How is the crime of shoplifting punishable in your state? Find out who is doing the shoplifting. Research statistics regarding the gender and age of those most often involved in shoplifting.
6. Read newspapers and consumer publications for news on product recalls, or research product recalls in a particular industry. What are some steps manufacturers take to ensure that vital information about a recall is communicated to its customers? What are the manufacturers' obligations to its customers? Does the consumer have the responsibility to stay informed? How can both the manufacturer and the consumer exercise their rights and responsibilities regarding product recalls? Contact a trade organization for specific information. Names and addresses of trade organizations are listed in the *Directory of National Trade and Professional Associations of the United States.* Check with your school or local librarian for this reference book.

PART FIVE

Your Shopping Decisions

Shopping for Food and Clothing 14

Overview: In Chapter 14, students examine a wide range of alternatives available to satisfy food and clothing wants and use the basic consumer decision-making process in making choices.

OBJECTIVES

This chapter will help you to:

1. Plan your diet to meet your nutritional needs.
2. Decide what food to buy after checking labels for nutritional information, grades, dates, and prices.
3. Plan to fill your wardrobe needs.
4. Buy clothes after considering fiber, care, fit, and construction.
5. Substitute resources to get food in the way that best satisfies you.

The supermarket was very crowded one Saturday—so crowded that Adam and Louis almost didn't see each other as they passed near the meat counter.

"Hey, what are you doing here on a sunny Saturday?" asked Adam, surprised to see his friend there with a cart full of groceries.

Louis laughed. "Now that football season's over, I do the shopping for our family every week."

"Really?" said Adam. "This is my first time here. My mom and dad both have the flu, and I'm trying to help out."

"You look a little confused," said Louis. "Having trouble choosing what to get?"

Adam grinned and shook his head. "You know, it's not as easy as those commercials make it look! I'm supposed to get steak, but there are so many kinds, and the prices are pretty different. Eye steak, chuck steak, sirloin, T-bone, Porterhouse—where's the plain old steak? How do I know which one to get?"

"Which one does your family like and what's your budget?" asked Louis. "And how many people will be eating it and how will it be cooked? Once you know that, picking which steak is easy."

"You're a big help," sighed Adam. "Now I'm really confused."

Louis suggested, "Maybe you should talk to the store's meat manager or the butcher. Either one of them could probably help. Better yet, why don't you buy some chicken?"

"Don't worry—I have to buy chicken, too," said Adam, looking more dismayed. "And that's worse! Do I want legs or thighs or a whole chicken? I wish flu season was over!"

Critical Thinking : What personal needs, other than basic subsistence, are met through food and clothing?

Historic Illustration: During the early days of our country's settlement, individuals had fewer food-related decisions to make. The type of meat they ate for dinner depended on the day's hunt. Their choice of vegetables depended on what they were able to grow, to store, or to gather.

CERTAIN BASIC NEEDS —our primary wants—must be satisfied for us to survive. We must have food, clothing, housing, and transportation. All of us don't satisfy these needs in the same way, but all of us must satisfy them somehow.

Figure 14.1 shows how the federal government estimates that low-, middle-, and high-income families divide their spending among the basic needs. Of course, these numbers are averages—individuals and families vary considerably. You may have special dietary needs that require you to spend more on food. A friend who is concerned with appearance may spend more than the average on clothing. Everybody, though, has to spend in all four categories. In this chapter we offer some hints on buying food and clothing. In the next chapter you'll learn how to shop for housing and transportation.

To help meet these basic expenses, you can use the *basic consumer* method:

Step 1. *Plan your purchases,* choosing which needs to satisfy and how to do so using the fewest resources.

Step 2. *Get information* about what to buy, so that you'll know what your options are and the costs and benefits of each.

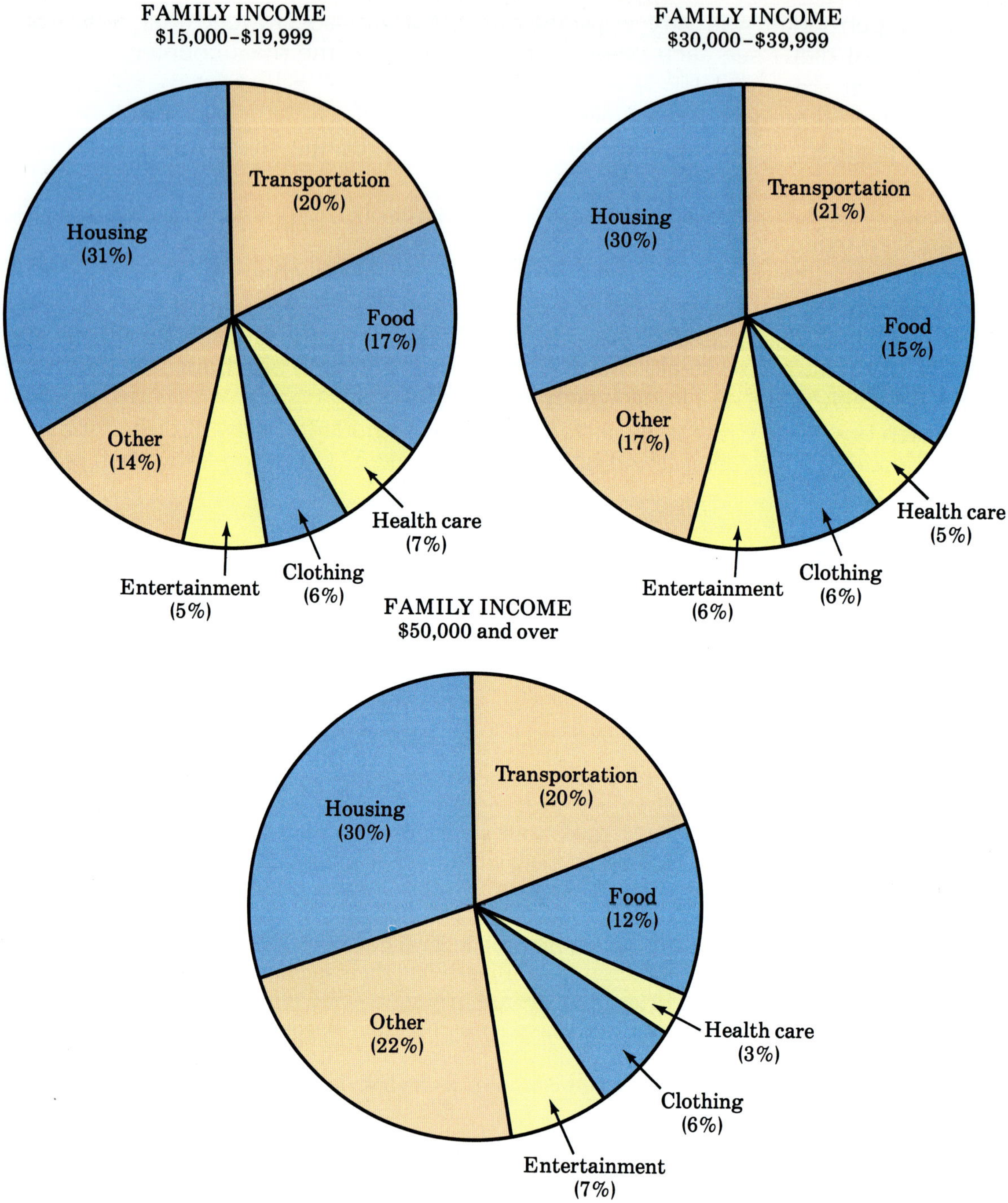

Source: Bureau of Labor Statistics

Figure 14.1 How Families Divide Their Spending Among the Basic Consumer Areas

Step 3. *Comparison shop,* checking out different sellers.
Step 4. *Determine how to pay* for the purchase, whether to use cash or credit or savings.
Step 5. *Make the purchase*—and if you've done a good job with steps 1 through 4, you'll make the best choice for you.

Math Activity: Use the pie charts on page 230 as the basis for enhancing students' math skills.

You can use all these steps in buying the basics, although the amount of time spent on each step varies with what you're buying. For example, getting information about the nutritional value and preparation of food is quite important. You usually don't have to think about shopping for credit to pay for food, though. On the other hand, when it comes to buying a new car, credit terms — how to pay — are very important.

Expansion: Our food-purchasing decisions involve several filters such as: (1) family preferences; (2) general nutrition requirements; (3) special needs of family members; (4) food availability; and (5) costs of alternatives.

Of course, making a purchase isn't the only way to satisfy a basic need. Use all your resources. You can use your resources to get food in other ways—grow your own, process raw foods yourself by canning or freezing, or go to a restaurant. This practice of substituting less costly alternatives applies to the other basic categories, too. For example, some people make their own clothes or recondition their old ones. Substitution is discussed more fully in the last section of this chapter.

SHOPPING FOR FOOD

Food involves all of our personal resources. We spend time, money, and skill to get and prepare the food, which gives us the energy we need to survive. In this section, you'll learn how to plan for the food you need and decide which types or brands of food to buy.

Activity: Encourage students to conduct a survey in your school to determine understanding about their nutrition needs. Publicize the results in the school newspaper.

Plan What Food You Want

Planning to buy food involves three stages: considering our nutritional needs, creating menus to satisfy those needs and our preferences, and making shopping lists.

Food Planning Considers Nutritional Needs Eating enough to satisfy the appetite isn't enough for health. Diet must provide **nutrients,** *the substances the body needs in order to stay healthy and to grow.* Nutrients, essential to all living cells, are the basis of *good nutrition.* People need the following basic nutrients:

Critical Thinking: Why would some food stores deduct double the value of coupons from the purchase price?

- **Protein**—*compounds that are needed for the growth and repair of body tissue.* Good sources of protein include meat, fish, eggs, milk, and dried beans.
- **Carbohydrates**—*starches and sugars that supply the body with quick energy and fiber to aid digestion.* Fruits and vegetables, breads, potatoes, and rice are good sources.
- **Fats**—*energy-rich compounds that carry vitamins and insulate body organs.* Fats are present in meats, butter, whole milk, and vegetable oil.
- **Vitamins**—*substances needed to prevent disease and regulate many body functions.* These are found in most raw foods and are added to many processed foods.

- **Minerals**—*elements needed to maintain the body's acid balance and fluid levels and to perform other important roles.* Good sources are green leafy vegetables, seafood, breads and cereals, and liver.
- **Water** *makes up most of the body's weight, transports nutrients and wastes, and is contained in the body fluids.* Water is supplied by all fluids in a diet and by fruits and vegetables that contain large amounts of water.

Critical Thinking: How do the diets of North Americans compare with individuals around the world? What affects the type of foods we eat?

The government has determined *how much of each nutrient a person should have each day.* This is called the U.S. **Recommended Daily Allowance,** or U.S. **RDA.** The U.S. RDA varies according to a person's age and sex. Table 14.1 shows the U.S. RDA for males and females in two age groups—the complete U.S. RDA chart covers all ages. U.S. RDA figures are revised periodically as researchers learn more about nutrition.

World Economy: In the 1980s the diets of more than 60 percent of the population in both Asia and Africa contained less than the minimum caloric requirements. In addition, less than a third of the population in LDCs had access to clean water.

Food Planning Includes Making Menus By eating the amounts of nutrients suggested in the U.S. RDA charts, you can keep your body healthy, but how can you be sure to eat the right amounts of food? Plan menus for all your daily meals to guarantee that you have a **balanced diet.** This is *a daily intake of the foods you need to stay healthy and strong.*

Having a balanced diet doesn't mean you have to measure how many milligrams of vitamin C you eat each day. An easier way of ensuring a balanced diet is to plan menus using the basic food groups, shown in Table 14.2. Each group includes many different foods, so there's plenty of variety. These food groups provide the basic nutrients.

Some of the foods we eat belong to a fifth group made up of fats and sweets. This group includes vegetable oils, butter, margarine, sugar, and candy. These foods provide fatty acids and low levels of vitamins, minerals, and protein.

Discussion: Discuss nutritional needs for different age groups, sexes, and people with special needs. Why do these needs differ?

While all the foods shown in Table 14.2 are good for you, it isn't a good idea to eat too much of one thing. Too much red meat isn't good for you, for instance. Vary your protein by choosing from the other sources—poultry, fish, eggs, and beans. Be especially careful with foods in the fats and sweets group—they provide calories, but few nutrients.

Table 14.1 U.S. Recommended Daily Dietary Allowances[a]

								Minerals	
	Age	**Protein (g)**	**Vitamin A (RE)**	**Vitamin C (mg)**	**Thiamine (mg)**	**Riboflavin (mg)**	**Niacin (mg)**	**Calcium (mg)**	**Iron (mg)**
Males	15–18	56	1000	60	1.4	1.7	18	1200	18
	19–22	56	1000	60	1.5	1.7	19	800	10
Females	15–18	46	800	60	1.1	1.3	14	1200	18
	19–22	44	800	60	1.1	1.3	14	800	18

[a] The allowances are meant to provide for individual variations among most normal persons as they live in the United States under usual environmental stresses. Diets should be based on a variety of common foods in order to provide other nutrients for which human requirements have been less well defined. The full chart gives the U.S. RDA for other age groups as well.

Source: National Academy of Sciences—National Research Council

Activity: Require each of your students to plan menus for their family for one week. Make sure that the menus are well balanced, include a variety of foods, and fit within the family's budget. Students will prepare a shopping list for their menus.

Emphasize: Shopping with a list is very beneficial. Without one, you will be more likely to buy something on impulse.

Discuss: Discuss which foods would most likely be bought fresh, canned, frozen, and already prepared. What other factors could influence your decision?

Table 14.2 Menus Should Include Foods from the Basic Food Groups

Food Group	Number of Servings per Day	Includes	Provides
Fruits and vegetables	4	Citrus, melon, berries, tomatoes, other fruits Leafy green, dark green, yellow vegetables	Vitamins A and C Fiber Minerals
Breads and cereals	4	Breads, cereals, pastas, especially whole-grain	B vitamins Iron Protein
Milk and cheese	2–4	Milk, yogurt, cheese, ice cream	Calcium Vitamins Protein
Meat, poultry, fish, and beans	2	Beef, veal, lamb, pork Chicken, turkey, duck, eggs Fish, shellfish Beans, peas, nuts	Protein Minerals Vitamins

Planning menus can also help to balance a budget. By knowing what foods you'll be eating at each meal and sticking to the plan, you can control your food costs. Menus help you buy only the food you've planned for. By planning carefully, you can be sure to include items that give value for the money.

A final consideration in making a menu is to include a variety of foods that you enjoy. This is just as important as having a balanced diet and a balanced budget. Buy healthful foods that you like—you can benefit from good nutrition only if you eat the food. If you like a food that costs more than a similar food from the same group, allow for that extra expense by saving money on another food that you care less about. You can spend a little more to buy chicken breast, for instance, if you save a little by buying a cheaper cut of beef.

Planning Ends with Making a List The final stage of planning to buy food is making a shopping list, the buying plan you'll take to the store. Following the list helps you remember everything you need and avoid things you don't. Base the list on the menus you've planned. Take these factors into account:

- *Packaging*—do you want to buy the item raw, canned, frozen, or already prepared? Fully prepared foods cost more; raw foods may take more time to prepare. Remember that some types of packaging can be recycled.
- *Quantity*—do you want enough for one meal or more than one meal? How many people will be served?
- *Availability*—is the item seasonal, making it cheaper when in season but unavailable or more costly at other times of the year?
- *Storage*—how long can the item be kept? Must it be refrigerated or frozen?
- *Price*—are there any special sales? Can you use coupons?

Deciding What to Buy: Learning about Foods

Even with a shopping list, you still have many decisions to make at the store. Most processed foods have labels that help in making these choices. The labels contain information about the item's nutritional value, grade, freshness, and price.

Nutritional labels are required by the government if the food has had nutrients added to it—like enriched bread—or if ads for the food claim it is nutritious. Some manufacturers who are not required to include these labels do so by choice. Figure 14.2 shows a sample nutritional label.

Meat, poultry, eggs, milk, dairy products, fruits, and vegetables are all graded by the United States Department of Agriculture (USDA). **Grades** are *quality categories for food based on taste, appearance, size, and age.* Prime grade is a more expensive cut of meat than Choice grade. The USDA also inspects meat and other foods for wholesomeness—deciding whether the

Critical Thinking: Less than 20 percent of the food coupons distributed in the United States are ever redeemed. If a larger quantity were redeemed, would this affect the overall price of these food items?

Math Exercise: Examine each of the following pairs and decide which would be less expensive: (1) 1 lb. of cereal for $1.49, or 12 oz. of cereal for $1.22; (2) six rolls of toilet paper for $0.89, or eight rolls for $1.10; (3) 1 lb. of boneless chicken breasts for $4.30, or 1 lb. of chicken breasts with bone and skin for $4.20.

Note: Labels define the producer's idea of a serving size. This may be somewhat misleading if you do not read the label carefully. For example, the can of tuna contains 1.9 cups of tuna. If you assume that one person eats the entire can, then all of the amounts claimed would change since these amounts are based on the can's 1.9 servings.

OceanFresh

Tuna

packed by Delicious Seafoods, Inc.

Nutrition Information

Serving size—1 cup (incl. liq.)
Serving per container—1.9

Calories	250	Carbohydrates	0 gm.
Protein	50 gm.	Fat	4 gm.
Sodium	275 mgm.		

Percentage of U.S. Recommended Daily Allowance (U.S. RDA)

Protein	110%	Calcium	*
Vitamin A	*	Iron	4%
Vitamin C	*	Vitamin E	10%
Thiamine	4%	Vitamin B^{6}	45%
Riboflavin	6%	Vitamin B^{12}	50%
Niacin	120%		

*contains less than 2 percent of U.S. RDA for this nutrient

Ingredients: solid white tuna, water, salt

Figure 14.2 What Shoppers Can Learn from a Nutritional Label

Figure 14.3 Sample Grade and Inspection Marks

food is healthful and whether it was produced under clean conditions. The USDA inspection stamp is required by law for meat sent across state lines to be sold. Figure 14.3 shows several kinds of grade and inspection marks. This grading system helps you to choose the appropriate grade for the type of dish you want to prepare. For instance, you wouldn't need the Prime grade of beef to make a stew. The Choice grade, which is cheaper, would be just fine.

Perishable foods have dates printed on their packages. **Open dating** is *a system of stamping a calendar date on a food package that indicates the last day on which the product should be sold or used in order to ensure quality or freshness.* Two dates are important:

- *Pull date* gives the last day on which an item should be sold. It allows time for home storage and use.
- *Expiration date* is the last day by which the product should be used.

Buying products near their pull dates can save money — they may be marked down for quick sale. Be sure then to use them before they spoil. Remember that if the product has been mishandled by the producer or the consumer, the dates may no longer apply.

The sizes and prices of grocery products vary widely. One way to compare different brands is to check the **unit price.** This is *the price of an item in terms of a certain unit of measure.* For instance, one can of tuna may contain four ounces of fish and cost $1.00. Another might have ten ounces and cost $2.35. Which is the better buy? With unit pricing, you can look at the shelf and see the price per pound of each can. The first costs $4.00 a pound; the second costs $3.76 a pound.

Deciding How Much to Pay

Consumers can save money on food in four ways:

- Buying house brands or generic products. These no-name or no-frills items offer similar quality for a lot less money than national brands.
- Buying cheaper meats, cheaper cuts of meat, or less expensive meat substitutes and extenders.
- Buying convenience foods that cost less—like concentrated orange juice—and avoiding those that don't.

Research: The grading standard for beef has been revised; lean beef is now considered USDA Choice. Have students research the old and new standards for "Choice" designation and analyze why these changes were made.

Discussion: Many times a product merely has a date. How do you know which date is given? How accurate is this assurance of quality?

Explain: Shelf pricing became popular in the 1970s. The store places a card on the shelf with the item price as well as the unit price. In turn, items were not individually marked. The cashier registers the price of the item through a machine that reads the UPC. This system allows for easier and more rapid price changes and faster check out of grocery items.

Shoppers can use unit-price labels to compare the prices of packages of different quantity.

Illustrate: Discuss other methods for saving on the food bill.

- Using coupons and noting which stores offer double value for them. Use coupons carefully. Sometimes one brand still costs more than another even with the coupon.

Explain: Using coupons can save money. However, the amount saved will vary depending on how much time and effort is required for redemption.

Remember, though, that you may want to make a trade-off between cost and preference. Don't skimp on the things you really like. Save money on something else that you don't care about as much.

There's one other way to save money on food—handle it properly. Store food in the way that will keep it freshest and tastiest. Refrigerate food that may go bad and freeze what won't be used for a while. Be sure to prepare the food before it spoils. These cautions save money and avoid wasting good food.

SHOPPING FOR CLOTHES

Note: Store and prepare food properly. Mishandling of food can cause serious illness.

As a basic need, clothing is important in three ways. First, it covers our bodies and keeps us warm or cool, protecting us from extreme temperatures or rain or snow. Second, it can improve our appearance and make us feel good about ourselves and how we look to other people. Third, clothing is used as a uniform for certain types of jobs. Even if a specific uniform is not required, some careers call for workers to dress in a certain way. Businesspeople, for example, often wear suits. Construction workers need more rugged clothes.

For all of these reasons, buying clothing—like buying food—requires us to plan, gather information, and choose what, where, and when to buy.

Illustrate: John's job required that he attend four to eight black-tie functions a year. After five years of renting ill-fitting tuxedos, at $80 per rental, John decided to buy his own tux. This purchase was not tax deductible even though John claimed that it was a uniform required by his job. The IRS does not allow a deduction for clothing that could be used for personal use, claiming John's tuxedo was a personal clothing purchase that John would use outside of business. Two years ago John resigned from his job; since that time the tuxedo has not been taken out of its bag and worn. Was John correct, or was the IRS? Does it matter?

Plan What Clothing You Need

Start planning your clothing needs by taking stock of the clothes you already own. Use four factors to determine what clothing you need:

- *Intended use*—you need different kinds of clothes to wear to work, to play a sport, or to go to a formal dance.
- *Flexibility*—look for clothes that can be mixed and matched into several outfits, avoiding both fad clothes that will become out of date and clothes suitable for only one season. Of course, you will need some seasonal items, like coats, gloves, boots, or swimsuits.
- *Style*—we all want to wear the clothes that look best on us. Sometimes a certain style can change our whole appearance. A heavy person would not want to wear tight-fitting clothing. Clothes with vertical lines, however, might make him look slimmer. A very tall person would look shorter if she wore a wide belt, but vertical stripes would make her seem taller.
- *Color*—hair, eye, or skin color can be set off by color in clothing. Redheads often wear green because it contrasts nicely with their hair. Blue eyes seem even bluer next to blue clothes. Clothing color can also make someone seem heavier or thinner—darker colors have a slimming effect, for example.

After considering these factors and looking into your closets and drawers, you should be able to decide what clothing you need to fill out your wardrobe.

Getting Information on Fibers and Their Care

Part of deciding what clothing to buy is finding out what a garment is made of. **Fibers** are the *hairlike strands of material that are woven together to make cloth.* Two kinds of fiber are used for clothes – natural and manufactured.

Discuss: Discuss the different types of clothing required during a person's **life cycle**. Do these clothing needs change? Be sure and include work, leisure, and sports needs.

Natural fibers, including cotton, wool, silk, and linen, are derived from plants and animals. Cotton is a natural plant fiber that is soft and strong and has many uses. Wool is made from the fleece of lamb or sheep. It is warm and resists wrinkling. Silk is the fiber excreted by silkworms as they build cocoons. Because it isn't very rugged, silk is more of a luxury fabric. Linen is made from the flax plant and is rough and uneven in texture. It is cool and comfortable.

In general, natural fibers are durable, comfortable, and good looking. On the other hand, cotton and linen tend to wrinkle, and wool and silk require professional dry cleaning. Natural fibers vary greatly in price, so the purpose for which the garment is to be worn is important. Some silk dresses, for instance, are fragile and costly—they may not be the best for everyday wear.

Discuss: Invite an image consultant or shopping consultant to discuss clothing with your students.

Manufactured fibers are found in a wide variety, but the most common are acetate, acrylic, nylon, polyester, and rayon. Acetate looks like silk and is used

Illustrate: Bring clothing manufactured from different fibers to class. Include manufactured fibers, natural fibers, and blends.

Expand: In the 1920s, Bakelite, the first of the synthetic plastics, was invented. The rapid evolution of synthetic fabrics followed: vinyl, 1928; acrylics, 1936; polyester, 1940; and nylon, 1940.

Expand: In 1938, DuPont announced the development of a silk hosiery substitute, nylon. This product was knit into stockings and finally sold to the general public on May 15, 1940 after an enormous public-relations campaign. The first day of sales saw long lines of women queued up waiting to buy nylon hose. First-year sales of this product were over three million dozen pairs.

Critical Thinking: During World War II silk and rubber were obtained from far eastern countries with whom we were fighting. Therefore, substitutes had to be found or invented. What would happen if oil were not available today?

in taffeta, satin, crepe, and brocade. Acrylic is much like wool and resists wrinkles. Nylon is light and strong and has many uses. Polyester is used in most easy-care clothing and is often blended with cotton. Rayon is cheap and strong and combines easily with other fibers.

The manufactured fibers vary greatly in their features. Some are very strong and others wash and dry easily. They also range in price, but they are generally cheaper than natural fibers. The main drawback of these fibers is that they don't "breathe" as natural fibers do. This can make them uncomfortable in hot weather.

Many garments are made from a blend of natural and manufactured fibers. This combines the virtues of both. For instance, a shirt made of cotton and polyester can be wrinkle free and easy to wash, yet strong and comfortable.

Several laws protect consumers by requiring clothing labels to give certain information. The Wool Products Labeling Act of 1940 requires the label to say by percentage what type of fibers are present in clothes containing wool. The Fur Products Labeling Acts, passed in 1951, says that a label must state the English name of the type of animal the fur came from, what country it came from, and whether the garment includes fur that was damaged, dyed, or bleached, or was made from scraps. The Textile Fiber Products Identification Act, passed in 1958 and later amended, requires manufacturers to label the percentages of the different fibers in a garment. The

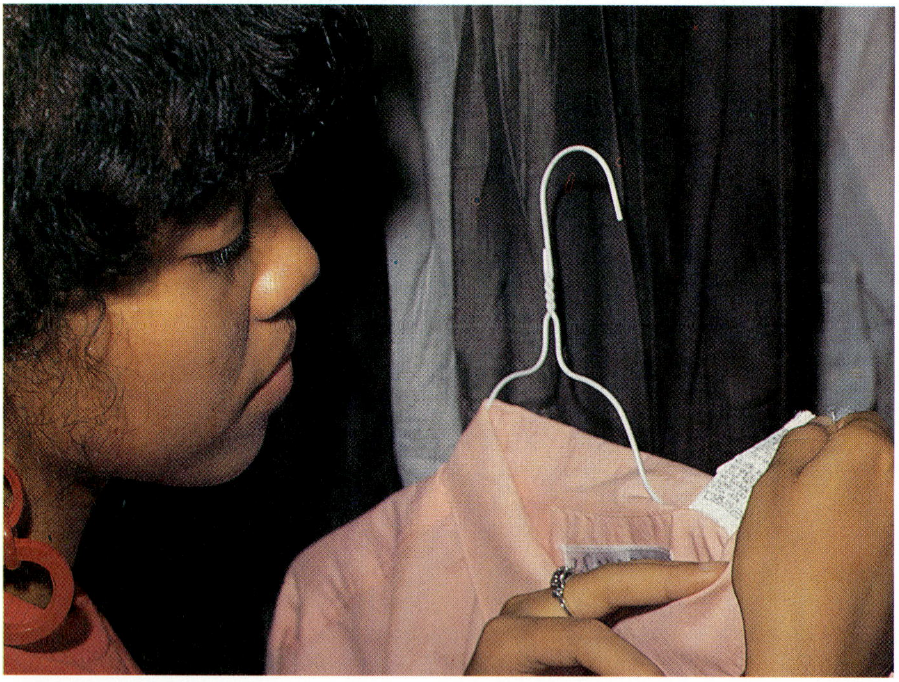

Federal law requires garment labels to state fiber content and care instructions.

Flammable Fabrics Act, first passed in 1953 and amended twice, establishes flammability standards for clothes. Since 1972, the Federal Trade Commission has required labels to include care instructions. Look for these labels when shopping, and follow the instructions carefully when cleaning your clothes.

Discussion: Invite a home economics teacher to discuss the construction of clothing. The teacher can advise students regarding what to look for in a garment.

Explain: Home sewing has declined for several reasons, but the most important are: (1) the availability of moderately priced, high-quality retail clothing; and (2) the higher opportunity cost of dual-income families.

Illustration: For years, surveys showed that consumers did not tear off the tags from pillows or mattresses. Early tags warned not to tear them off, and people were basically very law abiding. Today the tags warn that they are to be torn off only by the consumer, thus eliminating the confusion.

Deciding What to Buy: Fit and Construction

No garment, no matter how attractive, is right for you unless it fits. The only way to tell if it fits is to try it on. Try these tests:

- *Comfort*—a stylish shoe or garment is no bargain if you do not feel comfortable in it.
- *Tightness or looseness*—sizes can vary from manufacturer to manufacturer, so try clothes on even if they're your usual size.
- *Roominess at stress points*—move about, bend, sit down, and raise your arms above your head to test a garment for binding or twisting.
- *Attractiveness*—many garments look great on the rack, but because of the cut or pattern may not be right for you.

Also check the store's policy on alterations, if any are needed. Is there a charge for adjustments? If so, consider whether you can alter the garment yourself. By substituting your own time and skills, you may be able to save money. Of course, having the store do alterations saves time—decide which resource you'd rather use.

The **construction** of clothing is a sign of its quality. *How well clothing is put together shows us how good it will look and how long it will last.* Check these points:

- *Finishing*—make sure stripes and plaids match.
- *Stitching*—look for straight seams and small stitches; check also for loose threads.
- *Fasteners*—be sure all buttons, zippers, hooks, and snaps are secure, with no loose threads.
- *Hems*—examine all hems to see that they are fully finished and straight.
- *Linings*—make sure these are well sewn, with small, tight stitches.
- *Fabric construction*—clothing made from closely woven fabrics is usually more durable than clothing made from looser woven fabrics.

YOU INTERACT WITH THE ECONOMY: RESOURCE MANAGERS USE SUBSTITUTION

If someone asked you how the food got to your table, you would probably say that you bought it at the supermarket, cooked it on the stove, and served it. We tend to forget about the earlier stages in the food marketing system. In this section we'll look at all four stages and see how participants at each stage use the principle of substitution.

By substituting more efficient machines for human labor, U.S. farmers have achieved huge harvests.

Review: Earlier we mentioned the go-between and the costs and value these stages added. The food system is an excellent example of this.

Focus: The American food system is an excellent example of a market system. Each farmer is a firm; therefore, with the large number of firms in this market no one farmer is able to affect the price or market supply of the product.

These are the four stages of the food marketing system:

1. *Production*—growing the food or raising the livestock—is done by farmers and ranchers.
2. *Processing*—putting the food in edible form—is performed by canners or meatpackers, among others.
3. *Distribution*—getting the food to the consumer—is usually done by wholesalers and retailers.
4. *Consumption*—buying, preparing, and eating the food—is the stage consumers are most familiar with.

Participants at each stage use resources. Producers use seeds, human labor, fertilizer, and land, for example. Consumers use time, money, and skills. When one resource becomes too expensive, it is necessary to substitute a cheaper one. For the citrus farmer, human labor to plant, pick, and pack oranges can be very expensive. The farmer might decide to buy a machine to pick oranges faster and cheaper. The same sort of thing can happen at the processing stage. New technology can make orange juice more cheaply and quickly than hiring hundreds of people to squeeze oranges.

Behind all of these decisions is the same incentive—profit. The farmer and the juice packager all want to use the least resources to bring in the most income.

Emphasize: The concept of substitution is a very powerful one. Spend some time on the substitution of capital for labor when the relative price of labor goes up.

Critical Thinking: In 1990 the U.S.S.R. experienced food shortages in the cities. At the same time, there was food available in the rural areas and no indication of production failures. How could this occur?

Expand: The substitution of capital for labor is an excellent example of price as a signal. When the price of lettuce pickers rises high enough relative to the substitute capital equipment, it is a signal to the farmer to buy the appropriate equipment and use less labor. Thus, attempts to better the conditions of migrant labor may mean that capital will be substituted for this labor, and migrants will be out of a job.

List and Discuss: List the ways consumers can substitute their resources for others.

The profit incentive—and substitution—also helps these participants decide what food to grow, process, and sell. The farmer will grow grapefruits instead of oranges if grapefruit juice is more in demand and will make more money. The processor that makes the juice might decide to buy from another farmer who grows juicier oranges for a lower price. A grocery store chain might choose to sell a new kind of product, like frozen orange juice popsicles, if it seems likely to make money.

Consumers can substitute one way of using their resources for another, too. Each uses different amounts of resources:

- You can grow your own food. This may be inexpensive but costs much time, effort, and skill.
- You can buy raw food and process it yourself by canning or freezing. This is a little more costly and also takes much time and energy and some skill. Processing is a limited choice—you can only buy when the food is available and not all food can be processed safely.
- You can buy and cook prepared foods. This costs more in money but less in time and energy and requires varying amounts of skill.
- You can buy food ready to eat in a restaurant. This is the most expensive in terms of money but often the cheapest in time, and it doesn't take any skill!

How you choose to get your food affects the other participants in the food system. Consumers are buying more convenience foods and eating out more often, especially at fast-food restaurants. This is mostly because there are more families in which the husband and wife both work. These families have more money, but less time to spend getting food than in the past. So food producers, processors, and distributors have all changed the way they use their resources to meet these new consumer needs.

Wise shopping practices will save you money.

SUMMARY

- Consumers satisfy their needs for food and clothing by using the basic consumer method.
- Planning to buy food includes considering nutritional needs and preferences to create menus and then making a shopping list.
- A balanced diet includes all of the nutrients—protein, carbohydrates, vitamins, minerals, and water. An easy way of doing so is to include foods from the basic food groups—fruits and vegetables; breads and cereals; milk and cheese; and meat, poultry, fish, and beans.
- Check the labels on food products for nutritional value, grades, dates, and prices.
- To decide what clothing to buy, look at the intended use, flexibility, style, and color.
- Get information about the natural and manufactured fibers in clothing, and follow the care instructions on garment labels.
- Try on all clothing and check for proper fit—consider comfort, tightness or looseness, roominess at stress points, and attractiveness.
- Check garments for construction—inspect cut, stitching, fasteners, hems, and linings.
- Participants in the first three stages of the food marketing system—producers, processors, and distributors—use substitution when a cheaper resource can be used to increase profits and efficiency. Consumers also use substitution in choosing how to obtain food.

Key Terms

Match each of the following terms with the definition that most suits it.

balanced diet	fibers	open dating	U.S. Recommended Daily Allowance
carbohydrates	grades	protein	vitamins
construction	minerals	unit price	water
fats	nutrients		

a. the substances the body needs in order to stay healthy and to grow

b. compounds that are needed for the growth and repair of body tissue

c. starches and sugars that supply the body with quick energy and fiber to aid digestion

d. energy-rich compounds that carry vitamins and insulate body organs

e. substances needed to prevent diseases and regulate many body functions

f. elements needed to maintain the body's acid balance and fluid levels and to perform other important roles

g. the liquid that makes up most of the body's weight, transports nutrients and wastes, and is contained in the body fluids

h. a daily intake of the foods needed to stay healthy and strong

i. the government's quality categories for food based on taste, appearance, size, and age

j. a system of stamping a calendar date on a food package that indicates the last day on which the product should be sold or used in order to ensure quality or freshness

k. the price of an item in terms of a certain unit of measure

l. the hairlike strands of material that are woven together to make cloth

m. how well clothing is put together, which shows how good it will look and how long it will last

n. how much of each nutrient a person should have each day, which varies according to each person's age and sex

Review Questions

1. What are the four basic consumer needs? What method can you follow to satisfy these needs?
2. What nutrients do you need to consider when planning menus? How do you know how much of each nutrient you need?
3. How can you ensure that your menus provide a balanced diet?
4. Why should you be familiar with different grades of foods like meats and poultry?
5. What are the pull date and the expiration date? Why is open dating important?
6. How can unit pricing show you the best buy? Give an example.
7. What four factors help you determine your wardrobe needs?
8. What are the two kinds of fibers used in garments? Name three examples of each.
9. What are the two qualities you should look for when trying on clothes? How do you look for them?
10. What are the four stages in the food marketing system? What principle do participants at these stages use when a resource becomes too costly?
11. What options do consumers have in getting food?

Projects

1. Make a menu for all the meals you will eat next weekend. First, base the menus on foods that you like. Then check the menus against the five basic food groups to see whether they provide a balanced diet. Now, assume that your food budget is $10.00 a day. Make a shopping list for the weekend. Find out how much the foods on your menu would cost at your local stores. Can you stay within your budget and still have healthy foods that you like? Can you bring down the cost by comparison shopping? Can you save by subtituting raw foods that you cook yourself for processed foods?
2. More and more people are recycling in an effort to save the environment. Locate a recycling center in your area. Write down the center's name, address, and telephone number. Call the center—or do library research—to find out which types of packaging can be recycled and which cannot. Suggest one alternative to each of the types of packaging that cannot be recycled. Then find out what the recycled materials are used for. Present this information in a short written report. Prepare a poster that can be displayed in your school or community to inform others of the need for and benefits of recycling.
3. Comparison shop for a piece of clothing—a pair of jeans, jogging shoes, or a sweater, for instance. Go to at least three stores and note how different products compare in cost, fiber, fit, and construction. Is there a connection between price and quality? Is one product a good buy? Afterwards, tell the class what you found.
4. The food growing and distribution system in the United States has improved tremendously over the years. Now the average farmer grows enough food to feed about 77 people. What brought about this revolution in agriculture? Do some library research to find out what changes have occurred in the twentieth century in any one of these areas: food varieties that yield more crops, fertilizer, irrigation, efficient farm equipment, food processing, or food distribution.

Shopping for Housing and Transportation

15

Overview: Just as there are various types of housing, there are also various ways of paying for housing. Chapter 15 examines housing and transportation and suggests alternatives for both.

OBJECTIVES

This chapter will help you to:

1. Analyze your housing needs and decide whether to rent or buy.
2. Compare housing alternatives to meet your needs.
3. Protect your rights in leases and mortgages.
4. Plan to fill your transportation needs.
5. Shop for a new or used car that meets your needs at the right price.
6. Consider energy use in your future spending.

Jane and Denise both have full-time jobs, and they plan to continue their educations by taking night courses at the local community college. They are planning to move out of their parents' homes and get a place of their own. After a day of house-hunting separately, they met to see what each had found.

"I've got the perfect place," said Denise. "Two bedrooms, a nice, new kitchen—and there's a pool and clubhouse in the complex."

"Sounds terrific," said Jane, "but rent must be high, isn't it?"

"Well, it's a bit higher than we wanted—but it also comes furnished and it's near public transportation, so we won't need a car. What do you think?"

"Listen to what I found, first," Jane replied. "I looked near campus, thinking that if we're taking classes and using the library at night, we'd want to be nearby."

"That makes sense," Denise said.

"Anyway, I found an apartment upstairs in a two-family house. The owners live downstairs and take care of the place. It's got the two bedrooms we wanted, and we get to use the yard."

"What about getting to work?" Denise asked.

"It's right on the bus line, so that's no problem. And the rent is what we budgeted for—though we will need furniture. What do *you* think?"

"I don't know," said Denise. "I'd sure like that pool. They both sound good, but how will we choose?"

Discuss: What should Jane and Denise do next? How should they reconcile their different priorities?

Critical Thinking: Analyze the changes in housing needs in an individual's life cycle.

JANE AND DENISE have to make some choices about two basic consumer needs—housing and transportation. These, along with food and clothing, play central roles in our lives, and we spend a lot of our money, time, energy, and skills in getting them.

To satisfy these needs, we use the basic consumer method: planning to buy, getting information about the alternatives, comparison shopping to decide when and where to buy, deciding how to pay, and making the purchase. In this chapter, you'll learn how to apply this method to get the best housing and transportation for the least cost.

SHOPPING FOR HOUSING

There are lots of things to think about when looking for a place to live—size, location, cost, and much more. With careful planning, complete information, and systematic decision making, you can make satisfying choices.

Emphasize: Each individual must prioritize housing criteria. Problems arise when these priorities are not addressed in family decisions.

Planning Requires Analyzing Your Housing Needs

People determine what they want in housing by answering three sets of questions:

- *How many rooms and what type of rooms do you want?* To answer these questions, consider how many people will use the housing and what their

Discuss: Invite a realtor to class to discuss housing values, additional costs associated with more rooms, lot size, etc.

Critical Thinking: Debate the costs and benefits of renting housing vs. buying housing.

Explain: A lease for housing stipulates the length of time (usually a year) that a specific amount will be paid in order to inhabit the housing. Leases contain other conditions and, when signed by both parties, are binding. The lease is a legal contract and should be scrutinized carefully.

Extension: Do renters pay taxes? If utilities are included in the rent, does that mean that renters do not pay anything for the utilities they use? Do renters pay for upkeep? All these expenses are figured into the rental amount. If property taxes increase, then the next lease will include a higher rent payment. If the water, electricity, or sewage fees increase, so will next year's rent.

ages are. Will the number change in the near future? Do any special interests create the need for special rooms? An amateur photographer, for instance, might want space for a darkroom.

- *What type of housing do you want?* Is an old house preferable to a new one? A single-family home to an attached or multifamily home? Finally, what else do you want—a yard, basement, porch, or parking?
- *What kind of location do you want?* Would you like to live in an urban, suburban, or rural area? Of course, this decision is influenced by the convenience of an area—how close is it to where you work or go to school, to stores and recreational areas? What is the neighborhood like? What kind of taxes do residents of the locality pay?

Deciding Whether to Rent or Buy

The two ways to get housing are renting and buying. In renting, a **tenant** *agrees to pay a certain amount every month, called rent, for the right to live in a dwelling.* The rent is paid to a **landlord,** *the owner of property being rented.* The other option is to buy a home. A buyer often pays *a percentage of the price at the time of purchase,* which is called a **down payment.** The rest of the price is borrowed in a loan called a *mortgage* and paid back over many years.

Whether rented or bought, housing requires three kinds of expenses:

1. *Immediate out-of-pocket expenses*—a landlord may require that a security deposit and a month's rent be paid in advance. Buyers usually need to make a down payment and must meet closing costs and installation fees.
2. *Monthly expenses*—every month you pay rent or the mortgage payment, property taxes if you own your home, utility bills for phone service, electricity and gas, and insurance. Another monthly expense to consider is the cost to get to and from work or school to your home.
3. *Upkeep*—some expenses occur regularly, but less often than every month. Most of these affect homeowners and not renters. They include such costs as lawn care and repairs.

Once you've developed a budget to plan how to meet these expenses, you can decide which is better for you—renting or buying.

The Advantages of Renting People often start out by renting. Its advantages are the disadvantages of buying:

- *Smaller initial cash expense*—the security deposit and advance rent equal only one or two months' rent, but the down payment required for buying is generally larger.
- *Less financial risk*—as with any investment, a house may lose value over time or cannot be sold; renters avoid that risk.
- *Greater freedom to move*—renters can move when the rental agreement ends, which is often after a year. Owners must sell the house when moving, which may take time.
- *Less responsibility for upkeep*—renters don't need to worry about the work or cost of repairs or maintenance, which are the landlord's responsibility.

Analyze the Issue: **Rent control** restricts the amount that rent can be increased. For example, if rent on an apartment is $500, and rent control stipulates that rent can be increased no more than the increase in cost of living, then a 5% inflation rate would mean next year's rent could be no more than $525. Rent control laws benefit people who live in rent-controlled apartments. However, it has negative effects on the housing market. Anything that places a price ceiling below the market price means that the quantity of rental units supplied will be less than the quantity demanded.

Discuss: One of the most common disagreements between landlords and renters involves the quality and quantity of maintenance. The lease should stipulate each side's responsibility for damage and general maintenance as well as consequences for not complying with these conditions.

Many people prefer renting to buying because it gives them greater mobility.

Advantages of Buying The financial advantages of buying a home often increase over time. The advantages of buying point out the disadvantages of renting:

- *Possible investment income*—a house often gains value over time.
- *Equity*—**equity** means *ownership*. Mortgage payments can be partly recovered when the home is sold, but rental payments cannot.
- *Taxes*—homeowners can deduct interest and property tax payments from their federal income tax. Renters get no federal tax breaks, although some states allow them to deduct their rent.
- *Fixed payments*—mortgage payments stay the same or increase at an agreed-upon rate. Renters have less control over rent increases.
- *Freedom to remodel or redecorate*—homeowners can do whatever they want—within reason—with their building or land.

Getting Information on Available Housing

There are several sources of information on housing. Family, friends, coworkers, and schoolmates are all useful. For-rent and for-sale signs on buildings and houses are helpful, as are bulletin boards in shops and malls. Probably the source of housing information most often used, though, is the

Table 15.1 An Explanation of Some Terms Found in Housing Ads

	Rooms		
studio	One-room apartment (plus bathroom)	G&E	Gas and electric
BR	Bedroom	utils	Heat, gas, hot water, and electricity
bath	Bathroom	a/c	Air conditioning
kit	Kitchen	w/w	Wall-to-wall carpeting
din	Dining room	pkg	Parking space
bsmt	Basement	furn	Rent includes furniture
		unfurn	Unfurnished
	Features		**Conditions of Rental**
wsh/dryer	Washing machine and clothes dryer	immed occup	Available for rental immediately
d/w	Dishwasher	sec dep	Security deposit required
d/d	Dishwasher and garbage disposal	refs	Landlord wishes to see references for renter
hw	Hot water		
incl ht	Rent includes heat		
unhtd	Rent doesn't include heat		
h/hw	Rent includes heat and hot water		

Illustrate: It has been said that a house is a hole in the ground into which you pour money. Upkeep requires repainting, replacing tile or carpet, landscaping, refinishing floors, etc. These expenses should be estimated and included in the cost of buying a house.

Critical Thinking: What would happen if the IRS eliminated the mortgage payment deduction?

newspaper classified section. Table 15.1 explains some of the terms found in these ads.

Real estate agents have listings of places for sale and for rent. However, agencies charge a commission on a sale, which is added to the sale price. They also may charge a fee to renters.

Comparing Housing Alternatives

Housing comes in many forms. Most kinds can be purchased or rented, depending on what the owner wants to do.

- *Single home*—one-family homes are usually owned, but can also be rented.
- *Duplex or triplex*—a house with two or three living units. Sometimes the duplex can be bought; sometimes the owner lives in one unit and rents the others.
- *Multifamily dwelling*—this is a property with several units. Such a building is usually rented, but may be bought. Some are high rises.
- *Town home*—a single-family home that shares at least one wall with another single-family home and is usually more than one story.
- *Mobile home*—this small, movable house is usually bought. Mobile homes are often restricted to trailer parks by city zoning laws.

A **condominium** is *a form of ownership in which a person owns a living unit and a share of common property.* The buyer pays for his or her unit's upkeep and mortgage. Each owner also pays a monthly fee to maintain the common property, which is owned by an association of all owners. A **cooperative** is *a form of ownership in which each owner owns a percentage of the building.* The buyer buys shares in the corporation that owns the building to become a tenant-shareholder and lives in one of the units. The corporation still owns the apartment, but the tenant-shareholder is responsible for the unit. The tenant pays the cooperative to cover the mortgage costs and the upkeep of public areas. Tax laws may treat these forms differently.

Clarify: Newspaper ads are probably the most common method of locating rental housing. Home sales are to be handled through real estate agents. These agents handle advertising, sales, and closing responsibilities although you should hire a lawyer to review all legal documents on your behalf.

Discussion: Invite a local realtor to class to discuss the costs and benefits of the different forms of housing in your area. In urban areas, where land is scarce you will find multi-family dwellings are more common. In rural areas, single-family dwellings are more common.

Research: Ask students to research state law regarding condominiums or cooperatives. Are there legal differences regarding ownership?

Discuss: Laws prohibit discrimination based on race, religion, children, or marital status. Examine the laws based on your local area and discuss the reason for, and effects of, this prohibition.

Always inspect housing before agreeing to rent or buy it. Are the appliances included?

Once you've found housing that you're interested in, you must inspect the house, apartment, or unit. Never rent or buy without checking the condition of the housing personally. When you inspect housing, look for the following:

- Cleanliness and condition—is the property well maintained or run down? Is the structure sound?
- Size, number, and layout of rooms—does the layout match what you want and what furnishings you have?
- Energy use—how much does it cost to heat or cool the property at the temperature you want? Are there storm doors, storm windows, and insulation?
- Plumbing, electrical outlets, and appliances—does the plumbing work well? Are appliances in good order?
- Storage space—is enough closet and other storage space available?
- Outside features, like yard, patio, and parking—are these extras worth the extra money? Are they in good condition?
- Security systems in apartment buildings, or doors, windows, and locks in houses—will your belongings be safe?

In addition to your own inspection, you can talk to the previous owner or renter to ask how the furnace works or whether the landlord makes needed repairs promptly. You can also hire a specialist to inspect certain parts of the property, like the heating system.

Legalities of Renting and Buying

Getting housing involves complex legal contracts. Consumers must know their rights to act wisely.

Discuss: Why should both renters and buyers inspect housing carefully?

Activity: Ask students to design their ideal apartment. Include room layout, storage, amenities, security, and appliances.

Activity: Ask students to design the ideal housing they would like to own. Include location, condition, price, etc. Compare this with units currently listed for sale.

Explain: What causes deteriorated urban housing? Although there are many reasons, emphasize: (1) the exodus of prosperous families into the suburbs leaving urban areas inhabited by families without the resources to maintain property values; (2) declining urban property values with increasing costs of government services; (3) decreasing quantity of housing stock, declining in value and quality but not necessarily in price; and (4) rent controls.

Leases Tenants and landlords each have rights and responsibilities. Landlords have the obligation of providing a fit place for living. The housing must be safe and healthful and all equipment the landlord provides must be in good working condition. Landlords are responsible for making any repairs required by normal wear. In return, landlords have the right to receive the rent on time and to have the property cared for by tenants. Tenants have to maintain the property carefully and pay for any repairs caused by their actions.

Tenants and landlords often sign a **lease,** *a legal contract setting forth the terms of a rental.* By signing a year's lease, a tenant promises to reside at the property for a specified length of time, usually a year. If a tenant leaves early, the landlord can take legal action. A lease includes the following information:

- The names of the landlord and tenants.
- A description of the property being rented and its contents—the number of rooms and the appliances the landlord will provide.
- The beginning and ending dates of the lease, and any conditions for its renewal. The lease should also tell how soon one party must notify the other before a change can take effect. Many leases require 30 days' notice for the tenant to leave or for the landlord to raise the rent. Some require as many as 90 days.
- The amount of the security deposit and monthly rent and the dates they are due.
- Any promises either party makes regarding the upkeep of the property or its use.
- Any restrictions on either party. For instance, the tenant may promise not to keep pets.

The lease may prohibit the tenant from subletting. **Subletting** is *the tenant's renting all or part of a property to another person.* Tenants may want to sublet if their plans change and they need to leave before the lease ends. Unless the lease specifies otherwise, tenants have the right to sublet. The tenant who signs the lease — *not* the person who sublets — is still responsible for paying rent on time and keeping the place in good condition.

Some rentals have no leases. That gives a tenant more freedom to move, but both parties have less protection. The landlord can raise the rent more often than is possible with a lease, and each party's rights and responsibilities are not clearly spelled out.

Mortgages Complicated legal matters are also involved in buying a house. A buyer must have a **title search,** which is *an investigation into the deed to a property to establish a clear claim to ownership.* Then there's the **closing,** *the final step of the sale.* At the closing, legal details like title insurance, taxes, and service charges are arranged. These matters may cost the buyer extra money. People buying houses are wise to have a lawyer for advice. Although this is an extra expense, the help is valuable.

Focus: Since the majority of your students will, at some time, lease a unit, discussion of the contents of a lease is extremely important. The lease stipulates the responsibilities of the tenant as well as the tenant's rights.

Definition: **Subletting** is an important consideration in rental units. Rental units are often shared by more than one person. Even though all parties sign the lease, agreeing to split the rental cost, most leases are written stipulating that all parties are responsible for the entire rental amount. Thus, if any roommate fails to fulfill his or her responsibilities, the remaining roommates incur that additional cost. Often it is necessary to find a new roommate.

Most people need to get a mortgage to finance the purchase of a home. A **mortgage** is *a creditor's claim against real property bought with the money borrowed.* The property is security against the money borrowed, which is paid back in monthly payments for 25 to 30 years. If the buyer fails to meet the monthly payments, the lender can take possession of the property. There are several types of mortgages. The most common are:

- *Standard, fixed-rate mortgage* (often called a *conventional* mortgage)—the interest rate is set and monthly payments do not change for the length of the loan.
- *Variable-rate mortgage*—the interest rate is reevaluated and monthly payments may change at set times.
- *Graduated-payment mortgage*—monthly payments increase up to a fixed level in five or six years.

These different types of mortgages allow buyers and lenders to adjust to changes in interest rates. Of course, different lenders offer different mortgage rates. Home buyers must use their shopping skills to find the best terms.

The federal government helps some home buyers:

- The Federal Housing Administration (FHA) insures the private lender up to $67,500 for qualified home loans, making it easier to get a mortgage. These loans have a low down payment.
- The Veteran's Administration (VA) will guarantee a mortgage by a private lender to a qualified veteran. The VA doesn't require a down payment, but the lender may. Interest rates are set by the VA.

Some lenders use points to increase the rate on these low-interest loans. A **point** is *a charge of 1 percent of the amount of a mortgage.* If the government-approved rate is, say, 10 percent, but the rate for conventional loans is 12 percent, the lender may add two points to bring the lower rate up to the market price. Sometimes points are charged to cover the lender's paperwork and must be paid at the time of the sale.

Some buyers *assume* an existing mortgage from the seller. Not all states allow this. This can be quite helpful to the buyer if mortgage interest rates are rising. By assuming a mortgage that was taken out when rates were lower, the buyer can get a loan at lower rates. Sometimes sellers become lenders and offer the mortgages themselves.

SHOPPING FOR TRANSPORTATION

Obviously, transportation is affected by where we live. Like housing, the basic need for transportation requires us to plan and make careful choices. In this section you'll learn how to fill your transportation needs.

Planning to Fill Your Transportation Needs

Discussion: Invite a lawyer who specializes in mortgages and home buying to speak to the class.

Activity: Contact local banks, savings and loans, the VA, and the FHA to determine any changes in interest rates in your area over the past five years. Obtain rates for fixed-rate, variable-rate, and graduated-payment mortgages. Have students graph these interest rates over the five-year period.

Critical Thinking: Analyze requirements to obtain a mortgage considering different creditors and interest rates. Be sure to include: (1) down payment requirements; (2) income requirements; (3) changing payment amounts; and (4) any other requirements.

Activity: While surveying interest rate fluctuations, also determine whether or not points have been charged and, if so, the amount of points charged.

In planning for transportation, we need to consider many factors. The first choice is whether to use public or private methods.

Public mass transit systems are *local transportation methods regulated and sometimes run by government agencies for the public at a low cost to the user.* They are provided as a public service for all people who want to use them. Private transportation is obtained by individuals. It includes such methods as cars, motorcycles, bicycles, and walking, as well as carpools and taxis and private bus and train companies.

In choosing between public and private transit, consider the following factors:

- *Cost*—public transit is relatively cheap for each user. The cost of private means varies—cars require a large initial expense and fairly high operating costs, while walking is free.
- *Convenience and reliability*—the convenience and reliability of public transit vary, depending on where you live, though it does save on parking. Most private means are probably more convenient and reliable, however.
- *Time*—the importance of this factor depends on where you live and how far you need to go. Sometimes public transit is faster, but not always.
- *Flexibility*—here, private transit has the advantage over public transit. You can come and go when and where you please, without worrying about schedules or getting to and from bus stops and train stations.

There are many alternatives to buying a car, even for commuters.

Demonstration: Elasticity can be demonstrated with rubber bands. A thin rubber band (quantity demanded) can be influenced by pressure (price). The response is elastic. Using a thick (less responsive) rubber band, the band (quantity demanded) requires more pressure (higher prices) in order to be influenced.

Critical Thinking: A large U.S. city has an urban transit system with increasing costs and ridership which have steadily declined. Several years ago a regional 1 per cent sales tax was approved in order to subsidize the costs of this transit system. Recently, because of increased costs and decreased rider revenue, the transit system proposed a 25 per cent rate increase. Using a supply-and-demand graph, show how this rate increase will affect demand. Why is it important for the transit company to be aware of the elasticity of demand?

Discussion: What are the differences between public and private transportation?

- *Safety*—traffic safety and accident rates can be a concern for drivers, but public transit systems can't guarantee safety for people traveling alone and at night.
- *Social costs*—drivers need to think about how they add to gasoline use and to pollution. Users of public methods should consider the cost to the public of operating the system.

If we decide on private means of transportation, we have many options to choose from. Table 15.2 lists them and their pros and cons. The rest of this section will focus on buying cars because they are a big investment and buying them can be complicated.

Comparison Shop for New and Used Cars

Next to buying a house, buying a car is the second largest purchase most people make. Whether you're buying a new or used car, comparison shop carefully to get the best car at the best price. Remember to gather information, using objective sources like *Consumer Reports* and *Consumers' Research* that test different cars.

Deciding Which New Car to Buy There are so many sizes, makes, and models of cars that we should be able to find one for any purpose. Choosing a size requires us to evaluate our need for space, engine power, luxury, and economy. The larger the car, the more room it provides. Larger cars often have a more powerful engine than smaller cars, and some have more luxury features. Larger cars also cost more to buy and operate.

Once you've decided what size car you want, you need to compare models. To

Table 15.2 Comparing Alternative Forms of Private Transportation

Method	Advantages	Disadvantages
Walking	Free; no maintenance; good exercise	Not good for long distances or bad weather; takes time
Bicycle	Cheap; low maintenance; good exercise; faster than walking	Possibly dangerous in heavy traffic; not good for long distances or bad weather; takes time; little storage
Motorcycle	Usually cheaper than car; fast; can go long distances	Not as safe as a car; not good in bad weather; carries few people; little storage; needs insurance, gas, maintenance
Carpool	Fast; can go long distances; reduces operating costs by sharing with others	Not as flexible as one-car driver; may not lower ownership costs
Car rental	Fast; can go long distances; cheaper than buying for short-term use	Only temporary; no equity; needs insurance, gas
Car purchase	Fast; can go long distances; carries more passengers; equity; storage space	High cost; needs insurance, gasoline, maintenance

do so, you can use seven factors.

- *Mileage*—all makers state the estimated average miles per gallon (MPG) of gasoline for each model. While actual gas use probably won't match these figures, these estimates do help in comparing models.
- *Safety record*—has the model passed the federal government's crash tests? If not, it may be unsafe if an accident occurs. Also, what is the collision and injury record of the car—some cars suffer more damage in an accident than others.
- *Handling and braking*—how well does the car hold to turns or make emergency maneuvers? How quickly does it stop? Do its brakes perform more poorly over time?
- *Warranty and maintenance record*—does the model have a good repair record? Are parts easy to find when you need them or are they rarely stocked? Does it offer good warranty protection?
- *Operating costs*—expenses vary from model to model. A sporty car will probably cost more to insure than a sedan. One with air conditioning may need more servicing than one without.
- *Comfort and room*—how comfortable will driver and passengers feel? How much storage space does the car have?
- *Options*—an inexpensive compact can cost as much as a luxury model if it's loaded with options. These are *extra items added to a vehicle's basic model, which increase its cost.* Costly options include automatic transmission, power brakes and steering, and air conditioning. Some options can increase the value of the car if it is resold later. Remember that some options, like stereo, can be installed inexpensively by the owner.

You can get information to compare models two ways. First, check government and consumer publications that print the results of objective tests. Second, and very important, test drive the cars you're interested in. As with clothes, the ultimate test for a car is how it fits. Test drive the car on hills, around curves, in traffic, and at highway speeds. Back up, park, and ride over some bumps. Listen for noise and vibrations. Judge how the car handles and brakes, how it accelerates, and how smooth and quiet the ride is.

Deciding What Used Car to Buy Used cars can be a low-cost means of transportation. They can also create tremendous problems if the buyer doesn't shop cautiously. Remember to take your time and weigh your decision carefully. A used car that breaks down soon after it's bought provides no transportation. To shop for a used car, follow four steps.

First, decide what size car you want and what extras you're interested in. Of course, used cars offer buyers less choice on options—they're already equipped. Still, know which extras you want and which you don't. Consumer and car publications can help you find a reliable used car—they say what cars have a good history of reliability or have created problems for their owners. Find out if a car was ever recalled for faulty manufacture.

Of course, this information is general. To evaluate a particular car, take the second step—examine it carefully. Check the following:

- *Exterior*—look for signs of wear, rust, or body work done after an accident.

Expansion: Some would argue that public transportation benefits users of private as well as public transportation. Public transit makes private transportation easier and faster by taking automobiles off the highway (each of the public transportation riders could be an additional automobile).

Discussion: Spend time discussing transportation alternatives. Encourage students to prioritize the advantages depending on their individual needs.

Emphasize: Stress the need to obtain information on autos before beginning comparison shopping. This information will help you evaluate the sales pitch, ask the right questions, and provide additional information regarding price and quality.

Expand: Research indicates that size also influences safety. As long as there are both large and small cars on the highway, it appears that large cars will be safer. One of the features you trade off for fuel efficiency is weight and protection.

- *Interior*—be sure all equipment works properly—failure to perform may endanger your safety. Look for signs of extra wear or poor maintenance.
- *Engine*—run the engine and test how it starts, accelerates, and idles. Listen for noises and watch for stalling.
- *Lights*—test all the lights—these safety features are important.

Note: The average MPG for autos should be given for both city and rural driving. Ask your students why and how these conditions should affect the MPG of automobiles.

Next is the third step—test drive the car. Test driving is just as important on a used car as on a new one, if not more so. *Never* buy a used car if the seller won't let you test it.

The fourth step is to ask a trusted mechanic to look at the car and evaluate it. Sometimes major problems—in the transmission, for example—cannot be spotted except by an expert. Ask the mechanic what needs fixing and how much it will cost. If you're still interested in this car, use this information later to negotiate for a good price.

Extension: Find out what government studies and publications are required to be available in the automobile dealership's showroom. Discuss how these studies can be used in making a decision.

Deciding Where to Buy a Car

Car buyers also have to decide where to buy a car. New cars can be bought only at new car dealers, but shoppers have many dealers to choose from. There may even be more than one dealer nearby who sells a particular make of car.

Used car buyers have more sellers to choose from. New car dealers may also sell used models, and some businesses sell only used cars. Consumers can also buy from each other, using notices of car sales in local newspapers or on bulletin boards. Used cars can be bought at police auctions, when stolen goods that have not been reclaimed are sold to the public. Newspaper notices state the date and location of these auctions. Finally, some car rental companies sell their cars after they're done renting them.

Critical Thinking: Sometimes autos can be less expensive if purchased through a shopping service or in a larger city. However, you eliminate any local dealer contact or direct responsibility. How important is trading with a local dealer? How much would you be willing to pay for this?

Shop for Price

Whoever you buy a car from, shop carefully for price. Car prices vary quite a bit from seller to seller, even for the same model and year. By doing some research away from the dealer's pressure, you can save money by bargaining for a better price.

The law requires dealers to show consumers *the manufacturer's suggested selling price for a new car,* which is called the **sticker price.** Many cars, though, are sold for less than that. Check in the library for consumer publications that print the dealer's cost for the car and any options you want. Add these prices up and then add the cost of shipping the car from the manufacturer to the dealer—this is shown on the sticker. The result is the total dealer cost—the price the dealer paid for the car. It will be less than the sticker price. The difference between the dealer cost and the sticker price is the bargaining range. Within that area, you and the dealer can negotiate to find a price satisfactory to both. Table 15.3 shows the sticker price and dealer cost for a fictional car and some options for it.

Explain: Keep in mind that used-car dealers are required to attest to the condition of a car and are responsible for the accuracy of this verification. Individuals selling a used car are not held to this standard.

Smart shoppers look for two other ways of cutting the price of a new car. First, many car owners trade in their old car to the dealer in return for a

Table 15.3 Sample Comparison of Sticker Price to Dealer's Cost for a New Car

	Dealer	List
Panther (4-door hatch)	$ 9377	$10485
Panther LE	10574	11845
Options		
5-speed manual transmission	Included	Included
3-speed automatic transmission	469	552
4-speed automatic transmission	549	646
Turbo	595	700
Air conditioning	696	819
Power brakes	Included	Included
Power steering	Included	Included
AM/FM stereo	Included	Included
AM/FM stereo with cassette	176	207
All-season tires	63	74
Rear window defogger	132	155
Sunroof	348	409
Air bag	Included	Included

Emphasize: When shopping for a used car, bring someone who knows about autos. This person will be able to identify potential problems you might not foresee and will be able to examine the auto for you rather than your depending on the information provided by the seller.

List: Ask students to develop a list of sources for new and used cars in your area. Check if the sources listed in the text are available in your town or nearby.

Explain: The automobile is one of the few goods where Americans expect to negotiate the price. This sometimes puts individuals at a disadvantage because of their lack of practice at negotiation. Spend some class time examining the sticker price and the dealer cost of a given car as well as possible negotiation points.

Critical Thinking: What happens to used-car sales when the economy is booming? What happens during a recession?

lower price on the new model. A buyer planning to trade in a car should get an estimate of its worth from a different dealer first. Remember that you might get more by selling the car yourself. Second, buy when sales are slow. Automakers may offer rebates during a slow sales period.

Buyers of used cars can also shop for price. Once you have a car in mind, find the year and model in the National Automobile Dealers Association (NADA) *Official Used Car Guide.* That book publishes the average price of all models and years of used cars sold throughout the country in the previous month. The book also shows the add-on cost of key extras like automatic transmission and air conditioning. Of course, these figures are averages. A reasonable price for any car depends on its condition. A well-maintained model with few miles will sell for more; a cheaper car may need costly repairs. Still, you can use these averages as a guide. By taking into account the car's condition, you can determine how much you think the car is worth. There is usually room for bargaining between the buyer and the seller of a used car.

Once you've settled on a car and price, you still may need to shop for financing. Since cars are fairly costly, many people take loans to buy one. Car loans can be obtained from financial institutions or from the lending companies set up by automakers or dealers. Sometimes automakers offer special low rates to stimulate sales.

Another factor to consider when shopping for a car is the terms of the warranty. A warranty may protect you if problems arise after you have owned your vehicle for a period of time or if your vehicle turns out to be a lemon. All states have laws known as lemon laws. While these laws vary from state to state, each establishes what makes a car a lemon. The purpose of these laws is to enable the buyer of a lemon to take legal action against a manufacturer or dealer for a refund or replacement vehicle.

Insulating the home can help reduce the use of energy in the summer as well as in the winter.

YOU INTERACT WITH THE ECONOMY: CONSUMER DECISIONS AFFECT ENERGY USE

Explain: Examine the amount you could expect to receive if you sold your existing auto yourself, rather than using it as a trade-in. Many times, the dealer will offer a generous trade-in which merely reflects the range that he or she would be willing to bargain anyway.

Today, energy costs are a number-one topic. It's not clear just how the costs of energy will change, but the low prices of past years will probably not come back in the near future. Satisfying our energy needs requires us to manage our personal resources of time and money. Because energy is a national resource we also must take into account how our individual choices affect the whole economy.

People use energy primarily in two areas: transportation and housing. Each of us can do a lot to reduce the amount of energy we use. You can use your car less by planning better. You can combine trips rather than making many separate trips; carpool to school or work, cutting down on the number of vehicles on the road; use public transit, which helps conserve energy; and buy more fuel-efficient models and maintain cars properly so they perform at their best.

Consumers can take many steps to save energy in the home, too:

- Maintain higher summer temperatures and lower winter ones.
- See that the home is well insulated by using storm windows and by closing out drafts.

- Keep heating and cooling systems properly maintained.
- Close off unused rooms rather than using energy to heat or cool them.

Discussion: How might landlords encourage their renters to conserve energy?

Critical Thinking: Ask students to explore different sources of energy. Compare the costs and benefits of each source as well as the current knowledge regarding their use.

You can also cut your energy use in the daily operation of the home:

- Be efficient in cooking, using the stove or oven wisely.
- Turn off unnecessary lights and appliances.
- Use less hot water by washing dishes or clothes in large batches, attaching flow restrictors to shower heads, and heating water to a lower temperature.
- When shopping for new appliances, buy energy-efficient brands.

Our individual decisions affect the state of the economy as a whole. Wise consumers help put their own and the nation's resources to their best use.

SUMMARY

- As with food and clothing, satisfying the need for housing and transportation can be made easier by using the basic consumer method.
- Analyze housing needs by considering the number of rooms desired, the type of housing desired, and the location desired.
- Housing has three kinds of costs: immediate expenses, monthly expenses, and upkeep.
- People obtain housing by renting or buying. Renting generally offers greater freedom, while buying provides financial benefits. We must weigh the pros and cons of each method in light of our resources and wants.
- To get information on housing, turn to family, friends, coworkers, schoolmates, signs advertising rent or sale, and real estate agents. The most popular source is probably the classified ads in the newspaper.
- Housing alternatives include single-family homes, multifamily homes, town homes, and mobile homes. Most types of housing can be bought or rented.
- Before agreeing to buy or rent a property, always inspect the premises.
- Landlords and tenants both have rights and responsibilities. Many times these are spelled out in a rental agreement called a lease. Read a lease carefully before signing it.
- To buy a home, people usually take out a mortgage, which is a long-term loan. Different types of mortgages exist to cover changes in interest rates. Home buyers often get the help of a lawyer.
- Consumers choose between public and private transportation methods by analyzing each option's cost, convenience and reliability, time, flexibility, and safety.
- In shopping for a new car, consumers decide what size car they want and then compare different models' mileage, safety, handling and braking, warranty and maintenance record, operating costs, and options. Lemon laws protect consumers from being stuck with defective vehicles.
- In buying a used car, consumers gather information on good values, carefully inspect the car for signs of wear or accidents, test drive it, and ask a mechanic to look the car over.
- New cars are bought from dealers. Used cars are bought from dealers, from other consumers, at auctions, or from car-rental companies.

- In buying either a new or used car, consumers should do some research and bargain for a good price. Many cars are paid for with borrowed money—consumers must also shop for good credit terms.
- Individual choices about housing and transportation affect our nation's use of energy, a costly resource. Wise buying and wise use of our cars, homes, and appliances can save us—and the country as a whole—money.

Key Terms

Match each of the following terms with the definition that most suits it.

closing	equity	options	subletting
condominium	landlord	point	tenant
cooperative	lease	public mass transit systems	title search
down payment	mortgage	sticker price	

a. local transportation methods regulated and sometimes run by government agencies for the public at a low cost to the user
b. ownership
c. a lender's claim against real property bought with the money borrowed
d. a charge of 1 percent of the amount of a mortgage
e. a form of ownership in which a person owns a living unit and a share of common property
f. a form of ownership in which each owner owns a percentage of the building
g. an investigation into the deed to a property to establish a clear claim to ownership
h. the final step of the sale of real estate
i. a legal contract setting forth the terms of a rental
j. extra items added to a vehicle's basic model, which increase its cost
k. the owner of property being rented
l. a person who agrees to pay a certain amount every month, called *rent,* for the right to live in a dwelling
m. the manufacturer's suggested selling price for a new car
n. the tenant's renting of all or part of a property to another person
o. the percentage of an item's price that is paid at the time of the purchase when the rest is borrowed

Review Questions

1. What is the first step in planning to obtain housing?
2. What three kinds of expenses does housing require? Give an example of each type.
3. List two advantages of renting housing and of buying a house.
4. Where do consumers get information on housing?
5. What should you look for when inspecting housing?
6. Why do landlords and tenants sign a lease? What conditions are found in a lease?
7. What five factors can you use to decide between public and private transportation?
8. What factors are used to compare different models of new cars? How do you get this information?
9. What are the four steps of shopping for a used car?
10. How can you shop for the best car price?
11. What two areas of consumer spending have an impact on the nation's energy? Name four things you can do to conserve energy.

Projects

1. Using your newspaper—and any other sources you can find—make a list of available apartments or houses in your community that you feel you could reasonably afford now or in the near future. Choose places that seem right to you based on what you can gather from the ads. Be able to give reasons for your choices based on size, location, price, personal preferences, and any other relevant factors.
2. Invite a local landlord to speak to your class about tenant-landlord rights and responsibilities. Ask the landlord to explain the lease that he or she signs with tenants.
3. If you have a car of your own, list the costs of running it each month, including insurance, registration, gasoline, maintenance, parking fees, and any others. If you don't have a car, ask a family member or a friend who has one to supply you with these figures for his or hers. Compare the monthly operating costs of a car with how much alternative transportation (public transit, bike, or other) would cost you to make the same local trips. Compare what you discovered with your classmates' findings.
4. Conduct a survey on car prices. Pick one or two new or used car dealers nearby. Ask them to describe five cars they sold recently—what was the year and model, what options were included, and how much the buyer paid for the car, not including taxes and finance charges? Now go to the library and compare these prices to those listed in consumer publications or the NADA book. Tell the class what you found.
5. Make a drawing that shows the layout of your house or apartment, indicating the locations of doors, windows, stairs, heating vents, and major appliances. Indicate with a star any place where there has been an effort to improve energy efficiency. List some ideas for other such improvements.
6. Do your parents or caregivers have carpool arrangements to their jobs? Take an in-class survey of how parents get to and from work each day. Carpooling is becoming popular among people who live and work near each other. It reduces energy consumption and traffic congestion. Some employers even offer incentives for their employees who carpool. List the advantages and disadvantages of carpooling. Would you consider a carpool arrangement when you are ready to enter the world of work? How would you organize a carpool?
7. Study and clip display advertisements for apartments from the Sunday newspaper's real estate section. What conveniences and incentives are offered in newly constructed apartment complexes to convince people to rent there? Do they add to the cost of monthly rent? Prepare a bulletin board display of the ads you find and arrange them by their costs.

Shopping for Financial Services 16

Overview: Today, most people use one or more financial services. Whether you have a checking account, a credit card, or a Merrill Lynch account you are involved with financial services.

OBJECTIVES

This chapter will help you to:

1. Explain how financial, credit, and investment decisions are connected.
2. Describe the services offered by financial institutions.
3. Outline the characteristics of major types of financial institutions.
4. Comparison shop for financial services.
5. Describe how Federal Reserve policies affect you and the economy.

Connie was looking at her mail after she got home from her after-school job. "Look at this!" she cried out.

Mollie, her sister, looked up from reading the newspaper.

"What's the problem?" she asked.

"It's my bank," Connie said. "They're going to charge a service fee for savings accounts with a balance below $500—and I'm *far* below that! I already have to pay for the checking account—and now this!"

"Why don't you change banks?" Mollie asked.

"Why bother?" said Connie. "All banks charge the same fees—don't they?"

"Not at all," Mollie said. "You've got to shop for bank services just like you shop for anything else."

"Well, I don't have the time for it. Between school and the job, I can't afford to spend time bank-shopping."

"Can you afford to lose money by *not* shopping?" Mollie asked.

Illustration: Connie has found that different banks offer different services—and charge different amounts for these services.

AS CONNIE HAS LEARNED, financial institutions are competing for her business. In this chapter, you'll learn what services they offer and how those services overlap. You'll also learn about the different types of financial institutions that offer these services and how to compare them.

SHOPPING FOR FINANCIAL SERVICES

As Mollie advised her sister, to put money to its best use, you must comparison shop, just as you shop before buying a car. You need to shop for three reasons. First, financial institutions compete for your money, so you need to shop for the best one. Second, financial services are changing, so you need to keep informed. Third, financial services overlap, so you must shop for them as a package—though it isn't always wise to keep your money in only one location.

Note: An increase in alternatives brings a related increase in consumer decisions. Banking deregulation has forced banks to compete which has resulted in a wider variety of services and interest rates. Although the consumer's job has gotten more difficult, the benefits have increased.

Financial Institutions Compete for Your Money

Beginning with the banking deregulation law of 1980, the government has changed many of the rules that governed financial institutions. Because of these changes, institutions now compete eagerly for your dollars. One of their means of competition is the *benefits* they give—the interest rates and services they offer. Another is *costs*—the fees they charge for these services.

More competition helps consumers, but it means they must shop carefully. When shopping for a car, you first find the type of car that suits your needs and then shop for the best deal in price, warranty, and service. Do the same when you shop for financial services. First, decide what services you need.

Compare the costs and benefits of institutions to find the blend of services you want.

Research: Obtain summaries of the Electronic Fund Transfer Act of 1978, the Depository Institutions Deregulation and Monetary Control Act of 1980, and the Garn-St. Germain Depository Institutions Act of 1982. Trace the changes occurring in the financial services sector.

Financial Services Have Changed

Electronic banking has led to major changes in financial services. Automatic deposits and bill paying, and debit cards, have made banking easier and faster.

Another development of recent years is banking between states. In the past, banking institutions could operate only in one state or region. After the law was changed in 1980, large banks joined together to offer common services, such as linked automatic teller machines. Interstate banking helps many consumers—for instance, those who work in one state and live in another. It may also mean that large institutions will buy up smaller ones, which would reduce competition.

The Electronic Fund Transfer Act of 1978 set the rules for institutions and consumers using the new computer-aided methods of banking. The Depository Institutions Deregulation and Monetary Control Act was passed in 1980. This law removed most government restrictions on the interest and services that banking institutions could offer. The Garn-St. Germain Depository Institutions Act of 1982 took these changes even further.

Activity: Assign students to different financial institutions such as a: (1) national bank; (2) state bank; (3) savings and loan; and (4) nonbank bank (such as Sears Money Store). Ask them to gather information on the types of checking and savings accounts available, the interest rates, and other services.

Financial Services Overlap

People use money in many ways. You can spend it to buy goods and services you want or save it for the future. Money saved in a financial institution stays safe and earns interest—it grows. There's another way of making money grow—investing. To **invest** is *to use money in a way that we expect will increase its value.* Investing is taking the risk of losing some money on the chance that it will grow more than it would by saving it.

Define: In economics, **investment** is the process of producing and accumulating capital goods. The definition in the text refers to consumer investment. Articles in the business press generally refer to economic investment.

In the past, certain institutions were best for certain kinds of services. Some were used mainly for checking accounts and personal loans. Some were good for savings and home mortgage loans, others for investing. People usually knew from the service they wanted what kind of institution they would use.

Since deregulation, however, financial institutions have become more alike. Many offer a similar range of checking, credit, saving, and investing services. All compete with the interest rates they pay on savings and charge on loans.

As a result, you have many financial institutions to choose from. View your financial needs as a total package rather than as many separate items. Then shop for an institution—maybe more than one—that can best meet the needs of that package.

Although these services overlap, you need to study them separately to be able to understand them. In this chapter, you'll learn about all the financial services consumers look for. Chapter 17 will cover credit in more detail, and Chapter 18 will focus on saving and investing.

PLANNING WHAT FINANCIAL SERVICES YOU WANT

Generally, consumers want the following financial services: ways to obtain cash and pay bills, borrow money, and make investments. They also want convenience and security. Let's see what each of these services involves.

Activity: Review the financial institutions surveyed earlier. How many of these services were offered by each of the institutions?

Explain: To find out the value of a foreign currency, check the *Wall Street Journal.*

Extension: **Money Exchanges** cash checks for a fee for individuals with no bank account. The fee is usually higher than checking account fees.

Discuss: Some financial institutions offer more personal service than others. Expect to pay for this service in one way or another. It could be that you will be charged for formerly free services such as savings accounts below a minimum balance; it could be that the interest rate for loans will be higher, or the interest paid on savings will be lower.

Services for Obtaining Cash or Paying Bills

There are many different ways of getting cash and paying bills:

- *Checking accounts*—you deposit money in an institution and write checks for cash or to pay bills.
- *Special checks*—you buy cashier's checks, certified checks, or money orders to pay certain bills or traveler's checks to carry instead of cash.
- *Automatic teller machines*—you can use a special plastic card to deposit or withdraw money at a 24-hour teller machine.
- *Automatic bill paying*—you ask an institution to make certain fixed payments without writing checks.
- *Bank by phone*—you arrange with an institution to pay bills by using a push-button telephone.
- *Foreign exchange*—you *change the currency of one country into that of another*, which is called **foreign exchange.** Someone taking a trip to Mexico, for example, can ask a bank to change dollars into Mexican pesos.

Credit Services

Consumers look for many credit services:

- *Home mortgage loans*—these long-term loans enable you to buy a house.
- *Personal loans*—these short-term loans help you meet such goals as going to college or taking a trip.
- *Auto, home improvement, appliance, or furniture loans*—these medium-sized loans that run from two to five years help you buy high-priced goods and services.
- *Bank credit cards*—you can use these cards to buy goods and to get cash in an emergency.
- *Overdraft privileges on checking accounts*—you can arrange to be able to write checks for more than the balance in your checking account. This is similar to getting a short-term loan.
- *Passbook loan*—you can borrow money against the amount you have in a savings account.

These services are described in detail in Chapter 17.

Saving and Investing Services

There are many different ways to save and invest money:

- *Savings*—you can set money aside for future use by putting it in an account that earns interest or by buying United States savings bonds.
- *Stocks and bonds*—you can buy stock, becoming part owner of a business, or bonds, becoming a lender to business or government.

- *Mutual funds and investment clubs*—you can pool your money with other consumers and invest as a group.
- *Real estate and collectibles*—you can buy property or selected goods in the hopes they will grow in value.
- *Investment counseling*—you can pay someone to manage your investments or advise you.
- *Trust services*—you can create a **trust,** which is *property managed by someone for the benefit of someone else*. For example, an aunt may leave money to her niece in her will, but name an adult to manage the money until the child is old enough to do so.

These services are explained fully in Chapter 18.

Convenience Services

Some of the conveniences that people look for are:

- *Location*—you want services to be easy to reach. Look for an institution with nearby offices or one that offers banking by mail or by phone.
- *Business hours*—you want to be able to use financial services when you need them. Look for long hours, drive-in windows, and automatic teller machines.
- *Automatic teller machines*—these electronic machines, which can be used 24 hours a day, are a great convenience.

One convenience service offered by many banks is a drive-in window that has longer hours than the main office.

- *Direct deposit*—you may arrange to have your employer send paychecks directly to your account. Retired people can have their Social Security checks deposited directly.
- *Automatic transfers between accounts*—you can arrange to be able to transfer a certain amount of money from one account to another on a regular basis.
- *Bank by phone*—you can pay bills or make transactions over the phone to save time.

Critical Thinking: Several services offered by financial institutions are listed in the text. Can your students think of any other services that could draw customers? Who would be attracted by these new services? How could the services be paid for?

Security Services

Consumers want one more financial service—security. Federal and state governments offer **deposit insurance,** which *guarantees that deposits up to a certain amount will be returned to depositors if an insured institution goes out of business.* If an institution fails, depositors lose their money. If it is insured, though, these people receive the money they had in an account, up to a certain limit. A person with more money than the limit can open more than one account in order to be completely safe.

Research: Ask your students to research the history of the FDIC and the FSLIC. Highlight the problems caused by inflation in the 1960s and 1970s and the increase of bank failures in the 1980s.

Most institutions are insured, and they are required by law to post a sign in the window saying so. Table 16.1 describes the insurance plans for the four main types of institutions.

In the late 1980s, hundreds of savings and loan banks failed and government deposit insurance had to cover the losses of depositors. The losses were huge and put a great strain on already limited resources. In 1989, Congress passed a bill to restructure and strengthen the banking industry.

Most people want another security service—**safe deposit boxes.** These are *metal containers that people can rent from a financial institution for storing their valuables.* The contents are safe because only the owner can open the box. People use these boxes to store important papers like deeds and items like jewelry.

These signs in the window of a financial institution tell you if and how deposits are insured.

Activity: After surveying the rates and services of financial institutions in your area, ask students to develop a matrix using their criteria to evaluate these institutions. Then have them decide where they would open a checking and savings account.

Note: The banking deregulation law of 1980 blurred the distinction between these different financial institutions. S&Ls had begun competing directly with commercial banks; so to enable commercial banks to meet this competition, restrictions and regulations were relaxed.

Table 16.1 Deposit Insurance for the Four Main Types of Financial Institutions

Types of Institutions	Source of Insurance	Maximum Amount Insured
Commercial bank	Federal Deposit Insurance Corporation (FDIC)	$100,000
Savings and loan association	Savings Association Insurance Fund (SAIF)	$100,000
Mutual savings bank	FDIC *or* state insurance fund (maximum varies)	$100,000
Credit union	National Credit Union Administration (NCUA)	$100,000

Planning What Services You Need

Before shopping for financial services, you must decide what services you need. At the start of this chapter, Connie learned that she must rethink her banking. She still wants a checking account to cover her daily expenses and purchases. She also wants some way to save money for a car. To save time, Connie decided to ask her employer to deposit her paycheck directly into her account. She also decided she wanted an institution that had automatic teller machines near her home and her job. As for credit, Connie is thinking about applying for one or two store charge cards.

You must do what Connie did—plan the financial services you need. Make these plans while looking at financial services as a whole, instead of seeing them as separate problems.

SHOPPING FOR FINANCIAL INSTITUTIONS

People get most financial services from four main types of institutions: commercial banks, savings and loan associations, mutual savings banks, and credit unions. Consumers can also turn to several other sources.

Research: Some banks are national banks and some are state banks. Encourage students to investigate the difference between these designations.

The Four Basic Institutions

Commercial banks are *banks that have been authorized, by either the state or the federal government, to offer a full range of financial services.* They are also known as *bank and trust companies* or *community banks* and exist in all states. Most are corporations, owned by stockholders and managed for profit.

Savings and loan associations (S&Ls) are *savings institutions that used to specialize in savings accounts and home mortgages but now have a full*

Many people rent a safe deposit box from a financial institution to store their valuable possessions or important papers.

Research: Ask students to investigate the historical basis for having separate types of institutions such as commercial banks, savings and loans, and mutual savings banks. Is there a need for these differences today?

Explain: The most common trade-off considered in terms of savings is that of safety versus return. Generally, a higher return is an indication of lower safety. FDIC and FSLIC has eliminated much of the need for this consideration.

range of services. S&Ls are also known as *building and loan associations, cooperative banks, savings associations,* and *homestead banks*. S&Ls are authorized under state or federal law and are found in all states. Some are corporations, but most are owned by their members.

In the past, S&Ls offered fewer services than commercial banks. With deregulation, though, the differences between them are fewer. S&Ls now have checking accounts (including those that pay interest), time deposits, and some investments. In the past, S&Ls were allowed to pay slightly higher interest rates on savings than commercial banks, but this, too, has changed in most cases.

Mutual savings banks are *banks owned by their depositors and whose goal is to encourage savings*. Mutual savings banks are also known as *five-cents banks* and *dime savings banks*. They are found in only eighteen states and in Puerto Rico. They are organized under state laws.

Mutual savings banks provide most financial services. Like S&Ls, they used to be allowed to pay higher interest on savings accounts, but in most cases this is no longer true. Mutual banks make loans and offer checking accounts, bank credit cards, and high-interest savings accounts. In some states, they can also sell low-cost life insurance.

Credit unions are *nonprofit savings and lending cooperatives formed by people with a common bond*. The people may have the same employer, work in the same trade, belong to the same union, or live in the same area. Credit unions are found in all states. They make many types of loans, including personal and home loans at low interest. They also offer savings accounts at slightly higher rates than other institutions, but their services can be used only by members.

Note: Many commercial banks, savings and loans, and mutual savings banks offer **NOW** (negotiable order of withdrawal) accounts. NOW accounts pay interest on your savings, but also allow you to withdraw savings using a form similar to a check. These accounts may have restrictions such as a minimum amount that can be withdrawn at one time or a maximum number of withdrawals over a specified period of time

After deregulation, these institutions began to look almost the same. Still, different banks, credit unions, and S&Ls have different services at different prices. When shopping for services, check all your alternatives.

Other Sources of Financial Services

Remember to check other sources of financial services. For instance, credit can be obtained from retailers like department stores and oil companies. Finance companies offer personal loans for all sorts of purchases, and automakers help people borrow to buy new cars. The different sources of credit are discussed in detail in Chapter 17.

Savings and investment services can be found in many places, including stockbrokers, dealers in real estate and jewelry, and mutual funds. These are discussed in Chapter 18.

Checking accounts are also offered with some investments. These may require large funds to be invested, though. You can also get cash from some retail stores that cash paychecks for their customers. Money orders are sold at the post office. Traveler's checks can be bought from a number of sources, including the American Express Company and, in some states, the American Automobile Association (AAA).

EVALUATING FINANCIAL INSTITUTIONS

Critical Thinking: Why would financial institutions offer free checking only if a minimum balance is maintained in the account?

Connie first decided what financial services she wanted. Then she called and visited a few institutions and got information by reading booklets and asking questions. Now she must evaluate them for the services they offer, the interest they pay, and the fees they charge.

Connie found two institutions that were convenient—First State Bank and City Cooperative Bank. Both had branches near her home and automatic tellers near where she worked. Both had deposit insurance—Connie saw the sign in the window. Both accepted the direct deposit of paychecks. Connie liked the *quality* of services both supplied. Employees were helpful, courteous, and well informed. Now Connie had to compare the services they supplied and their costs.

She first looked at their checking accounts. Both institutions had interest-bearing checking accounts, but at both the minimum balance was $500. If the balance was below that amount, there was a service charge. Connie wouldn't be able to keep the minimum, so she looked at the regular checking accounts. First State Bank charged a fee for each check written. City Cooperative charged a fee only if the minimum balance wasn't kept, but this minimum was lower than the one for the account that paid interest. If Connie wrote many checks, a per-check fee would be costly. Since she would probably write few, the account at First State Bank seemed better.

Math Activity: Figure interest compounded daily and monthly on a deposit of $400.

Note: After a severe money panic in 1903, a commission was appointed to study the banking problems of the United States and to outline a solution. The final result of this study was the Federal Reserve Act of 1907.

Next, Connie compared savings accounts, which was more involved. Since both institutions were insured, she had to check three things: what the interest rate was, how often interest was compounded, and when her money began earning interest. Both institutions paid the same interest rate, so they seemed equal in this respect. City Cooperative compounded the interest every day, and First State did so only every month. Compounding means that interest is added to the balance so that it, too, earns interest. The more often interest is compounded, the more money savings can earn. Connie knew that daily compounding was better than monthly. She also found out when interest was calculated. First State paid interest only on the money in the account on the last day of each month. Connie knew she could earn more money at City Cooperative—it paid interest from the day she deposited money until the day she withdrew it.

Connie decided to open a regular checking account and a savings account at the City Cooperative Bank. It offered the services she wanted for the least cost. By opening both accounts there, she could apply the balance in her savings account toward the minimum required for free checking. As a result, Connie may be able to hold down the cost of financial services.

YOU INTERACT WITH THE ECONOMY: THE FEDERAL RESERVE SYSTEM

Clarify: The policy-making arm of the FED is its Board of Governors. Each of the board's seven members is appointed by the president and confirmed by the Senate. The staggered terms (one member is appointed every two years) are designed to ensure continuity and experience, while the 14-year terms are designed to divorce the board from politics and guarantee independence. The board is responsible for supervising and controlling the U.S. money and banking system.

The **Federal Reserve System,** often called the Fed, is *the federal agency that controls the nation's money supply and oversees the practices of its member banks.* The Fed is divided into twelve districts, each of which has a main reserve bank and two branches. (See Figure 16.1.) The rest of the system is made up of the 5,500 or so member banks. Let's look at the Fed's role in our economy.

The Fed Clears Interstate Checks

A check is written by a person (the *drawer*) to make funds in a financial institution (the *drawee*) payable to another person, a business, or an organization (the *payee*). The payee can cash or deposit the check at his or her own institution.

The check must then *clear.* This means the amount of the check must be subtracted from the drawer's account and added to the payee's account. If the drawee's and the payee's institutions are both in the same area, they will transfer the checks using a messenger or local *clearinghouse.* The clearinghouse collects all the checks written in one area and sends them to the correct drawee institutions. *The time it takes for a check to clear* is called the **float.** In this time, the drawer's account still contains the money, even though it has been subtracted from the checkbook balance.

Clearing checks for institutions in different states is the work of the Fed. The method is shown in Figure 16.2. In providing this service, the Fed saves institutions and depositors much time and money. Billions of checks are made out each year. Without the Fed, each local institution would spend

Expansion: Although consumers are more aware of the FED's check-clearing activities, activities which affect the country's money supply have more effect on our economy. Through the **Federal Open Market Committee (FOMC)** the system can implement policy regarding the sale and purchase of government bonds on the open market. FOMC members include the seven members of the Board of Governors plus five of the presidents of the regional Federal Reserve Banks.

Explain: The Federal Reserve Banks have three basic characteristics: (1) They are central banks. (2) They are quasi-governmental in that they have private ownership (shares of stock are owned by commercial banks in their region), but policy is set by a governmental body, the Board of Governors. They primarily serve the government and commercial banks. (3) They are bankers' banks. They accept the deposits of, and make loans to, banks and thrifts.

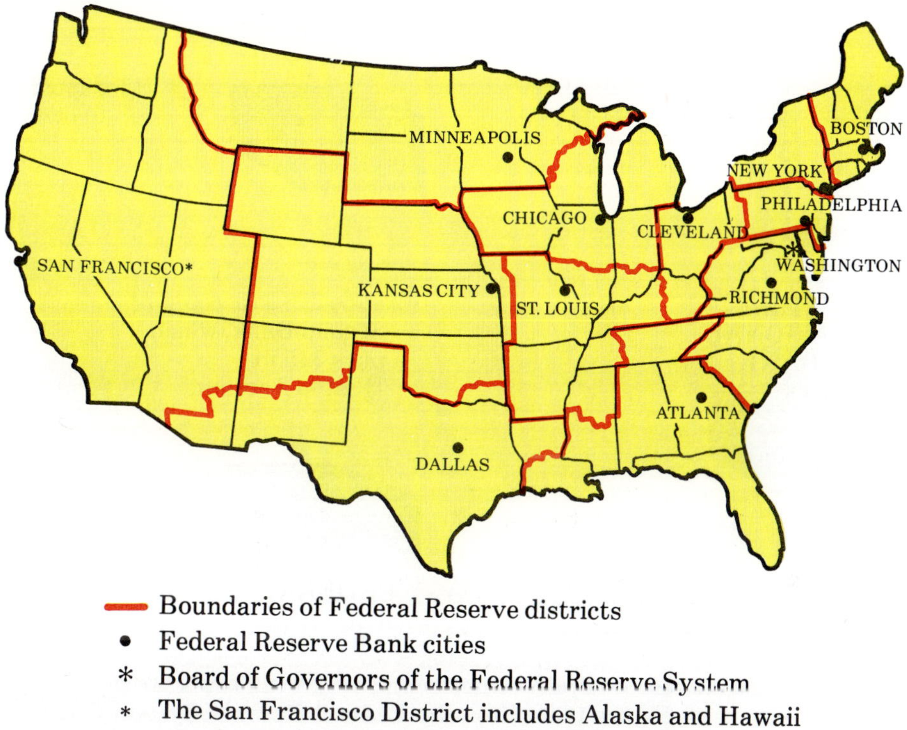

Figure 16.1 The Federal Reserve Districts and Main Banks

hundreds of dollars mailing checks to others. The cost of all this paperwork would drive up the fees these institutions charge.

The Fed Controls the Money Supply

More important, though, are the four ways the Fed can control the supply of money. The Fed can:

- Change reserve requirements
- Buy and sell government bonds
- Change the interest rate banks pay to borrow money
- Control some types of credit

A **reserve** is a *sum of money set aside by member banks that is equal to a certain percentage of their deposits.* In setting the reserve, the Fed restricts the amount of money institutions can lend—the money in reserve cannot be used for loans. In this way, the Fed can control the growth of the money supply. Let's see how this works.

If someone deposits $500, and the Fed requires a 10 percent reserve, the institution can lend only $450 of that deposit (the $500 minus $50, which is 10 percent). The money doesn't stop there. The person who borrows this $450 can put it in another institution, which can lend $405 (the $450 minus $45, which is 10 percent of the second deposit). Money continues to be created in this way, as Table 16.2 shows.

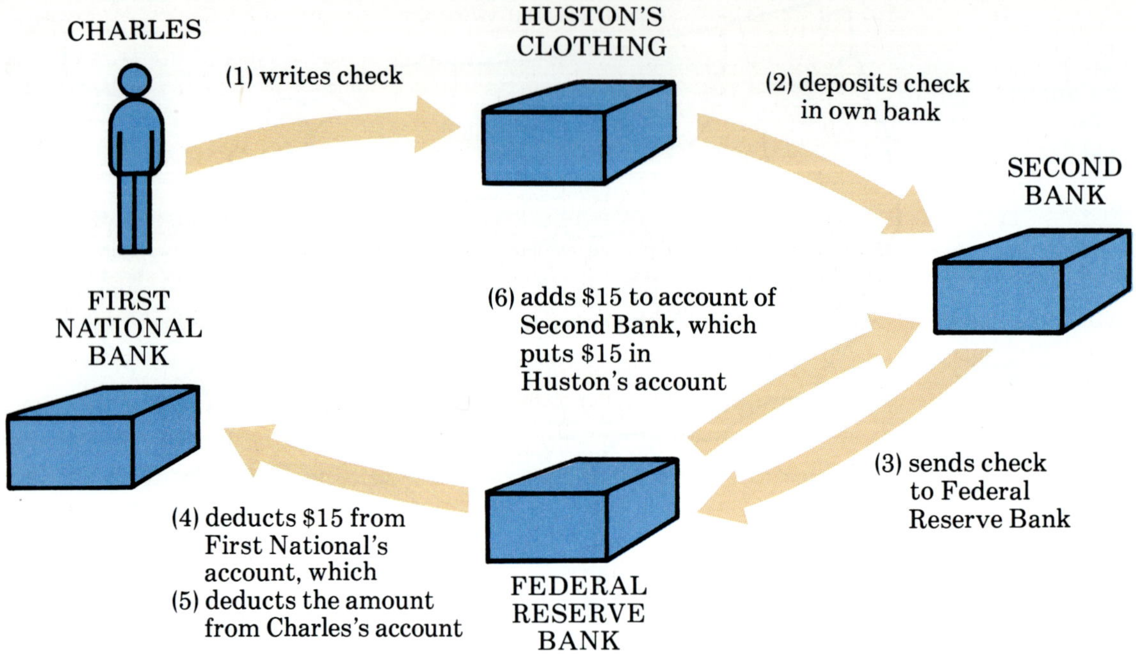

Source: Board of Governors of the Federal Reserve System

Figure 16.2 How the Federal Reserve System Clears a Check. (1) Charles, who has a checking account at the First National Bank, writes a check for $15 to Huston's Clothing. (2) Huston's deposits the check in its account at the Second Bank. (3) The Second Bank sends the check to the Federal Reserve Bank, (4) which subtracts $15 from the reserve account of the First National Bank. (5) Notified of this step, the First National Bank deducts $15 from Charles's account. (6) The Federal Reserve Bank adds $15 to the account of the Second Bank; that bank adds $15 to the account of Huston's Clothing.

Critical Thinking: What would happen if every depositor demanded all their money back from every bank at the same time?

Math Activity: Spend time on Table 16.2. Make sure students understand that a higher reserve requirement will mean a smaller money supply, and vice versa.

The higher the reserve requirement, the less money institutions have to lend. This means less money will circulate in the economy. A lower reserve increases the amount of money institutions can lend, which increases the money supply.

The Fed also affects the supply of money through *its power to buy and sell government bonds*. This method is called **open market operations** because the bonds are bought and sold on the open market. If the Fed wants to reduce the money supply, it sells bonds to consumers and institutions. The money paid for the bonds cannot be used for other purchases, so it goes out of circulation. The supply of money is reduced. When the Fed wants to create the opposite effect, it buys back the bonds.

The Fed's third method of controlling the money supply is changing the **discount rate,** which is *the interest rate that institutions pay the Fed to borrow money*. If the Fed lowers the discount rate, institutions can then charge less for loans they make. More businesses and consumers will borrow, and the money supply will grow. If the Fed raises the discount rate, the

Table 16.2 The Effect of the Fed's Reserve Requirement on the Money Supply

Bank	With 10% Reserve			With 20% Reserve		
	Deposits	Reserve	Money to Lend	Deposits	Reserve	Money to Lend
A	$ 500	$50	$450	$ 500	$100	$400
B	$ 450	$45	$405	$ 400	$ 80	$320
C	$ 405	$40.50	$364.50	$ 320	$ 64	$256
	$1,355			$1,220		

This is the total amount of money added to the money supply after only three transactions as a result of the initial deposit.

Critical Thinking: If all the country's resources were fully employed, and the FED increased the money supply, what would happen? If there is high unemployment and the money supply is increased, what happens?

Define: Government activities dealing with the money supply are called **monetary policy**. Government activities dealing with taxing and spending are called **fiscal policy**.

opposite occurs. Institutions will charge more for loans, people will borrow less, and the supply of money will decrease.

The fourth way the Fed controls the money supply is by using *selective credit controls*. People who wish to buy stock can borrow a percentage of the purchase price. By setting this percentage higher or lower, the Fed can make buying stock easier or harder, respectively.

The Fed takes these four actions in an effort to improve the performance of the economy. When prices are high, the Fed may try to reduce the supply of money. The goal is to reduce consumer demand, which will result in lower prices. If the economy is doing poorly, the Fed will try to increase the money supply and promote more consumer spending. Increased demand will lead businesses to produce more, and the economy will grow.

SUMMARY

- Just as consumers shop for other goods and services, they should shop for financial services.
- Financial institutions compete for consumers' dollars. Consumers can benefit from this by carefully evaluating the services offered by different institutions.
- The services offered by different financial institutions are changing rapidly. Keep aware of changes brought about by new laws and regulations.
- Financial services overlap, so consumers must consider and plan for their needs as a total package.
- Consumers look for the following financial services: obtaining cash and paying bills, credit, savings, and investment. Consumers also want convenience and security in the institutions providing financial services.
- The four basic types of financial institutions are commercial banks, savings and loan associations (S&Ls), mutual savings banks, and credit unions. Since deregulation, institutions have been offering similar services.
- There are other sources of financial services, such as retailers, finance companies, or automakers for credit; brokerage houses,

real estate and jewelry dealers, or mutual funds for investment; retailers or the post office for cash substitutes.

- Alternative financial institutions should be evaluated carefully for the availability, cost, and quality of their services, as well as convenience and security.
- The Federal Reserve System's most important role is to regulate the money supply, which it controls in four ways: by setting reserve requirements, buying and selling government bonds, setting the interest rate banks must pay to borrow from it, and controlling some types of credit. The Fed also aids consumers by clearing checks.

Key Terms

Match each of the following terms with the definition that most suits it.

commercial bank	Federal Reserve System	mutual savings bank	safe deposit box
credit union	float	open market operations	savings and loan association
deposit insurance	foreign exchange	reserve	trust
discount rate	invest		

a. changing the currency of one country into that of another
b. a metal container that a person can rent from a financial institution for storing valuables
c. a bank that has been authorized, by either the state or the federal government, to offer a full range of financial services
d. a savings institution that used to specialize in savings accounts and home mortgages but now offers a full range of services
e. a bank owned by its depositors and whose goal is to encourage savings
f. a nonprofit savings and lending cooperative formed by people with a common bond
g. the time it takes for a check to clear
h. a government program that guarantees that deposits up to a certain amount will be returned to depositors if an insured financial institution goes out of business
i. the federal agency that controls the nation's money supply and oversees the practices of its member banks
j. a sum of money set aside by Federal Reserve member banks that is equal to a certain percentage of their deposits
k. property managed by someone for the benefit of someone else
l. the Fed's power to buy and sell government bonds, used to control the supply of money
m. the interest rate that institutions pay the Fed to borrow money
n. to use money in a way that we expect will increase its value

Review Questions

1. What are the two main areas of competition among financial institutions for depositors' dollars? Explain what each area involves.
2. Identify the four most common types of financial services desired by consumers. Give two examples of each.
3. Identify three convenience services consumers look for in financial institutions.
4. How can a consumer identify a financial institution that carries deposit insurance? Why look for insurance?

5. What do wise consumers do first before choosing a financial institution? Why?
6. Identify the four basic financial institutions from which consumers receive most of their financial services.
7. Name a source other than the four basic financial institutions for (a) credit, (b) savings and investment, and (c) cash substitutes.
8. How does the Fed's check-clearing role help consumers?
9. What four methods of controlling the money supply can the Fed choose from? Why does the Fed want to control the money supply?

Projects

1. List the financial services you think you might need. Include cashing of paychecks, retail store credit, bill-paying needs, savings, and any other financial service. Shop for those services, trying at least two institutions. Decide what would be the package of services that would most suit your wants. Write a report summarizing your conclusions.
2. Deposits were first insured in 1934 because many banks had failed during the Great Depression. These bank failures wiped out depositors' life savings. At first, only savings accounts in commercial banks were insured, and only up to $5,000. Do some library research to find out when the limits were raised, when other financial institutions and types of accounts began to be insured, and why Congress made these changes. Prepare a report explaining your findings.
3. Do some research into the operations of the Federal Reserve. Look in newspapers or magazines for current information—what is the Fed doing? How do its decisions affect consumers?
4. Interview a banker or visit a bank to research up-and-coming banking services for the 1990s. One possibility might be "point of sale" (POS) terminals. Banks place these electronic terminals at retail stores. They allow you to pay for goods through a direct debit to your account at the bank. They also allow retailers to obtain an authorization from the bank that your personal check is covered by funds in your bank account. If your bank has POS terminals, it will give you a plastic card and a personal identification number so that you have access to the terminals. Another topic might be home banking. In home banking, consumers issue payment instructions to the bank from their personal computer at home. Today, only a small number of banks offer POS and home banking services.
5. Research the outlook for banking employment. In today's deregulated banking climate, there will be a need for banking personnel who are customer-oriented. Write to the American Bankers Association, 1120 Connecticut Ave., N.W., Washington, DC, 20036, for information on banking as a career. Share the information you find with the class.
6. Collect print advertisements from banks and arrange a bulletin board display. Analyze the appeals used in the ads. Who is the targeted customer in each ad?

Shopping for Credit 17

Overview: Chapter 17 introduces the use—and misuse—of credit. Obtaining information and using the decision-making process will help consumers maximize their satisfaction and minimize their problems with credit.

OBJECTIVES

This chapter will help you to:

1. Plan how you will use credit.
2. Relate your credit record to the amount of credit available to you.
3. Evaluate the types and sources of credit.
4. Explain the rights of creditors and borrowers.
5. Discuss how consumer credit affects the economy.

A few weeks after she opened her new checking and savings accounts, Connie asked her sister's advice. "I was thinking about the car I want to buy," she said. "Why wait until the end of the summer to buy it? Why don't I get a loan and pay it back from what I earn?"

"You're a little young to get a loan from a bank," said Mollie. "Even though you're working now, you haven't been for long. And you've never borrowed anything before, so you don't have a credit record."

"You don't think I could get a loan?" asked Connie.

"You might be able to," her sister said. "From someplace other than a bank. But they might charge more interest, so it may cost you more."

"That doesn't sound like a good idea." Connie said. "So how do I get a credit record?"

"It's usually a good idea to start small. You could get a charge account at a department store. If you buy small things and pay for them on time, you'll develop a good record."

"I guess that's the way to start," Connie agreed. "But I sure wish I could buy the car sooner."

"You can always shop around to see what terms you can get," Mollie said. "But if you take out a car loan, mom and dad will have to promise to pay if you miss payments—so you'll have to talk them into it, too!"

Clarify: Using credit is using tomorrow's income to pay for today's purchases.

CONNIE IS LEARNING—earlier than many of us—about the use and importance of credit. In this chapter, you'll learn what credit is and how to plan your use of credit. You'll also see why a credit record is important and learn about the types, sources, and costs of credit. Finally, you'll see how your credit decisions—and those of every consumer—affect the whole economy.

CREDIT MEANS BUYING NOW AND PAYING LATER

Explain: Connie could save her income (earning interest) until she has enough to buy the car; or, she could borrow the money (paying interest), buy the car, and pay the money back out of future income.

Before World War II, people generally bought only what they could buy with cash. Today, most consumers use some form of credit. Figure 17.1 shows how consumer credit buying has gone up. In fact, the economy of the nation depends on consumers using credit. When credit buying slows down, as it did in the early 1980s because of high interest rates and high unemployment, businesses can't sell their goods. The result is less production and more unemployed workers.

Why have consumers come to use so much credit? For one thing, personal income has been rising steadily. People with more income can get more credit. For another thing, businesses have found that offering credit has many benefits for them. Some businesses offer credit to meet or beat the competition. Others use it to encourage consumers to buy their goods or services. Still others have made a business of granting credit.

Critical Thinking: Why might some firms be more willing to accept a credit card than a check from an unknown customer?

Discussion: Lead a class discussion on the reasons for using credit. Invite students to give examples of situations they have had where the use of credit would have been beneficial.

Math Activity: Have students develop different types of graphs for the information in Figure 17.1.

Critical Thinking: The period from 1982 to 1988 saw the greatest increase in personal credit use. Invite your students to examine the economy during this time. Why did the use of credit grow so much during this period?

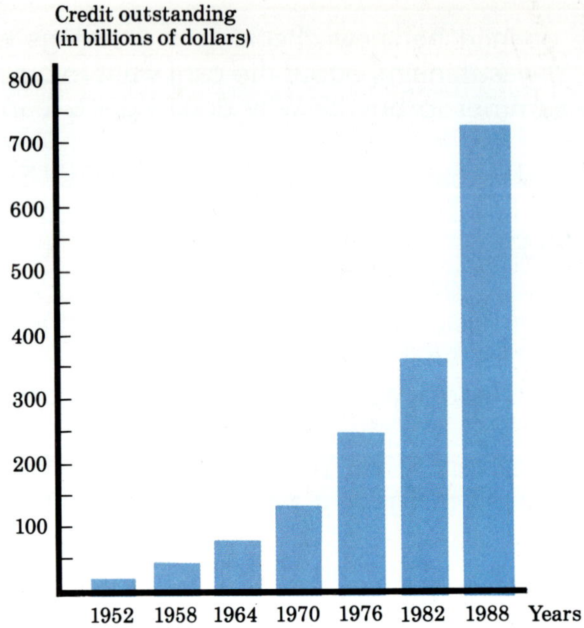

Source: Board of Governors of the Federal Reserve System

Figure 17.1 The Rising Use of Consumer Credit

Why People Use Credit

People use credit for five reasons:

- *To get something they want to enjoy now but cannot pay cash for*—if you want a new CD player for your room, you can use credit to buy the player now, and pay for it while you enjoy it.
- *Convenience*—it can be easier to charge an item than to carry a lot of cash around or get a personal check accepted.
- *Emergencies*—if your car breaks down while you're on a trip, for instance, you can use a credit card to pay for repairs.
- *To buy expensive items*—getting credit is the only way many people can manage the high purchase price of some things.
- *To build a good credit record* — a creditor looks at how someone has handled credit before deciding to lend to the person. A consumer builds a good credit record by repaying his or her debts on time.

There are two things to remember when using credit. First, credit usually costs money, and this cost must be considered when you decide whether to use credit. Second, misusing credit by charging too much or missing payments can cause serious problems—including the loss of all credit.

What's Involved in Using Credit?

Using credit is a decision. Make this decision by using the basic consumer method: plan, get information on the types and sources of credit, and compare the costs and terms of credit from each source.

World Economy: Do working people in LDCs use credit? Yes, they do; they must find a way to survive until the next crop is harvested. Usually they obtain credit from the local landowner at exceptionally high interest rates. Even though some governments have sought to introduce banks to finance these needs, the working people prefer borrowing from landlords who tend to be more sympathetic toward erratic or delayed payments (this may be why the interest rate is so high).

Consumers can use credit to take advantage of sales when they do not have cash.

Explain: A few years ago, businesses advertised discounts for the use of cash. In effect, cash purchases subsidized credit purchases (with their higher costs).

Plan what you'll use credit for and decide beforehand how much you can afford to charge. This prevents borrowing more than you can manage to repay. Learn all you can about the types and sources of credit, the costs involved, and the rights of borrowers and creditors. When shopping for credit, remember to compare the costs of different credit plans. Creditors are required by law to tell you the finance charge and the annual percentage rate (APR) of the loan — use those figures to find the most affordable credit.

USING CREDIT REQUIRES CAREFUL PLANNING

Carefully planning our use of credit helps us get the most out of our resources. Here are some tips for good credit planning:

- *Use credit only when necessary*—would you make the purchase if you were using cash? Use credit for things you really need or want that fit your budget. Don't use it for impulse buying.
- *Compare the credit cost of an item with its cash cost*—sometimes a discount is offered for cash.
- *Shop for credit*—take advantage of the competition in credit. Use the finance charge and APR to shop for the best terms.

- *Reduce the cost of credit*—the higher the down payment on an item and the shorter the time for repayment, the cheaper the loan. Plan your budget to take advantage of this. Remember, too, that some charge accounts offer free credit for bills repaid within a certain period of time.
- *Read all credit contracts carefully*—if you don't understand something, ask questions. Don't sign any contract that you haven't read or that has unfilled blanks. Keep a copy of every contract you sign.
- *Don't feel pressured*—when deciding to borrow, take your time. Don't let a salesperson hurry you.
- *Don't take on more major debts than you can handle*—space out purchases of high-priced items so that you can repay them more easily.

Note: Sometimes purchases are not added to your credit balance for a couple of weeks. If your credit company does not charge interest on a balance paid before the next monthly billing period, that means you have up to six weeks' free use of their money before you must start paying interest. If you pay the credit company for your purchase before the next billing period, you have an interest-free loan.

Planning how to use credit also means avoiding the trap of overborrowing—going into debt beyond your ability to repay. Someone who overborrows will have to cut back on necessities like food and clothing. If the problem is very serious, the consumer has several choices.

The first choice is to visit a debt counseling service. Some people get advice from their financial institution. Others turn to a consumer credit counseling service or a family service agency. Any of these sources offer advice on how to pay off debts.

Consumers with a number of monthly debts that they cannot meet may get a **debt consolidation loan.** This is *a high-interest loan for a sum large enough to settle all of a person's short-term debts.* The goal is to reduce many different monthly payments to a single, manageable one. The payment for the consolidation loan is less than the total payments for all the other debts. However, this loan takes longer to repay.

Focus: Credit contracts are legal documents and should be carefully examined. Make sure you understand the APR and other terms of the agreement (payment dates, minimum payments, balloon payments, etc.).

Consumers who cannot repay loans they used to buy cars or appliances may have the purchases repossessed. **Repossession** means that *the creditor takes ownership of the item that was bought with the borrowed money.* The consumer loses not only all the money paid on the loan until then, but also the item itself. Repossession also harms the consumer's credit rating, making it hard to borrow in the future.

As a last resort, consumers may declare bankruptcy. In **bankruptcy,** *a court sells a borrower's property—except for certain items protected by law—and pays the proceeds to his or her creditors.* While it removes all remaining debt, bankruptcy can make credit almost impossible to get for a long time afterward.

Critical Thinking: In examining the individual's life cycle, when do you think the use of credit will be the highest?

YOUR ABILITY TO BORROW DEPENDS ON YOUR CREDIT RECORD

The first thing to keep in mind is that businesses *want* to grant you credit. Banks stay in business by making loans. Retailers and restaurants find that credit increases their business. Credit is available. How much you can get depends on how well you use it.

How Creditors Get Information

Creditors decide whether or not to grant credit on the basis of information about the borrower's past use of credit. The person who wants credit supplies some of this information on an application form. This form has questions about the person's present and past employment, income, property, and credit references.

Creditors get more information from credit bureaus. A **credit bureau** is *a firm that collects credit information about consumers and gives it to other businesses that request it.* The credit bureau gathers information from local creditors in a file on each borrower. When someone applies for credit somewhere, the creditor asks the local credit bureau for that person's file. The credit bureau only gives information — it doesn't decide whether to grant credit. The creditor makes this choice, based on what it learns from the applicant and the credit bureau and using its own standards.

Focus: Honesty is always the best policy, especially in filling out credit applications. You may wonder if you have to fill in all the information that is requested. Do you really have to include all the credit cards that are asked for? The operation of credit reporting agencies has become extremely sophisticated. These agencies have extensive files dating from your first use of credit. They will know any major or national card you have, because all this information has been reported to them. They will be able to check their information against what you record on an application if they are asked to do so.

What Creditors Look for When Granting Credit

What creditors look for most in borrowers is their ability to repay the debt. Creditors consider the three C's of credit:

- **Character**—this is *how a borrower can be expected to act; whether a borrower is honest and responsible and has good judgment.*
- **Capacity**—this is *a borrower's financial ability to pay back a loan.*
- **Capital** — this is *the property someone owns, which a creditor uses as a guide to the person's ability to repay a debt.*

The three C's form the basis of a creditor's faith in a borrower. Without this faith, creditors will not grant credit — they lose money if loans are not repaid.

To measure someone's character, capacity, and capital, creditors ask questions. (See the samples in Table 17.1.) Creditors use facts about past borrowing, work and income history, and property to judge whether a person is a good credit risk. *The category of credit risk that a creditor assigns to a potential borrower* is the person's **credit rating.** The better the credit rating, the more money the creditors will be willing to lend.

Explain: Credit is based on trust and faith. If the creditor has a high degree of trust that you will repay on time, then you have a good credit rating. If the creditor feels there is a risk that you will not repay, then your credit rating will be lower. How poor your credit rating is depends on how risky the creditor feels your repayment is.

Table 17.1 Questions Creditors Ask Potential Borrowers

The Three C's	Questions Creditors Might Ask
Character	What credit has been granted to you in the past? Was it repaid on time? Were there any late charges, repossessions, or failures to pay? Where do you live? How long have you lived there? Do you have any personal references?
Capacity	What is your income? What is your current job? How long have you held it? What other sources of income do you have?
Capital	How much money do you have in savings or checking accounts? How long have you had these accounts? What real estate, cars, or other valuables do you own?

Many creditors use a point system to decide whether or not to grant credit. Each fact about an applicant is given a certain number of points. The higher the person's total score, the better the credit rating. Credit applicants get points for such things as living in one place for a long time, having a telephone, and keeping a bank account.

Discussion: Why would the lack of a credit history make it difficult to obtain a large loan?

Having a good credit history is probably the best way to convince a creditor to lend to you. One way to start is to follow the advice of Connie's sister at the beginning of this chapter and open a charge account at a retail store. These are easier to get than major credit cards. You can use it for small purchases, being sure to repay on time.

Focus: Many creditors require a co-signer for loans made to minors. Since young people have less experience, the state protects them by allowing them to abrogate contracts. Thus, creditors could have difficulty in getting their money back. By requiring an adult co-signer, creditors have more assurance that the money will be repaid since the adult cannot break the contract and must repay the loan.

Some reasons that creditors refuse to grant credit include:

- *No identification* — creditors don't like to loan money to someone without a driver's license, social security card, birth certificate, union card, or employee identification card.
- *A floating address* — a post office box number, a rooming house, or an address in care of a friend may lead the creditor to believe that the borrower won't be around long enough to repay the loan. An applicant who is new in town can avoid this problem by pointing to a more stable address in the past.
- *Unstable employment history* — someone who changes jobs frequently or has an unstable line of work may also seem risky.
- *Age* — for applicants under 18, or 21 in some states, creditors may ask an adult to cosign the loan. A **cosigner** is *someone who promises to repay a loan if the borrower fails to do so.*
- *Bad credit history* — a history of late payments, repossessions, or unpaid loans makes it very hard to get credit.
- *No credit history* — someone who never had credit before may also find it hard to obtain a large loan. This problem can be avoided by starting with smaller loans.

Research: Ask students to investigate state bankruptcy laws. What personal property is excluded? What is the process for declaring bankruptcy?

Someone who has been turned down by one creditor may still be able to get credit from another. Different creditors have different standards. Later in this chapter we'll see what rights people have when they've been turned down for credit.

GETTING INFORMATION ON CREDIT

An important step in the consumer decision-making process is gathering information about our options. This step is a big part of making decisions about credit. We should find out all we can about the various types and sources of credit.

Types of Credit

There are two basic types of credit: closed-end and open-end. **Closed-end credit** involves *a fixed amount borrowed at a fixed charge for a fixed period and repaid in fixed payments.* This type is also known as *installment credit* because the loan is paid back in fixed installments. Examples are car loans,

List: Ask students to list all of the purchases that closed-end credit could be used for. Then have them list purchases that would be paid for with open-end credit. Discuss the differences between the two types of purchases.

Explain: Home, auto, and appliance loans usually require collateral (usually the item being purchased), so that if the loan is not repaid the creditor can repossess the item and attempt to regain his or her money by reselling the collateral. Sometimes personal loans require collateral as well. The collateral would be some fully paid asset (a car that does not have a loan against it, for example) that could be repossessed

Focus: Examine the different types of open-end credit. This is the credit your students will be exposed to more often and is the type of credit where over-extension is common.

home mortgage loans, and major appliance loans. The time for repaying loans can run from one or two years for a major appliance up to 25 or 30 years for a home mortgage.

Home, auto, and appliance loans require **collateral,** *the pledge by the borrower of something of value to ensure repayment of the loan.* If the loan is not repaid, the collateral can be repossessed by the creditor. These loans are called *secured loans. Unsecured loans,* like personal loans, don't require collateral. Personal loans are used for a variety of purposes, from financing a college education to paying for a vacation.

Open-end credit is *credit in which the amount a borrower owes increases each time a purchase is made and decreases each time a payment is made. The maximum amount a person may charge* is called the **credit limit.** This is set by the creditor and differs for each borrower. Also called *noninstallment credit,* open-end credit lets the consumer borrow any amount as long as the total doesn't pass the limit. On a $500 limit, someone can borrow up to $500. If $350 has already been borrowed, he or she can borrow only $150 more. The borrower can repay the entire amount or only a part.

There are several types of open-end credit:

- *From service firms*—most doctors, dentists, and utilities offer free credit if a bill is paid within a certain time, usually a month.
- *Retailers' charge cards*—there are two kinds. An **open charge account** *requires the borrower to pay for the purchase at the end of the billing period, usually a month.* If the account is not paid in full, a service charge is added to the balance. A **revolving charge account** *allows a borrower to buy up to a certain limit and repay in installments.* Only a partial payment is due with each bill. Interest is charged on any unpaid balance.
- *Bank credit cards*—these cards, like MasterCard and Visa, are issued by banks and used to make many purchases and to get cash. Cardholders may pay a yearly fee. The cardholder gets one bill that covers all purchases made up to the closing date of the statement. A minimum payment is due, and interest is charged on the unpaid balance. The creditor sets a limit on how much the cardholder can charge.
- *Travel and entertainment cards*—these cards, like American Express, Diner's Club, airline cards, or service station charge cards, work very much like bank credit cards. The cardholder may be able to choose between paying the entire bill with no extra charges or paying a portion each month with added finance charges. Some cards require prompt payment of the entire bill. The cardholder often must pay a yearly membership fee.
- *Overdraft protection—a guarantee by a bank to cover a depositor's check up to a certain amount even if the check withdraws more money than is in the account* is called **overdraft protection.** The amount is set by the bank, and interest may be charged until the overdrawn amount is repaid.
- A *single-payment loan—a loan in which the entire amount plus a finance charge is repaid in one payment* is a **single-payment loan.** This type of loan is not often available, but it does carry lower interest rates.
- A *passbook loan—a cash loan from a bank using the money in a passbook savings account as collateral* is a **passbook loan.** The interest rate is often low because the loan is secured by the person's savings account.

Credit cards are widely accepted by sellers. They help consumers make more purchases and merchants sell more goods.

Research: Assign students to different types of credit. They will identify interest rates on these types of accounts. Some students (those with bank cards, for example) will have to do some exploring to find out the rate charged by out-of-town banks.

Because their own savings are at risk, borrowers have extra motivation to meet payments.

Sources of Credit

The four main types of financial institutions offer credit. Commercial banks offer all kinds of credit, including bank cards. Savings and loan associations grant home mortgages, home improvement loans, and personal loans and have bank cards. Mutual savings banks also offer a wide range of credit, including bank cards. Credit unions generally offer personal, auto, home mortgage, and home improvement loans.

Clarify: With the banking deregulation act, interest rates became more varied. Prior to this legislation, financial institutions could not compete on the basis of price. Now the price varies greatly as competition becomes more stiff.

The interest rates charged by these institutions vary. In the past, credit unions offered the lowest rates and commercial banks the highest. With the deregulation of banking, however, rates became more similar. As a result, you must shop carefully. Another reason to shop around is that standards for granting credit vary from creditor to creditor. Credit unions, however, lend only to their members.

There are other sources of loans, too:

- *Finance companies—financial institutions that specialize in granting credit to merchants and making personal loans* are called **finance companies.** The loan amounts are generally small and interest rates tend to be high, often two or three times higher than a bank's rates. The rates are high for two reasons. First, finance companies lend to poorer credit risks. Second, because the loans are often unsecured, there is no property for the creditor to repossess if the loan isn't repaid. The cost of bad debts can be met only by charging more interest.

- *Industrial banks—lending institutions originally set up to offer loans to industrial workers* are called **industrial banks.** These banks now lend to all kinds of people and perform many of the functions of commercial banks. Their rates are higher than those at regular banks but lower than those at finance companies. They may require a cosigner.
- *Retailers and service businesses*—this includes charge accounts from department stores, gas stations, and airlines. Credit from these sources is easy to get and there is usually no charge if the borrowed amounts are repaid on time. However, not all goods and services can be bought this way, and consumers are limited as to where they can buy.
- *Cash surrender value* of certain kinds of life insurance—the interest on these loans is very low, but the amount available may be low, too. If the loan isn't repaid, though, the amount is deducted from the policy benefits.
- *Families*—relatives may not charge interest, but there isn't always enough money available in a family for a loan. There can be problems — like family conflict or hardship — if a loan is not repaid. One way to prevent this kind of trouble is to put the details in writing.

There are two sources of credit to avoid:

- *Pawnbrokers* — creditors who give cash in return for some item of value, such as jewelry. When the borrower has cash again he or she can retrieve the item. If not, the pawnbroker sells the property. The loans do not nearly match the value of the item pawned, so this source should be avoided.
- *Loan sharks*—criminal dealers who offer cash loans for extremely high interest rates. They should be avoided at all costs.

Borrower and Creditor Rights

A number of laws spell out the rights of creditors and borrowers. We will describe the major points of each of these laws.

A major step in protecting credit rights was the Consumer Credit Protection Act of 1969, also known as the Truth in Lending Act. As amended in 1982, this act contains the following main points:

- For closed-end credit, the act requires that the creditor state the total dollar amount of the finance charge and the APR. Creditors must list the total of principal and interest paid by the borrower as the "total sales price." The creditor must also state the number, amount, due dates, and total of all payments, along with the amount and conditions of any penalty fees for late payments or early repayment. In addition, any collateral for the loan must be described.
- For open-end credit, the act requires the creditor to state the APR, the method used to figure the balance on which a service charge is based, and when finance charges begin. All information must appear on monthly statements along with a notice of the consumer's rights under the Fair Credit Billing Act, described later. Businesses are prohibited from mail-

Illustration: One of the first dilemmas of a new entrepreneur is, "Where can I get the money I need to start my business?" Financial institutions are seldom interested in providing "start-up" monies for new, inexperienced entrepreneurs. Venture capitalists are only interested in firms which have the possibility for rapid and extensive growth (usually in high-tech industries and manufacturing). That leaves the beginning entrepreneur with the list of sources on pages 284-285 plus refinancing the home, and selling or borrowing on any other asset available. This is the way most beginning entrepreneurs get their initial funding. Only after their idea has started proving its success are they able to obtain financial capital from financial institutions.

Discuss: Discuss the benefits and costs of these alternate means of financing. Compare and contrast them with financing from the four types of financial institutions.

ing or issuing credit cards that weren't requested. Finally, cardholders are liable for only $50 of unauthorized use if a credit card is lost or stolen. You are not liable for any unauthorized charges once you report the theft or loss of the card.

Note: The Fair Credit Reporting Act of 1970 states that you may review your credit file at no charge if you have been denied credit because of information in this file. If you have not been denied credit, but would like to review the information in the file, you may be charged a service charge.

The Fair Credit Reporting Act of 1970 was passed to protect consumers from the use of incorrect or outdated credit information:

- *Incorrect or outdated information*—you have the right to know the name and address of the credit bureau that gave information used by a business that denied you credit, insurance, or a job or one that decided to increase the cost of credit or insurance.
- *Credit file*—you have the right, with proper identification, to get the information in your credit file from the credit bureau. You can then correct any errors in it and place a personal explanation in the file. The bureau will send this new information to creditors who refused credit.

The Equal Credit Opportunity Act of 1975 forbids discrimination in lending. Originally, it was passed to protect women who wanted credit. Single women were often denied credit even if they had jobs. Married women were not able to build a credit record of their own, even if they managed the family's money. To prevent such abuses, the act forbids denying credit or changing the status of an account because of sex or marital status. In 1977

Federal law prohibits lenders from discriminating against women in the granting of credit.

the act was broadened to prohibit the denial of credit because of age, race, religion, or national origin.

Focus: The Fair Credit Billing Act of 1975 details procedures for settling billing disputes on open-end credit. It is important that students understand their responsibilities as well as their rights in this process.

The Fair Credit Billing Act of 1975 details the procedures for settling billing disputes with users of open-end credit:

- *Billing dispute*—you have 60 days from receiving a bill to inform the creditor in writing of any dispute over the bill.
- *Until the dispute is settled,* the creditor cannot close the account or give it to a collection agency, and you need not pay the part of the bill in dispute.
- *When the dispute is settled,* if you are wrong, you must pay the amount and any finance charges due.

The Fair Debt Collection Practices Act of 1977 covers the actions of **collection agencies.** These are *companies that specialize in collecting overdue loans.* They pay part of what they recover to the creditor and keep the rest. The act forbids these agencies to use threats, harassment, or abuse to collect debts. It also prohibits them from lying or implying that they are lawyers or government officials when they try to collect a debt.

COMPARING CREDIT COSTS

Clarify: Inflation leads to higher nominal interest rates; however, this does not necessarily mean that real interest rates increase. Suppose that last year the average APR was 9% (the nominal interest rate) and that inflation was 3%; this means that the real interest rate was 6%. This year the inflation rate has increased to 6.5% and the nominal APR is a whopping 12%; however, the real interest rate has dropped to 5.5%.

We can compare credit costs by looking at the total finance charge and the annual percentage rate (APR). The finance charge is the total dollar amount the borrower pays to use credit. The APR expresses the cost of credit as a yearly percentage. The creditor must state both on all papers related to a loan. While federal laws do not establish interest rates, they do help consumers compare credit costs by requiring creditors to provide this information.

Still, look beyond the APR to discover what affects the cost of credit. For instance, economic conditions influence the availability—and the cost—of credit. A large demand for credit, from either the government or business, will drive up interest rates for consumers. The rising prices of inflation tend to make interest rates rise.

Another factor is how long the borrower takes to pay off a loan—the more time, the higher the cost. The amount of risk the creditor takes that a borrower might not repay the loan also affects the cost of credit. Creditors charge higher interest rates to borrowers with poor credit ratings.

Consider all these factors and shop carefully, looking for the best terms. Always consider the alternative of not using credit. Waiting to buy means not being able to use an item until enough cash is saved. If you feel that the opportunity cost of using credit is small, wait to buy something and avoid the extra cost of credit. If you decide you need the item now, using credit—wisely—may be the solution.

YOU INTERACT WITH THE ECONOMY: CONSUMER CREDIT

Consumer credit helps the nation's economy as a whole. Borrowing by consumers increases the demand for goods and services, giving businesses the

Some industries, because their goods are fairly expensive, depend on consumers using credit to make purchases.

Note: Wide use of consumer credit will encourage the economy to expand as long as people continue to expand their use of credit. However, if the use of consumer credit slows or stops, then income will be used to repay the previous amount borrowed instead of purchasing additional goods and services.

Critical Thinking: What would happen to auto sales (and prices) if we could not use credit anymore? What would we have to do in order to buy a car?

desire and means to increase production. This results in economic growth and helps create prosperity.

A second benefit of credit comes from financial institutions. The income they earn from interest on loans is used partly to pay interest on savings.

Credit is also valuable in helping people to get the goods and services they want. Few of us are able to raise the cash needed to buy a house or a new car. Credit helps us enjoy more goods and services by paying for them as we use them.

In inflationary times, credit also gives consumers a chance to beat rising prices, which reduce the value of the dollar. During inflation, consumers who borrow $100 one day repay it later with dollars that are worth less than those they borrowed. Another trend offsets this advantage, though. Creditors may raise interest rates if they expect prices to keep rising.

Consumer credit does have some drawbacks too—not just for each of us, but also for the economy. For instance, because it increases demand, borrowing may boost inflation by pushing up the prices of goods and services. If everyone tries to beat inflation by buying now and paying later, the result may be higher inflation. At this point, the Federal Reserve Board may move to raise interest rates. By holding down borrowing, it hopes to reduce demand and lower the rate of inflation.

Consumer credit also pushes up the price of goods and services. Retailers who give credit must raise their prices to cover extra paperwork. They also need to cover the cost of losses from bad debts. These higher costs are borne by all consumers, whether they use credit or not.

Summary: Credit can be beneficial both to the consumer and to the overall economy. However, credit can be easily abused. The consumer should investigate credit options and use the decision-making process in order to make the best choices.

Basically, though, consumer credit is not good or bad in itself. How people manage credit is what matters. Used well and managed properly, credit can help raise our life-styles and act as an engine to drive a prosperous economy. Mismanaged or used carelessly, credit can cause problems for people and perhaps make inflation worse.

SUMMARY

- People use credit mainly to get something they want to enjoy now but cannot yet pay for. They also use credit for convenience, in an emergency, to buy costly items, and to build a good credit record.
- Two things to watch out for when using credit are that credit usually costs money and that abusing it can cause serious problems.
- Make credit decisions using the basic consumer decision-making process.
- Carefully planning how to use credit reduces the chances of overborrowing, which can lead to a consolidation loan, repossession, or bankruptcy.
- Creditors decide whether to grant credit on the basis of information they receive from the applicant and from credit bureaus.
- Creditors look for the three C's—character, capacity, and capital—when deciding whether to give credit to a borrower.
- Past borrowing, financial assets, work history, and residence all give creditors an idea of a borrower's earning power, stability, and trustworthiness.
- Types of credit include closed-end, which is installment credit, and open-end, which is noninstallment credit with a limit.
- Sources of credit include all types of financial institutions, finance companies, industrial banks, retail and service businesses, life insurance companies, and families. Pawnbrokers and loan sharks should be avoided at all costs.
- Various laws govern the rights of borrowers and creditors, and consumers should be aware of them. The Consumer Credit Protection Act, also known as the Truth in Lending Act, requires creditors to state all finance charges and to describe the cost of credit in terms of its APR. The Fair Credit Reporting Act gives consumers the right to see and correct credit information. The Equal Credit Opportunity Act forbids discrimination in the granting of credit. The Fair Credit Billing Act sets the rules for resolving disputes over open-end credit. The Fair Debt Collection Practices Act prevents abuses by debt collection agencies.
- Consumer credit benefits the economy by increasing demand for goods and services, earning income for financial institutions, and fighting inflation. Credit can, however, make inflation worse by pushing up prices through increased demand.

Key Terms

Match each of the following terms with the definition that most suits it.

bankruptcy	collection agency	finance company	repossession
capacity	cosigner	industrial bank	revolving charge account
capital	credit bureau	open charge account	single-payment loan
character	credit limit	open-end credit	
closed-end credit	credit rating	overdraft protection	
collateral	debt consolidation loan	passbook loan	

a. the category of credit risk that a creditor assigns to a potential borrower

b. a high-interest loan for a sum large enough to settle all of a person's short-term debts

c. what may occur when a borrower fails to repay a secured loan; the creditor takes ownership of the item that was bought with the borrowed money

d. a situation in which a court sells a borrower's property—except for certain items protected by law—and pays the proceeds to his or her creditors

e. a business that collects credit information about consumers and gives it to other businesses that request it

f. a type of credit in which a fixed amount is borrowed at a fixed charge for a fixed period and repaid in fixed payments

g. the pledge by the borrower of something of value to ensure repayment of the loan

h. a type of credit in which the amount a borrower owes increases each time a purchase is made and decreases each time a payment is made

i. the maximum amount up to which a person may charge in an open-end credit agreement

j. how a borrower can be expected to act; whether a borrower is honest and responsible and has good judgment

k. a type of open-end credit that requires the borrower to pay for the purchase at the end of the billing period

l. a type of open-end credit that allows a borrower to buy up to a certain limit and repay in installments

m. a guarantee by a bank to cover a depositor's check up to a certain amount even if the check withdraws more money than is in the account

n. a borrower's financial ability to pay back a loan

o. a loan in which the entire amount plus a finance charge is repaid in one payment

p. a cash loan from a bank using the money in a passbook savings account as collateral

q. a financial institution that specializes in giving credit to merchants and making personal loans

r. someone who promises to repay a loan if the borrower fails to do so

s. a lending institution originally set up to offer loans to industrial workers

t. a company that specializes in collecting overdue loans

u. the property someone owns, which a creditor uses as a guide to the person's ability to repay a debt

Review Questions

1. What are the reasons most people use credit?
2. Name the opportunity cost of not using credit. Give an example.
3. Give four hints for planning to use credit.
4. Give the possible results of overusing credit.

5. What are the three C's of credit that creditors look for in potential borrowers? Explain each.
6. List three things you can do to help your credit rating. Name at least three things that can cause trouble when applying for credit.
7. What are the two kinds of credit? Give two different examples of each.
8. Name at least four sources of credit or loans.
9. Name at least three laws that spell out the rights of borrowers and creditors. Describe the major purpose of each.
10. Give two benefits of consumer credit to the economy. Give two disadvantages.

Projects

1. Get an application form from a credit source in your community (bank, retail store, or finance company). Discuss the form in class—why would the creditor want certain information?
2. Invite an officer from a credit rating agency or local creditor to speak to your class. Prepare questions that will tell you what information he or she looks for from a potential borrower.
3. Suppose you want to buy a used car for $1,795. You have $400 for the down payment. Identify at least three places where you could borrow the remaining money. Make sure that each is a different kind of institution (in other words, don't use two commercial banks). Find out the costs, terms, and conditions of borrowing from each source. Decide which you would prefer to use, and explain to the class the information you got, how you got it, which source you would select, and why.
4. The Fair Debt Collection Practices Act of 1977 was passed to correct some abuses of debt collection that had harmed consumers in the past. Do some library research to find out what kinds of abuses had been practiced. Report to the class, describing some specific cases.
5. Consumers are not the only ones who use credit to finance their needs and wants. Businesses and other groups must also borrow occasionally. Even the federal government runs up debts during the course of its work. You've probably heard of the national debt. Do some research into government's use of credit and then debate the issue with your classmates. Is government debt helpful or harmful to the economy? How necessary is it in today's economy?
6. Warning: Are you headed for credit problems? Experts say you may be if you (1) spend more than 20 percent of take-home pay on installment loans; (2) can only pay the minimum amount due monthly on installment loans or credit cards; (3) are delinquent paying rent, household bills; (4) use credit cards to pay for groceries, bills, or other card balances. Arrange with your teacher to invite a credit counselor to class to discuss financial problems of fictitious families and the workable budgets the counselor recommends. Non-profit credit counseling agencies exist throughout the country to help people who have money problems. You can obtain a list of agencies in your area by writing to the National Foundation for Consumer Credit, 8701 Georgia Ave., Silver Spring, MD, 20910. Be sure to send a self-addressed, stamped envelope.

Shopping for Personal Investments 18

OBJECTIVES

Overview: In Chapter 18, students learn about long-term saving, using today's income for tomorrow's purchases.

This chapter will help you to:

1. Explain the advantages and disadvantages of various savings methods.
2. Define stocks and bonds and interpret stock and bond listings.
3. Explain how mutual funds and investment clubs work.
4. Summarize the advantages and disadvantages of investing in real estate and collectibles.
5. Establish your saving and investment goals.
6. Describe the effect of personal and business investment on the economy.

Connie asked for her sister's advice. "I'm putting the money for the car I want in a savings account," she said. "And it's earning money. But I wonder if there's a way I could earn *more*."

"It's possible," Mollie answered. "But that depends on how much money you have to invest, how long you have to let it grow, and how much risk you're willing to take."

"What does that mean?" Connie asked.

"Well, you know that your savings are safe," her sister said. "And you know exactly how much you're going to earn from your passbook account. With some investments, the amount you earn may not be guaranteed. And you risk losing your money."

"That's no good! I want to buy a car," Connie exclaimed.

"I didn't say you *would* lose your money," Mollie said quickly. "I only said you *might*. If you invest carefully, your money can still be fairly safe. You just have to decide whether you're willing to take any risk."

Explain: Both savings and consumer investment require trade-offs between risk and return.

MANY PEOPLE, like Connie, put their money aside in savings or investments to see it grow. In this chapter, you'll learn what methods of saving or investing you can choose from and how to decide which method to use.

WE HAVE MANY WAYS TO SAVE AND INVEST

Savings and investments are both ways to put money to work to earn more money, instead of spending it. **Saving** is *setting money aside for future use.* **Investing** is *using money in a way that we expect will increase its value.*

Clarify: The more risky the investment, the more important is prior information or knowledge. The opportunity cost of gaining this information must be weighed against the expected return. However, it is hoped that the increased information will lessen risk.

When we save or invest money, we have less available to spend at present. Our short-term buying power is decreased. If the investment works, however, we'll end up with more money, so our long-term buying power is increased. This is the opposite of how credit works. When we buy something now but pay for it later, short-term buying power goes up while long-term buying power goes down.

Saving and investing both aim to make money grow, but they differ in one respect. Saving emphasizes safety and liquidity—this means the money saved is protected and is easily available. Investments, some of which earn more than savings, may also be riskier. Those who invest their money may lose it. Also, many investments require the investor to have special knowledge—or get expert advice—in order to make the investment work.

PLANNING SAVING AND INVESTMENT GOALS

Consumers base their saving and investment plans on their goals. Without having a clear idea of what you want to do, you cannot choose among the many methods of saving and investing.

Many people save the money they need to take the vacations they want.

Critical Thinking: Why would an individual want to increase wealth?

Discussion: Most financial advisors recommend that you limit your higher-risk investments to those funds you are willing to lose. Risk means there is a chance of losing everything. So only put at risk those funds you are willing to lose.

People save for four reasons:

- *To build an emergency fund*—experts suggest having from two months to six months of income in such a reserve.
- *To buy high-priced items*—many people prefer saving the money for a costly purchase to buying with credit.
- *To build a retirement fund*—people often put aside money for the years when they won't be working.
- *To get into the habit of saving*—one way to be sure to have money for emergencies is to set a pattern of saving.

The goal of personal investment is to increase **wealth,** which is *the money and property a person owns*. People invest money hoping to get more back later. Most people don't start to invest until they feel they have a comfortable amount of money saved.

GETTING HELP WITH SAVING AND INVESTING

We need information and advice to plan and meet saving and investing goals. One of the first places to look for information is the daily newspaper. Newspapers carry ads from financial institutions, and the business section gives news on economic trends. There are also daily reports on stocks and

Activity: Most investment alternatives have brokers who act as intermediaries between buyers and sellers and who, in effect, make the market in which supply and demand interact. Ask students to explore how brokers of different types of investment make their money. Do they earn a percentage of the transaction price? Do they receive a set fee for each transaction they complete? Are they paid by the buyer or seller?

Expansion: The 1990 recipients of the Nobel Memorial Prize in Economic Science were Harry Markowitz, William Sharpe, and Merton Miller. Their work revolutionized the way investment portfolios are managed. Markowitz, in the 1950s, pioneered the use of risk and expected return in evaluating investments. Sharpe, building on Markowitz's theories, developed a model for determining risk. Their work proved that risk could be measured and controlled.

Smart consumers get plenty of information—some of it from newspapers—before investing.

bonds. Many papers publish articles with financial advice from experts. One, the *Wall Street Journal,* is devoted to financial news and advice.

Magazines also provide financial information. The business sections of *Time, Newsweek,* and *U.S. News and World Report* give up-to-date reports on business and finance. *Money* and *Changing Times* publish many articles on saving and investing. Magazines like *Business Week, Fortune,* and *Forbes* report on business and finances, although the articles may be very technical.

Knowledgeable friends can also give information, but the local library is probably the best source of all. There you can find current books, magazines, or newsletters on investing, even in very specialized areas. Newsletters are published by large investment houses and by some expert individuals. They are full of advice.

You can get direct advice on investing from many sources. A good place to start is a **brokerage.** This is *a business that buys and sells stocks and bonds on behalf of its customers.* Many financial institutions have advisors who will help you make and meet investing and saving plans. For a special form of investing, like rare coins or real estate, speak with people who know about that area.

You can also study investing to increase your skill in analyzing investments. Many community colleges and adult education institutions offer courses on personal finances.

GETTING INFORMATION ON METHODS OF SAVING AND INVESTING

Note: Evaluate the different alternatives based on liquidity, growth, return, risk, price, special knowledge needed for evaluation, and taxability.

Activity: When examining each of the savings/investment alternatives, refer to Table 18.3 on page 303. Ask students to identify the trade-offs involved in each alternative.

Discussion: Why does a passbook savings account have a lower rate of return?

Research: Ask students to research the present-day, local rate of return for each investment alternative.

There are a number of ways to save or invest. Some of the most common are discussed here. After you learn about these options, we'll explain how to compare them.

Financial Institutions Offer Savings Accounts

The most common kind of savings account, a **passbook account,** is *a savings account in which a fixed rate of interest is paid and money can be withdrawn at any time.* Some banks are beginning to require a minimum deposit to open the account, though this amount may be low. The money in these accounts is often insured, which guarantees its safety. The interest rate is low compared to other methods, however.

Interest-bearing checking accounts—often called NOW accounts—may pay as much interest as passbook accounts do. Most are insured. Because the account owner can write checks, money in this account is even easier to use than that in a savings account. Some institutions require a minimum initial deposit to open a NOW account, though not all do. Sometimes there is a service charge if a minimum balance is not maintained.

Financial institutions also offer time deposits. A **time deposit** is *money left on deposit for a set length of time to earn a fixed interest rate.* The size of the minimum deposit depends on the interest rate and the length of time the money is left in the account, but it is higher than for passbook accounts. The money in the account is insured. Rates are higher than for passbook accounts, but lower than for other investments.

The interest rate for time deposits is fixed for a set length of time. If the rates for other investments are falling within that period, time deposits are better. If other investments begin to pay more, though, a time deposit becomes less desirable. The depositor may not be able to change investments though. Withdrawing money before the end of the term often means paying a penalty.

You can also put money in money market deposit accounts, which may have different names at different financial institutions. This kind of account is insured and the investor can write a limited number of checks. Today most institutions require a small minimum balance to open an account. Once the account is established, there is no minimum balance, but a maintenance charge may be added if the balance falls below a certain level. Mutual funds groups (which you will learn more about later) have similar accounts that have lower minimums and do not limit the number of checks that can be written. Financial institutions guarantee a minimum interest rate; mutual funds do not. To open a mutual fund account, $1,000 is required, unless the account is opened as part of an IRA. After that, neither a minimum balance nor a minimum deposit is required.

Special accounts, like Christmas clubs, are offered, but may not be a good way to save. They don't pay interest unless the money is left on deposit until a certain date. The interest rate is often lower than on a passbook.

Critical Thinking: Interest on an IRA is not taxable until it is withdrawn, then the interest is taxed as income. Why would this be an advantage?

Savings Bonds

Another way to save is to buy United States savings bonds. There are several types, but the most common—the Series EE bond—is sold for half of its **face value,** which is *the full amount that a bond is worth.* It may be *redeemed,* or cashed in, for full value when it reaches the **maturity date,** *the date when the issuer of the bond promises to buy it back at face value.* These bonds mature after ten years.

Define: When a bond is sold for less than its face value and redeemed at the full face value, the term used is that the bond is **discounted**.

Savings bonds can be bought through payroll savings plans where you work or at financial institutions, where they are also cashed in. Series EE bonds can be redeemed at any time six months after purchase, but interest is lost if they're cashed before they reach maturity.

EE bonds come in many amounts, starting at $50. Rates vary. The government will pay at least 7.5 percent, and more if the rates for other government bonds are higher. Savings bonds are a safe way to save. They can be replaced if they're lost, stolen, or destroyed.

Explain: U.S. Savings Bonds have effectively no risk because they are backed by the full faith and credit of the United States of America (and the taxes of all citizens).

Retirement Accounts Delay Taxes on Savings

Individual Retirement Accounts (IRAs), Keogh Plan accounts, and 401(k) Plan accounts are ways to save for retirement and delay taxes. Any worker can set up an IRA, even if he or she already has a pension plan at work. The investment may not be tax deductible, however.

Critical Thinking: Why would the Internal Revenue Service insist on approving IRA trustees?

People can save up to a certain maximum every year in an IRA. Then they deduct this money from their gross income. Interest earned from an IRA is not taxed until they withdraw it.

The money in these accounts can be invested in any of the ways discussed in this chapter. You can also change from one type of investment to another at any time. The only restriction is that the Internal Revenue Service must approve the custodian or **trustee,** which is *the person or institution through whom the investment is made.*

There are two other options for money in these accounts. One is the United States Individual Retirement Bond. This is a government bond, similar to savings bonds, designed just for IRAs. The other option is to buy an annuity plan through an insurer. In an **annuity,** *someone invests a sum of money and is promised a payment each month after retiring.* The insurer often offers a low rate of earnings that it guarantees as a minimum. Then it offers a higher current rate for a short time—a few years, perhaps—that might change when the period is over. Sometimes the insurer charges when money is withdrawn, which may amount to paying a penalty.

It is not necessary to put money into an IRA every year. The money may be withdrawn starting when the owner is 59½ years old, or if the owner

Clarify: When corporations initially sell their stock, they receive funds for investment purposes. The corporation uses this money to accumulate or to produce capital goods or for additions to inventory.

Expansion: The 1980s saw a rash of forced takeovers and mergers. Company A would offer to buy the stock of Company B from stockholders at a specified price. These were "forced" when the management of Company A was opposed to the merger. By the end of the decade, many corporate boards of directors had approved various negative consequences to a forced takeover—consequences which usually protected the existing management of Company A. Many times these activities pitted management against stockholders and highlighted the fact that stockholders and the boards of directors who were supposed to represent them had grown neglectful and allowed management (with little ownership in the company) complete control over the firm.

becomes disabled. There is a penalty for any withdrawal made if the owner does not meet one of these conditions. Withdrawals *must* begin in the calendar year the owner turns 70½. Once money is withdrawn, it is taxed.

The Keogh Plan is similar to the IRA, but limited to people who are self-employed. People can save as much as 25 percent of their income, up to a maximum of $30,000, in this account each year.

The 401(k) plan is a type of retirement plan that is company sponsored. Only employees who work for a company that provides the plan can participate. Employees contribute to the plan through salary deductions; employers then contribute a portion of this amount. The money in this account is not taxed until it is withdrawn.

Investing in Stocks Means Owning Part of a Business

Stocks represent a share of ownership in a corporation. Corporations sell stock to raise funds. The buyers become stockholders and receive stock certificates as proof of their ownership. Indirectly, stockholders can influence a company's managers, but the real power of any one owner is limited if there are many stockholders, as is often the case.

Stocks are bought and sold in three ways. A **stock exchange** is *a place where licensed traders come to buy and sell stock for their clients.* The New York Stock Exchange (NYSE) and the American Stock Exchange (AMEX) trade the stock of national firms. Ten regional exchanges trade stocks of local companies. To be listed on an exchange, a business must meet certain standards. The largest companies tend to be listed on the NYSE.

Another way to trade stocks is over the counter. **Over-the-counter (OTC) trading** is *a system of dealers and brokers who use telecommunications to trade stocks and bonds.* This method handles about 30 percent of the nation's stock business.

People can also trade stocks among themselves. This method accounts for a very small percentage of stocks traded.

Stockbrokers are paid by investors to buy and sell stock. The customer tells the broker that he or she wants to buy or sell a certain number of shares of a stock within a range of prices. The broker's agent finds another agent on the exchange floor who is willing to trade within that price range. (In an OTC exchange, this would be done by phone.) The client is told of the exchange and sent a check if stock was sold or a bill if stock was bought.

The price of a company's stock is set entirely by supply and demand. A corporation sets a price for its stock when it is first issued. After that, the stock sells for whatever people are willing to pay for it. The value of a share of stock changes often, even from minute to minute.

Prices change for many reasons. Demand for a stock may rise if the company has produced a successful new product. For instance, Coleco stock soared when their *Cabbage Patch Kids* first came out. Demand for a stock falls if sales decline. This happened to Coleco when sales of the dolls slowed down. The overall condition of the economy and an industry also affects stock prices.

Daily changes in the prices of all stocks are listed in the newspapers and on cable TV. Table 18.1 shows a listing from a paper and explains how to read it.

Investors watch trends in the market carefully. A "bear market" means that stock prices are generally falling. It shows that investors feel that the economy is in a bad period—or heading for one. When stock prices are rising, a "bull market" exists. This shows that investors believe the economy is healthy or will be soon. To identify whether the market is bear or bull, investors watch indices like the Dow-Jones averages. These are averages based on the day's price and the number of shares traded for the stocks of selected firms in three areas—industrial, transportation, and utilities. Only the stocks of companies that are seen as most important to the economy are used for this average. A rise in the Dow average means economic health. A drop is a sign that the economy is doing poorly.

Investors hope to gain from stocks in two ways. First, they want to receive **dividends,** which are *a part of the profits of a corporation that directors*

Discussion: Invite a local stockbroker to class to discuss corporate stocks.

Activity: The Securities Industry Foundation for Economic Education in New York, sponsors a Stock Market Game in which students compete with students in other locations in building an investment portfolio. Weekly student trades are compared with computer tapes of actual trades on the stock exchanges, and student investments are evaluated based on this comparison.

Activity: Set up a stock-market simulation in your classroom. Allow each student $10,000 to invest for four weeks. Twice a week let students trade the stocks in their portfolio based on that day's market price as reported in the *Wall Street Journal* or your local newspaper. This activity will increase students' enthusiasm.

Table 18.1 How to Read Stock Listings

1		2	3	4	5	6	7	8	9	10
52 Weeks										
High	Low	Stock	Div	Yld	PE	Sales 100s	High	Low	Last	Change
19¼	6-3/4	GnData	—	—	—	294	17½	16½	17¼	+½
49-3/8	24¼	GenDyn	1.0	2.0	20	3205	u50½	49-1/8	49-3/8	+1.8
112-3/4	60	GenEl	3.40	3.1	13	3256	111-5/8	108-7/8	109-1/8	−1-5/8
47-3/4	33	GenFds	2.40	5.5	9	1947	43-5/8	43-1/8	43½	+1/8
55½	38-5/8	GnMills	1.84	3.4	12	282	54½	53-7/8	54	+1/8
66	39-5/8	GMot	2.40	3.7	14	7059	65-5/8	64-1/8	64-3/4	−5/8

1. The highest and lowest price per share over the past 52 weeks. Prices are shown in eighths of a dollar, which equals 12.5 cents.
2. The firm's abbreviated name: *GenDyn* is General Dynamics Corporation; *GenEl* is General Electric.
3. The annual dividend, if any, that the company is paying for each share of stock. The first entry, *GnData,* is currently not paying a dividend.
4. The yield, or rate of return on a stockholder's investment. This is figured by dividing the dividend by the current price per share.
5. The price-earnings (PE) ratio, which is a measure of investors' confidence in the company. It is found by dividing the closing price by the company's stated earnings per share.
6. The number of shares traded today, in hundreds of shares.
7. The day's highest price for the stock. The symbol *u* in the second entry shows that the price was the highest in 52 weeks.
8. The day's lowest price for the stock.
9. The stock's price at the end of the day.
10. The difference between yesterday's and today's closing prices. General Electric, in the third entry, lost 1-5/8 points from yesterday, meaning its stock sold for $1.62½ less than it did the day before.

decide to pay to stockholders. Table 18.1 shows how stock listings show what dividends a business has paid. Second, investors want the value of the stock to grow. If investors sell stock at a higher price than they paid for it, their investment has grown.

World Economy: The other major stock exchanges in the world are in London and Tokyo. With the rapid communications available today, the major exchanges are quite reliant on each other. If the Japanese market drops precipitously, it is likely that the London and New York exchanges will also drop.

Buying Bonds Means Lending to Business or Government

A **bond** is *a long-term note sold by governments or businesses to raise money.* The bond issuer promises to buy back the bond at its face value after a certain number of years. Whoever issues the bond may **default,** which is *to fail to meet interest payments or buy back the bond when it reaches maturity.* The investor has then lost the money used to buy the bond. Still, this risk is low because defaults seldom occur.

The issuer also pays interest at stated times during the life of the bond. Bonds are often sold at a price higher or lower than the face value. A $1,000 bond selling at $950 would be sold at a *discount.* If it sold at $1,050, it would be selling at a *premium.* Most bonds are traded over the counter. Table 18.2 shows bond listings from a newspaper and explains how to read them.

Definition: Brokers use computers for programmed trading. For example, the computers are programmed to detect if the market price for stock has dropped a certain amount; if so, the computer automatically sells the stock. This can intensify a bear market.

There are three types of bonds—corporate, federal, and municipal. *Corporate bonds* are sold by businesses to raise money for their operations. *Federal bonds,* which include Treasury notes and government bonds, are sold by the United States government to cover its expenses. *Municipal bonds* are sold by cities and states to raise money for some action, such as new roads, school construction, or low-income housing. The money earned on a municipal bond is not taxable. This makes them useful for investors with higher income tax rates.

Clarify: The stock market is a relatively good barometer of the country's economic condition, but it is not a perfect one.

Table 18.2 How to Read Bond Listings

1	2 Bonds	3 CurYld	4 Vol	5 High	6 Low	7 Close	8 Change
DowCh	8¼16	14	42	61-3/4	61	61	+5/8
DowCh	8-1/817	14	10	59	59	59	—
duPont	8.85s95	14	8	63-5/8	63-5/8	63-5/8	+½
Duke Pw	10-1/896	12	7	84	84	84	+7/8

1. The firm's abbreviated name: *DowCh* is Dow Chemical Company.
2. A description of the bond's terms. The first number is the interest rate; the second is the maturity date. The first entry is an 8.25 percent bond maturing in 2016. The third is an 8.85 percent bond maturing in 1995.
3. The annual interest of the bond divided by its current purchase price. This figure allows the investor to compare the value of different bonds.
4. The number of $1,000 bonds traded today.
5. The highest price for the bond today. In the first entry, 61-3/4 means the bond sold for $617.50. In the fourth, 84 means $840. All the bonds shown traded at a discount, which means they sold for less than their $1,000 face value.
6. The low price for the day.
7. The price at the end of the day.
8. The change from yesterday's to today's closing price.

Focus: Remind students that stocks are ownership in the company; bonds are debts of the company.

Some Investors Pool Their Money

Discussion: Investment pools generate a larger pool of money to invest as well as provide a way of pooling information about the market. Why would this benefit the investor?

Mutual funds are *groups in which many people pool their money, which is then managed and invested by professionals.* By combining the resources of many people, mutual funds can make large investments that earn higher rates. Thus, small investors can earn more money than they could on their own.

Some mutuals are *load funds,* which deduct a fee from the amount a person invests. *No-load funds* do not charge a fee—they invest the whole amount that an investor sends them. However, no-load funds may offer less personal service to customers than load funds do. Both types charge a management fee, which is deducted from the income that investments earn. The rest of the earnings is paid to the investors.

Explain: The value of real estate tends to fluctuate in concert with economic conditions. Therefore, the value of this investment tends to increase with inflation. In some cases, the value increases more than inflation. The value of fixed return investments such as bonds will not react in this way.

There are many kinds of mutual funds, which means you have many options to choose from. Some invest in stocks that are expected to grow over time. Others focus on bonds that pay high income. Still others invest only in tax-free municipal bonds. There are many more types, each with a different goal. Many companies manage more than one type of fund and allow investors to shift from one to another as their investment goals change.

An **investment club** is *a group of investors who form their own mutual fund by pooling their money and managing their own investments.* Members generally draw up a contract setting forth the terms of the club. The amount of money needed to become a member varies from club to club. The success of such a club depends greatly on the skill of the members.

Investing in Real Estate and Collectibles

Emphasize: There is an iron-clad inverse relationship between bond prices and the interest rate. If you own a $1,000 bond paying 5% interest and the interest rate is 5%, then you will be able to sell your bond for the face value ($1,000). However, if the general interest rate increases to 10%, then you will not be able to sell that bond for more than $500.

Many people invest in **real estate,** which consists of *buildings and land.* Others invest in **collectibles,** which are *personal goods that are expected to grow in value.* Collectibles include things like rugs, antiques, metals, gems, coins, art, and stamps.

Investing in real estate is a good idea because land generally rises in value. Buying a house has two extra advantages. First, you can live in it. Second, some costs of owning a home can be used to reduce taxes. Property owners can also earn income by leasing their property to others. Of course, a large amount of money is needed to buy real estate, although people can borrow some to make this easier.

Collectibles can be risky. Collecting stamps, coins, or antiques can be fun for the investor who has a personal interest in these objects. They may gain quite a bit of cash value. Still, collectibles are risky because prices vary greatly. These investments require knowledge and, like real estate, they cannot always be turned into cash quickly.

WE USE EIGHT FACTORS TO COMPARE INVESTMENTS

People use eight factors to compare investments. There is no one best investment. You must weigh all these factors to choose the best investment for you at a particular time. Remember to reevaluate your goals often. If your goals change, your investments should change.

Emphasize: We must prioritize our investment goals, as with all personal decisions. Under one set of circumstances, we may be willing to undertake more risk in hopes of higher return; under other circumstances, we may be more interested in liquidity. However, circumstances change, the economy changes, and our goals change. Investing is not an activity to enter into lightly or with expectations of little effort.

1. *Liquidity*—this involves changing your investment into cash easily, without a loss. A passbook account is more liquid than a time deposit because if you withdraw a time deposit early you pay a penalty. Stocks and bonds are more liquid than real estate because they are easier to sell.
2. *Growth*—this involves your investment's increase in value over time. If a house was bought for $85,000 and sold for $90,000, the investment grew—it was worth more. A savings account grows because the deposit and the interest earn interest. Growth is measured in two ways: how much the investment has grown and how certain it is to grow.
3. *Income*—this is the money you earn from the investment while it is held. For savings accounts, income is expressed as a guaranteed interest rate. For stocks, it is the dividend that might be paid. Income differs from growth—it refers to money earned during the life of an investment. Growth compares the value of the investment at the end of its life to its value at the beginning.
4. *Safety*—this involves whether the amount you invest is safe. Savings accounts, most of which are insured, and federal government bonds are very safe. Other investments are less so. On the other hand, greater risk may offer a chance for greater growth or income.
5. *Capital*—investments vary in the amount of cash you need to make them. A passbook account requires little capital; real estate requires more.
6. *Knowledge*—some investments require skill in order to be managed successfully. Someone who invests in stocks and bonds must know how well companies are performing and understand how other investors might behave. Savings accounts require less knowledge—although finding a good savings plan does require shopping skills. Of course, you can pay experts with this knowledge to manage your investments for you.
7. *Time*—you must decide how long your money can be tied up in the investment and when you want to meet your investment goals. Keep in mind that some investments charge penalties for early withdrawal.
8. *Taxability*—you may want to lower your income tax rate. Tax-exempt investments like municipal bonds are good for people with high incomes. Saving in IRA, Keogh, and 401(k) accounts also reduces taxable income.

Activity: Develop a series of case studies detailing families with different needs, goals, and expectations. Ask students to evaluate the investment needs for these families, and to suggest the best mix of investment alternatives to meet these goals.

Table 18.3 compares the different ways of saving and investing using these eight factors.

As we've said, there is no single best investment. In investing, there is always a trade-off between benefits. Liquidity may mean lower income; growth requires time; high income may involve risk. Balance the benefits and costs of each investment in light of your situation and goals.

Note: Individuals buy some stock because it offers security and other stock which offers a little more risk, but pays a higher return. Seldom do you find an individual portfolio containing all high-risk, high-return stocks.

To do this, decide what you want from your investments. When you know what you want and what you can afford, rank the eight factors just described in order of importance. This will help you make intelligent choices. Remember that it can be helpful to make more than one type of investment. Mix several kinds of investments to achieve different goals.

Table 18.3 Comparing Methods of Saving and Investing

Method	Liquidity	Growth	Income	Safety	Capital Needed	Knowledge Needed	Time	Taxability
Passbook savings	Good	Low; fixed	Low; fixed	Insured	Small	Shopping skills	Doesn't apply	Taxable
Interest-bearing checking account	Very good	Low; fixed	Low; fixed	Insured	Fairly high	Shopping skills	Doesn't apply	Taxable
Time deposit	Not good	Fairly high; fixed	Fairly high; fixed	Insured	Fairly high	Shopping skills	Penalty*	Taxable
Money market account	Very good	Fairly high; varies	Fairly high; varies		High	Shopping skills	Doesn't apply	Taxable
Special account	Good	Low; fixed	Low; fixed	Insured	Small	Shopping skills	Penalty*	Taxable
Savings bonds	Fairly good	Fairly high; fixed minimum	Fairly high; fixed minimum	Very safe	Small	Doesn't apply	Penalty*	Taxable
IRA, Keogh, or 401(k)	Not good	Varies	Varies	Varies	Varies	Varies	Penalty*	Investment reduces taxes
Stock	Good	Varies; not fixed	Varies; not fixed	Varies	Varies	Necessary	Most gains need time	Taxable
Bonds	Fairly good	Varies; fixed	Varies; fixed	Varies	High	Important	Doesn't apply	Taxable (municipals not taxable)
Mutual funds	Fairly good	Varies; not fixed	Varies; not fixed	Varies	Varies	Shopping skills	May not apply	Taxable
Investment clubs	Varies	Varies	Varies	Varies	Varies	Necessary	May not apply	Taxable
	Not good	Varies; not fixed	Varies	Varies	Very high	Shopping skills	Most gains need time	Taxable
	Not good	Varies; not fixed	None	Varies	Varies	Necessary	Varies	Taxable

*Penalty charged for early withdrawal

YOU INTERACT WITH THE ECONOMY: PERSONAL AND BUSINESS INVESTMENTS

Discussion: Use Table 18.3 to review investment alternatives.

Personal and business investments affect the country's economy in different ways, but they are related to each other in certain aspects.

Note: Business will invest in capital goods only when it expects the investment to be profitable. If a retailer expects low consumer demand, then it will not invest in a large inventory of stock. If demand for rolled domestic steel is declining, then a steel factory might not purchase a new roller until demand shows signs of increasing.

Discussion: Does consumer spending provide a stimulus to the economy? How does the economy react to consumer saving?

Critical Thinking: Analyze the reaction to a declining economy from the business perspective.

People invest extra income in order to increase their wealth, whether it be cash or property. Businesses invest part of their profits in order to grow. They invest by adding to their resources, which means they acquire more land, buildings, equipment, or information. With more resources, the company can produce more goods or services.

Some types of personal investing provide funds for business investment. When people deposit money into financial institutions, they create a pool of money that both businesses and other people can borrow from.

Other personal investments do not have a direct effect on businesses. The stocks and bonds that consumers trade do not directly benefit the company. A corporation sells 100,000 shares of stock at $10 a share to an investment group. It now has $1 million to use to expand. The investment group then sells the stock to investors. As time passes, the stock's value rises and falls, but if the price of a share grows to $12, the corporation doesn't get any more money. It already collected its $1 million. While changes in a stock's price may not have a direct effect on a corporation's finances, trading does show how much confidence investors have in the business. If confidence is low, the company will have a hard time issuing new stock.

The economy as a whole is affected by personal investment. The money that consumers save, as we saw, is lent to businesses, who use it to increase production, or to consumers, who increase demand. The income that people

The huge expense needed to build factories like this auto plant make businesses plan very carefully before they begin to invest.

earn from investments also gives them more buying power. This, too, pushes up the demand for goods and services, which boosts the economy.

Business investment, however, has a more direct effect on the economy. Because it often means more production, business investment creates economic growth. It means more goods and services and more jobs.

Summary: Individuals must decide what to do with their disposable income. If income is spent on consumption, then there will be nothing left to save. Individuals must decide how to save or invest income that is not spent on consumption so as to maximize their goals.

Businesses decide whether to invest by considering three factors:

1. *Expectations for the future*—will consumer demand and the health of the economy be such that investments will result in higher sales?
2. *Interest rates*—if the investment requires borrowing money, are credit costs too high?
3. *Innovation*—will new technology, which requires large investments, provide enough new sales to be worthwhile?

Business investment is based on informed guesses about consumer demand in the future. A factory may take many years to complete, so managers must judge what the demand will be five and ten years in the future. Therefore, they must make long-range estimates of trends in the economy.

Business investment, then, signals economic health and growth. This is why news reports—and investors—pay so much attention to business investment.

SUMMARY

- People may save or invest their money. Saving is keeping extra money safe and available for future use while it earns interest. Investing means putting extra money to work to increase in value.
- People save to be ready for an emergency, to make a large purchase, to prepare for retirement, or to get into the habit of saving. The basic goal of personal investment is to increase wealth.
- Investors look for information on investing in newspapers, magazines, trade publications, and newsletters in libraries, and from experts and informed friends.
- Investors can get advice on investing from financial institutions, brokers, dealers in collectibles, real estate brokers, community colleges, and adult education institutions.
- Savings accounts offered at financial institutions include passbook accounts, interest-bearing checking accounts, time deposits, money market accounts, and special accounts like Christmas clubs. The government sells U.S. savings bonds to savers.
- The retirement accounts available are the IRA, open to everybody; the Keogh Plan, open only to self-employed people; and the 401(k) plan, which is company sponsored. Money put in these accounts is not taxed until it is withdrawn.
- Investing in stocks means buying a share of ownership in a corporation. Stock prices vary, but investors hope for their investments to grow and produce dividends. Stocks are bought and sold on exchanges, over the counter, or among individuals.
- Buying a bond means lending money to business or government. Municipal bonds are tax-free. Most bonds pay interest.
- Investors may also invest in real estate and collectibles, which are risky but offer potentially high returns.

- Investors weigh eight factors when deciding what savings and investments to make: liquidity, growth, income, safety, capital, knowledge, time, and taxability.
- To decide how to save and invest, investors establish clear goals for what they want from their investments. They should reevaluate those goals occasionally.
- Investment by consumers affects the country's whole economy. Personal savings provide money that businesses borrow to help them grow.
- Business investment is designed to increase a company's resources so it can increase production. It has a direct effect on the economy by providing more goods or services and jobs.

Key Terms

Match each of the following terms with the definition that most suits it.

annuity	dividend	mutual fund	stock exchange
bond	face value	over-the-counter trading	time deposit
brokerage	investing	passbook account	trustee
collectibles	investment club	real estate	wealth
default	maturity date	saving	

a. setting money aside for future use

b. using money in a way that we expect will increase its value

c. the money and property a person owns

d. a business that buys and sells stocks and bonds on behalf of its customers

e. a savings account in which a fixed rate of interest is paid and money can be withdrawn at any time

f. a savings method in which money is left on deposit for a set length of time and earns a fixed interest rate

g. the full amount that a bond is worth when it reaches maturity

h. a place where licensed traders come to buy and sell stock for their clients

i. a system of dealers and brokers who use telecommunications to trade stocks and bonds

j. the failure of a bond issuer to meet interest payments or to buy back a bond when it reaches maturity

k. a long-term note sold by governments or businesses to raise money

l. a group in which many people pool their money, which is then managed and invested by professionals

m. a group of investors who form their own mutual fund by pooling their money and managing their own investments

n. buildings and land

o. personal goods that are expected to grow in value

p. the date when the issuer of a bond promises to buy it back at face value

q. the person or institution through whom an IRA investment is made

r. a part of the profits of a corporation that directors decide to pay to stockholders

s. a plan in which someone invests money and is promised a payment each month after retiring

Review Questions

1. Name two basic goals of saving. What is the basic goal of investing.
2. Name at least three sources of information or advice you can consult when planning to save or invest.
3. Name an advantage and a disadvantage of passbook accounts.
4. Name an advantage and a disadvantage of time deposits.
5. Name an advantage and a disadvantage of U.S. savings bonds.
6. List the main advantages of an IRA, Keogh plan account, or 401(k) plan account. Point out a disadvantage to these accounts.
7. Name the three ways in which stocks are bought and sold.
8. Give two ways to gain from investing in stocks. Name two disadvantages of stocks.
9. Name an advantage and a disadvantage of bonds.
10. Name an advantage and a disadvantage of (a) mutual funds and (b) investment clubs.
11. Give an advantage and a disadvantage of (a) real estate and (b) collectibles.
12. List the eight factors investors consider when choosing their saving and investment strategies.
13. Distinguish between personal and business investment. Which has the greater impact on the nation's economy? Explain your answer.

Projects

1. Assume you have $200 to invest. Rank the list of eight factors for evaluating investments according to how important you think each factor is. Now compare three investments using this ranking. Which one is preferable? Now, assume you have $1,000, and compare the investments again. Would your answer be different?
2. Divide your class into groups, each with an imaginary $1,000 to invest. Each group should decide what goals it wants and then invest the money to meet these goals. At the end of the semester, each group should report how much money it would have if it sold all of its investments.
3. Research in the library or in newspapers and magazines the current forecasts for business investments for this year. Are businesses planning to increase or decrease their investments? Is the amount of change from last year significant, either up or down? What do experts feel will be the effect on the economy of present business investment plans? Is the economy expected to grow or not? Will there be more jobs? Do businesses' estimates expect consumer demand to rise, fall, or stay about the same? Write a report summarizing your research.
4. Arrange with your teacher to invite a stockbroker, banker, or real estate agent to class to discuss investments. Ask the speaker to discuss the pros and cons of investments in their area of expertise.

Shopping for Insurance 19

OBJECTIVES

Overview: We all assume risks. Chapter 19 discusses risk and protection against the economic losses from risk.

This chapter will help you to:

1. Explain the basic principles of insurance.
2. List some ways to reduce risk.
3. Compare types of life insurance plans.
4. Determine what auto insurance you need.
5. Describe what medical insurance covers.
6. Outline the basics of property and liability insurance.
7. Explain how drivers can lower car insurance costs.

Michael was walking to school when he heard a car horn. Looking over his shoulder, he saw his friend Laurie pulling over to the curb in a blue car.

"You got it!" Michael exclaimed as he peered in the window.

"I just picked it up last night," Laurie replied. "Imagine—my first car!"

Michael opened the passenger door and got in. "You know, I may be getting one too," he said. "My parents are buying a new car next month. They said I can have the old one if I buy my own insurance. But I'm not sure how insurance works. What do you have to do?"

"It all has to do with risks," Laurie answered as she signaled and pulled into the street.

"Risks?"

"That's right," Laurie continued. "We know that automobile accidents are going to happen. Insurance companies even have a good idea how *many* accidents will happen. But no one knows *who* will have them. So a lot of car owners share the risk that an accident will happen to them. They all pay money to an insurance company. Then when one of them has an accident, the company helps pay for the damages."

"That's all there is to it?" Michael asked.

"Well, the company can also say how likely you are to have this or that kind of loss from an accident," Laurie said. "Then you decide which risks you want to guard against by getting insurance."

Explain: Michael will pay a higher price for coverage against risk than Laurie. According to records, there is a higher probability of young males being involved in an accident.

AS LAURIE EXPLAINED to Michael, accidents happen. When they do, they cause financial loss. We obtain auto insurance to protect ourselves from these losses. Other types of insurance protect us from the cost of health care, loss of property, or loss of income through the death of a family member. In this chapter, you'll learn how insurance works, what kinds of insurance you can get, and how you can get it.

INSURANCE SHARES RISK

Emphasis: In order to appeal to your students, emphasize auto insurance. Most states require insurance in order to license a car.

Insurance is based on the principle of pure risk. **Pure risk** is *the probability that an event will occur.* If we rolled a six-sided die, the number 4 would have one chance in six of turning up. Accidents or illnesses also have a certain chance, or probability, of happening. When they do happen, they may cost us money. In fact, they may cost more than we can afford. To protect ourselves from this risk, we buy insurance. Many people—called *insureds*—pay money to an *insurer,* who puts it into one fund. Money is paid out of the fund to cover the losses that any insured person suffers.

The money that a person pays for insurance is called a **premium.** The protection that person buys is explained in the **insurance policy,** *a written contract that details the terms of the insurance coverage.* The policy states what is covered, how much the premium is, how long the coverage will last, and what the conditions of coverage are. The insured is also called the *policyholder*.

The size of the premium depends on many factors:

Discuss: Invite a local insurance broker to class to discuss auto insurance and to show students sample insurance policies.

- *The law of averages*—the chance that illness, accident, or death will occur. For example, a young driver is more likely to be in an auto accident than an older driver. Thus, the younger driver pays a higher premium.
- *The number of people sharing the risk*—the more people insured, the lower the premium will be for each.
- *The cost of claims in the past*—usually, the more the insurer has had to pay out in the past, the higher the premiums will be.
- *The characteristics of the individual*—the age, health, sex, geographic location, and occupation of the insured affect his or her premiums. An older person would pay more for medical insurance, for instance, than a younger one would.
- *The value of what's insured*—higher value means higher cost. Insurance to replace a $100,000 home costs more than insurance to replace a $50,000 home.
- *The deductible—the amount of loss the insured agrees to bear before the insurer begins to pay claims* is the **deductible.** This means that the insured will pay for part of the loss, and the insurer will pay for all or part of the rest.
- *State regulations*—state laws may require a minimum amount of coverage and may set the premium for it.

Illustrate: Have you seen direct-mail offers for high-cost cancer insurance, flight insurance, or trip cancellation insurance? Consider the cost for protection against an event with such a low probability of happening.

Insurance protects people from the cost of car accidents, health care, loss of property, injuries to others, or loss of income due to death. Whatever the type of coverage that is being bought, the factors just described will help set the premium.

PLANNING INSURANCE NEEDS

To plan our insurance needs, we need to take two steps. First, we must see how we can lower the risk that a loss will occur. Second, we must decide how much risk we want covered by insurance.

Stress: Individuals can reduce risks through their own actions. Statistics show that the mortality rate for seat-belt users is lower than for those who do not use seat belts. If you use a seat belt, you are personally lowering your risks. Discuss other ways to reduce risks.

Reducing Risk by Planning

As resource managers, we can use resources like time, energy, and skills to cut how much money we pay for insurance. Reduce the risk of loss by planning in the following ways:

- *Life*—to take care of yourself, maintain your health, don't smoke, drive carefully and wear seat belts, keep your home free of hazards, and avoid dangerous activities.
- *Auto*—to drive sensibly, drive defensively, obey traffic rules, keep your car in good condition, don't drink or use drugs when driving, and wear seat belts.
- *Health*—to protect your health, eat nutritious food, exercise, practice good hygiene, and avoid drug and alcohol abuse.

- *Home and property*—to protect your home and property, prevent fires and install smoke alarms, make needed repairs, remove hazards, and improve security with good locks and burglar alarms.

Explain: You can reduce your insurance costs, without reducing your coverage, through **co-insurance**. This means that you will pay a portion of any insured payment. This differs from a **deductible**, meaning that your initial payment will be deducted from the amount due.

Determining Insurance Needs

To determine your insurance needs, you must decide how willing you are to risk that something will *not* happen. If you knew you wouldn't need medical care, there would be no need to buy health insurance. You can't be sure of that, though, so you must decide what health care you are *likely* to need and what care you are willing to risk you will *not* need. Ask yourself similar questions for other types of insurance.

One purpose of life insurance is to provide income for children in case a parent dies. To decide how much life insurance you need, answer these questions: who depends on your income? How able are they to earn their own income if you die? How much income must be replaced?

The need for auto insurance depends first on the minimum amounts required by state law. Before buying more, you need to answer these questions: how much protection do you want for yourself and your property? How much is your car worth?

Your need for health insurance depends on what health care costs you think you may incur. For instance, a young couple that plans to have children will want a plan that pays for maternity costs. An older person might

Homeowners must estimate the probability that a disaster will occur and then perhaps purchase insurance to protect themselves from losses that would result.

not. Many people want health insurance that covers major medical expenses, in case they or a family member get a serious illness.

The need for home and property insurance depends on the value of your property and the cost of replacing it if it's stolen or damaged. You must also ask yourself about the risk of liability suits. **Liability** means *a person's responsibility for injury to others*. Someone who falls on an icy walkway outside someone else's home may sue the homeowner for causing his or her injury. If that person wins the suit, liability insurance pays the money the court awarded for the injury.

GATHERING INFORMATION ON VARIOUS TYPES OF INSURANCE

Explain: Life insurance can be purchased with or without a savings plan (term). If the interest rate paid by the insurance company for the savings portion is equal to or higher than the rates of return on other investments or savings, then you should use insurance as savings. If the interest rate is less than other savings or investment alternatives, then you should not waste your money on plans that offer savings.

In this section, you'll learn about many types of insurance. Whatever the loss covered and whatever the details of coverage, each type protects us from loss.

Life Insurance Protects Against Loss of Income

Life insurance does not cover the risk of dying. Rather, it covers the risk to others in the event that someone dies. That is, it protects those who would suffer financial loss from the death of the insured. The insured pays the premium, but the benefits usually go to another person, called the **beneficiary.** This is *the person named in the policy to receive payments should the policyholder die*. These payments may be used for two purposes: to provide income for dependents and to pay the final debts of the insured. Some life insurance policies also work as savings plans. Those plans can then provide a fund for low-interest loans.

The amount of coverage a policy provides is called its *face value*. Premium rates are affected by the type of policy, its face value, and the insured's age, health, and life expectancy. Insurers often ask the insured to take a medical exam before they will sell a policy.

Critical Thinking: Why is it important that term insurance have a renewability clause?

Term Insurance *Life insurance that offers protection but no savings* is called **term insurance.** It covers the insured for a certain amount of time—the term—and then ends. The term can be a set number of years or the policy can last until the insured reaches a certain age.

A term policy may have two valuable extra features:

- *Renewability*—the insured may be able to renew the policy at the end of the term, though the premium may go up.
- *Convertibility*—the insured may be able to change the policy to a whole-life plan.

Whole Life Also known as ordinary life, **whole-life insurance** is *life insurance that is in force and is paid for during the insured's entire life*. The premium is the same amount each year and is paid every year until the insured dies. A 30-year-old man who wants $30,000 worth of life insurance might compare the cost of term and whole-life polices and find the following:

Insured's Age	Amount of Premium Due Each Year: Term (Renewable Each Year)	Amount of Premium Due Each Year: Whole Life
30	$ 85	$435
40	98	435
50	220	435
60	497	435

Critical Thinking: The text points out that the whole-life policy includes savings. However, this does not explain all the difference. What other reason could there be for the difference in rates?

As you can see, term costs less each year until age 60, when the insured would pay more for term than for whole life. Also, rates differ for smokers and nonsmokers.

Research: Ask students to survey insurance agents to determine the difference in price between various brands of insurance.

Some of the extra cost of whole-life insurance goes toward savings. These policies build up a **cash surrender value (CSV),** which is *the part of the premium that is savings*. The insured can collect this CSV while still alive or even borrow against it. Doing so, however, will lower the amount paid to the beneficiary if the insured dies. Figure 19.1 shows how the CSV grows.

Insurance companies use different methods to decide how much of the premium is savings. Minimum levels, though, are set by state law.

One type of whole life is called **limited-payment life.** This is *life insurance in which premiums are paid over a specified time, though coverage lasts*

Note: Refer to Table 19.1 on page 314 when describing each type of life insurance.

Activity: During which periods of the life cycle would larger amounts of life insurance be recommended?

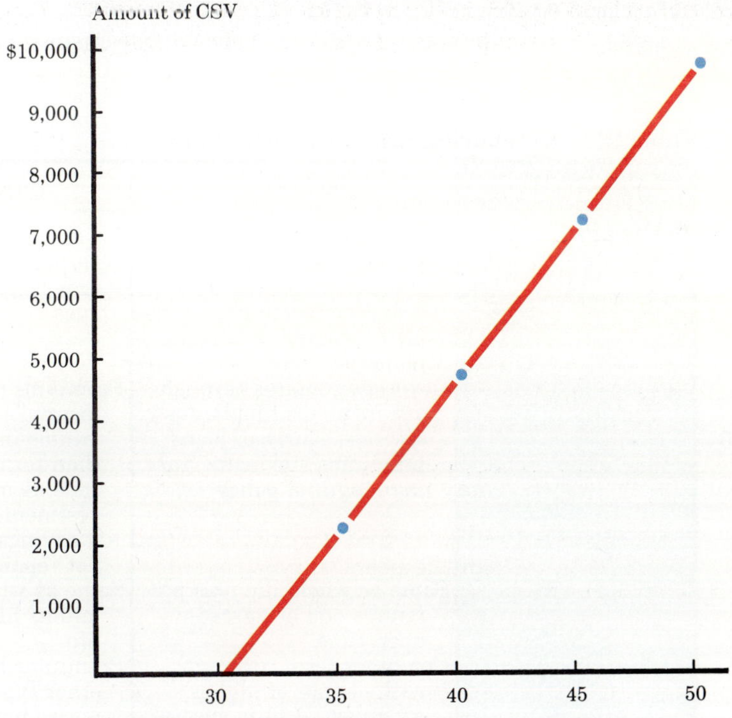

Source: Insurance Information Institute

Figure 19.1 Growth of the Cash Surrender Value for Whole-Life Insurance Bought by a 30-year-old Man

throughout the insured's life. All premiums are paid within, say, 10 or 20 years, or by the time the insured reaches age 60. The insurance is then said to be "paid up" and remains in force until the insured dies. The CSV grows faster with this type of policy than it does with whole life.

Some insurers sell a small whole-life policy along with a larger term policy. This way, people can start building savings yet buy more coverage for less money.

Endowment Another type is primarily a savings plan. **Endowments** are *life insurance policies in which premiums are paid for a fixed number of years and then the insured or the beneficiary collects the face value of the policy.* The CSV for this type rises more rapidly than in other plans, but premiums are higher. People use these plans to save for retirement or for their children's education.

Universal Life Insurers now *combine term coverage and an investment feature* in a plan they call **universal life.** Payments can vary but must at least meet a base amount. This base price provides term insurance. The rest is invested. Unlike whole-life insurance, which has a fixed interest rate, universal life offers a chance of higher income from investments.

The premium varies because insureds pay what they wish over the base amount. They may also decide to increase the amount of insurance, though they might be required to have another medical exam. This option is often not offered on whole-life policies.

Table 19.1 compares the different types of life insurance.

Activity: Ask students to describe an individual or family who might benefit most from each type of insurance.

Critical Thinking: How much life insurance is enough? This depends on family size and ages, age of the insured, income level, debt level, etc. Ask students to analyze the life insurance needs of different family structures.

Describe: Years ago, family policies were popular. A family policy included a $100,000 policy for Father, a $2,000 policy for Mother, and $1,000 policies for each child. This type of policy declined in popularity when families realized the costs involved in replacing the mother's services, and these family policies did not include a large enough policy to cover the costs. Families also realized they did not need life insurance on children.

Table 19.1 Comparing Life Insurance Plans

Type of Insurance	Advantages	Disadvantages
	Low cost for younger insured; renewable policies can extend period of coverage; convertible policies allow insured to change plans	Coverage only for limited period; no savings; premiums increased as insured ages
Whole life (or ordinary life)	Coverage remains throughout insured's life; builds savings; source of loans; premiums stay same during length of policy	Premiums paid throughout insured's life; higher premiums in early years than term; savings don't earn as much as other investments; benefits lower if savings borrowed and not repaid
Limited payment	Same as whole life *plus* premiums end at agreed-upon time	Same as whole life *plus* premiums higher than whole life
Universal life	Combines term coverage with chance of higher earnings; insured chooses amount going to savings; insured can increase coverage	Premiums higher than for other types; earnings still not as high as other investments

What Happens If a Premium Isn't Paid If a life insurance premium isn't paid on time, the insured may have a grace period of 31 days to make the payment. After that, the policy *lapses*—it is no longer in effect. Term policies that lapse may be reinstated by paying all back premiums. This must happen within a time limit set by the insurer. The insurer may also require a new medical exam.

Activity: Chapter 19 contains many terms. Encourage students to learn these terms and review the definitions by playing **Insurance Bingo**. Each student receives a blank Bingo card, and is allowed to place an insurance term on each space (with the middle space being a free space). After students have designed their own cards, the teacher then reads off the definition of a term. If the students recognize the term and have it written on their card they can cover the space.

If a whole-life policy lapses, the insured can reinstate the policy or choose one of four other options:

- Let the policy lapse and collect the CSV.
- Change the policy to term insurance, which will lower the premium.
- Reduce the face value of the policy to equal the amount of coverage that can be bought by all the premiums paid up to that time.
- Use part of the CSV to pay premiums until regular payments can be resumed.

Drivers Obtain Auto Insurance

The basic principles of auto insurance are the same as for other kinds of insurance. In this section you'll learn what losses it protects us from.

Basics of Auto Insurance You may be required to have auto insurance in order to drive. All states have *financial responsibility laws*. These laws require drivers to have a minimum amount of insurance or to post a bond if they cause an accident. Posting a bond means that the driver guarantees that money has been put aside to pay for losses or damages. More than half the states require drivers to carry liability insurance, which we'll describe shortly, in order to drive a car.

Note: Many people pay on a whole-life policy for years and eventually let it lapse thinking that they have discontinued the policy. Students should note that there may be a cash value on a lapsed policy.

In some states, insurers do not charge competitive rates for car insurance. Instead, the state government sets the rates. Even in these states, insureds must decide how much coverage they want, and they still have to shop around for the best insurer for their needs.

Who pays for the damage resulting from auto accidents? Traditionally, it depended on who was at fault. The insurance company of the driver who caused the accident paid the costs. This led to two main problems. First, there were many lawsuits to determine whose fault the accident was and who should pay. Second, it was not always easy or even possible to determine who was at fault.

Discussion: **No-fault insurance** laws guarantee that those injured in auto accidents can collect basic costs from their own insurance companies. Who would benefit from these laws? Who would not benefit?

These problems led some states to pass **no-fault insurance** laws in the 1970s. Under this system, *drivers who suffer injuries can collect up to a certain amount from their insurer, no matter whose fault the accident was.* This helps victims get their health care costs paid more promptly. If the bills are higher than the amount they receive from their insurer, accident victims can still sue the other driver or his or her insurer. The aim of no-fault is to speed the payment of medical bills and lost income resulting from accidents.

No-fault insurance applies only to personal injuries and to income lost because the injured person can't work. For other losses, no-fault coverage is the same as for other policies.

It is often very difficult to determine who was at fault in a car accident.

Review: Examine auto insurance coverage and identify possible duplications of coverage.

Critical Thinking: Germaine has a 10-year-old auto that is drivable, but "has seen better days." Should she purchase collision insurance? Why or why not?

Note: A deductible in an insurance policy will lower the price of the policy. The larger the deductible ($250 instead of $100, for example), the less the cost of the policy.

What Auto Insurance Covers Auto insurance covers injury to people involved in an accident. It also covers damage to the insured's car or to the property of others. We'll discuss these kinds of coverage in detail later.

Liability coverage pays for injury to others or damage to others' property that is caused by the insured. Liability has two parts. **Bodily injury protection** *covers injury to other people.* **Property damage protection** *covers damage to their property.* Many states require a minimum coverage of 30-60-10. This means $30,000 for injuries to one person, $60,000 for two or more people in the same accident, and $10,000 for property damages. Some insureds choose to purchase more coverage.

Medical payments coverage provides *medical and funeral expenses for the insured and anyone riding with him or her.* Typical state minimums for this type are $1,000 per person, but insureds can buy more coverage.

Collision coverage pays for *repairs to the insured's car.* If the car is wrecked beyond repair, the insurer will pay its *book value.* To find book value, the insurer reduces the car's purchase price according to its age, mileage, and condition before the accident. This type of coverage often involves a deductible. The insured agrees to pay a certain amount of repair costs before the insurer begins to pay. For example, with a $100 deductible, the insured pays the first $100 of a repair bill and the insurer pays the rest.

Uninsured motorist protection covers *the insured and family from the cost of injuries caused by a driver who has no insurance.* This type gives some protection when otherwise there would be none.

Discussion: Discuss ways in which motorcycle riders can protect themselves.

Explain: Comprehensive coverage tends to be more expensive in urban areas than in rural areas because of higher theft and vandalism rates. The geographic location of the car has strong effects on the rates of all types of coverage because of increased probabilities of some events occurring. There is low probability of floods in the desert, but high probability if the owner lives on a flood plain. Likewise, there is a lower probability of collision in a small rural town than there is in a large urban area simply because of the number of autos on the highway.

Critical Thinking: Is it fair to make 16-year-old males pay higher insurance rates simply because 16-year-old males have more accidents? What other ways could be used to determine insurance rates?

Motorcyclists can protect themselves by wearing helmets when riding their bikes.

Comprehensive coverage *protects the insured's car from theft and from damage caused by a number of disasters.* It protects against losses brought on by events like fire, vandalism, and flood. Taking a deductible can lower the cost of this coverage.

Wage loss and substitute services coverage is required in states with no-fault laws and can be bought in other states as well. This type *covers, at least partly, any income the insured might lose as a result of injury in an auto accident.* It also pays for the cost of services an injured person can't perform personally, such as child care.

Motorcycle insurance is similar to auto insurance but the coverage may differ. For instance, liability may not include passengers. Rates for motorcycle insurance are much higher than for auto insurance because motorcycles offer less protection than do cars. As a result, injuries are often more serious and more costly.

What Affects Auto Insurance Rates? Many factors affect auto insurance rates. Most are related to the chance of an accident occurring or to the value of the car:

- *The insured's residence*—insurance is often more expensive in urban than in rural areas. Cars in cities are more likely to suffer damage.
- *Driver characteristics*—the sex, age, marital status, driving experience, and occupation of drivers affect rates. Unmarried males under age 30 and

unmarried females under 25 pay the highest rates because they are involved in the most accidents.

- *Driving record of the driver*—good drivers of any age or sex pay lower premiums than drivers the same age and sex who have a history of traffic tickets or accidents.
- *How the car is used*—cars used for daily commuting have higher rates than cars used less often.
- *The car model*—cars that cost a lot to repair or that are often involved in accidents may have higher collision and comprehensive rates.
- *Driver education*—young drivers may be able to get a discount if they have passed certified driver education courses.
- *Size of the deductible*—the larger the deductible, the lower the premium will be.
- *Multiple car discounts*—insuring all of a family's cars in the same policy can lower rates.
- *Theft rate of vehicle*—certain car models are more frequently stolen.

Explain: During World War II, companies began providing health insurance as an employee benefit. This program was popular because: (1) the cost was tax deductible to the company; (2) the benefit was tax exempt to the worker; and, in theory, (3) by providing coverage to a large number of people, the cost per person would be reduced (spreading the risk).

Health Insurance Covers Medical Expenses

Illness and accident are two risks that we all face. Health insurance helps us meet the costs of these risks.

Basics of Health Insurance People get **health insurance** to cover *all or part of the costs of doctors' fees and hospital bills and other charges for health care*. In addition, this insurance may partly replace income lost because of a sickness or accident.

Medical insurance plans have limits—the insurer will pay claims only up to a certain amount. These limits may be yearly or cover a person's lifetime. They may apply to one person or a whole family. Be sure to find out.

Expansion: In some states, Blue Cross-Blue Shield has begun negotiating with health-care providers regarding the costs of this care. A new program, designating some health-care providers as **Preferred Providers**, guarantees that the providers will accept the insurance payment as full payment for their services (even though this payment may be lower than that generally charged for those services). In effect, this means that the insurers have negotiated a differentiated price (lower for their customers than for others).

Types of Coverage Health insurance pays for many kinds of health care costs. Policies vary in what they include, but here are the main types:

- *Hospital expenses*—pays for all or part of hospital charges. Different plans cover different charges. Limits on how much they'll pay vary. This type often pays the cost of a hospital room and meals, lab fees, and x-rays.
- *Surgical expense*—pays for operations. The insurer may limit how much it will pay for each type of surgery. The insured pays any charges above this limit.
- *Medical expense*—pays for office visits, prescribed drugs, and the like. Regular checkups often are not covered. Office visits may be covered only if there is an illness or injury.
- *Major medical expense*—pays for catastrophic illness or accident. If an illness costs more than the limits of other types of coverage, major medical takes over. It may have a deductible. It may also have a **coinsurance** feature. This means that *an insurer does not pay all the charges that a policy covers, but a large percentage of them*. Often the insurer pays 80 to 90 percent—the insured pays the rest.
- *Emergency service*—pays for the use of an ambulance or for emergency medical care.
- *Maternity care*—covers all or part of the costs involved in having a baby.

Activity: Ask students to prioritize the types of coverage discussed on pages 318 and 319. Check with the district insurance representative to identify the most, and least, common types of coverage and compare this with the students' prioritized list. Both lists should agree. In other words, employers decide the limits they can expend on health-care protection. These limits usually mean that companies must choose which types of protection they will provide (if they cannot provide all the benefits listed) based on the priorities of their workers. Your students' priorities should reflect the priorities of the general population.

Define: The typical health-care system operates on a fee-for-service basis. Service is provided to a patient and a fee is charged for this service. HMOs operate on a prepaid basis. A general fee is paid, and service is provided (at no additional fee or at a nominal fee) when needed.

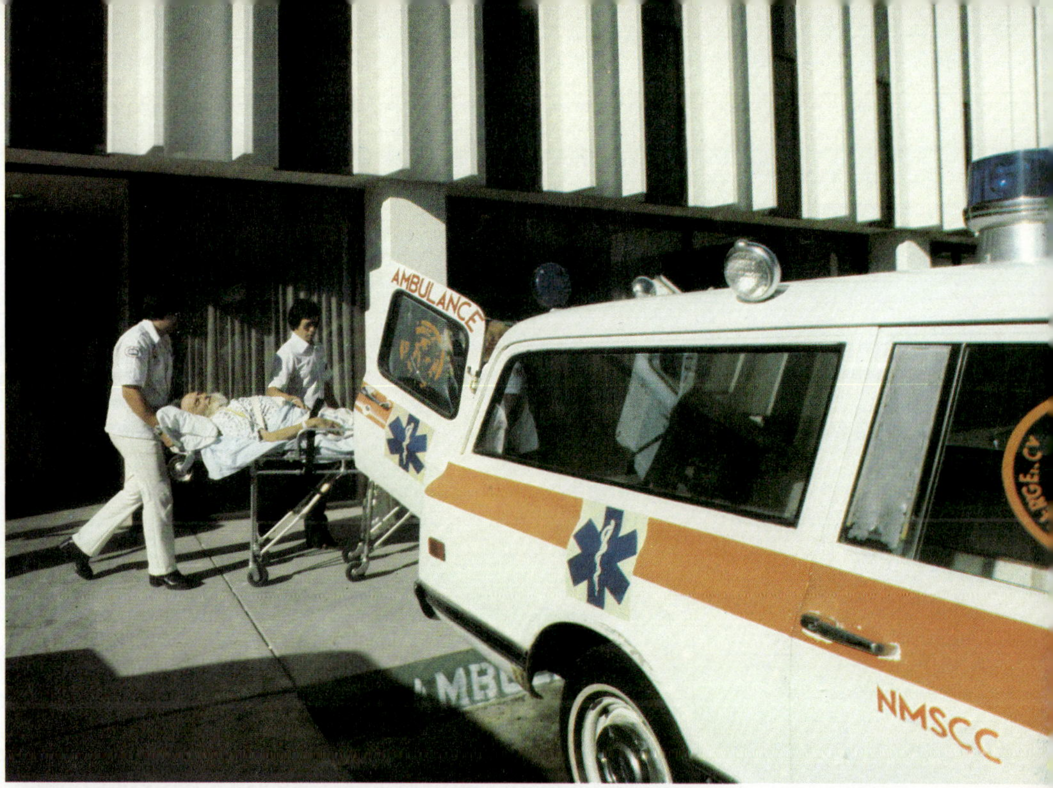

Health insurance covers the cost of health care, which can at times be needed when least expected.

It may pay the doctor's fees and the cost of the mother's and baby's stay in the hospital.

- *Disability insurance*—replaces some of the income lost if the insured becomes unable to work due to illness or injury.
- *Dental expense insurance*—helps the insured pay for most dental work. It usually has a deductible and a coinsurance feature.
- *Psychological care*—pays for mental health care. It might also pay for stays in hospitals or mental health facilities.
- *Alcohol or drug abuse treatment*—includes care received in drug treatment facilities and visits to professionals who offer this kind of care.
- *Home and nursing home care*—covers the cost of constant nursing care for older and disabled persons.
- *Comprehensive medical insurance*—a plan designed to provide all the health insurance needed in one package. These plans have the same rates and coinsurance features that separate policies have, but the deductible is often lower.

Another way to protect yourself from medical costs is to join a **health maintenance organization (HMO).** This is *a plan that provides all the medical care that members need for a fixed, yearly fee*. When HMO members use the plan's medical services, they usually pay only a nominal fee. HMOs hire their own physicians, and HMO members must choose their physicians from the staff. HMO plans offer some medical services, such as regular checkups, that other health plans do not cover. In addition to office visits, HMOs cover hospital and surgical costs. Employers that have group medical plans for at least twenty-five employees are required by law to offer an HMO if one is available in the area.

Explain: HMOs operate under the principle of preventive medicine. By not charging for check-ups and routine office visits, the HMO encourages clients to prevent illness, rather than wait until it is serious.

Home and Personal Property Insurance

Many people protect their homes and property by buying **homeowner's insurance.** This type of insurance *protects a person from property damage and from liability for injury to others.* A homeowner's policy has several sections:

- *Personal property* covers the contents of a house, including personal belongings, even if they're taken out of the house. For instance, a camera taken on a trip is covered—if it's stolen, the insured has protection. Property is protected from damage by fire and storm or loss by theft and burglary.
- *Additional living expenses* are covered up to a certain limit. This coverage would pay the cost of a hotel and meals while a home is being rebuilt after a fire.
- *Personal liability* protects the insured against lawsuits for injury or property damage to others.
- *Medical payments* cover the cost of treatment of a minor, accidental injury that a visitor suffers. Often there's a limit of $1,000 for these payments.
- *Property damage* covers minor damage that the insured—or a member of the insured's family—accidentally causes to someone else's property. Often there's a limit of $500 per accident.

Math Activity: The Glowe family purchased a home five years ago for $85,000. Their home insurance required 80 percent coverage. How much was the property value they had to buy coverage for? Now, five years later they discover that they can sell their house for $130,000. In order to comply with insurance requirements, they must increase the insured value of their house to what level?

Homeowner's policies cover the home, garage, and other buildings. They often pay the **replacement cost,** which is *the amount it will take to replace lost or damaged property at current prices.* The insurer may require that the policy cover at least 80 percent of the value of the property. If the value of the property goes up, the insured should increase the value of the policy.

The value of personal property covered is usually half that of the real property that is covered. In other words, a policy for $50,000 worth of damage to a house would also cover $25,000 worth of damage to its contents. The insurer generally pays the **actual cash value** of the item. That is *the replacement cost of a piece of property, reduced by its age and condition.* The insured may be able to buy coverage for full replacement cost by paying a higher premium. This would increase your personal property amount.

Definition: **Real property** is land, crops, buildings, or mineral rights connected to the land. **Personal property** is moveable articles of value such as furniture, jewelry, stocks, or bonds.

Liability coverage often has a minimum of $100,000, though insureds may buy more. Many people recommend coverage of $300,000.

Even though this type of insurance is called home*owner's,* renters can also get it. They, too, have property that needs protection and can be liable for injuries to others.

It is important to read policies carefully. Homeowner's policies have *exclusions,* which are losses that are not covered. Find out exactly what is covered before signing a policy.

Insured people can choose to buy extra coverage in what's called a *rider.*

This way they can insure especially valuable personal property, like a diamond ring.

COMPARING SOURCES OF INSURANCE

List: Ask students to list personal property which might require a rider (additional insurance coverage).

Review: Allow class time to review the basic consumer method of making decisions.

Critical Thinking: Provision of health care for the uninsured is the subject of extensive debate. Encourage students to research the need for health care for the uninsured, as well as alternate solutions. Divide the class into teams assigned to possible solutions and allow the teams to present various solutions to the class.

Note: Additional resource information can be obtained from *Consumer Reports, Consumer Research, Money Magazine,* the Insurance Institute, and your state agency on insurance.

Shopping for insurance requires careful comparing. We'll review some ways to get insurance here. We'll also see how to evaluate different plans.

Consumers Get Insurance Three Ways

You can buy insurance for yourself. You can get insurance through an employer, and you may be able to get insurance through the government.

First, you may buy coverage from private insurers. You will deal with either an agent who works for one company or an independent agent who is able to sell policies for several insurers. These agents will explain the various plans and costs. Remember that agents receive a commission for all insurance they sell based on the size of the policy. You can also buy insurance through the mail, although this may be risky. Before you buy, be sure to investigate the insurer.

Whoever you buy insurance from, be sure to compare prices and coverage. Shopping for insurance is just like shopping for anything else—go to more than one seller to find the best policy for you.

The second way to get insurance is as a fringe benefit from an employer. These plans have the advantage of lower premiums—in fact, the employer may pay all or part of the premium. On the other hand, the policy may not be tailored to your special needs. Also, coverage probably ends if you leave the job. Many plans, though, allow workers who leave an employer to switch from the group plan to personal coverage. Health insurance is the kind most frequently provided by employers, though many also offer life insurance. Few have auto or homeowner's plans.

Health insurance is also provided by the government through a program called Medicare. This program helps people over age 65 and some others. It has two parts:

- *Hospital insurance* helps pay for hospital care and for some care after the patient leaves the hospital. This program is funded through social security taxes.
- *Medical insurance* covers medical costs to older persons who enroll in the program and pay the monthly premium. The government pays two-thirds of the program's cost, which keeps the premium low.

Evaluating Insurance Policies

Shop around for insurance because coverage and rates vary. Good sources of information on insurance are the government agencies that regulate insurers in the state. You can also use published guides like *Consumer Reports* and *Changing Times*.

In shopping for insurance, be sure to check an insurer's history of settling claims. Companies that settle claims slowly are not helpful when they're needed. Checking books and magazines and talking to other consumers can help. Finally, read all policies carefully:

- Get all unclear terms explained.
- Get all conditions clarified. Double-check to see that you understand the extent of the coverage—look for deductibles, lifetime or annual limits on health costs, exceptions to property coverage loss, and the like. Be sure you understand the terms of payment—don't lose your coverage because of oversight or misunderstanding.

YOU INTERACT WITH THE ECONOMY: DRIVING RESPONSIBLY SAVES DOLLARS AND LIVES

Summary: We all must accept risk; however, we can be protected from some of the financial loss of risk through insurance. Chapter 19 introduced students to the four major types of insurance and the factors necessary for making decisions in buying these types of insurance.

Activity: Obtain a sample insurance policy and evaluate students on how well they are able to decipher the terms of the policy. Ask: Who is insured? What is the total value of the policy? What deductibles are given in the policy?

The annual cost of injuries and deaths from car accidents is more than $20 billion. When property damage and other losses are added, the cost is much higher. More importantly, accidents cost lives. More than 50,000 people die from motor vehicle accidents each year. Each of us can help lower these costs. Here are some steps you can take:

- *Observing speed limits*—driving faster than the limit is unsafe—accidents are more likely to happen. Remember to slow down in bad weather, when slick roads and poor visibility create more danger.

Drivers can best protect their children—and help hold down the cost of auto insurance—by using child safety seats.

- *Not mixing drinking and driving*—more than half of all fatal motor vehicle accidents involve a driver who's been drinking. Alcohol blurs vision and slows reflexes. The driver cannot control the car. Driving under the influence of alcohol is illegal. Underage drinking is also illegal. Stay away from alcohol and drugs when you drive. Persuade friends to do likewise.
- *Using seat belts and child restraints*—seat belts help protect you against injuries if you're in an accident. Some states require that small children be put in special car seats to protect them. Holding a child in the lap in the front seat doesn't protect the child.
- *Wearing a helmet when riding a motorcycle*—motorcycles don't offer as much protection as cars. Riders risk serious head injuries if they neglect to wear helmets.

By following these simple steps of prevention, you can benefit yourself and others. Driving responsibly gives you a good driving record and holds down your insurance premiums. It also saves society money—with fewer accidents, less is spent on emergency care, medical services, and lawsuits. The strongest argument for driving responsibly is that doing so saves our nation's most precious resource—lives.

SUMMARY

- Insurance is based on many people putting money into a fund that will be used to pay for the losses that only a few of them will have.
- The premium an insured pays is determined by the law of averages, the number of people sharing the risk, the cost of past claims, the characteristics of the person, the value of what's insured, whether there's a deductible, and the state laws.
- Resource managers can save money on insurance by taking action to reduce risk.
- To determine insurance needs, consumers take into account what losses may occur and what losses they are willing to risk will not occur.
- Life insurance protects dependents who would suffer financial loss from the early death of a provider and creates a fund to pay the insured's final expenses. Different types of life insurance include term, whole life, limited payment, endowment, and universal life. Term is the least expensive. The other types also act as savings plans.
- Auto insurance is required for all drivers in many states. It protects drivers from injury and property damage to themselves and others.
- No-fault auto insurance allows drivers who suffer injury to collect up to a specified amount from their insurers regardless of who is responsible for an accident.
- Automobile insurance includes liability coverage, medical costs for the insured, collision, uninsured motorist protection, comprehensive insurance, and wage loss and substitute services coverage.
- Auto insurance premiums are based on where the policyholder lives, driver characteristics, driving record, what the car is used for, its value, driver education, the amount of the deductible, multiple car discounts, the injury and collision loss history of the car model, and the theft rate of the vehicle.
- Health insurance covers hospital, surgical, regular medical, major medical, dental, and disability costs, among others. Comprehensive plans combine many of these risks.

- Consumers may also protect themselves from medical costs by joining an HMO.
- People buy homeowner's policies to protect themselves from property damage and personal liability.
- Consumers get insurance by buying it themselves, through an employer, or through the government.
- We can reduce our risk of having costly motor vehicle accidents by observing speed limits, not mixing drinking and driving, using seat belts, and wearing helmets when riding motorcycles. Good driving practices save lives and lower insurance costs.

Key Terms

Match each of the following terms with the definition that most suits it.

actual cash value
beneficiary
bodily injury protection
cash surrender value (CSV)
coinsurance
collision coverage
comprehensive coverage
deductible
endowment
health insurance
health maintenance organization (HMO)
homeowner's insurance
insurance policy
liability
limited-payment life
medical payments coverage
no-fault insurance
premium
property damage protection
pure risk
replacement cost
term insurance
uninsured motorist protection
universal life insurance
wage loss and substitute services coverage
whole-life insurance

a. the probability that an event will occur
b. the money that a person pays for insurance
c. a written contract that details the terms of the insurance coverage
d. a person's responsibility for injury to others
e. the person named in a life insurance policy to receive payments should the policyholder die
f. the part of a life insurance premium that is savings
g. a type of life insurance that offers protection but no savings
h. a type of life insurance that is in force and is paid for during the insured's entire life
i. a type of life insurance in which premiums are paid over a specified time, though coverage lasts throughout the insured's life
j. a life insurance policy in which premiums are paid for a fixed number of years and then the insured or the beneficiary collects the face value of the policy
k. a type of life insurance that combines term coverage and an investment feature
l. motor vehicle insurance allowing drivers who suffer injuries to collect up to a certain amount from their insurer, no matter whose fault the accident was
m. motor vehicle insurance covering injury to other people
n. motor vehicle insurance covering damage to others' property
o. motor vehicle insurance covering medical and funeral expenses for the insured and anyone riding with him or her
p. motor vehicle insurance covering repairs to the insured's car
q. the amount of loss the insured agrees to bear before the insurer begins to pay claims
r. motor vehicle insurance covering the insured and family from the costs of injuries caused by a driver who has no insurance
s. motor vehicle insurance covering the insured's car from theft and from damage caused by a number of disasters
t. motor vehicle insurance that covers, at least partly, any income the insured might lose as a result of injury in an auto accident

u. insurance to cover all or part of doctors' fees, hospital bills, and other charges for health care
v. the amount it will take to replace lost or damaged property at current prices
w. a plan that provides all the medical care that members need for a fixed yearly fee
x. an insurance package that protects a person from property damage and from liability for injury to others
y. a feature in which an insurer does not pay all the charges that a policy covers, but a large percentage of them
z. the replacement cost of a piece of property, reduced by its age and condition

Review Questions

1. Why do people buy insurance?
2. List three factors on which the amount of a premium depends.
3. Name at least one way resource managers can lower risk in each of the following areas: life, operating a motor vehicle, health, and maintaining home and property.
4. What is a deductible?
5. Name the forms of life insurance. Which is least costly? Which offers savings?
6. Who must get motor vehicle insurance? What do no-fault laws provide?
7. What types of coverage does automobile insurance include?
8. Name three types of coverage health insurance includes.
9. Explain coinsurance. What limits are there on health insurance?
10. What does a homeowner's policy cover? What must an insured constantly do to keep sufficient coverage?
11. Identify the three ways in which we get insurance.
12. What two things do consumers do when evaluating insurance policies and insurers?
13. Name four ways drivers can lower the risk of costly accidents. Who does this benefit?

Projects

1. Examine your auto insurance coverage, if you have any. If not, discuss with someone who has a car the kinds of coverage he or she has and why. Find out what minimum insurance your state requires. Do you carry more than the minimum? Why? Review what coverage you have. What are your premiums? What could you do to lower those premiums and maintain the same coverage?
2. Visit an HMO office or do some research in the library to find out what a particular HMO offers and how it matches the coverage in health insurance policies. How does it assign members to doctors, or can the members choose their doctor? What procedures are there for practicing preventive medicine? How does the HMO's cost compare with other types of health insurance? Based on your research, do you think that HMOs are a good idea? Why?
3. Make an inventory of your family's home or apartment and estimate how much money it would take to replace the property in it in case of a loss. Investigate at least three different insurers to find the coverage your family needs at the cost you're willing to pay. When you have chosen an insurer, compare its policy with the one your family already has. If your family does not have a policy, why not? Do you think it's a good idea to get one?

It's Up to You 20

Overview: Chapter 20 places what has been taught throughout this text in a future perspective. Chapter 20 helps your students begin thinking of how to apply this information to their future.

OBJECTIVES

This chapter will help you to:

1. Relate trade-offs, opportunity cost, and risk to your decisions.
2. Identify your values, goals, and resources before making decisions.
3. Apply your understanding of our economy's principles, participants, and forces to your decisions.
4. Protect your rights by keeping informed and protect the rights of others by acting responsibly.
5. Use this text as a tool for making future decisions.

Soon you'll be making many big decisions. First you'll decide what to do after high school. Will you get more schooling or start to work? In making that decision, you'll consider your long-term plans—what do you want to be doing five or ten years from now? What you decide to do now will make reaching that goal easier or harder.

In making your decision, you'll also consider your family. What goals does your family have? Can you help it achieve those goals? What resources does your family have? Can you use those resources to help reach your goals?

You'll need to make countless other decisions as well. Will you work productively and cooperate with others? Will you participate in group economic decisions? Will you use your time to increase your skills and maintain your energy? How much money will you plan to spend on food and how much on housing? How much will you save and where will you keep it? Will you apply for credit? How will you use the credit you're granted? How will you protect yourself against risk?

Note: Students may ask why they have to make decisions. In order to maximize their satisfaction, they have to decide on their own goals and the priority of those goals. If they let someone else make their decisions, chances are they will be less happy with the outcome.

THE DECISIONS NEVER END. Each decision you make creates the need for new decisions. What you learn in this text will help you make all those decisions. Throughout this book, we've presented three basic ideas:

- You need to make decisions, and you're better off if you make informed ones.
- To make informed decisions, you have to understand yourself.
- To make informed decisions, you have to understand our economy.

Each chapter of this text shows how each of these ideas applies in different situations you face. Let's look at them once more.

YOU NEED TO MAKE DECISIONS

You must make decisions because you have unlimited wants and limited resources. This conflict forces you to choose which wants to satisfy. You're more likely to satisfy your wants if you decide carefully.

Review: Review the suggestions contained in the annotations for Chapters 1 and 2 for possible activities and ideas for expansion.

Why You Make Decisions

Like everyone, you have wants—feelings that you must have something to survive or to live happily. Wants don't go away unless you take action to satisfy them. To satisfy your wants, you must give up some combination of your resources—money, time, energy, and skills.

The number of wants you can satisfy is limited by the amount of your resources. If days were 30 hours long, you could sleep 10 hours and still have 20 hours to work, eat, study, and play. Since they're only 24 hours long, you can't divide your time so easily. You're forced to choose what you'd rather do—sleep 10 hours and have only 14 hours for other activities, or take 16 hours for working, eating, and playing and sleep only 8. Because

Expansion: Our economic roles are sometimes in conflict. As union workers, we may want protection for our jobs and, therefore, agree with barriers on imports. However, as consumers, we may want access to less expensive products so that we will be able to use left-over resources to satisfy other wants.

Activity: Ask students to identify the conflicts between our economic roles in the following situations: increase the salary of the legislature (and increasing taxes) so that we can attract the best people to the jobs; union strikes on the railroads in time of war; voting for increased public services while voting against a tax increase.

List: Ask students to list their personal resources. Does this list differ from the one they developed at the beginning of class? What additional resources have they identified or developed?

Carefully choosing how you spend your time will help you satisfy your wants.

your resources are too limited to satisfy all your wants, you must decide which wants to satisfy.

You don't *have* to decide. You could just sleep until you wake up, whenever that is. Then you'd have to try to adjust your other activities to what's left of the day. That way, though, you probably wouldn't achieve your goals. You're better off choosing carefully. Simply take a few minutes at night to figure out what you want to do the next day and how much time you'll need. Then you can set your alarm clock to wake you up early enough to have time for these activities.

How You Make Decisions

Many decisions you make are economic—they involve getting or using resources. You make economic decisions while you play one of three economic roles. As a *worker,* you choose what career to enter, what job to take, and how to work with others. As a *citizen,* you vote for one candidate or another, pay taxes, and make your voice heard on issues you care about. As a *consumer,* you decide how to use your resources to satisfy your wants. In all three roles, your aim is to manage your resources to get the most out of them.

No matter what role you're playing or what decision you're making, you can follow the same method:

Step 1. Define your problem.
Step 2. Identify and rank your goals.
Step 3. Determine your alternatives.
Step 4. Analyze the consequences of each alternative.
Step 5. Choose the best alternative for achieving your goals.
Step 6. Put the decision into action.
Step 7. Evaluate the decision.

Activity: Ask students to identify a problem and work through the decision-making process to arrive at a solution.

Steps 4, 5, and 7 are complex. Let's look at them in more detail.

When you take Step 4—analyzing the consequences of your alternatives—you trade off costs and benefits. Benefits are the wants you satisfy by choosing a certain option. Costs are what you must give up to get an alternative—the resources you must spend. Cost is more than money. It includes all the resources you must use. All alternatives have both costs and benefits. You choose the alternative that offers you the most benefit for the least cost. You trade the costs you're willing to pay for the benefits you want to get.

Expansion: Your students have now learned that Step no. 4 really is a cost-benefit analysis. What they will be doing is identifying all the costs and benefits of each alternative. Their final decision will be the alternative where the benefits equal or exceed the costs. This process is conducted by business and by government.

Suppose you have a dollar to spend on an ice-cream cone. One store sells single-scoop cones for 85¢ and double scoops for $1.15. Another sells single scoops for 70¢ and doubles for 95¢. If you think the two brands are equal in taste, you'll buy a double scoop for 95¢. It gives you more benefits (more ice cream) for less money. If you think the more expensive brand tastes much better, you'll buy a single scoop of it. The second scoop you give up is worth the benefit you get (better taste).

To perform Step 5—choosing the best alternative—you consider the opportunity cost of each option. Since you don't have enough resources to satisfy all your wants, choosing one means losing the opportunity to satisfy another. This is called the opportunity cost. You can use this concept in choosing between saving to buy something you want later or using credit to buy it now. By saving, you give up the opportunity to use the item while you pay for it. By spending more to buy with credit, you lose the chance to buy something else.

Explain: The value in evaluating your decisions once they are put into effect is that you will learn what must be changed the next time you make the same or a similar decision. This is learning from our mistakes.

Of course, there are no guarantees that you'll be happy with the result of a decision. Step 7—evaluating decisions—helps reduce the chance that you'll be dissatisfied. Decisions in all three economic roles involve risk. Because the result of the decision is in the future, you don't know for sure what it will be. This uncertainty arises from two causes.

First, when you make a decision, you're limited by incomplete knowledge. No matter how much time you spend researching a problem, you can't know everything about it. This is especially true for many buying decisions. You can spend hours reading about and test-driving new cars before choosing one. Even if all reports about a particular model are favorable, you still might end up with a car that often stalls. The time you spend on research does lower the risk that you'll choose a car that runs poorly, but it can't eliminate the risk completely.

The second cause of risk is the chance that something unexpected may occur. People recognize this possibility when they buy insurance. Insurance protects people from financial loss caused by unexpected events like a fire, accident, or illness. This cause of risk applies to decisions you make in all three economic roles. You may choose to enter a career that has a promising future only to find that new technology has made the career outdated. The growing use of robots to make cars, for instance, is reducing the need for auto workers. To protect yourself from this kind of risk, learn all you can about what experts think the future will bring.

Activity: Can we ever have enough financial resources to meet all our wants? Ask your students to figure out how much annual income they would like to be making and what type of lifestyle that would provide. Then suggest that they just won the state lottery and will receive $50,000 per year for the next 20 years, after taxes. How will their lifestyle change? What if the lottery paid $100,000 per year for the next 20 years? Will they still have unobtainable wants?

Another way to protect yourself from risk is to evaluate your decisions. If something unexpected occurs, you may need to change your decision. If your resources or wants change, it may be time to reconsider the option you choose. You can benefit from evaluating the way you make decisions. Decision making is a skill, just like running fast, or painting, cooking, or piloting a jet. To improve your skill, you need to practice and to evaluate how well you perform. In these two ways, you can learn to become a better decision maker.

There's something else to remember: the decisions you make in each economic role affect those you make in other roles. The job you take determines how much income you'll earn. By voting and participating as a citizen, you influence the size of your taxes. After paying taxes, you have your disposable income. You use that money to satisfy your wants. You may also use some of it for education to improve your skills and get a better-paying job. You can give some to a political campaign, using your money resource to play a citizen role. Whatever actions you take, you'll get the most out of your resources by managing them carefully and planning how to use them.

YOU NEED TO UNDERSTAND YOURSELF

To be able to make decisions, you must understand yourself. Few people have enough money to satisfy all their wants. Your values—what you believe to be important in your life—influence your decisions about which wants to satisfy. You also must consider what resources you have or can get. After you've identified your values and resources, you can choose which want to satisfy. This becomes your goal—the destination you want to reach.

Emphasize: Risk can be lessened through information and through practicing and evaluating your decision-making processes. Every decision carries the risk that it will be a bad decision. However, the more decisions you make, the better you will get at making them.

Identify Your Values

Your values influence how you choose among competing wants. Suppose you get a part-time job. Your values will influence what you choose to do with the money you earn. If you value education, you may save your wages to pay for college. If you value your appearance, you may use much of your income for clothing. Many decisions also affect other people. Recognizing this, you often consider your family's values, wishes, and needs. You may choose to use part of your earnings to help your family buy necessities. You may decide to care for brothers and sisters instead of working.

Values play a part in choices you make in each of the economic roles. How you value your work affects how well you work: will you be efficient and productive or do as little as you can? If you put great value on your skill at cooking, you may choose to use your time to prepare meals rather

Many families discuss important matters so that each member has input in making decisions.

Extend: Increasingly, students will have to identify and act on their own values. Any activities you develop to help them in this process will be valuable.

than using your money to eat out. As a citizen, you compare your beliefs about the government's responsibility for defense, education, and the environment with the beliefs of various candidates. Then you support the one whose views match yours most closely.

Identify Your Resources

Activity: What will your students be doing this summer? Encourage them to identify resources they will gain from this summer activity or which resources will be improved. If they have no summer plans, encourage the class to brainstorm summer activities.

In deciding which want you'll satisfy, you must consider your resources. Resources are what you use to satisfy the want—and there's no point choosing to satisfy a want when you don't have the resources to obtain it. Resources don't stay at one level forever, however. You may have more resources tomorrow than you have today. So your decisions have to take future resources into account. Why do resources change?

First, some resources decrease as you use them up. The dollar you spend today cannot be spent tomorrow. For this reason, it is important to plan how to use your resources. Otherwise, they may be gone when you want them most. Planning—*managing* your resources—helps avoid waste. This is also true of how we use national economic resources. Using energy unnecessarily or working unproductively wastes valuable resources and harms the economy.

Second, resources increase when you invest one to build another. By saving or investing your money and letting it work over time, you can end up

Explain: Additional education or training is an excellent example of investment of time, energy, and knowledge (also personal resources).

Discussion: Ask: Why should you make such a big deal out of careers or what work you will do?

Extension: An area of study in economics is family resources. This is the study of the family unit, its resources, and the best use of these resources in order to maximize satisfaction. One conclusion is that families function best when all members are maximizing their resource contributions. For example, if outside income must be earned while at the same time functions within the household must be filled, then the family member with the lowest opportunity cost should perform each task. It could be that the outside income of husband and wife will be large enough so that the opportunity cost of hiring someone to stay at home is lowest.

You can use your resources of time, energy, and money to get more of another resource—skills.

with more money. By investing time and money in education, you can increase your skills. With better skills, you can get a better-paying job—and that means more money.

Remember that money isn't the only resource. Time, energy, and skills are also resources. Use them in combination to get the most use out of them. There are family and public resources, too. You can increase your resources by combining them with those of others.

Identify Your Goals

With your values and resources in mind, you decide which want to satisfy. That want becomes your goal. It's obvious why you need to identify your goals—how can you reach your destination without knowing where it is? Throughout this text, you've seen many examples of goal-setting. Budgeting is one—whether you're budgeting time or money, what you're doing is identifying goals for spending resources. Choosing the career you want is aiming at another goal. Whether you shop for food, clothing, investments, or insurance, you always start by identifying your goals—deciding what features you want in the good or service you're buying.

You have both short-term and long-term goals. Short-term goals are wants you plan to satisfy soon (this week or this year, for instance). Long-term goals will not be reached until future years. Remember that both kinds of goals affect each other. A long-term goal of going to a special training school, for example, may require the short-term goal of spending less money and saving more.

After identifying your goals, you need a plan to reach them. A plan is like a map you can follow to your destination. You plan for the job you want by drawing up a strategy. You plan for the food you want by making menus and a shopping list.

There are a few ways to avoid possible traps in planning:

Critical Thinking: Seldom have rules been given stating "how much should be spent" or "how much should be saved." Why is it better to provide tools for decision making rather than a set of rules to be followed?

- *Make the plan reasonable*—estimate wisely what resources you'll use. If it takes two hours each night to get your homework done, a time plan must allow for two hours, not one and a half.
- *Take your time when planning*—if you don't plan carefully, you're likely to make a plan that won't work.
- *Make your own plan*—you can get help in drawing up plans by reading books by experts or by talking to people you know. Whatever you learn from others is only general advice—adapt it to your own situation. You have your own values and resources to consider.
- *Follow the plan*—a plan is useful only if it's followed. You might get lost if you leave a road map in the car's glove compartment. You'll never reach your goal by ignoring the plan.
- *Evaluate the plan*—if circumstances change, a plan may become outdated—what you thought was a good idea yesterday may be a bad idea today. As you check how your plans turn out, you can help yourself make better plans in the future.

Focus: By focusing your students on the traps to planning they might encounter, you will enable them to be more successful in their own personal planning.

YOU NEED TO UNDERSTAND OUR ECONOMY

When you make decisions, you're making them within the society in which you live—a society that's made of millions of other people making decisions, too. Your choices affect them, and theirs affect you. Good decisions take this mutual influence into account. You need to understand the principles that underlie our economy, who participates in it, how it works, and what your rights and responsibilities are.

Explain: Your students will not be making decisions in a vacuum. They will be making decisions within an economic structure full of other individuals making decisions based on self-interest. In order for your students to succeed, they must understand the interdependence of all these decision-makers.

Understand Our Economy's Principles

Five principles describe how our economy should function in theory. Although it doesn't always work this way, these principles do describe what motivates most economic actors to act as they do.

- *Free choice* is the right to choose which wants to satisfy and how to satisfy them.
- *Self-interest* is the desire to satisfy yourself, what guides you in your choices. Because you can't reach all your goals through your own effort alone, it's in your best interest to cooperate with others and act responsibly toward others.
- *Competition* results from self-interest. In theory, some people, to pursue their self-interest, will go into business to produce a good or service for consumers to buy. Others, seeing the chance to make money, will begin

The economy is made up of millions of people making decisions, each one affecting all the others.

Critical Thinking: It has been said that "the consumer's best protection is competition." Why? Why does competition guarantee innovation and a wider selection?

World Economy: Ask students to research and report on the structure of government and the economic situation in other countries. Compare the GNP and the standard of living in these countries to the United States.

making the same good or service. The competition between sellers will result in more, better, and cheaper goods and services, which benefits consumers. In reality, the economy doesn't always work that way. Businesses can grow to tremendous size and gain greater power than theory predicts. The government may or may not decide to take action to limit that power.

- *Private property* is the right to keep the money you earn and to keep the purchases you make with that money.
- The last principle is *limited government*. The role of the government in the economy in theory is to protect property rights and ensure fair competition. In reality, the government's role has grown over the years. Some people argue that some steps the government has taken harm the economy and that its role should be decreased. Others believe it should do even more.

This disagreement points up one difficulty with group choices—not everyone will be happy with the choice made. Large groups are made up of many small groups with conflicting goals and differing strengths. These competing groups argue about the choices the government should make. Many individuals don't believe they can influence group decisions, so they don't participate in making them, but they forget an important fact. Everyone who takes part in group decisions is an *individual.* The only way to influence group decisions is to help make them.

Define: In economics, the circular flow of resources and goods and services illustrates that individuals sell their resources to firms in order to purchase goods and services produced by those firms. In turn, firms buy productive resources from individuals in order to produce the goods and services to sell to those individuals.

Critical Thinking: The discussion of actors in our economy ignores a large, and growing, sector: individuals who are not able to work. How are individuals that cannot participate in the economy cared for in the United States?

Discussion: The U.S. government provides for those who cannot provide for themselves in a variety of ways: (1) income supplements in the form of money; (2) subsidies specifically for food, housing, or child care; (3) job training. Ask your students to analyze these based on their efficiency and their success.

Understand Who Participates in Our Economy

To help make those group decisions wisely, you must understand who participates in the economy. The three types of economic actors are individuals, businesses, and governments.

Individuals are hired by businesses to do work. As *workers,* they help the businesses—called *producers*—to provide goods and services. Producers pay wages to workers. With these wages, the individuals buy goods and services. When they do so, they are called *consumers.* Both producers and consumers benefit. Producers try to sell goods and services for more than it costs to make them. The extra money is profit. Consumers use their money to save and to buy goods and services. In doing so, they satisfy their wants.

Governments collect taxes from both consumers and producers. With these taxes, they also hire workers (paying them income) and provide services for both individuals and businesses.

We all depend on others. People who make clothes depend on others who grow food. The choices you make, then, affect other people—not just yourself. Your consumer decisions also affect others. By complaining about a faulty or dangerous product, you help protect other consumers.

Government services, like the work this park ranger does, are provided out of the taxes that people pay.

Understand Economic Forces

The participants in the economy *act.* Individuals work, save, and spend; businesses produce goods and make profits; governments tax income and provide services. Their actions are shaped by the forces of supply and demand, which determine the prices of labor and of goods and services. The producers' need for workers with a particular skill (the *demand* for workers) is matched by the number of people who have that skill (the *supply* of workers). If producers want the skill very much, or there are few people who have it, the price of the skill—the *wage*—will rise. If the opposite is true—the supply is large or the demand is small—the wage will be lower.

The forces that set the prices of goods and services act similarly. If many people want to buy something, or if there are few units of it to buy, the producers who make it will be able to charge a higher price. If few people want it or if producers have too many to sell, the price will go down.

By understanding these forces, you can help yourself make better decisions. If you see that demand for something you want to buy is falling, you can time your purchase to get a lower price.

Review: If students are unclear about any of the points being made, refer back to the appropriate chapters.

Focus: If your students understand the interaction of supply and demand in our economy, they will be able to analyze a good many of the issues facing them in the future.

Critical Thinking: An analysis of supply and demand may help you decide what career or business venture will be most profitable. If the supply of engineers is large, and you know the demand for engineers is falling, then you may decide not to study engineering. If the demand for a specific product is high, and there are few suppliers, then that might be a good product to produce. Ask students to give specific examples of this in our economy.

Consumers can protect themselves by keeping informed of their rights.

Understand Your Rights and Responsibilities

Critical Thinking: The Year of the Bill of Rights is 1991. Although many people would say that the Bill of Rights is limited to political rights, ask your students to examine those rights and identify their economic implications.

Part of understanding the economy is knowing your rights. Everyone has basic rights that are spelled out in the Constitution. In addition, the federal government has created many laws that give people—as workers and as consumers—other rights. Fair hiring laws prevent employers from discriminating against certain groups of people when they hire new workers. Consumer credit law makes lenders clearly state the terms of loan contracts. Laws about warranties protect consumers from damage caused by goods that don't perform as they should.

The government, of course, doesn't follow each of us around every day to see if our rights are violated. You must protect your rights, which you can do in three ways:

- Know your rights in order to guard them.
- Exercise your rights in order to protect yourself and others.
- Keep informed in order to see if your rights are changed or threatened.

Remember that others have rights, too. Your choices affect others, so you must behave responsibly. If a worker doesn't produce on the job, other workers have to work harder. If people shoplift, store owners must raise prices to cover the money they're losing. If drivers don't drive sensibly, they—and others—have to pay for their mistakes in money and lives.

YOU CHANGE AND SOCIETY CHANGES

World Economy: In 1990, the Eastern European nations began the process of moving from a command economy to a market economy. Examine the pre-1990 economies of these nations and suggest what the people need to learn in order to succeed in a market economy.

You are different now than you were as a child. In 20 years, you will be different than you are now. The economy has changed dramatically since you were born, and it will change even more in the future. In school, you learn to use the tools that will help you identify and adapt to these changes.

In this text, we've provided you with some of those tools. We've explained how to get and evaluate information. For instance, we've shown how to find jobs and how to work with others on the job, but we cannot describe all the different jobs you'll have to choose from. First, there are too many. Second, you'll be faced with options that don't exist yet. The *way* you evaluate those alternatives—the things you look for in them—is less likely to change.

The same is true no matter what the topic: food, clothing, housing, transportation, financial services, or insurance. You'll be faced with new options as business develops new goods and services and government passes new laws. You can pick among those options by using the basic decision-making method.

Our responsibility is to help you learn to use the tools for evaluating your options. Yours is to identify the options and to use these tools. This responsibility will stay with you throughout your life. Keep informed of what's going on in the economy. Read books, magazines, and newspaper articles. Only by keeping up to date can you find alternatives that will satisfy you.

Since the world around us constantly changes and we will always need to make decisions, smart resource managers continue learning through their adulthood.

Your education can't end when you graduate. You must keep learning all your life.

SUMMARY

- The conflict between unlimited wants and limited resources forces you to make decisions.
- Your economic decisions occur in one of three roles: as worker, consumer, and citizen.
- Whatever decision you make, you can follow the same method: define your problem, identify and rank your goals, determine your alternatives, analyze the consequences of each alternative, choose the best alternative in light of your goals, put the decision into action, and evaluate the decision.
- To analyze alternatives, you weigh their costs and benefits. To choose among alternatives, you first identify what opportunity you must give up to obtain each one.
- Your decisions involve risk because you make them without complete knowledge and because the unexpected may occur. To protect yourself from risk, you need to evaluate your decisions. Evaluating how you make decisions helps you learn to make better ones.
- To make choices, you must understand your values—what you think is important in your life. Your values influence which wants you choose to satisfy.
- When making decisions, you consider what resources you have and how you can combine them to get the most out of them.
- The want you choose to satisfy is your goal. The surest way of reaching that goal is to make a plan and follow it.

- Our economy is based on five principles: your right to make your own choices, your right to pursue self-interest, the benefit of competition, your right to own property, and the limited role of government.
- The participants in our economy are individuals, businesses, and government. Individuals earn money by working and use it to buy the goods and services businesses produce. Governments tax both individuals and businesses and provide services for all.
- The interaction of producers' supply and consumers' demand sets the price of goods and services. Supply and demand also determine wages.
- People should know and use their rights to protect themselves and each other.
- Your own values, resources, and goals change over time. The economy also changes. You need to keep informed of these changes to ensure that you make wise decisions in the future.

Review Questions

1. What are the three basic ideas of this text?
2. What do wants make you do? How is your ability to do something about your wants limited?
3. What steps should you follow in making a decision?
4. How can you analyze and select alternatives?
5. What are two causes of risk? What two things help reduce risk?
6. What must you understand about yourself to choose which want to satisfy?
7. How do plans help you achieve your goals? What five steps can help you avoid traps in planning?
8. What principles underlie our economy? Does the economy work exactly as those principles say it should? If not, what's different?
9. What three actors participate in the economy? How are their decisions related to each other?
10. What economic forces determine price? Why should you learn about them?
11. What three things should individuals do about their rights?
12. Do you learn in school everything you need to know to make good personal economic choices? What else do you need to learn?

Projects

1. What will you do after high school? Make a decision, using the method outlined in this chapter. Write a report describing this decision that shows (1) how you analyzed your alternatives, (2) how you identified their opportunity cost, (3) what risks you foresee and how you intend to protect yourself from these risks, (4) how you based your decision on your values and resources, (5) the plan you have for putting the decision into action, and (6) how you took present and future economic trends into account. If you've already decided what you'll do, use these six items to analyze the choice. Does it look like a wise decision, or will you change it?
2. In the future, our society will change greatly. Focus on one area of economic life that interests you—careers in a certain field, a certain product, or services people use. Do some research in current books and magazines that tell how some experts expect it to change in the future. What will be different in the career, product, or service? How will these differences create the need for new skills on the part of the people who enter the career or use the product or service? Write a report.

Glossary

ability-to-pay-standard(5) the principle that people with more money should pay more in taxes than people with less money

acceptance(13) a party's agreement to accept what was offered in exchange for a promise to do something; a requirement of a contract

actual cash value(19) the replacement cost of a piece of property reduced by its age and condition

adjusted balance method(12) a way of finding the principal by subtracting any payments made during the billing period

advertising(10) a message meant to create interest in a product or service and to persuade consumers to buy it

agency shop(7) a workplace in which new workers are not required to join a union, but must pay the union a fee roughly equal to dues

alternative(1) a course of action that will at least partly fulfill a person's goals by using resources he or she has or can get

annual percentage rate (APR)(12) the yearly cost of a loan, expressed as a percentage of the principal

annuity(18) a plan in which someone invests money and is promised a payment each month after retiring

antidiscrimination laws(7) laws that forbid employers from refusing to hire workers because of race, age, sex, religion, or other traits

apprenticeship(6) job training that blends on-the-job experience and classroom study to teach a skill

arbitrator(7) an impartial person who examines the proposals of the two parties in a negotiation and makes a decision they must accept

auction(11) a selling method in which property or merchandise is bought by the highest bidder

automated teller machine (ATM) (12) a computer-run unit that takes deposits, gives cash, transfers funds, and gives account information

average daily balance method(12) a way of finding the principal by adding the balances of each day of the billing period and dividing the total by the number of days in the period

The number in parentheses shows the chapter in which the term is defined.

bait and switch advertising(10) an illegal practice in which a store advertises a low price on one item to lure shoppers in, only to talk them into buying a more expensive item.

balanced diet(14) a daily intake of the foods needed to stay healthy and strong

bank statement(12) the financial institution's record of all deposits and withdrawals made during a period in an account and the balance as of the statement's date

bankruptcy(17) a situation in which a court sells off a borrower's property—except for certain items protected by law—and pays the proceeds to his or her creditors

barter(2) the direct exchange of goods and services

basic consumer method(9) a seven-step process of planning and carrying out buying decisions

beneficiary(19) the person named in a life insurance policy to receive payments should the policyholder die

benefits(1) the goals that are met by an alternative

benefits-received standard(5) the principle that people should be taxed according to the share of government services they receive

Better Business Bureau (BBB)(10) a nonprofit corporation that protects businesses and consumers by helping businesses to regulate themselves

bodily injury protection(19) motor vehicle insurance covering injury to other people

bond(18) a long-term note sold by governments or businesses to raise money

bonus(8) an extra payment to a worker as a reward for superior performance by the worker or by the employer

boycott(7) the refusal to do business with an organization or to buy its products or services

brand(11) a name or trademark that identifies a product

breach of contract(13) the failure of either party to do what was promised in a contract

brokerage(18) a business that buys and sells stocks and bonds on behalf of its customers

budget(9) a plan to achieve goals by fitting expenses to income

business(4) an individual or group of individuals who produce goods and services for profit

buying power(9) the amount of goods or services a dollar will buy

capacity(17) a borrower's financial ability to pay back a loan

capital(17) the property someone owns, which a creditor uses as a guide to the person's ability to repay a debt

capital resources(2) the machines, equipment, and buildings used in the production of goods and services

carbohydrates(14) starches and sugars that supply the body with quick energy and fiber to aid digestion

career(6) a long-term commitment to a field, industry, or profession

cash surrender value (CSV)(19) the part of a life insurance premium that is savings

cashier's check(12) a check drawn on a financial institution's own funds

catalog selling(11) a method of offering a variety of products for sale through catalogs mailed to consumers' homes

certified check(12) a personal check that the drawee guarantees an account has enough money to cover

character(17) how a borrower can be expected to act; whether a borrower is honest and responsible and has good judgment

charter(4) a legal document that states a corporation's name, its business, and its procedures

check see *personal check*

check register(12) the record book for a checking account

citizen role(1) how a person decides to contribute to and use public resources

clearance sale(11) a situation in which sellers offer lower prices to unload unwanted supply

closed-end credit(12, 17) a type of credit in which a fixed amount is borrowed for a fixed period and repaid in fixed payments

closed shop(7) a workplace in which employers can only hire union members; an illegal practice

closing(15) the final point of the sale of real estate

coinsurance(19) a feature in which an insurer does not pay all the charges that a policy covers, but a large percentage of them

collateral(17) the pledge by the borrower of something of value to ensure repayment of the loan

collectibles(18) personal goods that are expected to grow in value

collection agency(17) a company that specializes in collecting overdue loans

collective bargaining(8) negotiation over the terms of employment, handled by officials of an employer and a labor union

collision coverage(19) motor vehicle insurance covering repairs to the insured's car

command system(3) an economic system in which economic choices are made by one or a few individuals who represent a central authority

commercial bank(16) a bank that has been authorized, by either the state or federal government, to offer a full range of financial services

commission(8) a rate of pay for work that is a percentage of sales made

comparison shopping(11) examining the price and quality of competing goods and services to find the best buy

competent(13) capable of bargaining effectively with others; a requirement of a contract

complements(3) related products

compound interest(12) a method of computing savings interest in which interest is added to the principal as it is earned so that it, too, earns interest

comprehensive coverage(19) motor vehicle insurance covering the insured's car from theft and from damage caused by a number of disasters

condominium(15) a form of ownership in which a person owns a living unit and a share of common property

consideration(13) something of value each party to a contract gives up in order to receive the benefit he or she wants

construction(14) how well clothing is put together, which shows how good it will look and how long it will last

consumer action panel(13) a group formed by the manufacturers in some industries to handle consumer problems

consumer role(1) how a person decides to use money, time, energy, and skills to get what he or she wants

consumers(2) people who purchase goods and services for personal use

contract(13) an agreement that can be enforced by the legal system

convenience stores(11) small food retailers that have long hours and neighborhood locations

cooperative(4) an enterprise owned by more than one person or business, which acts for the benefit of its members

cooperative(15) a form of ownership in which each owner owns a percentage of the building

corporation(4) a business owned by stockholders

cosigner(17) someone who promises to repay a loan if the borrower fails to do so

cost-of-living adjustment (COLA)(7) a periodic automatic increase in wages that is based on the current rate of inflation

costs(1) what a person must give up in order to have an alternative

credit bureau(17) a business that collects credit information about consumers and gives it to other businesses that request it

credit limit(17) the maximum amount up to which a person may charge in an open-end credit agreement

credit rating(17) the category of credit risk that a creditor assigns to a potential borrower

credit union(16) a nonprofit savings and lending cooperative formed by people with a common bond

debit card(12) a plastic card that enables consumers to pay instantly for purchases

debt consolidation loan(17) a high-interest loan for a sum large enough to settle all of a person's short-term debts

deductible(19) the amount of a loss that the insured agrees to bear before the insurer begins to pay claims

default(18) the failure of a bond issuer to meet interest payments or to buy back a bond when it reaches maturity

deflation(9) a decrease in the general level of prices

demand(3) a consumer's willingness and ability to buy a product at various prices over a given time

department stores(11) large retail businesses that sell a wide variety of products in one store

deposit insurance(16) a government program that guarantees that deposits up to a certain amount will be returned to depositors if a financial institution goes out of business

direct selling(11) a method of offering goods and services for sale to consumers in their homes

discount department stores(11) retail businesses that sell a variety of products at lower prices than department stores

discount rate(16) the interest rate that institutions pay the Federal Reserve System to borrow money

discount supermarkets(11) large self-service food stores that have lower prices than supermarkets but fewer services

distributor(4) a type of business that helps consumers and producers exchange goods

dividend(4, 18) a part of the profits of a corporation that directors decide to pay to stockholders

down payment(15) the percentage of the price of an item that is paid at the time of the purchase when the rest is borrowed

earned income(8) the total amount of money a worker is paid for his or her labor

economic system(3) the institutions and principles that determine how a society answers the basic economic questions

economics(1) the study of how people manage their resources to achieve their goals

effective annual yield(12) the actual yearly interest rate for savings, found by dividing one year's interest by the principal

emotional appeal(10) an advertising message that aims at consumers' psychological needs and desires

endorsement(12) the payee's signature on the back of a check

endowment(19) a life insurance policy in which premiums are paid for a fixed number of years and then the insured or the beneficiary collects the face value of the policy

entrepreneur(4) a person who has an idea, is willing to take risks, and is able to combine resources to produce goods or services for profit

equilibrium price(3) the price at which consumers are willing to buy as much as producers are willing to supply

equity(15) ownership

excise tax(5) a sales tax on a specific product

exemption(8) a reduction in taxable income allowed for each taxpayer, for his or her spouse, and for each dependent

exports(3) products sent out from one country to another country

face value(18) the full amount that a bond is worth when it reaches maturity

factory outlet(11) a store that sells specialized products at discount prices

fats(14) energy-rich compounds that carry vitamins and insulate body organs

Federal Reserve System(5, 16) a federal agency that controls the money supply and oversees the practices of its member banks

Federal Trade Commission (FTC)(10) the agency of the federal government that, among other tasks, protects consumers from ads that are unfair or deceptive

fibers(14) the hairlike strands of material that are woven together to make cloth

finance charge(12) the total dollar amount a borrower must pay, which includes interest plus any other lender fees, such as service charges or insurance

finance company(17) a financial institution that specializes in giving credit to merchants and making personal loans

fines(5) penalties paid to a government by those who break a law

firing(7) the permanent dismissal of a worker by an employer

fixed expenses(9) expenses that stay more or less the same over time and that must be met by a certain date

flea market(11) a gathering place where consumers sell used merchandise to other consumers

float(16) the time it takes for a check to clear

foreign exchange(16) changing the currency of one country into that of another

franchise(4) an arrangement in which one business sells another business the right to use its name and sell its products in a certain area

fringe benefits(8) insurance, vacation days, sick days, and other ways of paying workers that are not part of earned income

full warranty(13) a business's written guarantee to fix or replace a faulty product free within a reasonable time after being told of a problem

generic or unbranded products(11) goods that are identified only by the contents of the package, not by the store's or manufacturer's name

goals(1) the results a person wants from a decision

goods(2) products that people buy

grades(14) the government's quality categories for food based on taste, appearance, size, and age

grievance procedure(7) steps workers can follow to protest and appeal any employer decision they feel violates a labor contract

gross pay(8) the total amount of income an employer owes a worker for a given period

health insurance(19) insurance to cover all or part of doctors' fees, hospital bills, and other charges for health care

health maintenance organization (HMO)(19) a plan that provides all the medical care that members need for a fixed yearly fee

homeowner's insurance(19) an insurance package that protects a person from property damage and from liability for injury to others

human resources(2) the workers whose time, skills, and energy are used to produce goods and services

imports(3) products brought into one country from another country

income tax(5) a tax on the income that individuals and businesses earn

income tax return(8) the form people use to state their income and figure the tax they owe

income transfers(5) payments a government makes to groups of people who are judged to need more income

industrial bank(17) a lending institution originally set up to offer loans to industrial workers

inflation(9) an increase in the general level of prices

influences(10) forces inside and outside us that affect how we think and act

information(10) facts about goods and services that can be used to evaluate alternatives

injunction(7) a judge's decision ordering a person to stop an illegal action

insurance policy(19) a written contract that details the terms of the insurance coverage

interdependence(2) our reliance on others and theirs on us

interest(12) a fee for the use of money

interest-bearing checking account(12) a demand deposit account on which the institution pays interest on the balance

interview(6) a meeting that gives employers and job applicants the chance to talk to each other

investing(16, 18) using money in a way that we expect will increase its value

investment club(18) a group of investors who form their own mutual fund by pooling their money and managing their own investments

job(6) the position at which a person works to earn an income

job application(6) a form companies use to keep a record of similar information for all people who apply for work

job satisfaction(6) the enjoyment, pride, and sense of accomplishment workers get from their work

labor union(7) a group of workers who join together to bargain more effectively

landlord(15) the owner of property being rented

layoff(7) a temporary or permanent end to employment ordered by an employer for economic reasons

lease(15) a legal contract setting forth the terms of a rental

legal aid society(13) an organization paid for by the government to offer legal help free or for a small fee

liability(19) a person's responsibility for injury to others

license fees(5) fees charged to those who want to perform certain actions, including many that the government oversees

life-style(6) the way we live and how we spend our resources

limited partnership(4) a form of business in which the liability of some partners is limited to the amount they invested in the business

limited-payment life(19) a type of life insurance in which premiums are paid over a specific time, though coverage lasts throughout the insured's life

limited warranty(13) any warranty that is not full

long-term goals(9) goals to achieve in the distant future

loss(4) the amount by which a business's expenses exceed its income; the risk of going into business

loss leaders(11) items sold below cost to attract consumers into a store so they will buy other goods not on sale

mail-order clubs(11) sellers who offer specialized products to members through the mail

managers(4, 7) the people who turn an organization's goals into directions for the workers

market(3) a way by which goods and services are exchanged, usually for money

market demand(3) the sum of all the individual demands for a product in a market

market system(3) an economic system in which group economic choices are determined by the decisions of many individuals

maturity date(18) the date when the issuer of a bond promises to buy it back at face value

mediator(7) an impartial person who joins labor negotiations to help the two parties reach an agreement

medical payments coverage(19) motor vehicle insurance covering medical and funeral expenses for the insured and anyone riding with him or her

medium of exchange(2) an object that is generally accepted as payment for goods and services

merit services(5) services a government decides it should provide out of a belief businesses cannot or will not provide enough of them for all people

minerals(14) elements needed to maintain the body's acid balance and fluid levels and to perform other important roles

minor(13) a person who has not yet reached the age of majority

mixed system(3) an economic system that combines features of traditional, command, and market systems

modified market system(3) a mixed economic system based on the principles of the market system but having features of command and traditional systems

money order(12) a cash substitute that can be bought from financial institutions, the post office, or other sources

monopolistic competition(3) markets in which there are a few sellers, but each sells primarily to a specific group of buyers

monopoly(3) a situation in which only one firm provides a product or service and thus controls the entire market

mortgage(15) a creditor's claim against real property that is purchased with the money borrowed

mutual fund(18) a group in which many people pool their money, which is then managed and invested by professionals

mutual savings bank(16) a bank owned by its depositors and whose goal is to encourage savings

National Advertising Review Board(10) a group formed by the Better Business Bureau to hear and decide upon complaints about advertising

natural resources(2) the resources of the earth used in the production of goods and services

net pay(8) a worker's take-home pay, found by subtracting deductions from gross pay

no-fault insurance(19) motor vehicle insurance allowing drivers who suffer injuries to collect up to a certain amount from their insurer, no matter whose fault the accident was

nutrients(14) the substances the body needs in order to live and to grow

occupational ladder(6) the steps up from the lowest job in a career to the highest

offer(13) the promise one party makes to do something in exchange for something another party agrees to do; a requirement of a contract

oligopoly(3) a situation in which a few large firms produce most or all of a product or service and control the market

open charge account(17) a type of open-end credit that requires the borrower to pay for the purchase at the end of the billing period

open dating(14) a calendar date on a food package that indicates the last day on which the product should be sold or used in order to ensure quality or freshness

open-end credit(12, 17) a type of credit in which the amount a borrower owes increases each time a purchase is made and decreases each time a payment is made

open market operations(16) the Fed's power to buy and sell government bonds, used to control the money supply

open shop(7) a workplace in which employees are not represented by a union

opportunity cost(2) the value of the benefit that is given up when choosing one alternative over another

options(15) extra items added to a vehicle's basic model, which increase its cost

organization(7) a group of people working toward a common goal

overdraft(12) a check written for more money than an account contains

overdraft protection(17) a guarantee by a bank to cover a depositor's check up to a certain amount even if the check withdraws more money than is in the account

over-the-counter trading (OTC)(18) a system of dealers and brokers who use telecommunications to trade stocks and bonds

owners(4) people who have invested money in a business

partnership(4) a business owned by two or more persons at least one of whom has personal liability for the firm's debts

passbook account(18) a savings account in which a fixed rate of interest is paid and money can be withdrawn at any time

passbook loan(17) a cash loan from a bank using the money in a passbook savings account as collateral

payroll deductions(8) amounts subtracted from gross pay to cover regular payments that are required or voluntary

peer pressure(10) the influence created by our desire to be accepted by people our own age

pension plan(8) a retirement fund for workers created by contributions made by the employer

personal check(12) a written order drawn on an account in a financial institution to pay cash on demand

personal energy(9) our physical capacity to do things

personal liability(4) the principle that an owner is responsible for all of a business's debts

personal resources(1) the money, time, skills, and energy a person possesses

piecework rate(8) a set rate of pay for each unit of work produced

point(15) a charge of 1 percent of the amount of a mortgage

premium(19) the money that a person pays for insurance

prevailing wage(3) the equilibrium price of labor

previous balance method(12) a way of finding the principal in which payments made during the billing period are not deducted

price(2) how much money it costs to obtain a good or service and what it is worth compared to other goods and services

principal(12) the amount of money saved or borrowed, to which interest is added

principle of least cost(1) a method of deciding that involves choosing the alternative with the most benefits for the fewest costs

private employment agency(6) a business that tries to match employers with qualified job applicants

producer(4) a type of business that produces goods

producers(2) those who provide goods and services for consumers

product care and maintenance(9) the proper use and care of goods to stretch their lives

productivity(7) a measure of how many goods and services a producer produces using a given amount of resources

profit(4) the amount by which a business's income exceeds its expenses; the reward for taking a risk

profit-sharing plan(8) a fund some businesses create by setting aside part of their profits for workers

progressive tax(5) a tax that sets a higher rate for people with high incomes than for people with low incomes

promotion(7) an employer's decision to move a worker to a new job with more responsibility as a reward for working well in an old job

promotional sale(11) a situation in which sellers offer lower prices to stimulate demand

property damage protection(19) motor vehicle insurance covering damage to others' property

protein(14) compounds that are needed for the growth and repair of body tissue

public mass transit systems(15) local transportation regulated and sometimes run by government agencies for the general public at a low cost to the user

public monopoly(3) a single producer that controls a market through a right granted by a government to ensure that essential services are provided

public resources(1) the services that the government provides with the taxes we pay

public services(5) services that only a government can or will provide because the service must be provided for everyone, regardless of any person's inability or unwillingness to pay

puffing(13) exaggerated claims of a product's superiority that are clearly based on the seller's opinion

pure risk(19) the probability that an event will occur

raise(7) an increase in a worker's wage, either as a reward for good work or as called for in a contract

rational appeal(10) an advertising message that aims at consumers' practical needs in a logical way

real estate(18) buildings and land

real estate tax(5) a tax based on the value of land, buildings, and other real property that a business or consumer owns

rebate(11) the refund of part of a product's price given by producers to increase demand

recall(13) a situation in which a manufacturer discovers, or is made aware of, a flaw in its product and calls back all units that have been sold to fix them

reconcile an account(12) to match one's own records and figures for a checking account with those on a bank statement

references(6) people who know a job applicant's character and work

regressive tax(5) a tax that takes a higher percentage of money from people with low incomes than from people with high incomes

regular checking account(12) a demand deposit account offered by a financial institution

renting(9) paying a fee in return for the temporary use of some good or property

replacement cost(19) the amount it will take to replace lost or damaged property at current prices

repossession(17) what may occur when a borrower fails to repay a secured loan; the creditor takes ownership of the item that was bought with the borrowed money

reserve(16) a sum of money set aside by Federal Reserve member banks that is equal to a certain percentage of their deposits

resign(7) to leave a job to work somewhere else

responsibility(13) our duty to act in our best interest and that of other members of our society

résumé(6) a fact sheet that summarizes a job applicant's education, experience, and interests

retirement(7) a worker's decision to leave the work force at the end of his or her career

revolving charge account(17) a type of open-end credit that allows a borrower to buy up to a certain limit and repay in installments

risk(1) the uncertainty that results from not knowing for sure whether the alternative chosen will have the benefits and costs expected

safe deposit box(16) a metal container that a person can rent from a financial institution for storing valuables

salary(8) a rate of pay for work that is calculated by week, month, or year

sales pressure(10) the use of tactics by salespeople to persuade consumers to buy

sales tax(5) a tax paid by consumers when they buy goods or services

savings(9, 18) money set aside for future use

savings and loan association (S&L)(16) a savings institution that used to specialize in offering savings accounts and home mortgages but now offers a full range of services

scarcity(2) a situation in which the desire for a specific resource exceeds the ability to obtain it

services(2) actions of value that people pay others to perform

services(4) a type of business that performs actions of value for consumers or for other businesses

shoplifting(13) the crime of taking goods from a store without paying for them

short-term goals(9) goals to achieve in the near future

single-payment loan(17) a loan in which the entire amount plus a finance charge is repaid in one payment

skills(9) our talents and our ability to develop them

Small Business Administration (SBA)(4) an agency of the federal government that provides loans, advice, and information to small businesses

small claims court(13) an informally run court created to handle legal disputes over small sums of money

social insurance(8) social security and other plans that provide income for people who can no longer work

social security(8) payments by the federal government to eligible workers (or their families) who have retired, become disabled, or died

social security tax(5) a required contribution most workers make to the federal government's pension system

sole proprietorship(4) a business owned by one person

specialty stores(11) retail businesses that carry a wide selection of a few related products

sticker price(15) the manufacturer's suggested selling price for a new car

stock(4) a share or shares of ownership in a corporation

stock exchange(18) a place where licensed traders come to buy and sell stock for their clients

stockholders(4) people who purchase shares of stock in a corporation

stop-payment order(12) an instruction from a checking account owner to have the financial institution refuse to pay a check

strike(7) an organized stoppage of work by employees

sublet(15) the tenant's renting of all or part of a property to another person

substitutes(3) products that replace existing ones

substitution(2) replacing one way of satisfying a want with another that uses less of valuable resources

sue(13) to ask a court to settle a dispute

suggested list price(11) the price at which a manufacturer recommends that retailers sell its products

supermarkets(11) large self-service stores that carry a wide variety of products, but primarily food

supply(3) a producer's willingness and ability to sell a product at various prices over a given time

systematic decision-making method(1) a step-by-step way of identifying, analyzing, and choosing among alternatives, then later evaluating the choice

tariff(5) a fee charged on imported goods

tax deductions(8) expenses that reduce the income on which taxes are due

taxes(5) contributions required by a government, which uses them to provide services

tenant(15) a person who agrees to pay a certain amount every month, called *rent,* for the right to live in a dwelling

term insurance(19) a type of life insurance that offers protection but not savings

testimonial(10) an advertising technique in which someone proclaims his or her satisfaction with a product

time deposit(18) a savings method in which money is left on deposit and earns a fixed interest rate

tips(8) payments, usually voluntary, by customers to service workers

title search(15) an investigation into the deed to a property to establish a clear claim to ownership

trade and professional associations(10) groups of people or businesses who join together to promote their common interests

trade-off(1) giving up something a person wants in order to get something he or she wants more

traditional system(3) an economic system in which economic choices are based on the customs or habits of the group

transfer(7) an employer's decision to assign a worker to a job in a different place

traveler's checks(12) checks in fixed amounts that are protected by the issuer against loss or theft

trust(5) a situation in which one or a few businesses control an industry

trust(16) property managed by someone for the benefit of someone else

trustee(18) the person or institution through which an IRA investment is made

unemployment compensation(8) payments by the state government to workers who have lost their jobs and are willing but temporarily unable to find new ones

uninsured motorist protection(19) motor vehicle insurance covering the insured and family from the costs of injuries caused by a driver who has no insurance

union shop(7) workplace in which new employees must join a union within 30 days of their hiring

unit price(14) a system of stamping the price of an item in terms of a certain unit of measure

universal life insurance(19) a type of life insurance that combines term coverage and an investment feature

user fees(5) fees charged by a government to those who benefit from specific services

U.S. Recommended Daily Allowance (U.S. RDA)(14) how much of each nutrient a person should consume each day, which varies according to each person's age and sex

values(1) a person's beliefs about what is important in his or her life

variable expenses(9) expenses that change each month and that we may be able to control

vending machines(11) coin-operated machines that sell products from apples to soft drinks

vitamins(14) substances needed to prevent disease and regulate many body functions

voluntary exchanges(2) trades that are made between willing participants who both think they will benefit

wage(2) how much producers are willing to pay and workers are willing to accept for their time and skills

wage loss and substitute services coverage(19) motor vehicle insurance that covers, at least partly, any income the insured might lose as a result of injury in an auto accident

wages(8) an hourly rate of pay for work

wants(2) our feelings that we lack something that will satisfy us

warranty(10, 11, 13) a promise by a manufacturer or seller that a good meets certain standards

warranty of fitness(13) a guarantee that protects a buyer who relies on the seller's judgment when making a purchase

warranty of merchantability(13) a guarantee that the good is fit for the ordinary purpose for which it is used

water(14) the liquid that makes up most of the body's weight, transports nutrients and wastes, and is contained in the body fluids

wealth(5, 18) the money and property a person owns

W-4 form(8) the form a worker uses to instruct an employer how much income tax to withhold

whole-life insurance(19) a type of life insurance that is in force and is paid for during the insured's entire life

work permit(7) a document that allows a person under the minimum working age in a state to hold a job

worker crime(13) the crime of stealing supplies or products from employers or falsifying time or work records

worker role(1) how a person decides to use time, skills, and energy to earn money

workers(4) the people who make the products or provide the services that a business sells

workers' compensation(8) payments by the state government to cover the medical costs and lost income of a worker who is injured on the job

W-2 form(8) a form filled out by an employer that lists a worker's gross pay and payroll deductions for the previous year

Index